T0323073

They Eat Our Sweat

CRITICAL FRONTIERS OF THEORY, RESEARCH, AND POLICY IN INTERNATIONAL DEVELOPMENT STUDIES

Series Editors

Andrew Fischer, Giles Mohan, Tanja Müller, and Alfredo Saad Filho

Critical Frontiers of Theory, Research, and Policy in International Development Studies is the official book series of the Development Studies Association of the UK and Ireland (DSA).

The series profiles research monographs that will shape the theory, practice, and teaching of international development for a new generation of scholars, students, and practitioners. The objective is to set high quality standards within the field of development studies to nurture and advance the field, as is the central mandate of the DSA. Critical scholarship is especially encouraged, within the spirit of development studies as an interdisciplinary and applied field, dealing centrally with local, national, and global processes of structural transformation, and associated political, social, and cultural change, as well as critical reflections on achieving social justice. In particular, the series seeks to highlight analyses of historical development experiences as an important methodological and epistemological strength of the field of development studies.

They Eat Our Sweat

Transport Labor, Corruption, and Everyday Survival in Urban Nigeria

DANIEL E. AGBIBOA

OXFORD
UNIVERSITY PRESS

OXFORD

UNIVERSITY PRESS

Great Clarendon Street, Oxford, OX2 6DP,
United Kingdom

Oxford University Press is a department of the University of Oxford.
It furthers the University's objective of excellence in research, scholarship,
and education by publishing worldwide. Oxford is a registered trade mark of
Oxford University Press in the UK and in certain other countries

Published in the United States of America by Oxford University Press
198 Madison Avenue, New York, NY 10016, United States of America

British Library Cataloguing in Publication Data
Data available

Library of Congress Control Number: 2021939075

ISBN 978-0-19-886154-6

DOI: 10.1093/oso/9780198861546.001.0001

Printed and bound by
CPI Group (UK) Ltd, Croydon, CR0 4YY

Casa De Fernandez, © Amanda Iheme.

For my son, Fintan,

whose arrival heralds the next great adventure.

Acknowledgments

It has taken roughly a decade to finish this book. During that time, I have amassed a Sisyphean amount of debts from friends, colleagues, and mentors, which I must now pay.

I am eternally grateful to the late Abdul Raufu Mustapha, under whose supervision at the University of Oxford much of this research was completed. Upon my successful DPhil (PhD) *viva*, you sent me a lovely text: "Congratulations Dr Agbiboa! Very well deserved success. May this be the beginning of many important achievements for you." But what I never envisaged was you not being around to share these achievements with me. Without your clear direction and critical interventions, this book would not have been possible. A heartfelt thank you, too, to Olly Owen and Abiodun Alao, who examined an earlier draft of this work.

I owe an enormous debt of gratitude to all the faculty and staff (especially Gary and Penny) at the Oxford Department of International Development, which provided funding for this research through the Queen Elizabeth House Departmental Scholarship. I am also grateful to St. Antony's College, which awarded me a STAR grant to defray some of my fieldwork expenses. And to all my fellow DPhils who provided a genuine camaraderie during my years at Oxford, particularly Nelson Oppong, Zainab Usman, Sa'eed Husaini, Ola Akintola, Akin Iwilade, Alpha Adebe, among others: I say a big thank you.

A significant portion of this research was done during my year-long postdoctoral fellowship at the University of Pennsylvania's Perry World House. To my fellow inaugural postdocs, Aaron Rock-Singer, Julia Macdonald, and Rita Konaev, thank you for making that year a special one. Special thanks, too, to William Burke-White, Michael Horowitz, LaShawn Jefferson, and Katelyn Leader for creating the space for us to thrive.

I spent two wonderful years as Assistant Professor at George Mason University's Jimmy and Rosalynn Carter School for Peace and Conflict Resolution. There, I benefitted immensely from (in)formal interactions with colleagues and friends, especially Terrence Lyons, Tehama Bunyasi, Doug Erickson, Kevin Avruch, Susan Hirsch, Marc Gopin, Karina Korostelina, Richard Rubenstein, Solon Simmons, Arthur Romano, Daniel Rothbart, Patricia Maulden, Sheherazade Jaffari, and Ernest Ogbozor, among others.

A very special thanks to my colleagues at Harvard University's Department of African and African American Studies, especially superb mentors including

Tommie Shelby, Jacob Olupona, and Emmanuel Archeampong. Jean and John Co-maroff invited me to present part of this book at the African Studies Workshop in February 2019, and invited my wife and me for dinner afterwards. I want to thank them both, as well as the discussant of the day, Parker Shipton, and all the organizers, students, and participants at that workshop.

Part of this work was also presented at the Urban Security Assemblages Conference at the University of Amesterdam in February 2019. I want to thank Rivke Jaffe for inviting me, and all the participants including AbdouMaliq Simone, Diane Davis, Atreyee Sen, Laurens Bakker, Tessa Diphoorn, Nida Kirmani, and Maya Mynster Christensen.

At various points in my academic career, I have benefitted from the near and far support and inspiration of excellent scholars such as Wale Adebanwi, Ebenezer Obadare, Cyril Obi, Kenneth Amaeshi, and Ugo Nwokeji.

I am eternally grateful to the entire editorial team at Oxford University Press, especially the Series Editors for "Critical Frontiers of Theory, Research, and Policy in International Development Studies"—the official book series of the Development Studies Association (DSA) of the UK and Ireland. I am deeply indebted to Commissioning Editor Adam Swallow, whose guidance and clear communication kept me on task throughout the ups and downs, even loneliness, of writing. Special thanks, too, to my copyeditor, Meridith Murray, whose eye for details, particularly proper punctuation, is second to none. In like vein, I want to whole-heartedly thank all the peer-reviewers who devoted their time to reading and commenting on this book. I hope you can be proud of the end product.

I am thankful for all my field interviewees for taking the time out of, even during, their busy schedules to share their lifeworlds with me. To the brave road transport workers who, against all odds, keep Lagos in perpetual motion, I say *Èkó ò ní bàjé*.

To my family who have always supported me through the highs and lows of life: my mother, Esther Glory Agbiboa; my sisters: Ann Afadama, Philomena Ewea Agbiboa, Helen Iyesomi Agbiboa; and my brother: Patrick Osi Agbiboa. Thank you for being my rock.

Finally, to my wife, Mollie, the source and summit of my inspiration. I can't thank you enough for putting up with me throughout the protean process of writing and my fixation with fonts! What an indescribable pleasure it is to share ordinary life with you. I hope this book partly atones for those times when I have crept out of the bed in the wee hours of the morning to do some writing. To have seen further is to have stood on your shoulders.

Cambridge MA, 2021

Contents

List of Figures

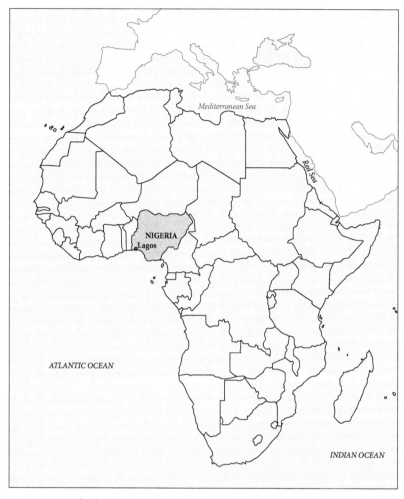

Fig. 1. Map of Africa showing Nigeria and Lagos

Introduction

Rethinking Corruption

Scholarly works on corruption in postcolonial Africa harp excessively on the failure of leadership. This bad leadership argument maps well onto muckraking narratives of powerful political patrons and so-called "big men" in postcolonial Africa gorging on state resources at the expense of the multitude who are generally assumed to be innocent victims of corruption. In *The Trouble with Nigeria*, acclaimed author Chinua Achebe places the blame squarely on the failure of leadership, maintaining that "(c)orruption goes with power, and whatever the average man may have it is not power. Therefore, to hold any useful discussion of corruption we must first locate it where it properly belongs—in the ranks of the powerful" (1983: 1). While Achebe's work emphasizes the mutual intertwining of corruption and elite power in Nigeria, it nonetheless robs non-elite groups of political agency or the capacity for action (Mustapha 2002). The banality of power, as Africanist scholars Achille Mbembe (1992), Jean-François Bayart (1993), and Célestine Monga (1996) tell us, dwells precisely in the conviviality of the ruler and the ruled. Rather than defining power in terms of narrow materialist rational choices of African elites (a view offered by Booth & Cammack 2013), the logic of conviviality reclaims Michel Foucault's non-elitist notion of power as emanating everywhere (1978: 93).

The clichéd image of the dysfunctional[1] African state as the root of all evil precludes a complex understanding of corruption as a transgressive category that implicates citizens as well as public officials, both of whom exercise a degree of power and political expectation. As the Nigerian sociologist Ebenezer Obadare points out, it would be disingenuous to limit corruption to the politics and business of elite alone since, as he argues, corruption is the key thread that binds elites and commoners in Nigeria's political economy (Obadare 2019: 165). This salient point is taken further by the economist Mushtaq Khan (1996a, 1996b, 2000), who argues that in many developing countries the state is weak relative to its clients and hence it lacks the capacity to maintain autonomy from powerful business interests, professionals, and other rent-seekers, giving rise to unproductive

---

[1] The "good governance" agenda in Africa is based upon the idea of the dysfunctionality of African states. This agenda rests simply upon an imagined disconnect between modern institutions and traditional African society, with the latter seen as precluding efficient and sustainable African bureaucracies (Anders 2009: 3).

They Eat Our Sweat. Daniel E. Agbiboa, Oxford University Press.
© Daniel E. Agbiboa (2022). DOI: 10.1093/oso/9780198861546.003.0001

rent-seeking activities. Khan (1996a, 2000) calls this the "clientelist patron-client networks" in contradistinction to "patrimonial patron-client networks," characterized by strong states able to maintain control over the management of rents. Using the example of India, Khan shows how a range of intermediate classes have come to occupy powerful positions in civil society and have mastered the art of exerting political pressures on the state. These intermediate classes have the power to influence the process of rents disbursement by the state (in the form of subsidies, tax breaks, and licenses) and prevent the state from eliminating unproductive rents (Jeffery 2002: 22).

In Africa, clientelist patron-client networks and intermediate classes are exemplified by powerful and politicized transport unions (e.g. Nigeria's Union of Road Transport Workers [NURTW] and Uganda's Taxi Operators and Drivers Association [UTODA]), which have come to wield disproportional power and influence over the central state, according to a bidirectional logic described as "double capture"[2] (Goodfellow 2017). That concept of double capture runs athwart the prevailing conception of interest groups and professional associations in Africa as poorly organized and comparatively weak. As Nicholas van de Walle claims, most African states are largely autonomous from social pressures because they have managed to outlaw, emasculate, or co-opt economic interest groups such as unions, business, and farmers associations (2001: 95). For van de Walle, the "absence of mass organizations in Africa weakens the political influence of lower-class groups who have little leverage over the 'patrons'" (2001: 72). The idea of double capture reinforces Erik Bähre's empirical analysis of the violent and shifting mutualities at the core of state-civil society relations, specifically the relationship between Cape Town's mafia-like taxi unions and state agencies (Bähre 2014). Far from redistributive, the clientelist patron-client networks that arises from such political settlements and elite bargains produce a "trickle-up" economy that largely benefits only a select few.

From Africa to South Asia and the Baltic, ethnographies of corruption have shown that corruption is simultaneously banalized and denounced in daily life. Anthropologist Daniel Jordan Smith argues that many average Nigerians who condemn corruption also participate in its social reproduction, and that too with ease (2007: 55). Comparing corruption in Ghana to the bodily function of coitus, Jennifer Hasty (2005a: 360) describes how the act of corruption is simultaneously decried and desired, hidden and exposed. In India, the same people who criticize the nation's weakened moral fabric are also open about the contradictions that surrounds their own discourses of corruption (Das 2015: 323, 340). This paradox of complicity is evident in Klavs Sedlenieks' ethnographic study of corruption in Latvia, where his informants expressed a disgust for corrupt activities alongside a

---

[2] This concept moves us beyond a one-sided view of state capture, that is, African leaders using state resources to co-opt different civil societies to maintain political stability (van de Walle, 2007: 50).

readiness to participate in them if the opportunity were to arise (2004: 120). The simultaneous criticism and complicity of corruption articulates with a growing corpus of works that have conceptualized corruption as a "collective action-social trap" problem (Mungiu-Pippidi 2006; Persson, Rothstein, & Teorell 2013), where any self-interested social actor will reason, "Well, if everybody seems corrupt, why shouldn't I be?" (Myrdal 1968: 409).

Theories of collective action postulate that when the dominant perception in any society is that public officials are hopelessly corrupt, this generally creates a social expectation that everybody pays a bribe, and therefore behavioral norms tend to override any ethical objections that individuals may have. The direct outcome is a "low-level equilibrium trap" (Rose & Peiffer 2014), in which people who resent corruption are resigned to accept it since the decision not to engage in corruption is considered to be "illogical or even ridiculous" (Marquette 2012: 22). The cost of not falling in line with the status quo is too high, as people risk being treated as outsiders (Kuran 1997) or punished (Wade 1985: 483). When a society is systemically corrupt, it becomes optimal to participate in corruption despite the presence of anti-corruption policies and legislation. This way corrupt behavior becomes the pragmatic norm (Mishra 2005: 30; cf. Booth & Commack 2013). So entrenched is the social norm of corruption in many developing countries that street-level bureaucrats (e.g. police) often find it difficult to resist the "erotics of corruption" (Miller 2008). Of the characteristic policeman on the streets of India, it is observed that his work puts him in constant interaction with people considered to be immoral. In a context where corruption is not only widespread, but deeply enmeshed with the practice of everyday life, "the policeman need not make opportunities; they are constantly being proffered to him routinely..." (Bayley 1974: 88).

The collective action-social trap framework constitutes a compelling critique and an alternative to the conventional "principle-agent" theory (seen in Klitgaard 1988; Rose-Ackerman 1978), which generally assumes the presence of "principled principals" in civil society and in positions of power who, by their very nature, are interested in holding agents to account and combating corruption (Marquette & Peiffer 2015: 2). Yet, in many developing countries where corruption is systemic and social and political trust are low, the absence of "principled principals" is conspicuous (Booth & Commack 2013; Booth 2012). Far from being a problem of individual deviation from the system, corruption becomes the system and virtually everyone is implicated in corruption (Prasad et al. 2019: 99). As Anna Persson et al. (2013: 457) explain, in a society in which corruption is the equilibrium norm, we can expect anti-corruption laws to be largely ineffective since there is little to no incentive to hold corrupt actors responsible. Across Africa, principals and agents are bound by a conceptualization of public office and state resources in terms of food (e.g. "national cake"), exemplified by the crudely avaricious mentalities of "It's our time to eat" (Kenya) and "*I chop you chop*" (I eat and let others eat also) (Nigeria).

In a thoroughly corrupted Nigerian society where nine out of ten people say public officials are corrupt and most people fear retaliation if they report corruption to local authorities (Afrobarometer 2018), the very instrumentalities of survival by average citizens tend to mirror the ones adopted by leaders to accumulate wealth and power. The vivid and visceral display of power and predation in contemporary Nigerian politics incorporates the dominant and the dominated, the elite and the subaltern, in an "intimate tyranny [that] links them in the desires that are shared across all its disparate groups" (Rowlands 1995: 38). In this light, then, any serious study of corruption in Africa must go beyond written rules and formal positions of power to examine how the practices of governments and publics are interwoven and mutually reinforcing (Mbembe 2001a: 133).

The Social Norms and Moral Economies of Corruption

To curtail corruption, we have to reorder the mindset of all [Nigerians]… those who are critics today are most times not better than those they criticize. When they are availed the same or similar opportunities, they act likewise. In other words, those who didn't have the opportunity criticize and blow whistle but when they get into office; they become victims of the same thing they criticize… This points to the fact that curtailing corruption might require a more broadened social engineering.

—President Muhammadu Buhari (*Leadership* 2015)

Buhari's statement underlines the oft-neglected social element of corruption, which is neither new nor specific to Nigeria. In fact, according to the World Development Report (2015: 60), there is a shared belief in many countries that "using public office to benefit oneself and one's family and friends is widespread, expected, and tolerated. In other words, corruption can be a social norm." Norms represent the standards of appropriate behavior in any society and have been defined as patterns of behavior which people conform to on the condition that they expect that most people in their reference network will conform to it also (Bicchieri & Mercier 2014). Social norms dictate the extent to which individuals engage and expect others to partake in corruption. In Nigeria, social norms have cultivated a fertile ground for the breeding of corruption (Ocheje 2018); this partly explains why corruption has defied post-1999 institutionalist anticorruption campaigns, most prominently the Independent Corrupt Practices Commission (ICPC) and the Economic and Financial Crimes Commission (EFCC). In as much as social norms in the wider society continue to favor or even reward corrupt practices, anti-corruption institutions and campaigns, though well-intentioned, will remain spineless and toothless.

At this juncture, a distinction must be made between moral norms and social norms, lest we fall into the culturalist trap of seeing corruption as the "culture" (i.e. moral beliefs and value codes) *of* the people/nation, and lest we conflate corruption as ingrained in the moral fabric of a society and its people, with corruption seen as a series of "standard operating procedures" that compels people to do things that they think are morally wrong (Rothstein 2018: 41). On the one hand, moral norms are clusters of moral judgements that justify the "relevant normative principle," while on the other hand, social norms are clusters of normative attitudes that consist of the "presumed social practice" (Brennan et al. 2013: 89). The significance of this distinction is confirmed by Bo Rothstein (2018: 40): "If travelling in a country where the 'presumed social practice' for getting medical treatment for one's children is to pay bribes to health personnel; most parents would likely pay the bribe. However, they could still be morally upset and convinced that doing so is ethically wrong. Similarly, a doctor in a systematically corrupt health care system may morally disapprove of the practice of taking money 'hidden in an envelope,' but it makes little sense to be the only honest player in a system where there is the presumed social practice." In a similar way, many average Nigerians who participate in corruption feel the context of political and moral economies in which they live compel them to do so. Although they recognize and denounce corruption in the abstract, these lowly Nigerians feel locked in a patronage system that determines the allocation of state resources (Smith 2007: 56). The political scientist Rasma Karklins (2005) puts it succinctly: "The system made me do it." To be clear, the system we are talking about here is one that has deprived millions of able-bodied people of jobs, food, and shelter, reducing them to bare life, to the struggle for daily survival. This is what Jean-Pierre Olivier de Sardan (1999: 48) describes as "the general feeling of helplessness in the face of an infernal mechanism." No wonder Monica Prasad and colleague's meticulous review of the corruption literature concluded that corruption often results from ordinary people trying to meet their legitimate, day-to-day needs (2019: 99).

The concept of *moral economy* originated from historian E.P. Thompson's seminal work on the eighteenth century hunger riots in England. Thompson (1971) defines moral economy as "a consistent traditional view of social norms and obligations, of the proper economic functions of various parties within the community, which, taken together, can be said to constitute the moral economy of the poor." The concept of moral economy was later popularized in James C. Scott's influential work on peasant life-strategies in Southeast Asia. In this work, Scott (1976: 167) apprehends moral economy as a kind of alternative social order based on two core principles: "the right of everyone to have access to the means of subsistence and survival, and the accompanying obligation to give and receive, thus obeying the norms of reciprocity" (Wutich 2011: 5). Since this work was published, a phalanx of scholars has applied moral economy to a broad selection of issues. In Africa, moral economy has been applied to theft (Newell 2006), political imagination (Isichei 2004), witchcraft beliefs (Austen 1993), and the relationship between famine, climate, and political economy (Watts 1983). Beyond Africa, moral economy has been used to make sense of racial health disparities in the United States (James 2003); poverty, immigration, and violence in France (Fassin 2005); the culture of entrepreneurship in Nepal (Parker 1988); the reciprocity of water insecurity in Bolivia (Wutich 2011); and ancestral worship among Chinese migrants (Kuah 1999). The broad application of moral economy has increasingly made it something of an empty signifier, a popularly invoked concept without substantial meaning. Scholars such as Didier Fassin (2009) and Chris Hann (2016: 3) have criticized the trivialization and thoroughly muddled nature of moral economy in the social sciences. Yet, behind the muddle lies a powerful analytic concept that can help illuminate the dynamics of corruption.

Africanist scholars Jean-Pierre Olivier de Sardan and Steven Pierce have reclaimed the concept of moral economy to understand the complexity of corruption. While Pierce's (2016: 174) account invites us to pay close attention to how and why particular public moral communities emerged over time, Olivier de Sardan (1999: 26) puts the emphasis on "as subtle as possible a restitution of the value systems and cultural codes by those who practice it." For Olivier de Sardan (1999: 32), corruption is difficult to address because it is engrained in social habits and, thus, deeply inscribed in the moral economy. Habits constitute the moral fabric of any society and the rational order of social relations (Camic 1986: 1057; Weber 2012: 300). Habits connect social patterns, conventions, and orders with everyday experience (Darmon & Warde 2018: 1039). Moral economy is loosely interpreted in this study as "the production, distribution, circulation, and use of moral sentiments, emotions and values, and norms and obligations in social space" (Fassin 2009: 15). This interpretation enables us to focus on the social evaluation of moral conduct and the moral judgment of social conduct (Smith 2016: 565). Moving us beyond the usual focus on material/economic conditions, Didier Fassin's interpretation allows us to interrogate voices and lived realities on the margins of society. In short, the moral economy approach moves us beyond simplistic notions of *homo politicus* and *homo economicus* by focusing on "the cognitive worlds of the poor" (Isichei 2004: 10).

In adopting the notion of moral economy as an explanatory model, my aim is to account for the ways in which corrupt practices are often embedded in sociopolitical mutualities and cultural forms that grant them legitimacy. Furthermore, I seek to interrogate corruption as a central arena in which the state and ideas about interaction with it are discursively constructed in everyday life (Gupta 1995; Masquelier 2001; Sedlenieks 2004: 119). Going beyond unitary, monolithic, and sedentarist conceptions, the state is reimagined here as an inherently translocal institution, which localizes itself in a multiplicity of sites, encompassing the village land registry where the subaltern in India encounter corrupt bureaucrats (Gupta 1995: 379; Ferme 2013), the poor condition of roads or the vast mine-affected areas of Angola's Moxico province that frequently claim lives and keep passengers aware of state abandonment (Neto 2017: 137), the checkpoints in Sri Lanka where both armed soldiers and civilians anticipate violence (Jeganathan 2000), and the local dispensary in rural Niger whose emptiness reminds residents of the withdrawal of the state (Masquelier 2001). Lastly, moral economy sheds light on how corruption gives rise to relationships of obligation and reciprocity (Carrier 2018: 30). A moral economy approach advances our knowledge of how the ruler and the ruled share the same "moral" universe whose values are not only linked to the ethic of economic survival but also reciprocal exchanges that are embedded in and reflective of a wide range of social relations and norms (Mauss 2000; Polanyi 1968). As James Scott notes:

> This moral context consists of a set of expectations and preferences about relations between the rich and the poor. By and large, these expectations are cast in the idioms of patronage, assistance, consideration, and helpfulness. They apply to employment, tenancy, charity, feast giving, and the conduct of daily social encounters. They imply that those who meet these expectations will be treated with respect, loyalty, and social recognition. (Scott 1985: 184)

The Politics of Corruption: Between the Grand and the Petty

Until now, there have been surprisingly few studies of corruption in relation to the overlapping logics of negotiation, gift-giving, solidarity, predatory authority, and redistributive accumulation (Olivier de Sardan 1999: 25). This is partly due to the origins of research on corruption in the analytical toolkits of economics and political science. Not so long ago, the field of anthropology accounted for a mere two percent of existing literature on corruption. In fact, save for Scott's early work on clientelism, "corruption" was eerily muted in the anthropological literature until the 1990s, when we saw a "corruption eruption" (Naim 1995; Torsello 2016: 1). On the one hand, economists are interested in examining the structures of economic incentives that make corruption more likely and assessing the impact of corruption on efficient economic outcomes (Mauro 1995; Bardhan 2015). Economists expect to see corruption when the benefits are high and the costs are low (Rose-Ackerman 1975). The costs of corruption are seen as primarily rent-seeking and social in nature. While the former describes the cost of the resources expended in seeking the rents or navigating around the restrictions, the latter derives from the rents and restrictions created by public officials (Khan 2006). On the other hand, the task of analyzing the roots of corruption has fallen to political scientists, who tend to define corruption in relation to state legitimacy, civil society engagement, and the manner in which political power is imagined, exercised, and contested (Szeftel 1998; Heidenheimer et al. 1989). Political scientists argue that corruption is a problem of weak states, which are characterized by security, capacity, and legitimacy gaps. Both economists and political scientists are united in the view of corruption as illegality, that is, the violation of the formal rules governing the allocation of public resources by officials in response to offers of financial gain or political support (Khan 1998; Nye 1967). This conventional notion of corruption—which overlooks how people everywhere come in contact with the state and imagine it—is directed by Max Weber's conception of the modern bureaucracy, particularly its bifurcation of the public and private realms:

> Legally and actually, office holding is not considered ownership of a course of income, to be exploited for rents or emoluments in exchange for the rendering of certain services... Rather, entrance into an office... is considered an acceptance of a specific duty of fealty to the purpose of the office (*Amstreue*) in return for the grant of a secure existence. It is decisive for the modern loyalty to an office that, in the pure type, it does not establish a relationship to a person, like the vassal's or disciple's faith under feudal or patrimonial authority, but rather is devoted to impersonal and functional purposes... The political official—at least in the fully developed modern state—is not considered the personal servant of a ruler. (Weber 1978: 959)

Political scientists and economists typically converge on a basic distinction between two corruption typologies: grand (high-level) and petty (everyday) corruption. Grand corruption involves large financial sums. The most extreme forms are instances where the state becomes an "apparatus of capture" (Ferme 2013: 957) and a conduit for private accumulation (Joseph 1987; Scott 1972; Osoba 1996). In Nigeria, for instance, political coalitions and clusters have historically been engaged in determined efforts to capture the state apparatus[3] for the purpose of using its redistributive powers to enrich themselves and their cronies (Joseph 1987). Between 1960 and 1999, an estimated USD400 billion was stolen from Nigeria's public accounts, and between 2005 and 2014, about USD182 billion was lost through illicit financial flows from the country (Hoffmann & Patel 2017: iv). Given its vital role in capital accumulation, efforts to capture the state in order to deploy a set of rent-seeking practices have intensified in the wake of the oil boom of the 1970s, when

---

[3] Like the concept of corruption, Foucault's concept of "apparatus" (*dispositif* in French) is at once a most ubiquitous and nebulous concept. However, in his *What is an Apparatus? And Other Essays*, Giorgio Agamben illuminates the notion. "I will call an apparatus," he writes, "literally anything that has in some way the capacity to capture, orient, determine, intercept, model, control, or secure the gestures, behaviors, opinions, or discourses of living beings" (2009: 14).

the expanded national revenue base from oil earnings rose dramatically, account-ing for about 75 percent of national revenues (Lewis 1996). Accordingly, political capital became intertwined with economic power, so much so that the premium on the former soon became a matter of life and death. As Nigerian historian Toyin Falola notes:

> The only way to grow rich was through state patronage. Consequently, today's business elite struggles to identify with power in a variety of ways: by joining po-litical parties, befriending military chieftains, and humoring the people in power. Either to protect wealth acquired corruptly, or to prevent their rivals from us-ing power to destroy them, the entrepreneur class continues to strengthen its connections with the protective powers in the government. (Falola 1998: 63–64)

It has been argued that public officials in sub-Saharan Africa barely view them-selves as rule-bound bureaucrats in the Weberian sense but instead have a pri-mordial loyalty to family, kin, ethnic groups, and party supporters (Chabal & Daloz 1999). The logic for this so-called deviant behavior was explained by the Nigerian sociologist Peter Ekeh; his central thesis is that the legacy of colonial-ism in Africa culminated in the coexistence of two distinct publics: the primordial and the civic. The former is perceived to be amoral and devoid of the generalized moral imperatives at play in the private realm and in the promoridal public (Ekeh 1975: 92). While Africans experienced a moral obligation to the ethnic primor-dial public, the westernized civic public was largely seen as a contested terrain for private accumulation. The dialectics of the two publics are implicated in the distinctive woes that troubles Africa today, where people's first loyalty is to their ethnic identities at the expense of the nation state (Ekeh 1975: 92). Corruption is the "acme of the dialectics," and derives directly from the legitimation of the need to nourish the primordial public (e.g. one's kin) with largesse seized from the civic public (Ekeh 1975: 110). Public officials in Africa are generally expected by their own community and adherents to acquire fortunes through corruption and cronyism. In Uganda for instance, stealing state funds is commonly seen as "smart," not immoral. The one who fails to cash in on his position might be told, *Ngor nyak I boto pa lawok* (literally, "peas yield in a toothless person's garden") (Baez-Camargo et al. 2017: 27). In DR Congo, a policeman who does not accept bribes is called *yuma*, which means stupid (Alexandre 2018: 568).

Ekeh's thesis rings true in contemporary Africa, where people often express far stronger loyalty to their ethnic kinsmen than to the nation state. In Nigeria, the only time when people appear to share a sense of national identity is when the national football team—nicknamed the "Super Eagles"—is playing a match. Here, government business is no man's business. In fact, a standing joke is that Nigeria is a career rather than a national identity. In this light, stealing from the state ap-paratus to nourish one's community is widely justified, even a respectable crime.

Not to do this is to risk being criticized and ostracized as a person without esteem (Tankebe 2010: 301; Tankebe et al. 2019). The huge pressures on African public servants to break with conventional norms of civil service is evident in Nigeria, where the higher one ascends the social ladder, the more one is expected to do for one's people. High-placed government officials and street-level bureaucrats are under immense pressure to provide gifts of money, jobs, and social amenities to their ethnic communities (Agbiboa 2011: 498). In Cameroon, elites feel constant pressure from their local village or ethnic communities to use every means, both moral and immoral, to "redistribute" as a way of demonstrating their commitment toward development (Orock 2015: 562). In Kenya, the state and society are intimately linked by a gluttonous and immoral mentality: "It's our time to eat" (Wrong 2009; Lindberg 2003).

Yet, Ekeh's thesis is not without flaws, perhaps the most obvious one being its over-simplification. Though influential, his argument has been criticized for disregarding the real experience of cleavages, inequalities, and ethnic hierarchies shaping the life chances of Africans, and making ethnic mobilization an attractive proposition for many elites and non-elites (Mustapha 2012). African civil societies, for instance, have been accused of ethnic fragmentation and primordial attachments (Osaghae 2006: 17). Moreover, Ekeh's two publics overlooks the reality of multiple overlapping publics and counter-publics in postcolonial Africa (Mbembe 1992: 4; Mustapha 2012)—a far cry from Jurgen Habermas' (1991, 2006) unitary theorization. In short, Ekeh's approach represents an inadequate heuristic for locating popular politics in contemporary Africa.

Despite the above shortcomings, Ekeh's theory has influenced major theoretical frameworks and debates that seek to understand how and why patron-client networks[4] persists in Africa today through the merger of formal bureaucratic procedures with traditional neo-patrimonial norms (Mamdani 1996). Such theories—known as "politics of the belly" (Bayart 1993), neopatrimonialism (Bratton & van de Walle 1994; Medard 1986), "embedded autonomy" (Evans 1995), "instrumentalized disorder" (Chabal & Daloz 1999), and "disorientations of civil society" (Osaghae 2006)—have sought to explain state pathologies and politics in Africa by alluding to the dynamics of internal social structures. Invariably, they have crystalized in the view of corruption as woven into the fabric of the African polity (Chabal & Daloz 1999: 99), reinforced by political and moral economies in which the spoils of the state are expected to be (re)distributed through social networks

---

[4] Patron-client networks generally describe "a set of transactions which may overlap with and yet are analytically distinct from corruption. Patron-client relationships are repeated relationships of exchange between specific patrons and their clients. A number of features distinguish patron-client exchanges from other types of exchange. First, such exchanges are usually personalized. They involve an identifiable patron and an identifiable set of clients. Entry and exit are considerably less free compared to normal market transactions. Secondly, the exchange is between two distinct types of agents, distinguished by status, power, or other characteristics" (Khan 1998: 23).

embedded in the state (Joseph 1987; Bayart et al. 1999). In Nigeria, patron-client networks constitutes much of the social fabric for informal and party politics and controls the possibility for political participation and social mobility (Forrest 1993: 5; Gatt & Owen 2018: 1198). The result is a personalized form of rule where political elites are able to shore up patronage by selectively distributing government resources to their local communities. In this perspective, corruption occurs when social expectations are unmet or when the spoils of the state ("national cake," as Nigerians like to say) are not appropriately and timeously redistributed. In this light, redistribution becomes the litmus test for political candidates and political accountability.

It is against this backdrop that Olivier de Sardan (1999: 18) has argued that the logic of solidarity networks in Africa includes an obligation of mutual assistance: "I scratch your back, you scratch my back." This logic of solidarity and reciprocity is richly documented in ethnographies of the state and socio-economic life in southwest and southeast Nigeria. On the former, anthropologist Karin Barber (1981: 724) writes: "The dynamic impulse of political life is the rise of self-made men. Individuals compete to make a position for themselves by recruiting supporters willing to acknowledge their greatness [...] but the self-made man, rather like the Big Man of New Guinea, is only 'big' if other people think so. He has to secure their attention by display and redistribution of wealth and by using his influence as a Big Man to protect them and intervene on their behalf. If he is not able to do this, he will not attract a following." On the latter, Smith (2007: 65) writes: "A man who enriches himself through emptying government coffers is despised in his community only if he fails to share enough of that wealth with his people through direct gifts to individuals and community development projects, but also through more ceremonial distribution such as lavish weddings for his children, spectacular burials for his parents, and extravagant chieftaincy installations ceremonies for himself. At such events, his people enjoy his wealth—they *chop* (eat) his money." In both ethnographies, the power of the big man intertwines with the people, putting both actors in a precarious[5] position.

Richard Joseph (1987: 191) challenged what Crawford Young and Thomas Turner (1985: 451) before him referred to as the state's moral entitlement to legitimacy, arguing instead that insecurity is a common denominator for those in positions of political power, the included, and those on the margins of the state, the excluded. This "precariousness of prebendalism," as David Pratten (2013) frames it, explains in part why political patrons in Nigeria often rely on mobilizing and

---

[5] The Latin word *precarious* means "given as favor," or "depending on the favor of another person." The earliest meaning of the English word "precarious" relates to the idea of being given something— the right to occupy land, or to hold a particular position—"at the pleasure of" another person, who might simply choose to take it back at any time. In its more modern usage, precarity means "subject to or fraught with physical danger or insecurity; at risk of falling, collapse, or similar accident; unsound, unsafe, rickety" (Oxford English Dictionary 2012; see also Standing 2011).

arming marginalized youth[6] during election times as political thugs. In Nigeria, big men are under constant pressure to remember and reward these rugged youth, since the big man status is unfixed and multiple: "followers may discard Big Men when they do not deliver. At the same time a follower is not loyal to just one Big Man, but typically enjoys different relationships with different Big Men" (Utas 2012: 8). This is precisely the sense in which bigmanity in Africa has been linked to being for someone else or other people; in Mende, "stand for them" or "be for them" (*numui lo va*). As one young man put it: "'being for' someone implies that you have made yourself subject to the person. You work for him, fight for him, etc. And he is in turn responsible for you in all ways [such as court fines, clothes, food, school fees, or bridewealth]" (Bledsoe 1990: 75). Similarly, regarding Mende social practices: what is most important is that everyone is accounted for by someone else, that is, that everyone is connected in a relationship of patronage or clientship (Ferme 2001: 106). In return, the patron, the person who stands for someone else, expects a level of respect, support, and privilege, as well as a share in any wealth that the client might accumulate (Hoffman 2007: 652). This "wealth in people" (Utas 2005a) is captured in an ethnographic study of the politics of plunder in southern Nigeria, which finds that one's achievements for one's people (*se enye anam*) constitutes a key social marker of personal wealth (*ackpokpor inyene*), showing how the personal and the social are interconnected. This explains why the obituaries of big men (*akamba owo*) often recount their achievements for their local communities. The logic is simple: wealth begets social responsibilities (Gore & Pratten 2003: 219–20). Similarly, in his seminal study of political consciousness among the poor in Ibadan, southwest Nigeria, Gavin Williams found that "the values and goals in terms of which the success of the rich is defined are to a large extent shared by the poor and define their aspirations, thereby legitimizing the rewards of the rich" (1980: 112).

What emerges from the above is a notion of corruption as a breakdown of traditional moral economy in which those who have (well-off elites) are obliged to provide for the have-nots (deprived non-elites). Perhaps, nowhere is this more evident than in the rise of advance fee fraud ("419") in Nigeria and "the magical allure of making money from nothing" (Andrews 1997: 3). The figure "419" signifies "Section 419" of Nigeria's Criminal Code Act 1990, Chapter 38, which states that: "Any person who by any false pretense, and with intent to defraud, obtains from any other person anything capable of being stolen, or induces any other person to deliver any person anything capable of being stolen, is guilty of a felony, and is liable to imprisonment for three years." Built upon duplicitous illusions, 419 e-mails blur the putative lines between "the forged and the far-fetched, the spirit and the letter of the counterfeit, the fetish and the fake" (Comaroff & Comaroff 2006: 15).

---

[6] In Nigeria, the concept of "youth" occupies a category of risk; it labels a dangerous, insurgent, and unpredictable force that threatens the social and political fabric (Pratten 2013: 245).

Although the name Nigeria has become a synonym for criminality and fraud in the global imagination, 419 scams are not unique to that country. In fact, "post-colonies are quite literally associated with a counterfeit modernity, a modernity of counterfeit" (Comaroff & Comaroff 2006: 13).

While economists and political scientists have indubitably contributed to a globally circulating set of anti-corruption campaigns, policies, and perception-based surveys, they have either explained away the social embeddedness of corruption or lost sight of the local terrain and systems of action and meaning that animate corrupt practices and imbue them with social significance (Pierce 2016: 18). We still know remarkably little about how corruption is routinely encountered and negotiated in concrete instantiations in state margins. Yet survey evidence from Africa shows that ordinary citizens are most burdened by corruption when trying to gain access to indispensable basic social services in their own country; in particular, poor people who use public services in Africa are twice as likely as the rich to pay bribes, particularly in urban areas (Global Corruption Barometer 2015: 2–3). In Nigeria, the average citizen expects to pay a bribe (*egunje*) to gain access to public services, even those marked as free. The thread of corruption runs through schools, courts, churches, hospitals, police stations and checkpoints (Obadare 2019: 165). Survey evidence from the Nigerian Bureau of Statistics (NBS) shows that roughly a third of adult citizens who had come into contact with public officials had been asked for a bribe. According to the NBS, a total of 82 million naira (USD200,000) was paid in bribes to public officials in Nigeria in the previous twelve-month period. This equates to an average of one bribe per person per year (BBC 2017). Another survey by the UN Office on Drugs and Crime (UNODC), in association with the NBS, found that poor Nigerians paid an estimated USD4.6 billion in bribes to public officials between June 2015 and May 2016, concluding that "bribery is an established part of the administrative procedure in Nigeria" (UNODC 2017: 5–6). Nigeria is not alone. In Kenya, it is estimated the average urban resident pays sixteen bribes per month (Ellis 2006: 204). President Daniel Arap Moi, during his twenty-four years in power, is widely credited with reducing Kenya to the home of the bribe, *nchi ya kitu kidogo* ("land of the 'little something'") (Wrong 2009: 2). An empirical study of Uganda's health care system found that nothing can be obtained without paying a bribe. In fact, almost half of all people who contacted the health sector in Uganda paid a bribe (Marquette, Peiffer, & Armytage 2019). Soliciting a bribe from a poor woman with acute chest pain, a Ugandan nurse is quoted as saying: "These days there are no free things, [not] even at the main hospital. Give me 20000 [schillings] and I will take you to the doctor" (Baez-Camargo et al. 2017: 12). To receive medical treatment, poor Ugandans often have to find a *musawo nga mukwanogwo* (health worker who is your friend). Beyond Africa, in the Philippines, poor people often have to pay bribes ranging from 3,000 to 5,000 pesos (USD58 to USD60), with some yielding up to three months' wages to their superiors in gratitude for their job (Quah 2006: 176).

By happenstance rather than by design (Haller & Shore 2005: 6),[7] a growing body of anthropological literature on corruption has emerged relatively recently. These ground-level studies have questioned the neat divide between the public and the private, the legal and the illegal (Gupta 1995; Ruud 2000; Bocarejo 2018), especially neo-Weberian assumptions about the nature of state institutions or the significance of a clash between patrimonial and bureaucratic political logics (Pierce 2016: 18; Piliavsky 2014). This "anthropological turn" pivots on how corruption, as a transgressive category, manifests in "gray practices" (Routley 2016; Muir & Gupta 2018). Anthropologists have also called attention to how people and NGOs navigate the ambivalence of corruption through tactics such as cultural construction (Lamour 2008), mis-recognition (Hansen 1995), negotiations (Routley 2016; Anjaria 2011), irony, rumor, and laughter (Gupta 2012), categorization (Werner 2000), straddling of political and economic spheres (Bayart 1993), and everyday deception (Smith 2007). These anthropological analyses extend to why corruption has taken on the forms it has and how cultural systems and value codes permit the legitimation of corruption. By anchoring corruption in everyday life, anthropologists call our attention to the social worlds that allows corruption to flourish.

Unlike the central focus of economists and political scientists on grand or high-level corruption, anthropologists are generally interested in petty corruption, defined as "everyday abuse of entrusted power by low- and mid-level public officials in their interaction with ordinary citizens, who often are trying to access basic goods or services in places like hospitals, schools, police departments, and other agencies" (Transparency International n.d.). Known in Greece as *fakelaki* ("little bribery envelopes"), in Nigeria as *egunje* (involuntary gifts), in Kenya as *kintu kidogo* (something small), and in Angola as *gasosas* ("soft drinks," often demanded at police checkpoints), petty corruption involves forms of bribery and extortion in daily life. In developing regions such as Africa and South Asia, petty corruption (particularly by law enforcement officials) is the "most visible face of corruption" and a primary source of "public irritation" (Khan 2006). At the same time, petty corruption has been labelled "quiet corruption," a term used by the World Bank (2010: 2) to capture forms of everyday corruption and malpractices that are neither easily observed and quantified nor necessitate monetary exchange, but which hold major, long-term ramifications for service delivery, regulation, and households. Visible or quiet, petty corruption has become a way of life and a mode of business and politics in much of the developing world (Ellis 2006: 204). In Nigeria, petty corruption is commonly regarded as a necessary evil or simply "the way things are done" (Hoffmann & Patel 2017). As early as 1950, future Nigerian prime

[7] Many anthropologists say they stumbled upon or noticed corruption while researching other topics. For example, in his *Moral Economies of Corruption*, Steven Pierce (2016: 5–6) notes that "The starting point of this project came while I collected oral histories about local government across the twentieth century."

minister Tafawa Balewa noted that the "twin curses" of bribery and corruption "pervade every rank and department" (Watts 2019: 554). Two years later, in 1952, the Commission of Inquiry into the Administration of the Lagos Town Council ("Storey Report") observed widespread practice of giving an unofficial cash gift or a fee (bribe) for services rendered:

> Hospitals where the nurses require a fee from every in-patient before the prescribed medicine, and even the ward servants must have their *dash* [bribe] before bringing the bed-pan; it is known to be rife in the Police Motor Traffic Unit, which has unrivalled opportunities on account of the common practice of over-loading vehicles; pay clerks make a deduction from the wages of daily paid staff; produce examiners exact a fee from the produce buyer for every bag that is graded and scaled; domestic servants pay a proportion of their wages to the senior of them, besides often having paid lump sum to buy the jobs."
> (Storey Report 1953)

Despite attempts to trivialize petty corruption, empirical studies show that this form of corruption saps the legitimacy of the state and damages confidence in public institutions and the political system (DFID 2015: 83).[8] Further, petty corruption disproportionately affects the poor in developing countries, while increasing transaction costs and general lawlessness (Khan 2006). Every stolen money robs the poor of an equal opportunity in life and precludes investment in human capitals by governments (World Bank 2020). While grand corruption did not prevent the rapid development of the East Asian countries, each of these countries took steps to address bureaucratic corruption (Kang 2002; Prasad & Nickow 2016), illustrating the cumulative threat of petty corruption.

Grand and Petty Corruption: Two Poles of a Continuum

The disparities between high-level and petty forms of corruption notwithstanding, this book interrogates both basic typologies as interconnected (Torsello & Venard 2015: 40), or, as Olivier de Sardan (1999) puts it, "two poles of a continuum." In her study of corruption in Accra, Jennifer Hasty (2005a: 342) argues that the ubiquitous nature of petty corruption "performs mimetic and contagious relations with the episodic spectacles of grand corruption—and vice versa. This enchanted relation is essential to the durability and proliferation of corruption." The implication

---

[8] Empirical research has shown that citizens who lack confidence in public institutions may be more likely to accept bribery and less likely to participate in political processes (DFID 2015: 83).

is that neatly categorizing corruption into only two typologies reduces its complexity and fluidity. As Davide Torsello and Bertrand Venard (2015: 37) tell us,
"focusing on one type of corruption puts any social reality into a static state without
taking into account its environment, when corruption is in fact a dynamic social
reality linked to its social and political setting, which by nature changes over time."
Moreover, the distinctions between grand and petty corruption downplays the in-
terplay between elite and popular politics, especially the cultural forces that shape
elite-subaltern interaction (Obadare 2019: 164). A case in point is Lagos, where
transport trade unions and local and state governments are deeply embroiled in
a complex relationship that evokes Bähre's notion of violent and shifting mutualities in Cape Town. According to Bähre (2014: 576), mutualities produce particular
economies that cannot exist without some level of social networks of trust, reciprocity, and protection to deal with the risks and radical uncertainties that average
citizens and public officials face on a day-to-day basis. Mutuality is most visible in
developing countries, where the state may be unable or unwilling to deliver political goods. In such a seemingly weak environment, the state and (un)civil society
are often implicated in political and moral economies of corruption. As Adebanwi
and Obadare note regarding Nigeria:

> Given the incapacity of the state, its divisive nature, and the pervasive poverty
> which these (re)produce—much of which is also explained by corruption—many
> Nigerians survive on the patron-client relationships and other identitarian con-
> nections which link them to particular members of the elite. This means that
> while Nigerians are generally socially supportive of anti-corruption efforts, many
> are politically or economically connected to the corruption complex directly or
> indirectly. (2011: 195)

As a fundamental aspect of social relations, the logic of mutuality has yet to penetrate the existent literature on corruption in Africa, which all too narrowly pivot
on the idea of the state while overlooking the people who populate it. In fact, "the
very idea of elites suggests qualities of agency, exclusivity, power and an apparent separation from mass society" (Shore 2002: 4). Yet, as scholars such as Philip
Abrams (1988) and Timothy Mitchell (1991) remind us, states in their abstract
form do not actually exist as distinct entities but rather as socially embedded and
relational sets of persons that animate state institutions. No wonder, then, that
George Marcus (1983: 12) calls for a rethinking of elites as socially situated groups
in relation to other non-elite groups. In a like vein, Sandipto Dasgupta (2019: 562)
argues that "public officials are not abstracted from private power relations in society, and private actors are not bereft of public political capacities." From Africa
to Latin America and South Asia, corruption is embedded within the logics of
negotiation and bargaining, and ordinary citizens simultaneously encounter the
state as an extension of disciplinary power and an epicenter of negotiation and legitimation of spatial claims (Anjaria 2011: 58; Olivier de Sardan 1999: 253, 256).

In Cameroon, for example, Orock points to how the social expectation that elites provide development projects "evokes the assumptions of conviviality that underlie social relations between the well-off (elites) and the less privileged non-elites" (2015: 541).

About this Book

This grounded, bottom-up study examines corruption in the context of everyday encounters and interactions between state (e.g. law enforcement agents) and nonstate (e.g. transport unionists and tax collectors) actors in Nigeria's road transport sector. The study is about the commonplace struggles and instrumentalities of survival of informal road transport workers (e.g. drivers, conductors, owners, unionists) refracted through a "thick" discussion of corruption, coercion, and complicity on the congested and dangerous roads of Lagos. Located within the above anthropological critique of corruption, the book argues that average Nigerians (in particular, road transport workers) are not passive in the face of corruption, but rather appropriate it in a variety of ways to minimize risk, maximize profit, and impose order on their workaday world. The study takes an actor-centered approach that explores how transport workers encounter and respond to the situation defined by extortion and violence in which they ply their trade. The book's overarching focus is, thus, on the role and impact of corruption in the context of the everyday life of informal road transport workers, particularly how these mobile but immobilized actors bend the rules to manage their precarious dwelling-in-motion. By so doing, the book takes up Olivier de Sardan's (1999: 25) call to explore the social mechanisms of corruption and its processes of legitimation from the actors' viewpoint.

As used in this study, the concept of "informal" means the self-organizing capacity of social actors who operate "inside the system, but outside the law" (Rasmussen 2012). Across African cities, informality is a way of life and a survival tactic for growing numbers of people on the margins of society, accounting for an estimated 86 percent of total employment, or 72 percent, excluding agriculture. In fact, nine out of ten jobs in Africa today are informal (Lindell & Adama 2020: 3–4). Despite the vital role of the informal sector as the main driver of job growth in urban Africa, informal workers are commonly stigmatized as illegal and undesirable occupants of urban spaces and thus targeted by state restrictions and eviction campaigns based on neoliberal policies aimed at modernizing and ordering the city.[9] To survive, informal workers often resort to giving bribes to secure protection from daily harassment and arrest. I want to suggest up front that the insights of this book are equally about corruption as they are about the struggle

---

[9] These actions run contrary to the basic thrust of the "New Urban Agenda" of the UN Habitat III, which seeks to promote inclusive cities that "leave no one behind" (UN Habitat III 2016: 7).

for daily survival—the two intertwine in the context of informal transport and commuter journeys in Lagos, where giving *egunje* (bribes) is generally viewed as a legitimate survival strategy. In other words, this book is less a systematic account of corruption than an empirically grounded analysis of the politics and poetics of survival in everyday, urban Nigeria.

In addition to the "demand side" of corruption (e.g. bribe solicitation by police officers), this book engages the oft-neglected "supply side" (e.g. facilitation payments). In Uganda, for example, so high is the supply side that the courts, in a bid to combat it, have plastered signs all over the courthouse. "Most court services are free," the inscriptions read. "Do Not Corrupt Us. Offender will be Prosecuted" (Tabachnik 2011: 23). In Freetown, Sierra Leone, it is common for motorbike-taxi (*okada*) drivers to supply bribes to police officers *ex ante*. Known as *bora* and *ajo*, this advance payment eases their passage through road checkpoints (Lipton 2017: 93). In Bukavu, the DRC, most taxi drivers lack the required driving particulars. So, they supply USD1 as bribe to each police station before driving. In this way, they are able to drive without police harassment. Police stations, for their part, must remit a weekly bribe of USD60–120 to the traffic police headquarters in Bukavu, depending on the lucrative location of the police station (Alexandre 2018: 564).

The concepts of demand and supply are used loosely in this study, since average citizens can, and regularly do, "demand" corruption on the part of people in positions of power or control (e.g. drivers). To illustrate, during my fieldwork in Lagos, I was struck by how often passengers of the yellow minibus-taxis (*danfos*) persuaded their driver[10] to follow the illegal "one way" route in order to beat traffic jam (*go-slow*, as they say in Lagos). The same passengers do not hesitate to insult the driver when he is pulled over by the policeman for a traffic violation. They will demand that he "settles" (bribes) the officer to avoid delay. This, of course, is a rational response on the part of passengers, since bribing a law enforcement agent to avoid a penalty for a traffic violation is generally less costly, risky, and time-consuming than would be going through "due process" for the violation (Hoffmann & Patel 2017: 10). When a driver chooses to maintain his correct lane, whether slow or fast, the same passengers are often incensed and start to repeatedly berate him. These passengers are aware that following "one way" is illegal and dangerous. Yet, they demand it because they see others doing so or expect others to do so. They rationalize "one way" as a practical response to the existential angst of being stuck in traffic and "packed like sardines" for any number of hours. This social expectation is conveyed by the popular Nigerian saying, *Naija no dey carry last* ("Nigerians strive to finish first").[11] The central point here is that corruption

---

[10] In Lagos, the taxi-driver is a "big man" in relation to the passenger. For, as Olatunde Lawuyi (1988: 5) observes with regard to Yorùbá taxi-drivers in southwest Nigeria: "The travelers themselves know that, if angered, the driver may refuse to take them to their destinations, for a certain power inheres in the owner's control of the vehicle and in a sense makes him a privileged citizen."

[11] "Naija no dey carry last" is the title of a book satirizing Nigeria by the late Pius Adesanmi.

is often a tactical weapon wielded by both the strong and the weak, by those in the proverbial driving seat and those being chauffeured around the city. In short, as Olivier de Sardan (1999: 250) argues, corruption is so widespread in Africa that the average citizen has a routine experience of dealing with it.

The above necessitates a dialectical approach that pays attention to the practical and social life of corruption, and the strategies of the various actors involved. That dynamic approach will shed much-needed light onto "gray practices" that challenge *idées reçues* of corruption. Thus, a dialectical approach to corruption lays bare the complicated web of social norms, value acceptances, power relations, negotiations, and social networks that animates local discourse and practices of corruption. In this light, then, corruption is best approached as a window onto how the postcolonial state is imagined and experienced in everyday life (Gupta 1995: 385; Masquelier 2001: 269). So conceived, any serious study of corruption in Africa today must move us beyond the idea of the state as an autonomous and unified entity and, instead, explore thoroughly its embodied and hybrid realities.

A Culture of/against Corruption

This book grounds corruption on the survival tactics of marginalized transport operators in Lagos as they socially navigate[12] a bumpy terrain embroiled in manifold risks, ranging from travel to unfamiliar places and, most of all, other city dwellers. In so doing, this book breaks with cultural primordialist analyses of corruption in Africa (in the form of Patrick Chabal & Jean-Pascal Daloz [2006] and Jean-Francois Bayart [2005]) that tend to misconstrue culture as path dependent, that is, as a set of primordial phenomena rather than of contested and protean attributes, both shaping and being shaped by socio-economic aspects of daily human interactions. Citizens and public officials run the risk of essentializing rather than explaining culture when they apply it as a "primordial trap, a mystical haze, or a source of hegemonic power" (Rao & Walton 2004: 3; see also Meagher 2006) in justification of otherwise despicable acts of corruption. While corruption saturates the political economies of African countries, it is not somehow organic to African culture. As Smith (2007: 224–25) notes, Nigeria is as much a culture *against* corruption as it is about a culture *of* corruption. Corruption is neither rooted in primordial traditional culture nor is it a desirable feature of everyday life. If by culture we mean the general moral orientation of the population in question, then the vast majority of Nigerians, nay Africans, are against rather than in support of corruption (Rothstein 2018: 39). Gift giving in Africa is not infrequently

---

[12] Henrik Vigh defines navigation as the striving "to direct and control the movement of one's life rather than having it be directed and moved by the shifting of the unstable social environment it is immersed in" (2006: 130).

rationalized by political elites and street-level bureaucrats as "part of our culture," and outsiders are warned not to conflate it with bribery. However, Chief Olusegun Obasanjo, a former Nigerian president (1999–2007), debunked this viewpoint:

> I shudder at how an integral aspect of our culture could be taken as the basis for rationalizing otherwise despicable behavior. In the African concept of appreciation and hospitality, the gift is usually a token. It is not demanded. The value is in the open and never in secret. Where it is excessive, it becomes an embarrassment and it is returned. If anything, corruption has perverted and destroyed this aspect of our culture. (cited in Pope 2000: 8)

Obasanjo's observation is not evidently insincere. A 2005 Afrobarometer survey[13] in Kenya found that 84 percent of all respondents think that a public official who demands a favor or an additional payment for some service that is part of his job is violating his responsibility to the public (Figure 2). Kenyans are also less accepting of a public official who gives a job to someone from his family who does not have adequate qualifications, with 72 percent considering this a punishable action. The study concluded that, "Clearly, traditional cultural practices, whether of gift or other varieties, do not, in the eyes of the public, entitle government officials to take advantage of them" (Afrobarometer Data 2006a: 1).

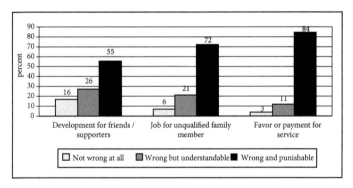

Fig. 2. What is corrupt?
Source: Afrobarometer (2006a: 2).

Similarly, in his analysis of corruption and the use of monies in Mongolia, David Sneath contrasts "acceptable enaction" (e.g. helping family and friends) with "unacceptable transaction" (e.g. bribing an official). He offers this example: "The gift

---

[13] The Afrobarometer survey was conducted between September 2 and 28, 2005. It involved face-to-face interviews with 1278 Kenyan men and women of voting age, selected through a scientific random sampling procedure in accordance with international polling standards. Interviews were conducted in all eight of the country's provinces, and 51 of its 72 districts. Citizens of each province are represented in the weighted sample in proportion to their share in the national population (Afrobarometer 2006a: 1).

of a bottle of vodka to a relative who uses a company truck to help a family move, for example (a very common form of assistance among rural kin), is expressive of the supportive relationship between the parties concerned and is not thought of as an exchange. But giving cash to a railway baggage handler to load an over-weight package onto a train is clearly understood to be a transaction—in this sense a potentially corrupt one" (Sneath 2006: 89). In a study of the social life of corruption in India, Arild Ruud (2000: 282–83) shows that, even from a culturally sensitive perspective, ordinary people from many different backgrounds often denounced corrupt practices such as bribe-taking, rule-bending, and favoritism. In his study of the relationship between corruption and culture in the Pacific Islands, Peter Lamour (2008: 229–30) quotes a Prime Minister in the State of Samoa who said: "What determines an acceptable gift is 5 percent policy/law and 95 percent common sense," adding "a bottle of whisky or ten tala [USD3.60] is considered to be acceptable gift, while a gift of say 3,000 tala [USD1,080] would certainly be regarded as unacceptable and this would be seen as a bribe." The foregoing challenges the common recourse to some generalized notion of culture to explain the banalization of corruption and supports the call for an avoidance of the "dual trap of condemnation and relativism" in the corruption literature (Das 2015: 323).

The Afrobarometer (2006b: 33) survey shows that most Africans think that corruption is "wrong and punishable"[14] (Figure 3). Hence, to blame corruption on the culture of a nation is tantamount to saying that its people are inherently fraudulent or prone to corruption, which is hardly a sound point of departure for inclusive policy change (Rothstein 2018: 40). In the case of Nigeria, ordinary citizens are largely supportive of anti-corruption campaigns, even if for ethnic, religious, or political reasons, they may not want to see certain politicians held accountable (i.e. punished) for their corrupt behavior (Adebanwi & Obadare 2011). This observation problematizes the moralizing, culturalist view that Nigerians are somehow more prone to corruption than others. This view is best exemplified by remarks made by former United States' Secretary of State Colin Powell, who suggested that corruption and crime are natural to Nigerians, because "it is in their natural culture" (cited in Gates 1995). But, as Stephen Ellis (2016: 3) asks, "Can culture be an explanation for such behavior? In any case, how does a specific culture come into being? Didn't the experience of colonial rule play some part?"

The above-cited Afrobarometer survey is buttressed by further survey evidence from Africa and South Asia which demonstrates that ordinary citizens in these societies do not only take a clear stance against corruption but also conceive of corruption in a similar way to global organizations such as the World Bank and

---

[14] The Afrobarometer surveyed individuals from Nigeria, Benin, Botswana, Cape Verde, Ghana, Kenya, Lesotho, Madagascar, Malawi, Mali, Mozambique, Namibia, Senegal, South Africa, Tanzania, Uganda, Zambia, and Zimbabwe.

For each of the following, please indicate whether you think the act is not wrong at all, wrong but understandable, or wrong and punishable.	Category	Response (%)
▪ A public official decides to locate a development project in area where his friends and supporters live.	▪ Not wrong at all	3
	▪ Wrong but understandable	12
	▪ Wrong and punishable	82
	▪ Don't know	4
▪ A government official gives a job to someone from his family who does not have adequate qualifications.	▪ Not wrong at all	1
	▪ Wrong but understandable	6
	▪ Wrong and punishable	91
	▪ Don't know	1
▪ A government official demands a favor or an additonal payment for some service that is part of his job.	▪ Not wrong at all	1
	▪ Wrong but understandable	8
	▪ Wrong and punishable	88
	▪ Don't know	3

Fig. 3. Thinking about corruption
Source: Afrobarometer (2006b: 33).

Transparency International (Rothstein & Torsello 2014: 276). In its Annual Meeting's address in 1996, former World Bank President James D. Wolfensohn adduced the *vox populi* as the primary reason why the World Bank reinvented itself as an anti-corruption organization:

> And let's not mince words: we need to deal with the cancer of corruption. In country after country, *it is the people who are demanding action on this issue.* They know that corruption diverts resources from the poor to the rich, increases the cost of running business, distorts public expenditures, and deters foreign investors. They also know that it erodes the constituency for aid programs and humanitarian relief. And we all know that it is a major barrier to sound and equitable development. (Wolfensohn 1996; my emphasis)

While the above evidence shows that most people in the developing world disapprove of corruption, it persists nevertheless because it is tied to the pursuit of daily survival.

My own findings from "hanging out" in the congested bus stations-*cum*-markets of Lagos suggest that the everyday and political life of corruption are intertwined, giving rise to systemic corruption. For instance, during my fieldwork, minibus-taxi drivers and passengers stressed that the dreaded motor park touts (*agberos*)—who violently extract bribes from drivers in the name of the National Union of Road Transport Workers (NURTW)—are powerfully linked to politicians and police chiefs. The cash bribes they collect each day serves to grease the union-state-police mutualities. As one resident of Lagos opined: "There is an apparent collusion between these touts, law enforcement agencies and some highly influential persons and politicians in the state. That is the reason why at some bus stops, unionists are deployed to collect illegal tolls and levies on behalf of influential persons, even law enforcement agents" (*The Guardian* 2017). This observation points to the limitation of the anthropology of corruption, especially its tendency to overlook political science literature, including political culture, thought, and language.[15] As Susan Rose-Ackerman (2010) observes: "Ethnographic research tends to concentrate on cultural and social expectations to explain the prevalence of personalistic ties and quid pro quo transactions to the exclusion of looking at the dynamics of 'grand' corruption, its systematic qualities, or the central role played by the state."

A Critical Ethnography of the State

This study takes a critical ethnography of the state perspective, which focuses on how the postcolonial state is constructed from below through the practice of everyday corruption and discursive productions. The state becomes an agent that simultaneously exists in and is continuously created by society. As Ruud (2000: 282) argues, "the state as it appears locally in the eyes of its citizens is colored by the circumstance of corruption as one of the means of mediation between the state and individuals."

This study is positioned within an emergent corpus of works that have articulated the theorized shift from government to *governance* in the developing world, whereby the state is increasingly hollowed out as functions are dispersed to supranational entities and nonstate actors (Ferguson 2006; Bagayoko et al. 2016). By governance, I mean the hybrid arena in which formal and informal, and state and nonstate, actors interact to make decisions and regulate the public realm. In this light, bifurcated notions of the state as either strong or weak pale into insignificance when compared with a hybrid form of governance, and "language of stateness,"[16] that is neither hegemonic nor subaltern (Hansen & Stepputat 2001; Jaffe 2013: 736). This hybrid system is, perhaps, most discernable in the decentered notion of power that underpins state-society dialectics.

Rejecting Nietzsche's notion of power as relations of domination, that is, that power descends in a linear direction from those who have it to those subjected to it (Sluga 2005: 232), this book operates from the Foucauldian mobile understanding of power as profoundly relational. Power is a product of complex struggles and negotiations over authority, status, reputation, and resources, which requires the participation of networks of actors and constituencies (Long 1999: 3). Far from

---

[15] A notable exception is Claudio Lomnitz's brilliant article on "Ritual, Rumor and Corruption in the Constitution of Polity in Modern Mexico," which argues that there is a general relationship between "political ritual" and localized appropriations of state institutions (corruption) (1995: 20–21).

[16] Hansen and Stepputat (2001) distinguishes practical languages of governance (such as the monopoly over violence) from the symbolic languages of authority (such as the institutionalization of the law).

being a universal or autonomous source of power, the state is nothing else but "a multiple and mobile field of force relations" (Foucault 1978: 102). Until recently, studies of corruption pivoted on how the state "sees" citizens (Scott 1998), how "stateness" is performed (Hansen & Stepputat 2001), how power is "sustained and articulated" (Rademacher 2008: 106), and how the aura of sovereign ultimacy is "internalized" (Chalfin 2008: 250). Less well known is how socio-economic practices at the margins shape the state itself (Das & Poole 2004) and, related to this, how the state is localized or made visible in discursive practices (Gupta 1995). This book contributes to bridging this lacuna in the existent literature.

Toward the Corruption Complex

> Corruption is behavior which deviates from the formal duties of a public role because of private-regarding (personal, close family, private clique) pecuniary or state gains; or violate rules against the exercise of certain types of private-regarding influence. This includes such behavior as bribery (use of a reward to pervert the judgement of a person in a position of trust); nepotism (bestowal of patronage by reason of ascriptive relationship rather than merit); and misappropriation (illegal appropriation of public resources for private-regarding uses). (Nye 1967: 419)

> Corruption is a kind of behavior that deviates from the norm actually prevalent or believed to prevail in a given context, such as the political. It is deviant behavior associated with a particular motivation, namely that of private gain at public expense. But whether this was the motivation or not, it is the fact that private gain was secured at public expense that matters. Such private gain may be a monetary one, and in the minds of the general public it usually is, but it may take other forms. (Friedrich 1989: 5)

Contained in the above conventional definitions of corruption are two fundamental assumptions: first, that mutually exclusive public and private interests exist and, second, that public servants must necessarily abstract themselves from the private realm if they are to properly function (Bratsis 2003: 11). These assumptions rest simply on a Weberian-style modern bureaucratic state which assumes—in contrast to the patrimonial state—the existence of a public office that is distinct from the private domain. As Weber notes, "The patrimonial office lacks above all the bureaucratic separation of the private and the official sphere. For the political administration, too, is treated as purely personal affair of the ruler, and political power is considered part of his personal property, which can be exploited by means of contributions and fees" (cited in Hyden 2006: 95). The Weberian rational legal state reifies corruption and overlooks its situation in overlapping publics and their distinct but interdependent logics.

Ethnographic studies of corruption have presented bottom-up evidence to show that the public/private bifurcation is often context-dependent (Gupta 1995; Muir & Gupta 2018; Bocarejo 2018). Evidence from my own fieldwork in Lagos suggests that the public/private dichotomy represents a normative demand rather than an empirical reality. "Corruption entails of very many things we don't believe to be corruption. If you influence a pastor of your church it is corrupt. You want him to do a special prayer for you, so you buy tubers of yam or bags of rice and take it to him. Some think it is a gift, but I call it corruption." That was how a minibus-taxi (*danfo*) driver in Lagos explained corruption to me. His words strike at the profoundly ambiguous concept of corruption (Haller & Shore 2005). The anthropology of corruption has shown that the concept of corruption covers a confusingly wide spectrum of practices (Gupta 1995; Bocarejo 2018; Sneath 2006; Smith 2007), including criminality and fraud. In this light, then, Olivier de Sardan's influential concept of the "corruption complex" (1999: 26) remains, perhaps, the most nuanced and productive theoretical lens for interpreting corruption in Africa. By definition, the corruption complex designates a number of illicit practices (such as nepotism, abuse of power, graft, and various forms of misappropriation), all of which are technically distinct from corruption but yet have in common with corruption their link to the state. Thus, the corruption complex describes practices that are deemed corrupt but may or may not be illegal as such (Routley 2016: 119; Pierce 2016: 8, 22).

One of the earliest observations of the corruption complex in Nigeria was among the Hausa-speaking people of northern Nigeria. Anthropologist M.G. Smith (1964: 164) argues that Hausa people lack a term for political corruption *sensu stricto*, which makes it difficult to isolate corruption from other conditions of its context for formal analyses. The Hausa people do, however, have several terms denoting a range of political conditions and practices related to corruption: "*Zalunchi* which refers to oppression, *tilas* to compulsion, *zamba* to oppression and swindling, *rikice* to fraud and confusion alike, *ha'inci* to bribery, *cin hanci* to taking bribes, *yi gaisuwa* to making greetings or gifts, *tara* to fines, *cin tara* to taking (keeping?) fines, *wasau* to forcible confiscation of property, *manafunci* to treachery and breaking of political agreements, *hamiya* to political rivalry, *kunjiya* to a faction or group of supporters, *baranktaka* to political agency, *kinjibbi* and *kutukutu* to differing types of intrigue, character assassination, and so on" (Smith 1964: 164). This semantic variability of corruption adds weight to Steven Pierce's diagnosis of corruption as "epistemologically shifty," as it refers to various meanings and phenomena (Pierce 2016: 5, 20).

Four decades after M.G. Smith's work, D.J. Smith corroborated the corruption complex among the Igbo people of southeast Nigeria. He observes that the talk of corruption in Nigeria extends beyond the abuse of public office for private gain to include "a whole range of social behaviors in which various forms of morally questionable deception enable the achievement of wealth, power, or prestige as well as much more mundane ambitions. Nigerian conception of corruption encompasses everything from government bribery and graft, rigged elections, and fraudulent business deals, to the diabolical abuse of occult powers, medical quackery, cheating in school, and even deceiving a lover" (2007: 55). In urban Nigeria, it is quite common to hear the word "corrupt" being used to describe a man that "carries woman"—a womanizer. This polyvalence of corruption *talk* is hardly specific to Nigeria. In Lubumbashi in DR Congo, corruption is so rife that people have developed an elaborate terminology for it: "Beans for the children, a little something, an encouragement, an envelope, something to tie the two ends with, to deal, to come to an understanding, to take care of me, to pay the beer, to short-circuit, to see clearly, to be lenient or comprehensive, to put things in place, to find a Zairian solution" (Riley 1999: 190).

There is no one-size-fits-all interpretation of corruption, so to ask what *exactly* is the meaning of corruption amounts to an exercise in futility. The real boundary between what is corruption and what is not is fluid and context-dependent (Olivier de Sardan 1999: 34). Thus, Torsello (2016: 15) is well within his rights to ask: "[W]hy stick to a single definition [of corruption] if the phenomenon is in constant mutation?" My ethnographic tendency is not to impose a universal meaning of corruption on the local context and then arrange my data accordingly (*etic* approach). Instead, my objective is to explore the range of behaviors that locals deem corrupt and to weave a grounded analysis based on what they do or say (*emic* approach). This approach is consistent with Mushtaq Khan's unanswered call for an analytical frame, which allows corruption to have different meanings and effects in different countries.[17] If, indeed, corruption has a uniform meaning and effect everywhere, argues Khan (1998), then we should reach this conclusion at the end of an evaluative process rather than make a presumption *ab initio*. The *emic* inclination of this study addresses the argument that corruption can only be fully grasped when it is situated within the setting where it appears and with which it continually interacts. This nuanced contextualization of corruption is fundamental, since more often than not, what strikes us as a clear case of unethical corrupt exchange turns out to be morally acceptable and socially legitimate when seen from the vantge point of local culture and the everyday lives of ordinary people. This reality, says Manuel Velasquez, calls for "greater caution when we are tempted to issue universal and absolute moral condemnation of corruption" (Velasquez 2004: 148). The title of Velasquez's essay is particularly telling: "Is Corruption Always Corrupt?"

---

[17] This approach is particularly apt in East and Southeast Asian countries, which combine high levels of corruption with good economic performance, challenging the popular assumption that corruption is associated with poor performance (Khan 1998).

Corruption, Language, and Social Action: Toward a Dialogical Approach

Inspired by calls to localize corruption in everyday discourse and practices, this book sees corruption as a social malpractice whose meaning is co-constructed by social actors and which emerges from specific social interactions. Corruption is intertwined with the evolving process of negotiation between citizens, public officials, and semi-private actors in particular settings and sectors. In other words, corruption generally unfolds in the "wider matrix of power relations in society" (Nuijten & Anders 2007: 2) and positions itself in the liminal space of interaction between the public and private realms. Given its embeddedness in everyday life and networks of sociocultural relations and logics, corruption is deeply interwoven with language and idiom.

Language emerges as "a powerful vehicle of thought and a crucial instrument for accomplishing social interaction, as an indispensable means of knowing the world and of performing deeds within it" (Basso 1992: xii). From the perspective of linguistic anthropology, language, culture, and society are mutually constituted; language shapes and is shaped by sociocultural factors and power dynamics (Ahearn 2001: 110–111). If the questions that social scientists seek to answer—for example, issues of bribery and corruption—are invariably posed first in ordinary language, it follows that "stipulating or legislating the meaning of a social science concept without first explicating the range of its ordinary language meanings is a dangerous practice" (Fearon and Laitin 2000: 5). Similar to speech and language, the discourse of corruption does not merely reflect an already existing social reality; it also helps to create that reality (Ahearn 2001: 111; Gupta 1995). Speech and idioms have the capacity to grasp corruption in its complexity because they too are embedded within the larger socio-economic fabric of society.

Understanding corruption as a complex, both practically and discursively, constitutes a radical break with normative analytical models based on comparative macro-level econometric-based data (Bardhan 2015; Mauro 1995). This study challenges the continued reliance on perception-based data and the conflation of data aggregation from various surveys into one figure used in international corruption barometers such as Transparency International's Corruption Perception Index (CPI). Instead, this study responds to recent calls to "refine and gather more experience-based measures of corruption" (Triesman 2007: 213; UNODC 2017: 11–12). Rising to the occasion, critical ethnographies of the state have established a symbiotic relationship between everyday corruption and the state's generalized informal functioning (Blundo & Olivier de Sardan 2006). For example, in his study of corruption in contemporary India, Gupta finds that the public/private spatial separation is weak to non-existent among public officials: "One has a better chance of finding them [the officials] at the roadside tea stalls and in their homes than in their offices" (1995: 384). It is against this backdrop that corruption is best situated within the wider pattern of interaction between centers and margins.

Beyond the Corruption Perception Index (CPI)

The CPI measures the perceptions of businesspeople and country experts regarding the degree of corruption among public officials and local politicians. A high score indicates greater levels of corruption. Self-styled the "survey of surveys," the CPI was originally compiled on the basis of sixteen different polls and surveys from eight independent institutions comprising businesspeople, country analysts, and the public (Lambsdorff 1999). The CPI has undoubtedly contributed to a worldwide movement and widespread consensus against corruption, tapping a decisive nail or two into the coffin of self-styled revisionists who, during the 1960s and 1970s, advocated the functionality of corruption for newly independent states in Africa and Asia (Leff 1964; Huntington 1968).[18] The CPI brought corruption into greater international prominence. As Fredrik Galtung writes:

> The CPI was a formidable instrument in raising awareness about the international scope and shared burden of corruption and driving corruption onto the front pages of newspapers throughout the developing world. The CPI levelled the playing field by comparing, for the first time, disparate and distinct countries on the same scale. The international shaming that ensued encouraged a race to the top, that is, to lower levels of corruption... and for some selected countries at the bottom of the league table (e.g., Bangladesh, Nigeria, and Paraguay) it has spurred a determination to shed the label of being "one of the world's most corrupt countries." (2006: 106)

Quoting his taxi driver in a piece on corruption in Pakistan, one journalist shared this joke:

> "You know," asked Ahmad, "swerving around a crater that could have swallowed his little taxi, "how Pakistan was No. 2 in the world in corruption?" I said that I'd heard something about it. Pakistan had been ranked second only to Nigeria in a 1996 "global corruption index" by an outfit called Transparency International. "Actually," Ahmad went on, "we were No. 1. But we bribed the Nigerians to take first place." (Stein 1997: 15)

---

[18] Revisionists argued that it is "natural but wrong to assume that the results of corruption are always both bad and important ... Where bureaucracy is both elaborate and inefficient, the provision of strong personal incentives to bureaucrats to cut red tape may be the only way of speeding the establishment of a new firm" (Leys 1965: 222). Today, however, there is no denying the "self-defeating" nature of corruption in the long run (Caiden 1988: 21, Agbiboa 2012).

Despite the CPI's impact on corruption, concerns abound about whether a polyvalent and hidden phenomenon such as corruption can be measured at all, let alone reduced to a single number (Haller & Shore 2005; Nuijten & Anders 2007). The problem with an evaluation such as the CPI is that corruption varies so much from country to country, no single number can accurately compare the wide range of forms that corruption takes from one country to the next (Johnston 2001: 63). A proper understanding of corruption must first locate it within the local contexts out of which it emerges and with which it routinely interacts. The focus of this study is not so much grand corruption as petty corruption, which is easier to observe but harder to quantify because it varies enormously and is embedded in complex social networks, which are in turn embedded in the state. In this light, then, there is no substitute for a critical ethnographic approach which interrogates not only "the social mechanisms through which corruption takes place" but also "the wider interactions of different spheres (economic, political, legal, social and cultural) and the symbolic reconstruction of this interaction" (Torsello 2016: 16). The very nature of ethnography develops through interactions with local populations, which evolve into the building of mutual trust and understanding with them (Torsello & Venard 2015).

Research Setting and Methodology

> Roads connect food, goods, markets, people, families, communities, and lives. They connect politicians, civil servants, the police and the military, the judiciary, and governments. But roads can lead from heaven to hell, as the ugly heads of greed and envy often seize the material opportunities for graft and corruption in the development, maintenance, and operations of roads. (Paterson & Chaudhuri 2007: 159)

This study grounds corruption in the "politics of transporting" (Peace 1988), that is, the micropolitics of relationships between drivers, passengers, unionists, law enforcement agents, and local politicians. The study is guided by the overriding premise that transportation has been as much about defining state-society relations as it has been about controlling people. In this perspective, mobility embodies the melding of the "high politics of the state" with the "deep politics of society (that is, the relations between rich and poor, powerful and weak)" (Lonsdale 1986: 130). If mobility makes states (Vigneswaran & Quirk 2015: 7), then the state itself is nothing but "a mobile entity capable of mirroring the mobility of subjects in the regulation of them" (Gill, Caletrio, & Mason 2014: 6). More and more, especially in conditions of endemic crisis, being on the move is the very condition of your survival and continuing relevance. If you are not on the move, the chances of survival are diminished (Mbembe 2018). This echoes the idea that bottlenecks—or *embouteillages*—can be seen as a literal and metaphorical entry point into how young taxi men in Dakar, Senegal, increasingly configured mobility as "a social value and a resource in itself: it was *through mobility* that one was able to stake claim to urban permanence and social presence" (Melly 2017: 5).

In Lagos, the law-abiding driver who refuses to pay cash bribes at checkpoints or roadblocks will find himself stuck, both physically and existentially. All drivers must stop at checkpoints for inspection. But what is being inspected is neither their vehicle contents (*wetin you carry?*) nor their compliance with the rules and protocols (*wetin you do?*), but rather their readiness to break them. Experienced drivers know how to deploy strategies—such as humor, strategic ingratiation, situational friendship, and appeal to ethnicity— to negotiate checkpoints. In other words, they know that "the first law of survival in Nigeria is understanding that a police officer at a checkpoint is, quite literally, above the law" (Obadare 2021: 184). Drivers that dare to resist this "first law" and challenge the shakedowns that they endure at endless checkpoints are labeled "enemies of the state" and arrested on the move or subjected to violence, which is often lethal. At the checkpoint, the driver is both a victim and a participant in a state-society "dance." The fact that many drivers across Nigerian cities have been shot dead for resisting police demand for bribes reinforces people's collective fears of state caprice and coercion, even blackmail. It is in this context that Mbembe and Roitman have argued:

> Those who follow the rules scrupulously sometimes find themselves in a snarl, facing figures of the real that have little correspondence to what is publicly alleged or prescribed… Every step or effort to follow the written rule is susceptible to lead not to the targeted goal, but to a situation of apparent contradiction and closure from which it is difficult to exit either by invoking the very same rules and authorities responsible for applying them, or by reclaiming theoretical rights supposed to protect those who respect official law. (1995: 342)

This study is set in the megacity of Lagos in southwest Nigeria (Figure 1). Lagos is home to an estimated 18 million people, projected to rise to 25 million by 2025 (World Bank 2011). This would place the city as the third largest agglomeration in the world, behind only Tokyo and Mumbai. Over the years, Lagos has evolved into a "cultural amalgam in which different ethnic groups and classes, and types of persons attempt to make their own lives, 'find their own ways,' express themselves as they can and experience the many-sided realities that are both theirs and others" (Aina 2003: 176). The megacity displays the grit, determination, and inventive responses that is critical to urban survival in the global South. In the words of Robert Campbell, "There is certainly no more industrious people any where, and I challenge all the world besides to produce a people more so, or capable of as much endurance" (1860: 16). Following Nigeria's transition to civil rule in 1999, Lagos experienced a major urban reform that sought to order its chaos by upgrading mass transportation (among other things), mainstreaming revenue reform, and renewing the social contract between the state and the people. In short, the post-1999 urban renewal plan in Lagos aimed to "convince the majority of… people that the government exists to serve rather than to prey upon them" (Maier 2000: xxviii). However, this approach to neoliberal urbanism neither had a place for the poor nor recognized informality as, above all, a way of life and an organizing logic (Roy & AlSayyad 2004).

Lagos relies heavily on road transportation, precisely because the state is composed of a collection of islands separated by creeks and the Lagos lagoon, with bridges connecting the islands to the mainland. Historically, Lagos has endured the yoke of a poorly coordinated public transportation network and, until 2008, was the largest city in the world without any form of government-organized mass transit (Cheeseman & de Gramont 2017). Instead, millions of urbanites seeking to traverse the megacity each day are served by privately run and alternatively regulated paratransit vehicles, including *danfos*, motorbike-taxis (*okadas*), and tricycle-taxis (keke NAPEPs, which derives from the National Poverty Eradication Program). These informal modes of transport are vital to everyday survival and sociability. In Nigeria, public transportation is mainly a road-based affair, accounting for three-fourths of mobility needs. In Lagos alone, no less than 16 million passenger trips are made each day (Nigeria Transport Policy 2010). Paratransit vehicles afford vibrant spaces of exchange, interaction, production, and predation, entangling the life of the road with the life of the people. Just like the vehicles that ply them daily, roads are spaces of mobility and stuckedness, of survival and death.

Lagos is home to a variety of violent extortionists, from NURTW tax collectors (motor park touts, or *agberos*) to mobile policemen (also known as "Kill and Go"), who "eat the sweat" (i.e. hard work) of informal transport workers on a regular basis. Corruption and coercion are most rampant at motor parks (bus stations), bus terminals, junctions, and checkpoints, where touts and law enforcement agents exercise biopower—the ability "to make live and to let die" (Foucault 1976: 241). Despite a hard day's work averaging up to twenty hours per day ("24 Hours on the Road," as one *danfo* slogan puts it), many transit workers make meagre returns, due to a mixture of bribe-eating and trigger-happy police officers; daily payments made to vehicle owners based on a hire-purchase contract; and the extortionate powers of politicized and violent transport unions. Not surprisingly, most drivers in Lagos view their work as just daily income. As one driver puts it: "What you get today you use today, and tomorrow you start again from scratch."

Fieldwork Approach: Mobile Ethnography

The fieldwork for this book was conducted over a twelve-month period in Lagos. Two local government areas (LGAs) were selected, based on their centrality to urban flows and fixities (Figure 4). One of them was Oshodi, the central terminus for intra-city and inter-city circulation in Lagos. Prior to its radical transformation in 2007, under the post-1999 Lagos state urban renewal campaign, Oshodi was widely seen as "the most radical urban condition on the planet" (Probst 2012: 138), a space that functions without a script (Aradeon 1997: 51). The other field site was Alimosho, the largest LGA in Lagos, with more than two million people. The area is predominantly inhabited by the *Egbados* (*yewa*), a subset of the larger Yorùbá ethnic group. Both Oshodi and Alimosho LGAs are known for their massive *go-slows*, complicated by an interminable tug of war involving drivers, conductors, commuters, touts, street vendors, and police. The overlapping circuitries of movement and standstills in Oshodi and Alimosho are central to political-economic and cultural processes in Lagos. Data for this book were collected from the coercive and vibrant spaces of bus stations, bus stops, checkpoints, and junctions. These are not only spaces of opportunities but also of terror. Here, the instrumentalities of daily survival conform to what Zygmunt Bauman calls the postmodern strategy for warding off death: "Daily life becomes a perpetual dress rehearsal of death" (1992:186).

Daily headlines about incidents at motor parks and bus stops in Lagos, and the transport union gangs riding roughshod over informal transport operators, are particularly revealing. A quick Google search produces the following results: "At Lagos Bus Stops, It's Extortion Galore by Police, Agberos," "Alcohol, Smoking Rule Night Life at Motor Parks [in Lagos]," "Three Killed in Lagos Brutal NURTW, Gang Clashes, 75 Arrested," "9 Dead as NURTW Fractions Clash in Lagos," "NURTW Members Fighting over Commercial [Motor] Park," and so on. The Yorùbá people have a popular saying: *omoluabi kan ki hu iwa omo garage* (a person of good character does not behave like a child of the garage [garage is another word for motor park]). This reinforces the argument that parks, markets, and roadsides (all of which bleed into each other in Lagos) evokes "danger and pleasure, segregation and communitas, sincerity and irreverence" (Gandhi & Hoek 2012: 4). It is no coincidence, therefore, that Robert Kaplan's influential though problematic essay, "The Coming Anarchy," was set in West Africa's bus terminals:

> Each time I went to the Abidjan bus terminal, groups of young men with restless, scanning eyes surrounded my taxi, putting their hands all over the windows, demanding "tips" for carrying my luggage even though I had only a rucksack. In cities in six West African countries, I saw similar young men everywhere—hordes of them. They were like loose molecules in a very unstable social fluid, a fluid that was clearly on the verge of igniting. (Kaplan 1994)

Africa's bus stations and terminals are fluid spaces where the everyday and the political intertwine in extremely dense ways (Stasik & Cissokho 2018; Quayson 2014; Ismail 2009). They have a dual quality, being simultaneously at the center and at the margins of the state. During the course of my fieldwork, I experienced

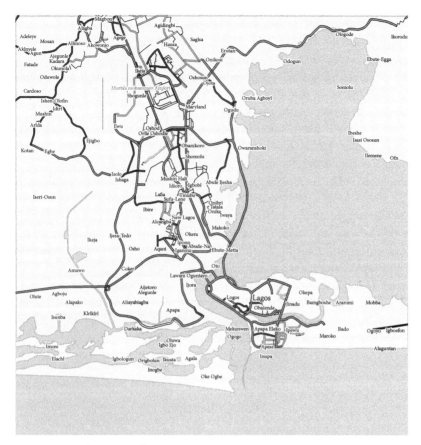

Fig. 4. Map of major roads in Lagos

motor parks, bus terminals, and junctions as vibrant sites of party politics at both the union and state level. Here, as in the bazaars of India and countless other public spaces, "'talking politics' turns from abstract reflection and idle rumor-mongering into focused discussions where political views and desires are forged and outcomes intermittently secured" (Piliavsky 2013: 109).

My fieldwork followed a "mobile ethnography" (Novoa 2015) approach, encompassing walking and traveling with people as a form of sustained engagement with their worldview and lifeworld. Through such "co-present immersion," the researcher moves with modes of movement and employs a range of observation and recording techniques. This method of research can also involve "participation-while-interviewing," in which the ethnographer first participates in patterns of movement, and then interviews people, individually or in focus groups, to show how their diverse mobilities constitute their patterning of daily life (Urry 2007: 40). Taking to the road allowed me to experience the world of the road transport worker as he negotiate "the multiple relations of power that intersect in complex ways to position individuals and collectivities in shifting and often contradictory locations" (Stasiulis 1999: 194). At its core, the road is a contested space where humans and nonhumans, and visible and invisible forces, intermingle and confront one another (Mbembe & Roitman 1995: 329). I found Julien Brachet's (2012) work very helpful in conceptualizing mobility as a "field site," that is, as a privileged moment of observation and discussion of spatial practices, such as corruption, that are otherwise confined to the sphere of "the implicit, the unsaid, and the inadmissible" (Blundo 2007: 36). Studies have shown that matters concerning corruption are often characterized by secrecy: "Real conversations take place elsewhere: off display, behind closed doors" (Piliavsky 2013: 105). By participating in a moving field-site, that is, following minibus- and motorbike-taxi drivers back and forth, asking questions on the way, and taking notes of mobile exchanges with NURTW officials and law enforcement agents, I gained a deeper understanding of the precarious lives and exploitative nature of informal transport work in Lagos. This "go-along" approach (Kusenbach 2003) allowed me to experience firsthand the violent and shifting mutualities between law enforcement agents, transport unionists, and mobile individuals, particularly as it relates to situations and practices of corruption and coercion, of control and taxation (Brachet 2012: x).

Data Collection

For data collection, I used a combination of participant observation, in-depth interviews, critical discourse analysis, court records, archival records, and anecdotal evidence. Participant observation—or what Clifford Geertz (1983: 127) refers to as "the dialectic of experience and interpretation"—necessitated continuous movement between the "inside" and the "outside" of the relationships under study (Baviskar 1995: 8). In turn, this helped not only to situate respondents within contexts that they are most familiar with, but also to experience their lived realities through the partial eyes of the "outsider within." Unlike Walter Benjamin's (1985) *flaneur*, the detached observer of modern city life, I entered into the workaday world of informal transport operators by means of what Gerd Spittler (2001) calls "thick participation." To wit: I did a two-months stint as a *danfo* conductor in a busy motor park along Oshodi-Ikotun route (Figure 5). This learning by doing is consistent with the "apprenticeship" approach that emphasizes the participant dimension of fieldwork (Downey, Dalidowicz, & Mason 2015: 184), turning researchers into "observing participants" more than "participant observers" (Woodward 2008). Working and learning by doing exemplifies the unresolved tension in participant observation. The fact that I was a bus conductor

Fig. 5. A conductor hangs out of a minibus-taxi (*danfo*) in Lagos.
Photo credit: Author

raised the kind of self-reflective questions that Laura Routley (2016) encountered: "Was I an observer or a participant? Was I working with them, or studying them?"

My conductor work came through a chance encounter with "TJ" (short for Tunji), a childhood friend of mine whom I encountered on the streets of Alimosho. TJ had graduated from being a conductor to being the proud owner of two *danfos*. After informing him of my research, TJ invited me to work as his bus conductor to experience the business from within. Though the prospect was daunting, I accepted his "informal" offer, mindful of the point that by actively participating in the lived experiences of drivers and conductors, I can come closer to experiencing and understanding their point of view (cf. Hume & Mulcock 2004: xi). By hanging out and hanging about with TJ, weaving in and out of the go-slows and potholed roads of Lagos, I operationalized Kusenbach's "go-along" method. As a conductor, I directly experienced the coercive exchanges and unreceipted fees that drivers had to make per trip to police officers and touts (*agberos*) at checkpoints and bus stops, and the violence administered to those who refused to comply. A common sight at most checkpoints in Lagos is that of a soldier poking the muzzle of his AK-47 into a driver's eyes for refusing to supply the exact cash bribes, or motor park touts attacking a conductor with a glass bottle for refusing to "settle" his dues. In two months, I witnessed firsthand the violent death of four conductors in the hands of *agberos* due to disputes over the illegal *owo load* ("loading fee"). "I just pay them and go on my way," said a crestfallen TJ. "What else can I do? They are kings of our roads." For many drivers like TJ, mobility is experienced as a contradictory resource, that is, as both a source of agency and a form of constraint. My physical appearances (black) and gender (male) combined with my fluency in Yorùbá (the lingua franca in southwest Nigeria), English (the official language of Nigeria), and Nigerian Pidgin English (a more or less national lingua franca) ensured that I retained a level of anonymity on Lagos roads, a vital element of "surreptitious ethnography" (Neto 2017). Participant observation is most authentic and reliable when the researcher is able to go unobserved (Kusenbach 2003: 461), because it provides much-needed access to "naturally" unfolding events (Becker 1958).

As a *danfo* conductor, I was able not only to witness violent extortion on the roads that my mobile interlocutors regularly traversed, but also to call on some of the "tactics" (in the de Certeauian sense) that they use in the face of agents of corruption who seek to impose fear on transport operators and make them less mobile or free to move. In this sense, movement and the blockades that impede it were central to my fieldwork and constituted an entry point to corruption and the strug-gle for survival. As a conductor, my duties involved (un)loading the bus, calling bus stops, negotiating the various fees demanded by battle-ready touts, collecting bus fares, attending NURTW monthly meetings, and the occasional extravagant *faji* or *jaiye jaiye* (social enjoyments) where people *chop awof* ("eat for free"). On the busy Ikotun-Oshodi routes, which I plied daily with TJ, I grappled with the sheer demands on conductors, especially the ability to multitask on the go: hold-ing money, counting change, opening and closing the poorly oiled sliding doors (sometimes the doors would slide off in motion, resulting in a "stop-go" process), attending to passengers, and watching the driver's blind spot—many *danfos* are without functioning gadgets. Amid all of this, I had to be alert to potential passen-gers along the road; to discern when to hang from the door and scan for passengers and when to shut the door and squeeze in to avoid police fines; and the tactic of "no shaking" (courage) in the face of menacing shouts of *owoo da?* ("Where is your money?") by the tax-collecting *agberos*. I also developed a "thick skin" in the face of insults from passengers with fixed notions of conductors as *con*-ductors. In short, throughout my fieldwork in Lagos, I was constantly aware of my precarious positionality as a researcher navigating an unpredictable and risky terrain, as well as the social stigma attached to driving work.

When I was not walking around the motor parks and bus stops, I joined Lagosians by the crowded roadsides, where nearly every inch has been appropri-ated by a vibrant informal market amid a failure of urban planning. As one traffic policeman complained to me: "In Lagos, people will just see space and occupy it." According to Filip De Boeck and Marie-Francoise Plissart, "The process of ran-dom occupation of space also reveals the organic approach [of urbanites] to the production of the city. Space, in a way, belongs to whomever uses it, despite the half-hearted attempts at the city authorities to control the... denser use of that space" (De Boeck & Plissart 2004: 230). The boundaries between motor parks and markets in Lagos are often so blurred that it is hard to tell where one ends and the other begins. This blurring facilitates corruption by expanding the extortion rackets of touts and police, who now tax not just informal transport workers but also street vendors. "Their code is to tax anything taxable," said a street vendor in Oshodi. Without a start-up loan to rent expensive retail spaces, street vendors such as the sellers of *paraga* (a local alcohol beverage) often set up collapsible kiosks by the roadside, while itinerant vendors cash in on the Lagos *go-slows* to adroitly weave in and out of traffic to sell their goods. There is a baffling mobility amid the endless traffic jam: drivers pull in their side-view mirrors to squeeze through incredibly tight spaces, and mobile street vendors move between stranded commercial vehicles. The *okadas* (motorbike-taxis) weave through the gaps as their passengers hang on for dear life. All this makes navigating Lagos roads an *art* of improvisation and, above all, a relentless practice of *"shinning your eyes well well"* ("Open your eyes," never drop your guard). Fela sang about the confusion, contradiction, and danger of navigating Lagos:

> *Bi mo ba wa moto ni London o, ma tun sese wa ko ti wa n'ile*
> (Even if I drove in London, I would have to learn driving anew when I return home)
> *Bi o ba wa moto ni New York o, wat un sese wa ko ti w anile*
> (Even if you drove in New York, you would have to learn driving anew on return)
> *Tori Turn Right l'Eko o, la'ju e, Turn left l'ori o*
> (Because "Turn Right" in Lagos, open your Eyes, is really "Turn Left")
> *Tori Turn Right l'Eko o, ore mi, Turn left lo ri o*
> Because if you see "Turn Right" in Lagos, my friend, it is really "Turn Left" you see
> *Tiw a tun yato si tiyin o se e ngbo e o, eko ile*
> Ours is different from yours, you hear, Lagos home.
>
> (Olaniyan 2004: 40)

Rhythmanalysis of Lagos

Henri Lefebvre tells us that wherever place, time, and energy interact, rhythm is invariably present. And every rhythm indicates a "relation of a time to a space, a localized time, or if one prefers, a temporalized space" (2004: 15, 89). This triumvirate of time-space-energy has its ultimate reference point not only in human bodies (2004: 67), but also in the non-human vessels that move those bodies on a daily basis (such as the *danfos*). Drawing on Lefebvre's concept of "rhythmanalysis"—a method for analyzing the rhythms of urban spaces and the effects of those rhythms on dwellers in motion—I sought during my fieldwork to capture the manifold, overlapping rhythms that manifest themselves in the sense-world surrounding Lagos, especially what they tell us about this "no man's land." Senses of place are intrinsically interwoven with cultures and shared bodies of local knowledge and wisdom, with which places are rendered meaningful and socially important by individuals and whole communities (Basso 1996). As such, with my digital camera and sound recorder, I was able to capture the hypervisuality and soundscape of Lagos life, which result as one moves about (often in a zig-zag style) within the megacity. These spatio-auditory sensations included the colorful and wry vehicle slogans and mottos, the blaring Fuji music of *danfos*, and loud sirens of police vans, revealing the confluences between music, mobility, and urban spatiality (Chapman 2013). It is a symphony of sound and sight: the syncopated cries of *pya wata pya wata* ("pure water, pure water") by itinerant female vendors, some with small children on their backs, handing small bags of water through the windows of (im)mobile *danfos* to the keenly outstretched arms within; the foul-mouthed and flirtatious conductors calling out their respective termini, jostling for passengers, and warning passengers to *wole pelu shenji e o* (enter with the exact fare); the rag-tag touts shouting *owoo da?* (where is your money?); the *okada* drivers weaving in and out of fast and slow lanes without regard for human life; the impatient bleats of vehicle horns (on the roads of Lagos, there is a competition as to which vehicle has the loudest horn. Here, loud horning gives you right of way); and the hordes of people dwelling in a kind of *perpetuum mobile*.

Beyond enabling my stint as a conductor, TJ was also helpful in connecting me to other security personnel and transport operators in his social network—a strategy variously known as "snowball technique," "referral sampling," or "chain of recommendations." Studies of corruption elsewhere demonstrate that "despite extensive knowledge of corruption, this topic is usually confined to close circles of acquaintances, friends and relatives" (Sedlenieks 2004: 120). TJ prided himself in his "long legs" (connections), both horizontally and vertically. He belabored the point that Lagos operates according to an epistemic logic of "man-know-man." "When you run into *wahala* (trouble)," he insists, "your life comes down to 'whom-you-know.'" In an urban context where everyday life is characterized by a state of emergency (Simone 2004a: 4), "Woe betide the man who knows no one, either directly or indirectly" (Olivier de Sardan 1999: 41). Using the snowball technique meant that I was able to draw on TJ's interpersonal networks to vouch for my own reliability and trustworthiness. This is vital in a Lagos environment where epistemological uncertainties and widespread anxieties over the authenticity of information and the veracity of claims abounds. This is largely due to the culture of deception, political chicanery, and advance fee fraud ("419" scams), for which Nigeria is deservedly notorious. Survey evidence shows that four of five Nigerians (80 percent) are naturally very careful when dealing with other Nigerians and only nearly one in seven citizens (15 percent) believe that most Nigerians can be trusted (CLEEN 2013).

I relied on face-to-face, in-depth interviews and informal conversations to garner real evidence on the corrupt and coercive relationships between commercial drivers and conductors on the one hand, and transport union tax collectors (*agberos*) and law enforcement agents on the other hand. My main dramatis personae, commercial drivers and conductors, were interviewed at both fixed and moving sites: at motor parks and bus stops, as they waited in line to load passengers; on the road, as they wove in and out of traffic gridlocks and water-logged potholes. By navigating (bodily and mentally) these flows and fixities, I came to experience how mobile operators in Lagos physically made the place (as actual and imagined) by routinely moving through it (Buescher & Urry 2009; Kusenbach 2003). This mobile ethnography supports the call for field-work in a deterritorialized world that focuses not so much on bounded fields as on shifting locations. The invitation here is to see familiar things in unfamiliar ways and in unlikely places (Gupta & Ferguson 1997: 35–40). As the character Ezeulu, in Chinua Achebe's *Arrow of God*, quipped: "The world is like a mask dancing. If you want to see it well you do not stand in one place" (1964: 46).

Aside from commercial drivers and conductors, a broad range of social actors within Lagos's transport sector were interviewed, including passengers, touts (*agberos*), street vendors, mobile police and traffic inspectors, Vehicle Inspection Officers, and officials of the National Union of Road Transport Workers (NURTW), the Road Transport Employers Association of Nigeria (RTEAN), Kick Against Indiscipline (KAI), and the Lagos State Traffic Management Authority (LASTMA). All interviews were conducted in English, Yorùbá, and Pidgin (or a combination of all three), depending on the preferences of my informants. The services of a field translator were not required, as I am conversationally fluent in all three languages. Beyond its capacity to reflect urban social realities, there is a performative side to language that gives it an active function in social interactions (Petit 2005: 473; Quayson 2014: 20).

With the consent of my informants, I initially recorded interview sessions in order to assist the natural limitations of my own memory and note-taking. However, most informal transport operators felt uneasy about being voice-recorded. Their anxieties are understandable, considering that many commercial drivers in Lagos operate without licenses. Any time I brought out my digital voice recorder, I could sense their discomfort. As a consequence, I adjusted my approach and started to take extremely detailed hand-written notes after all interviews. This proved easier and less obtrusive, as many of my interlocutors were more forthcoming in an unrecorded interview setting. Hence, for the rest of my fieldwork, I used methods similar to those described in Robert Desjarlais' award-winning *Shelter Blues: Sanity and Selfhood Among the Homeless*:

I spent much of my time hanging about, listening to conversations, and then finding a place to write down the gist of these exchanges... My notes on these conversations, which typically contained quasi-verbatim accounts, lacked the precision that tape or audio recordings could have provided. However, as many anthropologists have found, especially those who have worked among homeless populations, the advantages of unassuming participation in daily activities, during which one can develop lasting, informal ties with people, often outweigh the benefits of information obtained through surveys and more intrusive methods. (1997: 41)

I found interviews inherently flexible, allowing me to use probes to solicit depth and to foster relationships of trust. Interviewing allowed for flexible responses, where my interlocutors could guide the interview toward the topics they considered relevant. Given the sensitive, almost taboo, nature of corruption talk (Myrdal 1968: 938–39), I soon adjusted my interview strategy to what I call an "alienation effect," that is, requesting the reactions of operators to a practice observed on the road. With this approach, respondents were more relaxed about talking about their mobile encounters, relieved that they were not being directly accused of corruption. Other ethnographers of corruption have shared a similar experience. In India, Veena Das found that while her interlocutors spoke easily of elite corruption and massive graft, it was much more difficult to speak freely about everyday or immediate forms of corruption (2015: 340). In his study of corruption in contemporary Bolivia, Sian Lazar found that, "Corruption is always somewhere else, perpetrated by someone else" (2005: 212). Despite the serious dilemmas presented by corruption, Jennifer Hasty observed that people in Accra, Ghana, often burst into laughter when instances of corruption are discussed in public: "There's something humanly embarrassing, self-ironizing, and mutually implicating in the anxious bathos of corruption" (2005b: 359). Other times, my alienation effect was simply to ask my interlocutors to tell me about their day-to-day challenges and how they navigated around them to make the most of their time. More often than not, corruption emerged organically, overshadowing every other articulated concern.

I also sourced data using an interpretative analysis of vehicle slogans, combined with content analysis of court records involving the Lagos State Government versus *okada* unions. Press materials were key to understanding local attitudes toward corruption, since they denoted a discursive and changing field that enables corrupt practices to be labeled, discussed, decried, justified, and denounced. Data assembled from these newspapers informed my interviews and helped to triangulate my data to derive a nuanced perspective. Social scientists should not only strive to collect many instances of an identified phenomenon but also seek to gather "many kinds of evidence" to enhance the validity of a specific conclusion (Becker 1958: 657). I approached my data analysis using an iterative strategy, that is, a systematic, repetitive, and recursive process in qualitative data analysis (Mills,

Durepos, & Wiebe 2010). In practice, this meant that I transcribed and analyzed my data as I collected them, using this analysis to inform further research. This iterative process helped me to spot and address gaps in my interviews while I was still in the field and while the discussions were still fresh in my mind. As suggested above, corruption is a sensitive topic, more so in a sector such as public transport, where marginal men with a criminalized identity are stigmatized as "dirty workers" (Hughes 1958). As such, I have used pseudonyms and altered the context of specific interviews to protect my interviewees.

Subjugated Knowledges

This book reclaims the power of "subjugated knowledges"[19] (for example: stories, rumor, and gossip) for uncovering inaudible and unspeakable truths about corruption. Writing about the Mende in Sierra Leone, Mariane Ferme calls this "the underneath of things." Interestingly, the Mende word for meaning, *yembu* (that which lies underneath), emphasizes the vital role of the concealed, the subjugated, in making sense of the visible (Ferme 2001: 4). Far from being mere deceptions of reality (Taussig 1980: 229), subjugated knowledges are a powerful means through which average citizens in many African countries encounter the state, a state which, like the Mawri stories of man-eaters, "illicitly appropriate the vitality of those subordinated to them" (Masquelier 2000: 89). Subjugated knowledges are most visible in postcolonial contexts where the state lacks popular legitimacy and, thus, relies on (the threat of) violence to compel compliance and induce loyalty. Here, citizens prefer to source information from unofficial (e.g. rumor) rather than official channels since the latter lacks any credibility (Lomnitz 1995: 36).

Through subjugated knowledges, ordinary people not only make explicit their fears, aspirations, and anxieties about politics, which is widely seen as corrupting those involved, but also partake in moral evaluations of their political leaders (Turner 2007: 93). Corruption involves a kind of "public secrets" (Taussig 1999), a public knowledge that cannot be articulated: "everyone knows that this cannot be known" (Newell 2012: 100). Secrecy is a politicized domain; "In a context where speaking truth to power can lead to arbitrary danger and death, secret domains are also where popular cultural creativity produces alternative discourses that limit the exercise of political power, through the systematic intrusion of unpredictability" (Ferme 2001:6).

---

[19] Michel Foucault coined the term "subjugated knowledges" to describe insufficient or disqualified set of knowledges; in other words, "naïve knowledges, located down on the hierarchy, beneath the required level of cognition or scientificity." He believes that "it is through the re-emergence of these low-ranking knowledges, these unqualified, even directly disqualified knowledges... that criticisms perform its work" (1980: 81–82).

A long standing criticism levelled against the anthropology of corruption is that "observer effects" can bias research findings (LeCompte & Goetz 1982; Rose-Ackerman 2010). Thus, critics claim that the "thick" presence of a researcher could influence the behavior of those being studied, making it difficult for ethnographers to document social phenomena in any accurate, let alone objective, way (Wilson 1977). Yet, such critics too often miss the fact that, however staged for or influenced by the observer, informants' performances reveal profound truths about sociocultural phenomena such as bribery and corruption. In analyzing these performances, we gain a better understanding not only of how local people perceive themselves but also of how they would like to be perceived by others. As an *omo eko* ("child of Lagos"), I tapped into my own longstanding embodied experiences of the quotidian rhythms of Lagos life to enrich my data analysis. To bridge other knowledge gaps, I regularly performed pragmatic validity checks by comparing corruption discourse to daily practice and triangulating articulations from multiple informants, looking for any (in)consistency. In so doing, I was able to "forge links between different knowledges that are possible from different locations and trace lines of possible alliances and common purposes between them" (Gupta & Ferguson 1997: 39).

Limitations of Study

My fieldwork in Lagos spanned an extremely difficult four-month period (July to October 2014), when the sprawling metropolis suffered the outbreak of the deadly Ebola Virus Disease (EVD). The resultant fear of contagion in everyday life forbade intimacies and the usual gathering of Lagosians, from public spaces (e.g. motor parks) to sacred grounds (churches and mosques). The tentative mood during this period was palpable in the unwillingness of many Lagosians to be interviewed by a random stranger. I was a *danfo* conductor in Oshodi during these difficult Ebola months and recall many occasions when a poor passenger would pay for two extra seats—one to his left, the other to his right—so as to reduce the chances of bodily contact with fellow passengers. In an effort to prevent EVD in the motor parks of Lagos, the NURTW called on all operators to practice social distancing by stopping the overloading of passengers, a practice that increases the chances of contagion. The call was surprisingly heeded, calling into question the hopelessly lawless picture that is often painted of informal workers. *Ta lo fe ku?* (Who wants to die?), one driver in Oshodi said. In sum, the Ebola months in Lagos affected the quality of social interactions. As one journalist neatly sums it up: "Once rated in a United Nations survey as the 'happiest people' in the world, Nigerians seem to have lost their natural good humor and increasingly more people are scared of shaking hands with or hugging other people, especially strangers, for fear of getting infected with the virus" (Punch 2014b). At that time, of course, few people could have foreseen that another viral disease, COVID-19, would tear across the entire world, threatening all that is normal and disrupting daily routines and social practices in every corner of the globe.

The politicized and violent nature of the NURTW presented its own challenges as I navigated crowded bus stations and junctions—spaces where collective fear has become a way of life for many. In Lagos, as in much of Africa, bus stations are commonly seen as spaces of danger and intimidation and bastions of criminals, drug dealers, prostitutes, and withcraft (Stasik & Cissokho 2018: xiii–xiv; Ademowo 2010). Yet, at their core, motor parks, and the markets that surround them, are microcosms of social life, which facilitate the unceasing flow of goods and passengers (Beck 2013: 426). Conversations with some union touts were frankly quite intimidating, and some rival union gangs did not particularly appreciate my constant presence in the motor parks and terminals of Lagos. This created considerable fear and anxiety within me, as I was uncertain about whose toes I was stepping on at any point in time. As my fieldwork unfolded, it became increasingly clear that I was becoming too familiar with a mafia-like world where people could suddenly disappear without trace, and that keeping me out enabled those implicated, the NURTW and law enforcement agents, to maintain "a unified front that hid the internal politics that are inevitably part of mutualities" (Bähre 2014: 578) in Lagos's transport sector. As the old adage goes, "knowledge is power," and the NURTW maintains control of transit spaces, in part, through its opacity. This explains why, despite its enormous political clout, the NURTW has managed to escape scholarly gaze. But does one abandon urgent research simply because a predatory trade union and a complicit state government do not want their extortion racket to be documented and exposed?

The Road Ahead

The rest of this book is organized in six chapters. Chapter 1, *Corruption and the Crisis of Values*, has two parts. In the first, corruption wide, I examine the definitional challenge of corruption, with particular attention to confusion over what is private and what is public, what is legal and what is illegal. The chapter finds its purchase in the critical examination of "culturalist" research and approaches to corruption and the state in Africa, particularly the common but problematic amalgamation of Africa's political failings or deficits under the concept of neopatrimonialism (e.g. patronage, rent-seeking, and clientelism). In the second part, corruption close, I explore the political economy of oil, elite corruption, and the economic crisis in Nigeria since independence in October 1960, especially the systematic plundering of state wealth and the resulting crisis of values in everyday life, typified by the magical scramble for money among included politicians and excluded Nigerian youth eager to make money by any means (e.g. "419ners" and "Yahoo" boys). The analysis in this chapter extends to the checkered story of post-1999 institutionalist efforts under civilian rule to fight corruption and repair Nigeria's tarnished international image. This chapter shows how economic crisis and material acquisitiveness have coalesced to entrench the "survival of the fattest" in the Nigerian psyche.

That corruption is, first and foremost, a "language" that is inscribed in daily life remains an obvious but often overlooked fact in the corruption literature. Drawing upon critical discourse analysis, Chapter 2, *The Language of Corruption*, analyzes the popular semiology of corruption in Africa. It examines how corruption is commonly scripted in corporeal metaphors of eating and bodily fluids (literally and metaphorically), confirming the generality, banality, and commensality of corruption on the continent. By paying attention to the local language and idioms used to imagine and articulate acts of bribery and corruption, we gain a more grounded and sophisticated understanding of the corruption complex and, crucially, popular reactions to it. Foregrounding corruption as "food for thought," this chapter reclaims the ambiguous and multivocal power of language in how we think and talk about corruption. In so doing, it sheds new light onto what counts as corruption in the value acceptances of everyday people, thereby advancing our knowledge of the meanings that people everywhere ascribe to corruption or its rough equivalents in other languages.

Chapter 3, *The Politics of Informal Transport*, examines the role of the informal urban transport ("paratransit") sector in Africa, as a groundwork for the rest of the book's attention to the micropolitics of transportation and road exploitation in Lagos, Nigeria's commercial capital. This chapter argues that an analysis of the organization and politics of informal transport provisions affords a unique window onto the precarious unfolding of urban life in Africa, including issues of "transport poverty," the stigmatized identity of drivers and conductors, the extortionate powers of politicized transport unions in cahoots with state governments, and how plans to modernize public transit systems across the continent generally ignore the motley array of unregulated carriers that have become the fulcrum of Africa's urban fabric. The paradox in this chapter is not lost: while Africa's informal transport workers are often regarded as criminals, they are actually daily victims of corruption themselves.

If corruption is a constitutive element of everyday life, then it behooves us to understand what exactly that everyday life is. Despite their centrality to the imagination and popular experiences of informal road transport workers, there are, surprisingly, few studies on the ubiquitous and aphoristic slogans painted on passenger vehicles as a window onto the political economy of everyday life in urban Africa. Chapter 4, *The Art of Urban Survival*, explores what an interpretative analysis of vehicle slogans can tell us about the everyday spaces of maneuver, survival, and opportunities of road transport workers, including the particular circumstances which may have informed the driver's choice of a particular slogan.

This chapter explores how popular culture manifests itself through these slogans, as a means to interpret the everyday experiences of marginalized transport workers in Lagos as well as an expression of their "social theory." Through a textual analysis of minibus-taxi slogans in Lagos, we are able to relate to the precarious lifeworlds of operators, including their daily encounters with agents of corruption and fear on dangerous roads. Seeing *danfos* as mobile bodies of meaning, the chapter finds that *danfo* slogans not only provide unique windows onto the exploitative labor of informal transport workers in Lagos, but are also effective means through which these marginal men carve out meaningful temporalities, stand out in a cutthroat business, and expand their capacity to aspire and become.

Chapter 5, *Nigeria's Transport Mafia*, focuses on the origins and changing dynamics of the dreaded NURTW's tax collectors—the *agberos* or motor park touts—and the intimidating and violent tactics they deploy to extort illegal fees of all sorts from transport operators in Lagos. Situating the emergence and reach of *agberos* within the widespread crisis of the structural adjustment program (SAP) of the 1980s in Nigeria, this chapter directly relates the transformation of *agberos*, from callers of passengers to violent extortionists, to their adverse incorporation into the NURTW as tax collectors and political thugs, which altered their initial role in the road transport sector. Efforts by the Lagos State Government to rid the roads of *agberos* since 1999 are inspired by its controversial neoliberal urban renewal project which responds to the logic of the market rather than the needs of the Lagos subaltern. Yet, the role of "big politics" (in form of the unholy alliance between the NURTW and the state government) helps explain the botched attempts to remove *agberos* from the roads. The chapter also pays attention to the ways in which political agency is exercised at different levels, that is, both within the NURTW and toward transport workers and state agents.

Chapter 6, *The Paradox of Urban Reform*, critically examines the impact of the Lagos State Road Traffic Law of 2012, introduced by the Lagos State Government to restore "sanity" to Lagos roads, on the spaces of livelihoods of informal transport workers, with particular attention to motorbike-taxi (*okada*) drivers and their associations. On the one hand, the chapter explores the corrupt and brutal manner in which law enforcement agents in Lagos (for example, "Kick Against Indiscipline") have enforced the Traffic Law. On the other hand, it examines how and why the largest association of motorbike-taxi drivers in Lagos—the All Nigerian Autobike Commercial Owners and Workers Association (ANACOWA)—is appealing to state laws as a weapon of combat against the Lagos State Government and its agents. This chapter sheds light onto the way in which informal transport workers and their associations exercise agency and their "right to the city" in a collective attempt to intervene in the corrupt and unequal processes of neoliberal urban legislation. Further, the chapter shows how urban reform can reproduce rather than address corruption and precarious existence in everyday life.

The concluding chapter, *Learning from Corruption*, advances some final critical reflections on the broader theoretical and empirical implications of the ideas presented in this book, particularly the need to go beyond the essentialist, culturalist, and functionalist explanations that constrain dominant approaches to corruption in Africa and the global South generally. The conclusion offers an approach to corruption "from below" that is not detached from but inextricably linked to corruption "from above." In this dialectical perspective, corruption is a multi-faceted phenomenon located in "gray zones" between the legal and the extralegal, and shaped by mutualities between formal and informal actors and rules. Such mutuality is at work in the collusion and collision of the NURTW and the Lagos State Government, affirming corruption as an effective arena for exploring the fault lines of statecraft, urban political engineering, and the pursuit of daily survival.

1

Corruption and the Crisis of Values

Defining corruption is an extremely difficult undertaking, since the very word "corruption" evokes vastly different meanings and connotations. While corruption exists in all polities, the form it takes, its extent, and its political and socio-economic functions vary enormously across time and place. In a thorough review of the empirical literature on corruption, Monica Prasad and associates distill three major observations about how and why corruption persists. First, corruption persists because diminished state capacity forces average citizens to partake in it to meet basic survival needs. This they call the "resource challenge." Second, corruption persists because of the unsettled debates over what is corrupt and what is not corrupt, what is private and what is public. This they call the "definitional challenge." And third, corruption persists because of counteracting moral pressures, such as the interrelated pressures associated with looking after one's own ethnic group (tribalism) or with patrimonial client networks. This they call the "alternative moralities challenge" (Prasad et al. 2019: 98).

This two-part chapter analyzes the relationship between political corruption, economic crisis, and anti-corruption reform in postcolonial Nigeria. The first part, "corruption wide," critically scrutinizes the definitional and alternative moralities challenge of corruption. The second part, "corruption close," examines elite corruption in Nigeria since independence in October 1960, especially the systematic plundering of state wealth and the consequent emergence of a crisis of values in everyday life. The analysis in this chapter extends to the checkered story of post-1999 institutionalist efforts to combat corruption.

Corruption Wide: Complicating Our Understanding of Corruption

Corruption is widely defined as "behavior which deviates from the formal duties of a public role because of private-regarding (personal, close family, private clique) pecuniary or status gains; or violates rules against the exercise of certain types of private-regarding influence" (Nye 1967: 419). This public-office view rests simply and squarely on the illegality of corruption. "Illegality" here denotes that there are rules governing the conduct of public-office holders and the process of selection to public office (Theobald 1990: 16; Underkuffler 2005). There

They Eat Our Sweat. Daniel E. Agbiboa, Oxford University Press.
© Daniel E. Agbiboa (2022). DOI: 10.1093/oso/9780198861546.003.0002

are three essential elements of the public-office conception of corruption: (a) payments to public officials beyond their salaries; (b) an action associated with these payments that violates either explicit laws or implicit social norms; and (c) losses to the public either from that action or from a system that renders it necessary for actions to arise only from such payments (Glaeser & Goldin 2006: 7).

Despite its popularity, the public-office view is fraught with difficulties that sit awkwardly with our purposes. To start with, the questions raised by Michael Johnston fifty-odd years ago remain relevant today: "Which norms are the ones that will be utilized to distinguish corrupt from noncorrupt acts? If the definitions are public-centered, then whose evaluation of the public's interest is to be operationalized?" (1970: 6). Another objection notes that the very concept of public office is basically "Western." In the developing world, it is argued, public office as an institution and the ethos surrounding it remains weakly established. In this light, nepotism, patronage, and minor forms of bribery disguised as gift-giving, far from attracting opprobrium, are generally socially approved (Theobald 1990: 3). The division between public and private—the basis for common definitions of corruption—does not carry the same moral weight in all societies (Ruud 2000: 291). To the extent that public officials in sub-Saharan Africa or South Asia often find themselves committed to upholding two contradictory sets of values—on the one hand, those of the modern bureaucracy, which they have sworn to uphold, and, on the other hand, those foisted on them by their traditional, cultural setting (Anders 2009)—they become "polynormative" (Olowu 1988: 219), and in many cases this translates into "normlessness" (Riggs 1964). Further, in many African states, loyalty to the family or ethnic kinsmen overrides individual rights or personal accountability. The civil servant, in this context, may become engaged in corruption in a desperate effort to generate the additional resources he or she needs to meet obligations to members of their family members or ethnic group (Alam 1989: 445; Wrong 2009). Studying Malawi, Gerhard Anders (2009) points to the co-existence and interaction of multiple sets of contradictory rules that a Malawian civil servant is required to negotiate on a daily basis, including the official rules, kinship rules, and the unofficial code of conduct.

The understanding of corruption as illegality is simultaneously too narrow and too broad in scope, since that which is illegal is not necessarily corrupt, and that which is corrupt is not necessarily illegal. As such, an overly legislative approach to corruption ignores the sociocultural forms that corruption takes (Olivier de Sardan 1999; Routley 2016; Baez-Camargo et al. 2017) as well as changes in corruption across both time and space (Pierce 2016). This may explain why, despite boasting higly sophisticated accountability organs and anti-corruption legislation, a country such as Uganda is still consistently ranked in the bottom third of countries perceived to be the most corrupt in the world.[1] Uganda's formal anti-corruption bodies score 99 out of 100 points in the Global Integrity 2009 index; yet the country is consistently ranked among the most corrupt in the world. If corruption is the "secret of law" (Nuijten & Anders 2007), that is to say, corruption and law are not opposite but constitutive of one another, it follows that an approach that purely reads traditional state-centered *état de droit* as the only panacea for corruption is grossly inadequate (Torsello & Venard 2015: 3; Bocarejo 2018: S49). Although legally culpable and widely reproved, practices that fall within the gamut of the corruption complex are nonetheless seen by those who participate in them as legitimate, and often as not being corrupt at all (Olivier de Sardan 1999: 34).

Consider Janet Roitman's study of the "ethics of illegality" in the Lake Chad Basin, which comprises Nigeria, Cameroon, Niger, and Chad. While unregulated economic activities and violent modes of extraction are commonly viewed as "illegal," *Bedskin* drivers and road bandits (*coupeurs de route*) also imagine these practices as "licit" and "rational behavior" (Roitman 2006: 251–61). Similarly, Eric Bähre's study of Cape Town's taxi associations show that taxi owners generally embrace illegality and informality as being vital to doing business (Bähre 2014: 576). In their study of the educational sector in the DRC, Kristof Titeca and Tom de Herdt found that formal state-backed rules and agreements only played an indirect role in governing the system, even if all actors in the educational sector systematically refer to these rules and agreements (2011: 214). These African case studies find affirmation in ethnographies of corruption in South Asia and South America, which show that people generally see corruption as a "legitimate way of going about doing things" (Kondos 1987: 17). In India, Veena Das finds that, while people openly admitted that their actions (such as tapping electricity from high-tension wires) violate the law, they nonetheless "have a completely lucid answer to allegations of corruption levelled at them by bureaucrats—what is the poor man to do—he is only trying to earn *rozi-roti* (income for food), he is somehow feeding his wife and children. Surely that cannot be illegitimate?" (2015: 340). Similarly, in her ethnography of corruption among Columbia peasants (*campesinos*), Diana Bocarejo (2018: S53) finds that *campesinos* accept the law neither as "fixed" nor as an a priori legitimate set of discourses and practices.

How do we make sense of the above pervasiveness of an "ethics of illegality" in the Global South? One rather incomplete explanation that has been adduced time and again is that the full panoply of laws and administrative apparatus in many developing countries is "copied entirely from the West" (Scott 1969: 319; cf. Anders 2009). Only a few African countries have proposed alternative standards of

---

[1] The Afrobarometer (2015) reported that 69 percent of Ugandans think that the government is performing badly or not doing enough to crack down on corruption in the public sector.

public service morality. Instead, many of these postcolonies have each "striven to ensure that their public bureaucracies conform to the ethical standards and codes inherited from their erstwhile colonial masters" (Olowu 1988: 216).[2] Social science studies (of corruption) are not immune from this Western-centric critique. David Sills and Robert Merton have already called attention to the dearth of social science materials from non-Western cultures:

> The social sciences themselves are primarily products of Western civilization, and Africans, Asians, and other non-Westerners who work in social sciences [myself included] generally use the theory and methods of the Western social sciences as their framework... Certainly a major challenge for the social sciences—if not for all of the sciences—is to find ways of incorporating the basic ideas of African, Asian, and other non-Western thought into the Western paradigm.[3] (cited in Schatzberg 2001: 25)

The Shadow State

In much of the Global South, the public/private bifurcation that underpins Western-centric understandings and explanations of corruption have little daily utility. Developing regions have remained "decidedly 'non-Weberian'" (Khan 2012b: 10), despite attempts at improving formal enforcement. Africa, for instance, is commonly seen as a place where formal rules have little constraining effect on political conducts which are generally viewed as governed by the expectation that "constitutional rules or administrative regulations can, and probably ought, to be evaded" (Jackson & Rosberg 1984: 425). The dominance of informal institutions in the so-called developing world has been cast in light of the "weakness" of the state to enforce formal institutions (Khan 2012a; Robbins 2000: 425).

William Reno (1995) famously used the concept of the "shadow state" to describe personalized rule in Sierra Leone, where the "real" state is constructed behind the façade of formal statehood. Such a dualistic understanding articulates with the distinction between *pays légal* (a legal structure) and *pays réel* (where real power is wielded) (Bayart 2000), or the bifurcation of "official" and "practical" norms (Olivier de Sardan 2008). Viewed in this perspective, the "indigenous" is perceived to be implicated in "the corrupt." The crisis of governance is situated within the irreconcilable clash between, rather than the hybridity of, "African-traditional" and "Western-modern" forms of governance, a clash that is then interpreted as the root cause of corruption in Africa, *tout court* (Routley 2016). As

---

[2] The problem of this viewpoint is its tendency to reify the dichotomy between Western state institutions and African society rather than sharpen our focus on "the lives of people in the midst of processes that restructured state institutions all around the globe" (Anders 2009: 150).
[3] The very assumption of a *purely* western paradigm is dubious (Comaroff & Comaroff 2015).

Jean and John Comaroff puts it, "In Africa, the epitome of post/colonial misrule in European eyes, metaphors of malfeasance—kleptocracy, neopatrimonialism, clientelism, prebendalism—have long been the accepted terms, popular and scholarly alike, for indigenous modes of governance" (Comaroff & Comaroff 2006: 6–7). The continued delinking of Western and African elements, colonial legacies and traditional practices, and the local and the international, persists because "it enables claims to be made based on the value attributed to association with one side of the dichotomy or the other" (Routley 2016: 5).

The image of "shadow" has long been a favored discursive trope (particularly among Western scholars) to imagine and articulate contemporary African realities. The study of Africa is awash with problematic images of darkness, black holes, and phantoms (De Boeck, Cassiman, & Van Wolputte 2009: 36). In addition to Reno's influential "shadow state" concept, Western scholars of Africa have written about shadow economies and shadow networks (Duffield 2002), twilight institutions (Lund 2007), shadow cities (Neuwirth 2006), global shadows (Ferguson 2006), and shadows of war (Nordstrom 2004). The danger with these popular representations is that "the notion that 'real' meanings, events, and entities are deferred to other domains may lead to the reification of those other, unavailable sites. This facilitates all sorts of mystifications" (Ferme 2001: 6). Often, the word "shadow" has been headlined by these authors with little sensitivity to its racist undertones and the sensibilities of the millions of Africans of whom they write. Looking at these titles, one cannot help but recall the words of the late Kenyan writer Binyavanga Wainaina, in his now renowned satire of Western writing about Africa titled: "How to Write about Africa." Wainaina (2006) begins this piece with: "Always use the word 'Africa' or 'Darkness' or 'Safari' in your title."

Criticizing the state deficiency argument for its weak explanatory power and "pernicious Eurocentrism," Paul Robbins calls for an alternative approach by examining corruption not as "the absence of rules" but as "the presence of alternative norms." Studies of corruption, he argues, must transcend the absence of strong state institutions to critically examine "the presence of differing institutions which vie for legitimacy and trust amongst diverse players within both the state and civil society" (2000: 426). Other Africanist scholars have likewise challenged the idea of state failure, rejecting a priori views about what the state should look like. The "Weberization" of the African state, they argue, precludes an understanding of "real governance" in Africa (Olivier de Sardan 2008: 2; MacGaffey 1991). The understanding of African politics as deviant evokes cultural primordialism (Meagher 2006), that is, a generalized notion of corruption as "the form of politics" in Africa (Bayart 1993: 89) or the state in African as "naturally corrupt" (Szeftel 1998). It is exactly this essentialism and cultural determinism that Olivier de Sardan condemned when he said: "Should one therefore impute corruption in Africa to some kind of 'African culture?' Nothing should be more absurd. The notion of culture is extremely polysemic." Instead, he argues in favor of the avoidance of "both of these opposed and symmetrical stumbling blocks: an explanation of 'culture,' or the denial of any 'cultural factor' whatsoever" (1999: 44). While the notion of "shadow state" has become ingrained in studies of African politics, it is problematic to assume that official norms invariably fall outside the purview of real governance and are thus irrelevant. As Olivier de Sardan points out: "For the researchers and actors alike, the official norms are part of the definition of the situation. They cannot be dispensed with under the pretext that the level of adherence to them is scant, nor is it possible to focus on the practices as if it were the case that the official norms did not exist" (2008: 7).

Beyond the Cultural Turn

Analysts of corruption in Africa (e.g. Bayart, Ellis, & Hibou 1999; Bayart 2005; Chabal & Daloz 2006) take various positions that essentialize rather than explain culture. But let my position be clear: the idea of culture is fluid and relational, and there is no overarching value system that induces the deportment of African people. Two key debates have shaped culturalist analyses of corruption in postcolonial Africa. On the one hand, scholars have argued that corruption is a consequence of the endurance of "traditional" social practices and logics in a modern context (McMullan 1961; Bodruzic 2016). Advocates of this school of thought often point to the predominance of patronage politics and patrimonialism in the African polity, including primordial traditions of gift giving (Ekpo 1979) and the culture of supportive values (Le Vine 1975). On the other hand, scholars observe that corruption in postcolonial Africa is the result of a historic rupture that formed with the importation of the colonial state (Ekeh 1975; Mamdani 1996). In the first few pages of *This Present Darkness*, Stephen Ellis (2016: 4) wrote, "[…] we need to study the colonial experience of Indirect Rule if we are to understand the origin of later practices of organized crime and corruption."

The resort to culture in interpreting corruption conjures up the specter of expediency, which has become an "easy explanatory trap" for many African leaders (Ocheje 2001). For example, under Ghana's Kwame Nkrumah, corruption was politically constructed as "indigenous forms of 'African' resistance to the abstract formalism of the state" (Hasty 2005b: 295). Syed Alatas criticizes approaches that use cultural practices for the purposes of corruption rather than being the cause of corruption (1968: 96–97). Following a review of the cultural aspects of corruption, Johann Lambsdorff (1999: 13), the inventor of the Corruption Perception Index, noted that culture can only explain "a certain fraction of the level of corruption…" Michael Thompson and colleagues enumerate three crucial ways in which culture is misused in corruption debates. First, culture can be invoked as an "uncaused cause" when an individual is said to have acted corruptly "because his culture told him to" (2006: 332). Such explanation fails to address the prior question of what caused the culture to be like that (Lamour 2012: 159). Second, culture is invoked as "an explanation of last resort" (Thompson, Verweii, & Ellis 2006: 322). In other words, having exhausted other explanations of corruption, we conveniently turn to culture as some sort of "residual category" (Lamour 2008: 228). Third, culture is often invoked as a "veto on comparison" (Thompson, Verweii, & Ellis 2006: 323). For example, in his ethnography of corruption and culture in the Pacific Islands, Peter Lamour (2008: 228) describes how he routinely experienced a "blocking" character: "To say 'corruption' is part of a culture is not unlike saying 'back off: this is none of your business.'"

Revisiting Neopatrimonialism

No discussion of the relationship between corruption and culture in modern Africa will be complete without a look, if cursory, at neopatrimonialism, a concept often deployed as a one-size-fits-all explanation for political failings in Africa, especially in relation to issues of corruption (Mkandawire 2015: 563; Pitcher, Moran, & Johnston 2009; deGrassi 2008). The concept of neopatrimonialism is often evoked as a general explanation for a range of practices that are seen as typical of African politics, such as despotism, clannish behavior, 'tribalism,' regionalism, patronage, 'cronyism,' 'prebendalism,' corruption, predation, and factionalism (Bach 2012: 221). While neopatrimonialism is not easy to define, a "conceptual muddle" as Aaron deGrassi (2008: 112) calls it, Jean-François Medard (1986) used the now viral concept as an explanatory model for the contradictory nature of the state in Africa, in which bureaucratic process sits cheek by jowl with the patrimonial management of public resources. Perhaps the most authoritative formulation comes from Christopher Clapham, who defines neopatrimonialism as "a form of organization in which relationships of a broadly patrimonial type pervade a political and administrative system which is formally constructed on rational-legal lines. Officials hold position in bureaucratic organizations with powers which are formally defined, but exercise those powers... as a form of private property" (1985: 48).

In postcolonial Africa, neopatrimonialism is usually interpreted from two interrelated perspectives, the society-centric and the state-centric. The society-centric perspective describes "practices and norms in African society that prevents the embrace and sustained application of 'rational' policy choices capable of promoting economic development and political liberalization" (Olukoshi 2005: 182). Richard Marcus (2010: 117) refers to this approach as "cultural representation in the political process." The state-centric perspective locates the problem of neopatrimonialism in the state itself, pointing to the ways in which the state encumbers society on account of the predatory and personalized politics which it nurtures (Olukoshi 2005: 184). This perspective has given rise to essentialist narratives of Africa as "a society with no sense of the public good, one that condones corruption and is inhabited by individuals who focus on their own bellies" (Mkandawire 2015: 6). This functionalist state-centric school of thought has also contributed to a pervasive international cynicism about a culture of political corruption in Africa (Le Vine 1993: 274) and neopatrimonialism as the "core feature" of African politics (Bratton & van de Walle 1997: 62). In turn, such de-historicized and uncritical views have paved the way for jaundiced questions such as the one raised in *The Economist* (2000): "Does Africa have some inherent character flaw that keeps it backward and incapable of development?"

To be clear, the argument here is not that no African state is neopatrimonial—in fact, many are—but that "analysts need to avoid a priori assumptions about the existence of neopatrimonialism and hasty invocations of the phenomenon [...] without thorough documentation of the precise forms, characters, origins, transformations, contestations, extent, and other important features of neopatrimonialism" (de Grassi 2008: 122; see also Pitcher, Moran, & Johnston 2009). The concept of neopatrimonialism in Africa has been criticized for its perfunctory appeal to culture, with no explanation for the arbitrary restriction of the domain of individuals' rational behavior. As Thandika Mkandawire points out: "Culture is comprised of such a broad repertoire of actual and potential practices that any social practice can be accounted for by reference to it. Given the wide range of African political practices, the neopatrimonial model involves a select choice of cultural elements, though the selection process is itself never specified. The subjective choice of cultural elements included often says more about the preanalytical predispositions of the analysts than of the society being observed" (Mkandawire 2015: 572). Moreover, casting all political failings and democratic deficits in Africa in light of neopatrimonialism occludes the real problems facing the continent: "corruption, vertical and horizontal inequality, ethnic and gender discrimination, weak state capacity, wrong ideas, political chicanery, and the machinations of the many external actors who seek to exploit Africa in some form or other" (Mkandawire 2015: 602; see also Szeftel 1998: 236). In a similar vein, A.R. Mustapha calls into question the logic of neopatrimonialism, particularly its tendency to reduce the political community in Africa to struggle for spoils among predatory elites, thus robbing non-elite groups of political agency (Mustapha 2002).

Despite its shortcomings, the concept of neopatrimonialism holds strengths that are useful for our purposes. One of these is its emphasis on how the state, society, and the economy are interrelated. It also foregrounds the problems of state capacity in how we come to think of corruption (de Grassi 2008: 108), especially in the way the state is appropriated by personal interests (Koechlin 2013: 69). Thus, the notion of neopatrimonialism calls our attention to how corruption is commonly a product of state capacities that have not been "strong enough" to prevent the subversion of essential state functions and interventions (Khan 1989, 1996a, 1996b). Neopatrimonialism presents scholars in the Global South with an opportunity to account for the complex relationship between patronage politics and democratic values, between patrimonial domination and rational-legal bureaucratic domination (Piliavsky 2014; Adebanwi & Obadare 2011: 189). The question of why patronage continues to hold sway in local political life in the global South is a salient one (Piliavsky 2014: 14). In many postcolonial settings, writings on civil society continue to pivot on "a normative emphasis on the tension between patronage (arising from 'tradition') and the more abstract, individual-oriented values, including openness, equity, and efficiency, commonly associated with democratic (and capitalist) forms of rule" (Gillmartin 2014: 128–29). In South Asia, for example, the distinguishing feature of corruption is "the close intermeshing of economic and political calculations in exchanges between patrons and clients at different levels" (Khan 1998: 27).

Having explored the definitional and alternative moralities challenge of corruption, the next part shifts attention to how corruption in postcolonial Nigeria has been politically generated through intense elite struggles for power and resources. The analysis in this section is inspired in part by Mushtaq Khan's argument that forms of economic corruption and their effects in developing countries are intrinsically interwoven with forms of political corruption (Khan 1998). While corruption is certainly older than Nigeria (see, for example, Tignor 1973; Njoku 2005), there is no denying that Nigeria's international image as the epicenter of corruption and fraud is coterminous with its oil boom of the 1970s and the meteoric rise of advance internet fee-fraud.

Corruption Close: State Robbery, the Crisis of Values, and Reform in Nigeria

There was corruption! Corruption! And corruption! Everywhere and all the time! Corruption was not only rife, it had eaten so deeply into the marrow of our existence that looters and fraudsters had become heroes, and it seemed we could no longer place any faith in honesty and decency and hard work. (President Olusegun Obasanjo, cited in Obasanjo 2000)

To most outsiders, the very name Nigeria conjures up images of chaos and confusion, military coups, repression, drug trafficking, and business fraud, [turning the country into] a giant, heaving multiethnic symbol of the archetypal Third World basket case. (Maier 2000: xviii)

Prolonged military rule—about thirty out of forty years (between 1960 and 1999)—played a central role in putting Nigeria on the global corruption map. Nigeria, the self-styled "Giant of Africa," was crippled by decades of corrupt and oppressive military rule, which left "a legacy of executive dominance and political corruption in the hands of Nigeria's so-called 'godfathers'—powerful political bosses sitting atop vast patronage networks who view the government primarily through the lens of their own personal enrichment" (Kew 2006). Driven by a desire for personal gain and hobbled by cronyism, military elites, aided by civilian minions, brazenly looted state property, diverted state funds into their private accounts, and awarded questionable contracts to companies owned by them and their cronies. Former president Olusegun Obasanjo was blunt in his assessment of the military's role in entrenching corruption in Nigeria: "One of the greatest tragedies of military rule in recent times is that corruption was allowed to grow unchallenged and unchecked even when it was glaring for everyone to see" (Akinwale 2017). Unfettered by the rule of law, military elites circumvented virtually all mechanisms designed to promote accountability. Accumulating wealth was all that mattered, and no effort or means was spared in pursuing that ignoble goal. In the pointed words of Nigerian playwright Wole Soyinka, "Only a community of fools will entrust its most sacred possession—nationhood—yet again to a class that has proven so fickle, so treacherous and dishonorable" (Soyinka 1996: 9).

While the Nigerian military has often seized power through unlawful means, they have justified their actions by claiming them to be corrective and *pro tempore*. It is common practice in Africa for regimes that take power to justify their claim on office by criticizing the corruption of the previous administration and promising to wage a war on corruption. They then proceed to reproduce the same corruption that they denounced (Szeftel 1998: 236). This contradiction is not specific to African leaders but permeates all levels of society, from the president to the taxi driver. As Smith notes, "The same [Nigerian] who rails against [rulers such as] General Abacha or President Obasanjo, can in a different moment, lament or laugh about their own involvement in corruption" (2007: 55).

The twin woes of corruption and bad governance were the main reasons adduced by the Nigerian military to rationalize their incursion into politics in 1966 (Adekanye 1993; Ikoku 1985; Ojiakor 1980; Luckham 1971; Agbese 1992). Major Chukwuma Kaduna Nzeogwu, who masterminded the 1966 guardian coup that ousted the First Republic (1960–66), assured ordinary Nigerians that the sole objective of the military was to purge society of "irresponsible and opportunistic politicians, and incompetent and corrupt civil servants; restore respectability, professionalism, transparency, and accountability to Nigeria's public service; and then return to the barracks" (Mbaku 1998: 21). To be sure, Nigeria's First Republic was the "most perfect example" of kleptocracy (Andreski 1968: 108). The popular expectation in Nigeria was that soldiers will use their monopoly of coercive power to literally intimidate people into compliance with the laws and rid the country of the corruption cankerworm. Some scholars argued that the good reception of the Nigerian military should not be mistaken for a public preference for military over civilian rule. Instead, "it reflected a total disenchantment with the uncertainty, violence, corruption and waste that had marred civilian rule since 1960" (Dudley 1973: 109). Others have insisted that the Nigerian miltiary have always enjoyed popular public support any time it outsted an elected government (Siollun 2013). This claim is not without merit. Max Siollun cites former Nigerian head of state General Ibrahim Badamosi Babangida who revealed the extent to which military incursion in Nigerian politics was goaded on by civilian preference for military rule over democracy:

> We in the military waited for an opportunity. There was the media frenzy about how bad the election was, massively rigged, corruption, the economy gone completely bad, threat of secession by people who felt aggrieved. There was frustration within society and it was not unusual to hear statements like, "the worst military dictatorship is better than this democratic government." Nigerians always welcome military intervention because we have not yet developed mentally the values and virtues of democracy. (Siollun 2013)

Ironically, the military, which seized power in 1966 promising to root out corruption, left Nigeria a "culture of corruption" that threatened the continued existence of the country as an independent nation. Soyinka has argued that victory in the Nigerian civil war (1967–1970) consolidated the values of the ruling elites so that corruption became synonymous with "Nigerianism"—national identity and even patriotism (Pratten 2017: 206). Indeed, after one civil war, seven military governments, and three botched attempts to establish democracy, there is one recurrent factor in the failure to govern Nigeria: elite corruption, or what some have described as "the quest for power for the sole purpose of enriching government functionaries, their families, and their close associates, to the detriment of national economic growth" (Iyoha & Oriakhi 2008: 656). In fact, since 1966, most military heads of state have behaved basically as the civilian leaders that they ousted from office: "They have either been engaged in many forms of opportunism to enrich themselves at the expense of the people or have allowed members of their regime to turn governmental structures into instruments of plunder" (Mbaku 2000: 23). Nowhere is this more evident than during the oil boom years of the 1970s and the subsequent economic crisis from the 1980s onwards—a crucial period that not only entrenched corruption but also undermined citizens' trust in their government.

The Vampire State: Oil and Blood Money

Since 2001, hundreds of academic studies have yielded robust evidence showing that natural resource (such as oil) windfalls heighten corruption, hurt state institutions, and make authoritarian regimes more durable (Ross 2015; Sala-i-Martin & Subramanian 2008). Nigeria became the perfect example of this thesis. The mid-1970s in Nigeria was a period of rapid, albeit uneven, economic expansion based on "petrodollars" (Apter 2005). In 1973, at the height of the oil boom, former Nigerian president General Yakubu Gowon famously announced that "Nigeria's problem is not money, but how to spend it" (*The Guardian* 2014a). By 1981, however, the country's relative prosperity came to a halt with the unexpected drop in oil prices. By the end of the decade, the inflation rate had risen steeply, and Nigeria was well on the way to becoming a net debtor for the first time, with its external debt rising from USD1.3bn to USD34bn between 1981 and 1991. This was equivalent to 75 percent of its GDP and nearly 200 percent of its export earnings. For the first time, Nigeria was listed by the World Bank as a low-income country (Nelson 1992). Meanwhile, extreme poverty figures from the country made for a grim reading, rising steadily from 28 percent in 1980 to 66 percent in 1996 (Gandy 2005: 46, 48). This difficult period of "oil bust" coincided with record unemployment in Nigeria, with political patronage becoming "the only way to secure any important employment or contract" (Falola 1998: 60). In Lagos, Nigeria's commercial capital, the population snowballed as rural migrants flocked to the already overloaded city, settling wherever they could get a foothold in the spreading shanty towns on the margins of railway tracks or highways, in moribund bus stations, under the bridges, or in shacks precariously extended over the filthy canals, ditches, and waterways. The various social infrastructure programs inspired by the petrodollars—such as ports, airports, roads, bridges, oil refineries, and steel mills—were generally abandoned and left to decay. A mix of falling oil revenues, widespread corruption, and severe hardship left average Nigerians distressed about the present and fearful for the future (Mustapha 1999).

Despite the drop in oil revenue, Nigerian government spending continued to rise. Shortfalls were made up by borrowing, which plunged Nigeria into even greater debt (Lloyd 2004: 217). Oil effectively transmogrified from "black gold" into the "devil's excrement" (Watts 2008), from the lifeblood of the nation into "a mischievous substance turning politicians into corrupt potentates and making the national political process crumble from the inside" (Apter 2005: 250). The oil bust furthered massive graft by intensifying competition over increasingly scarce petrodollars (Smith 2005: 733). This, in turn, stoked discontent over the consequent poverty and inequality trap. Nowhere was this crisis more evident than in the civilian rule of President Shehu Shagari (1979–1983). As Ali Mazrui notes:

[The] Shagari administration was one of the most economically corrupt and incompetent in Nigeria's history. The nation's oil resources were rampantly abused, its finances substantially depleted, its laws of contract desecrated, its laws against corruption ignored, its teachers unpaid, its people impoverished. Never was a country's economic promise so quickly reduced to economic rampage. Shagari's balance sheet was stark: impressive political freedom against incredible economic anarchy… Shagari's economic sins of anarchy were doomed to be more relevant than his political virtues of freedom. (cited in Siollun 2013)

It was under the Shagari government that "subjugated knowledges" (in form of stories, rumors, and gossip) started to circulate in everyday life about the rise of a "vampire state" (Frimpong-Ansah 1992), where elites were not only sucking the state dry, but literally using human blood for money ritual (blood money or *owo eje*). This underscores what Masquelier (2001: 269) calls the "omnivorous potentialities of the postcolony." In his *Eating and Being Eaten: Cannibalism as Food for Thought*, Francis Nyamnjoh (2018) tells us that "to feed on someone's life chances is tantamount to feeding on someone's flesh." This metaphorical link between cannibalism and corruption in Nigeria is best studied as part of an evolving process of commodity fetishism, in which people see money as the ultimate value and become obsessed with its accrual. As the ultimate fetish of privilege, money reifies the process by which the products of human labor are alienated from their producers, and thus can be amassed by the powerful—not as a result of their own labors, but by virtue of the sweat of others (McCall 2003: 83). As Apter puts it:

> The notion of effortless gain at the expense of even "consumption" of others is echoed in various witchcraft beliefs as well, but the underlying template motivating it is the conversion of blood into money—bad money to be sure… As the cost of living rose, real incomes fell, and the professional middle class gradually withered away, oil was transformed from the life-blood of the nation into the bad blood of corrupt government. (Apter 2005: 251–52)

In particular, the 1990s saw widespread and visceral stories of "money medicine" and "money doubling" that sometimes read like pages from Amos Tutola's "magical realism" novels. The stories generally related actual practices in which human blood and (private) body parts were trafficked in macabre rituals for the creation of instant wealth (Bures 2008: 60). As we know from studies elsewhere, "these body parts are used for the preparation of magic potions. Parts of the body may be used to secure certain advantages from the ancestors. A skull may, for instance, be built into the foundation of a new building to ensure a good business, or a brew containing human parts may be buried where it will ensure a good harvest" (Ralushai et al. 1996: 255). In January 1998, the front cover of *Fame*, a popular tabloid in Nigeria, displayed grisly pictures of a woman whose eyes had been gouged out for money medicine. The boom in Nigerian home videos (Nollywood) of the 1990s pivoted on evil occult forces. One of the biggest blockbusters of that decade, *Blood Money I and II*, tells the story of Mike and his immersion in the "vulture cult," involving human sacrifice, the mutation of men into vulture, and the transmogrification of children into chickens who vomit money. Another blockbuster, *Egba Orun* ("The Necklace"), tells the story of a woman who uses her daughter for money ritual purposes. For the most part, videos such as *Blood Money* and *Egba Orun* are not cast as allegories or fanciful representations, but as accounts of real occurrences. In these movies, as in the many other stories circulating in the Nigerian press and public discourse at the time, the main theme came down to "excessive riches obtained from evil occult power—riches that are represented as anti-social, destructive, and ultimately unprofitable" (Marshall 2009: 188). Money magic became the ultimate signifier of Nigeria's unproductive wealth (Apter 2005: 269). By characterizing sudden wealth as bewitched, average Nigerians engaged in an active critique of a wicked world in which "ends far outstrip means, in which the will to consume is not matched by the opportunity to earn, in which there is a high velocity of exchange and a relatively low volume of production... in which the possibility of rapid enrichment, of amassing a fortune by largely invisible methods, is always palpably present" (Comaroff & Comaroff 2000: 293).

The 1990s also saw an "epidemic of penis theft" that swept across Nigeria and West Africa generally (Diouf 2003: 10). In a typical incident, someone would suddenly shout: "Thief! My genitals are gone!" Then a culprit would be identified, apprehended, and summarily killed. In the streets of Lagos, it was not unusual to see men holding on to their genitalia while women held on to their breasts, either openly or discreetly (Bures 2008). To this day, rumors of magical penis theft and blood money hold sway in Nigeria, calling our attention to "a world in which humans seem in constant danger of turning into commodities, of losing their lifeblood to the market and to the destructive desires it evokes" (Comaroff & Comaroff 1993: xx). During my fieldwork in the bus terminals of Lagos, *danfo* drivers often related numerous stories of big men in their area who used the blood of children (*eje omode*), relatives (*eje ara ile*), or strangers (*eje alejo*) to "kill money" (*pa owo*) and acquire fame. These frequent accusations reflect a Nigerian society where power and the occult are interconnected: "all 'big men' that have 'eaten well' are understood to have links to secret and occult forms of power!" (Marshall 1998: 304). Jean and John Comaroff (1999), writing about post-colonial South Africa, describe this as "occult economies," that is, an economy in which wealth is achieved by "eating" someone else's productive and navigational capacity.

The connection between witchcraft and corruption is well documented in post-colonial African studies; it underscores "the secret world of obscure rituals" that characterize corruption and power on the continent (Nuijten & Anders 2007: 19; Geschiere 1997; Bayart 1993; Schatzberg 2001: 50). In Malawi, accusations of magic and corruption are often aimed at people whose wealth appears suddenly or inexplicably (Nuijten & Anders 2007: 19). In Cameroon, the opulent are accused of having strong *evu/djambe* (sorcery). Accusing the wealthy of sorcery is potentially dangerous, since they can use their sorcery to "eat," that is, punish the accuser (Rowlands & Warnier 1988: 123). "Those who can 'eat' materially are able to do this because they can 'eat' their victims spiritually" (Schatzberg 2001: 5). My aim in this section was not to reduce political life in Nigeria and Africa to sensationalist impressions, but to show how the ambiguous sources of wealth and its socially unproductive nature in Nigeria generated a public obsession with evil ritual practice and occult forces.

Rugged Materialism

The economic crisis of the 1980s, especially the frantic looting that took hold amongst the ruling cabal, created a cohort of disaffected Nigerian youth variously labeled as a "lost generation" (Cruise O'Brien 1996), a "coming anarchy" (Kaplan 1994), and a category without importance, at the mercy of global, political, and economic fluctuations. The inordinate quest for fame and fortune among Nigerian leaders taught many youth that being an honest and law-abiding citizen does not pay (Osoba 1996: 384), that "it is better to sell your soul to the devil than to be scrupulous. The cunning required to meet immediate needs has replaced the respect of any righteous moral code" (Nzeza 2004: 21).[4] The mentality of *owo kia kia* ("fast money") or money by any means became the lifestyle and trademark of a new precarious class in Lagos. In this no man's land, money became an "uncontained agent" that penetrated all relations (Oestermann & Geschiere 2017: 109). In Lagos, *owo* (money) transmogrified from *idi gbogbo buburu* (root of all evil) into *ewa* (beauty). This reclaims Cyprian Ekwensi's timeless novel *Jagua Nana* (1961), which paints a sinister picture of Lagos as a vanity fair where money is an "idol worshipped in every waking and sleeping moment" (1961: 30). Ekwensi compares Lagos to Tropicana, a nightclub where people's first loyalty was to money. According to Ekwensi, village people come to Lagos to "make fast money by faster means, and greedily to seek positions that yielded even more money" (1961: 15). *Jagua Nana's* sharp contrast of the immorality of the city to village traditional morality foreshadows Ekeh's (1975) distinction between primordial and civic public.

The displacement of traditional cultural values by "rugged materialism" (Assimeng 1986: 249)—that is, a condition of aggressive preoccupation with material accumulation without regard to values of probity and propriety—offers a useful historical angle to the Nigerian "politics of plunder" endemic since the beginning of the oil boom (Gore & Pratten 2003: 102). About four decades ago, William Brownsberger criticized studies that explained third-world corruption by reference to anachronistic traditions and to the special pressures on public officials. He argued, instead, that the roots of corruption in Nigeria go deeper, to "a materialism and political fragmentation that are the products of a moment in development" (1983: 215). The "dazzling status of the white man (and the successor black elite)," argues Brownsberger, "burned into the [Nigerian] populace a desire to appear and act as did their dominators, and this led the most successful to corrupt excesses" (1983: 215–33). This observation is confirmed in several roadside conversations during my fieldwork in Lagos. I was struck by the strong connections that (elderly) commuters made between corruption and the loss of

---

[4] In *This Present Darkness*, the late Stephen Ellis (2016) tells us that the 1970s and' 80s precipitated the expansion of a "criminal diaspora" of the educated but jobless youth—Nigerian criminality and fraud went global at the same time when the issue of "organized crime" was becoming the cynosure of media eyes.

value, with many lamenting the neglect of traditional moral values of *ise* (work) before *owo* (money). These commuters parsed corruption as a direct result of the inordinate desire for *owo kia kia* without patience for due process.

Nigeria's *owo kia kia* mentality came out clearly in two interviews I had in late 2014, the first with Balogun, a Senior Vehicle Inspector Officer, in Alimosho: "As far as I am concerned," said Balogun, "we Nigerians are a problem to ourselves. We look for where we can find easy money. Nobody wants to apply themselves to apprenticeship work anymore... That is why I said we need to seriously work on the psyche of the average Nigerian. A lot of people today are just interested in what brings in fast cash, without regard for what happens on the long run." In the other interview at a bus terminus in Oshodi, a veteran *danfo* driver bemoaned the fact that "Nigerians no longer work for their food. They just want money here and now, at all cost. Even when they have to use their loved one for money ritual, most will not hesitate. They forget that they must first learn to crawl before walking. During our time, we learnt that work cures poverty. Our youth have lost the virtues of work and patience. They embrace *jibiti* (fraud)."

IBB, SAP, and the Politics of Deception

In an effort to re-impose political order and decency in Nigeria, the Buhari-Idiagbon regime (1984–85) toppled Nigeria's Second Republic (1979–83) and mounted a public propaganda "war against indiscipline" (WAI), along with a special paramilitary squad—"WAI brigade"—for its execution (Falola 1998: 62). WAI's goals were to boost national unity, promote economic self-sufficiency, and instill cultural, personal, and moral discipline so as to control indolence, corruption, and criminal practices (Agbaje & Adisa 1988). Be that as it may, the regime ultimately dug its own grave by "trying to arrest the country's economic and social decline by doctrinaire and anti-people policies like massive retrenchment of workers in the public service, the introduction of many new taxes, levies and fees on citizens, drastic reduction in public expenditure, especially on social welfare and agricultural subsidies, and the widespread destruction of the means of livelihood of small privately employed persons like motor mechanics, food vendors, and petty traders by pulling down their makeshift sheds, kiosks, and bukas in the name of urban environmental sanitation" (Osoba 1996: 381). By August 1985, the regime faced an intense crisis of legitimation (Jega 2000; Diamond, Kirk-Greene, & Oyediran 1997).

Enter General Ibrahim Badamosi Babangida ("IBB"), through a bloodless coup. IBB's regime (1985–1993) derived much of its popularity and legitimacy from a self-proclaimed "corrective mission" (Graf 1988; Mustapha 1999). To put a halt to Nigeria's downward economic spiral, IBB implemented a structural adjustment program (SAP) in 1986, alongside a Transition to Civil Rule project—what many

Nigerian observers have called a "transition without end" (Mustapha 1999)—to meet the demands of the International Monetary Fund (IMF) and the World Bank. Premised on the alleged rationalistic logic of the supremacy of market signals in economic management, the SAP was a reform package aimed at strengthening the economy by increasing domestic production and instituting financial and import restrictions. Core elements of the SAP included currency devaluation and exchange rate deregulation, significant reductions in public expenditure, especially in social services sector, and privatization and commercialization of public enterprises and services. Yet, the SAP in Nigeria proved largely "inconsistent and irregular and economic management was soon overshadowed by political discord" and domestic discontent, reflected in strikes and student protests (Lewis & Bratton 2000: 2; see also Mustapha 1999; Apter 2005).

The role of the personality of leaders is often muted in many analyses of how and why the SAP failed in Nigeria, and Africa generally. Nigerian iconoclastic musician Fela Kuti described IBB and his regime as *wayo* (fraudulent). Apter (2005) indexes the many ruses deployed by IBB—infamously nicknamed "the evil genius"—to loot the treasury and lead a democratic transition that ultimately left the juntas in charge. On the economic front, IBB deviously exploited both the local expectations for development and the World Bank and IMF's demand for SAP to establish programs that diverted resources back to his pocket and those of his cronies (Smith 2005). For about seven years, IBB involved average Nigerians in a political transition to civilian rule whose cost is estimated at N30 billion. "It became clear in the end that [IBB's] Machiavellian maneuvers were ultimately aimed at perpetuating his personal grip on power, even at the cost of fragmenting the country along regional, ethnic and religious lines" (Mustapha 1999: 278). IBB's wife, Maryam Babangida, was not left out of the act. Maryam created the "Better Life for Rural Women" program—sarcastically dubbed by average Nigerians as "Better Life for Rich Women" or "Better Life for Ruling Women"—wherein "the first lady, together with the wives of governors, launched their projects in state capitals while sporting the finest lace and fanciest head ties, forever out of reach and out of touch" (Apter 2005: 248). The personalization of state institutions under IBB ensured that only those with "long legs," the right connections, could hope for economic security and selective justice from the state. Petro-naira, political patronage, and repression became the regular trademarks of IBB's kleptocracy. His regime sanctioned corruption by issuing a pardon to officials convicted of corruption by his predecessors and reinstating their seized properties (Ocheje 2001: 171–3). General Buhari had it right when he said:

> The regime that came to power in 1985 that ushered in General Ibrahim Babangida destroyed all national institutions, which in its own opinion, stood in its way. It tolerated, encouraged, entrenched and institutionalized corruption and glorified its perpetrators… At the end of its tenure in 1993, the military

government had established an image of corrupt, unreliable and unaccountable lords of the manor. (cited in Mustapha 1999: 278)

The abuses of the IBB regime created a society where mastring the art of deception became the conditio sine qua non for survival and success (Smith 2005: 735–36). Obsession with deception and fraud gathered momentum from the 1980s onward; advance fee fraud and confidence tricks involving forgery and impersonation, covered under the article "419" of the Nigerian criminal code, exploded with the deregulation of the banking and foreign exchange system under IBB's SAP (Marshall 2009: 186). "419" became the ultimate symbol of "world-as-misrepresentation" and the second source of foreign export in Nigeria in the 1990s, after oil (Apter 2005: 248).

Today, popular discourse in Nigeria is dominated by fantastic stories of someone who was conned by a "Yahoo," that is, a person that uses Yahoo email for fraudulent activities online. Variations include "Yahoo-Yahoo" and "Yahoo Boys". In general: "They tend to be young men conducting get rich quick schemes out of cybercafés. These scams go by the nickname '419' after Nigeria's penal code for fraud. Many are imposters on online dating sites, sell items that don't exist, buy items that are 'paid for' with fake Western Union receipts, or carry out phishing schemes. So, if you ever receive an email from a dying African prince who seeks to bequeath his $5 million fortune to someone deserving but initially needs a wire transfer of $500 as proof of life, it was probably sent by a Nigerian Yahoo boy" (Bell 2019). One Lagosian traced the rise of "419" practices to the crisis of values under IBB's venal rule:

> All the 419, fraud, corruption practices you see today have their roots in the IBB era. Those things were not only acceptable, they were the norm. You could defraud anyone as long as you were smart enough. All kinds of wrong things began to happen—smuggling, bunkering, drugs—and Babangida encouraged it. Fraud and corruption became the prevalent ways to really make money. The society descended into utter depravity.

One of the primary and lasting consequences of 419 scams in Lagos is "epistemological insecurity" (Pratten 2013), that is, anxieties over the authenticity of information and the veracity of claims. During fieldwork in Lagos, almost every wall had the warning sign: "This Land is Not for Sale. Beware of 419." To quote Mbembe (2001a: 148), a visible characteristic of everyday life in Nigeria became its "simultaneous multiplicities"—in other words, the incongruence between "what one sees and exposes, and the real value of things… the unexpected is the rule." The economic crisis of the 1980s exposed not only the contradictions of Nigeria's oil-dependent economy and petro-naira, but also spotlighted a simulated government that unproductively accrued wealth.

As the oil economy imploded and collapsed, the signs of wealth and development became increasingly estranged from their referents, infusing the value forms of everyday exchange with ghostly simulacra—food that did not satisfy, clothes and uniforms that disguised, financial instruments that had no legitimacy, banks lacking capital, hospitals without medicine, and finally democracy that had no demos. (Apter 2005: 274)

IBB was forced out of office in June 1993, following his botched attempt to subvert his own deceitful Political Transition Program. An official report issued after IBB's exit declared that an estimated USD12bn from public funds went missing under his rule (Nairaland Forum 2006; Apter 2005: 247). IBB was replaced by the unelected Interim National Government (ING), which was later toppled in November 1993 by General Sani Abacha (1993–1998), IBB's minister of defense and Nigeria's last despot.

A Coup from Heaven

By the time Abacha seized power, the Nigerian economy was in free fall. This, however, did not prevent Abacha from deepening the trigger-happy democracy, through which incumbent juntas in Nigeria manipulate political processes to re-constitute themselves as elected democratic governments (Alao 2000). In light of the popular opposition which his regime endured from the beginning, Abacha quickly adopted populist, nationalist, and draconian measures to contain the series of crises threatening his grip on power. For example, the regime enacted "Decree No. 12 of 1994, which officially removed the authority of the courts to investigate, let alone challenge, the actions of members of the regime" (Badru 1998: 151). Under Abacha, corruption was no longer an aberration but rather the way the system works (Diamond 1987: 581), the object of governance. Robert Guest (2004: 121), for example, describes how "[Abacha] used to send trucks around to the central bank with orders that they be filled with banknotes." When this happens, says the distinguished Nigerian scholar Claude Ake (1995: 2), "the state effectively ceases to exist as a state and compromises its ability to pursue development." Not surprisingly, in both 1997 and 1998, Transparency International listed Nigeria as the most corrupt nation in the world. Jane Guyer (2002: xi) points to the deleterious impacts of Abacha's negligent, repressive, and rapacious regime on Nigeria's urban life, including:

Petro shortage, personal insecurity, long interruptions in electricity and water service, multiple road blocks… and sheer worry about the futures… the shocking waste of hope and energy as children failed to get medical care, very brilliant students failed to shape careers, farmers and traders failed to get goods to market

before they rotted... Life was fearful and profoundly discouraging. (cited in
Animasawun 2017: 240)

Dubbed a "coup from heaven," Abacha's sudden death (apparently poisoned while
in the company of three prostitutes, see Weiner 1998) in June 1998 was followed,
four weeks later, by that of Chief M.K.O. Abiola in July, the other leading protagonist in the intractable political crisis that had plagued Nigeria since June 1993.
Following his death, the Swiss government repatriated the sum of USD700 million out of a reported USD3 billion stolen by Abacha and deposited in several Swiss
banks—over a million dollars for each day in office, including weekends (Africa
Confidential, 2000). Abacha alone stole the equivalent of 2 to 3 percent of Nigeria's
GDP for every year that he was president. The Nigerian government has also recovered more than USD100 million of the funds stolen by the late dictator and his family from the autonomous British island of Jersey and an estimated USD150 million
from Luxembourg. Other funds belonging to the despot remain frozen in accounts
in Liechtenstein, Luxembourg, and the United Kingdom. In November 2009,
Abacha's son was convicted by a Swiss court for his involvement in a criminal organization and USD350 million in assets stolen from Nigeria were seized (Ocheje
2001: 171). Abacha's turning of state power into "a weapon for stealing the nation
blind" (*Tell* 1998, cited in Adebanwi & Obadare, 2011: 191) was characterized as
"army robbery—the highest stage of armed robbery" (Osoba 1996: 383): 383).

In the decades between 1960 and 1999, Nigeria's post-independence rulers had
either stolen or mismanaged an astronomical USD400 billion in what Paul Collier
(2005) cleverly calls a "survival of the fattest." If you were to put four hundred billion dollar bills end-to-end, you could make seventy-five round trips to the moon!
(United Nations Office on Drugs & Crime n.d.). Also, this amount is equivalent to
six times the Marshal Plan, the sum total needed to rebuild devastated Europe in
the aftermath of the Second World War (Adebanwi & Obadare 2011: 190). This
serial pillaging of the national treasury created a paradox in which "the scandalous, almost legendary, wealth of key ruling class members exist[ed] to mock
the unspeakable mass poverty, misery and degradation of the Nigerian people"
(Osoba 1996: 383). Military kleptocracy accelerated Nigeria's dramatic decline
from a middle-income country with an annual per capita income of USD1000
in the early 1980s to an impoverished nation with a per capita income of only
USD310 in 1999 (Suberu 2001: 207–8). In 2000, the standard of living in Nigeria
equaled what it was in the early 1970s, a period following three years of bloody
Civil War (1967–1970) (Ocheje 2001: 176).

Abacha's death opened the door for democratic reforms. Enter General Abdul-
salami Abubakar, who succeeded Abacha as the de facto Head of State (1998–
1999). Abubakar moved quickly to release hundreds of unjustly detained political
prisoners (including Olusegun Obasanjo, who had been imprisoned in 1995 for
opposing Abacha) and repealed notorious military decrees weaponized against
the opposition, such as Decree 2 of 1984, which allowed detention without trial. In

his greatest achievement, Abubakar oversaw a transition to civilian rule program that returned the country to democratic rule on 29 May 1999. The presidential election of 1999 was comfortably won by Chief Olusegun Obasanjo, the PDP (People's Democratic Party) candidate. Obasanjo was a former military Head of State (1976–1979) who handed over power to Shehu Shagari (1979–1983), a democratically-elected civilian president, hence becoming the first military head of state to transfer power peacefully to a civilian administration in Nigeria.

A Mixed Bag: Anti-Corruption Initiatives, 1999–2007

Studies have shown that new leaders are often more inclined to reform and less tied to existing patron-client networks (Lawson 2009: 78; Bienen & Herbst 1996; Kjaer 2004; Taylor 2006; van de Walle 1999). Obasanjo's case is no exception. By May 1999, when he acceded to power, Nigerians were poorer than when the oil boom began, and the country was saddled with debts of over USD30 billion (Guest 2004: 124). The percentage of Nigerians living below the poverty line, less than USD1 a day, was estimated to be 70 percent (Sala-i-Martin & Subramanian 2008). Against this backdrop, Obasanjo was widely expected to cauterize the country's elite corruption epidemic and usher in a new era of transparent governance and national unity. Obasanjo was seen as the main bridge between the military and civilians, and between the north and south; in short, "a new broom who would sweep out the corruption and abuses of military brass hats who had lost any sense of purpose beyond plundering the national treasury and brutally pummeling innocent citizens into submission" (Adebajo 2008: 5). At his inauguration, Obasanjo vowed to leave no stones unturned in his effort to defeat corruption and change the "business as usual" mentality in Nigeria. There will be "no sacred cows," he declared, adding that "corruption, the greatest bane of society today, will be tackled head-on at all levels… No society can achieve anything near its full potential if it allows corruption to become full blown cancer as it has become in Nigeria" (Omotola 2006: 221). Very early in his term, Obasanjo identified Nigeria's debt issue as a major impediment to economic development. With his committed finance minister Ngozi Okonjo-Iweala (2003–2006), Obasanjo led negotiations with the Paris Club of Creditors that wiped out Nigeria's entire USD30 billion external debt by paying USD12.4 billion and having $USD17.6 billion canceled (Center for Global Development 2017). This was the largest such financial deal in Africa.

War against Corruption: The ICPC and EFCC

Obasanjo began his war against corruption by establishing the Independent Corrupt Practices and Other Related Offences Commission (ICPC) and the Economic and Financial Crime Commission (EFCC) in 2000 and 2003, respectively.

The ICPC and EFCC were meant to complement each other. While the ICPC had a judicial approach to anti-corruption, the EFCC adopted a law enforcement approach. As stated on its website, the ICPC's mission is "to rid Nigeria of corruption through lawful enforcement and preventive measures." However, the Commission struggled to leave a dent on the solid walls of corruption investigation and prosecution, with a low conviction rate—only eight convictions (Aina 2014). In sharp contrast to the ICPC, the EFCC went about its work with "unusual zeal" (Adebanwi & Obadare 2011: 192), like a "corruption-exposing X-ray machine that was striking fear into the hearts of national leaders" (Mazzarella 2006: 475). Headed by senior police officer Nuhu Ribadu, the EFCC was empowered to "rid Nigeria of economic and financial crimes and to effectively coordinate the domestic effort of the global fight against money laundering and terrorist financing." This mission was timely, given the upsurge of advance fee fraud ("419") in post-1999 Nigeria, coupled with the country's inclusion in the list of non-cooperating nations by the Financial Action Task Force (FATF).[5] Empowered by the EFCC (Establishment) Act (2004), the EFCC's mission is multilayered, including: to "curb the menace of the corruption that constitutes the cog in the wheel of progress; protect national and foreign investments in the country; imbue the spirit of hard work in the citizenry and discourage ill-gotten wealth; identify illegally acquired wealth and confiscate it; build an upright workforce in both public and private sectors of the economy; and contribute to the global war against financial crimes."[6]

True to its mission, the EFCC secured over 250 convictions in four years, mostly in respect to the advance fee fraud and Internet crimes (Adebanwi & Obadare 2011: 195). During Obasanjo's tenure, more than two thousand people responsible for "419" email scams were arrested, and over 130 were convicted of fraud (Ploch 2010: 12). The EFCC recovered USD5 billion in stolen assets and prosecuted many high-profile persons, from businessmen to politicians and police officers. In unprecedented moves in 2005, Tofa Balogun, Nigeria's Inspector General of Police, was convicted of corruption, having stolen N10 billion from the Nigeria Police Force; Senate Speaker Adolphus Wabara was forced to resign after taking over USD400,000 in bribes from the Minister of Education, Fabian Osuji (who was also dismissed in relation to corruption allegations); Alice Mobolaji Osomo, the Minister of Housing, was fired for allocating 200 properties to senior government officials instead of public sale, and for bribing legislators to pass a budget. In partnership with the London Metropolitan Police, the EFCC exposed

---

[5] Set up in 1989 at the G-7 Summit in Paris, the FATF is an intergovernmental organization that develops and promotes national and international politics to combat money laundering and terrorist financing.

[6] EFCC, Official Website.

a number of high-profile cases of corruption among Nigerian governors, two of which are examined here.

The first case involves Joshua Dariye, former governor of Plateau state (1999–2004), who was found to operate twenty-five bank accounts in London alone to juggle money and evade the law. Like many governors of his ilk, Dariye used front agents to penetrate Western real estate markets, where he purchased choice properties. The London Metropolitan Police determined Dariye had acquired 10 million euros in benefits through criminal conduct in London, while domestically EFCC were able to restrain proceeds of his crimes worth around USD34 million. In June 2018, the Nigerian High Court sentenced Dariye to fourteen years imprisonment on charges of criminal breach of trust and misappropriation of funds (N1.6 billion). The Court of Appeal later reduced Dariye's sentence to ten years (*Punch* 2018).

In the other case, former governor of Delta state James Ibori (1999–2007), pled guilty in London to charges of money laundering and other financial crimes totaling N12.4 billion (USD79 million) he had committed during his eight years in office. Ibori was sentenced to thirteen years in prison, with the Crown Prosecution Service noting that Ibori had acquired his wealth "at the expense of some of the poorest people in the world" (BBC 2012). Richard Dowden (2008: 445) was right after all: "Politics in Nigeria is a business career: Any politician who does not end up a multi-millionaire is regarded a fool." At the same time, politics in Nigeria drives home a frequently overlooked fact that corruption in the developing world is not infrequently aided and abetted by Western donor governments and the World Bank (Bonner 2009). "For every minister trousering a bribe [in Africa] there had to be a Western company ready to pay it" (Wrong 2009).

The EFCC's relative success in the fight against corruption was boosted by several factors, including the collective disdain for corruption by ordinary Nigerians, the strong backing of the Nigerian federal government under President Obasanjo, and the renewed interest in Europe and America to monitor money laundering in the wake of 9/11 attacks and terrorism financing. Under Ribadu, the EFCC relentlessly called on the international community to "continue to support our work. That then sends a strong message to our elite that the world is watching what is happening in Nigeria, and that protects us" (Lawson 2009: 90–91). In 2007, Ribadu told the World Bank:

> What we need is training, equipment, and exposure for our staff. We also need your support at the international level. So much of grand corruption is out of our control, as the money goes out of our jurisdiction. If the World Bank can help us retrieve stolen money and ensure there is no safe haven outside, it will help us immensely in our fight internally. There should be no hiding place for the corrupt; treat them like terrorists. (Lawson 2009: 90)

The EFCC benefited from the financial support of key international actors such as the European Union, the United States, the United Nations Development Program, and the World Bank. The European Union, for example, donated a total of USD32 million to the EFCC between 2004 and 2008, representing 85 percent of its foreign support. In 2005, a USD5 million grant from the World Bank "allowed the EFCC to target political corruption among high-stakes elites, including members of the executive branch of government and members of parliament... at a time when these very same officials halted the appropriation [sic] of the EFCC to stop us from pursuing leads" (*allafrica* 2007). Also, the personality of Ribadu was key to success. An unusually courageous and devoted man, Ribadu pledged his life to fighting corruption in Nigeria. "I am ready to give my life..." he declared in 2003 when he was appointed to lead the EFCC. "When you go into the Army, you known you are going to be killed or you are going to kill. And I look at it not too different from that. This work is worth doing. I am ready to give my life for Nigeria" (Adebanwi & Obadare 2011: 198). For his efforts, Ribadu was named "Man of the Year" for 2006 by the respected Nigerian *Vanguard* newspaper. In 2007, a poll found the EFCC to be the second most trusted institution in Nigeria (cited in Lawson 2009: 91).

Corruption Fights Back

Obasanjo's efforts to overcome corruption began to reap dividends on the international stage. In one year—2005—Nigeria jumped from third to sixth position in Transparency International's CPI rankings of the world's most corrupt nations—an improvement on its poor showing in 2004 and 2003 when it occupied second and first position, respectively, on the list. Praise for the Obasanjo administration came thick and fast. Antonio Maria Costa, former Executive Director of the United Nations Office on Drugs and Crime (UNODC), noted that "Nigeria's anti-graft war is proving that there are no sacred cows left when it comes to tackling corruption. That sends a strong message of hope across the continent and beyond" (UNODC n.d.). Daniel Kaufmann, former head of global programs at the World Bank, expressed hope and admiration for the transformative power of Obasanjo's anti-corruption war: "Nigeria is changing for the better... if the current momentum is maintained and deepened, the progress made in the fight against corruption could become irreversible" (News24 2005).

Alas, the anti-corruption momentum was neither maintained nor deepened; if anything, it was reversed. Obasanjo's government soon became littered with postures of reform, with grandiose promises and conspicuous lack of delivery. Finance minister Okonjo-Iweala, now Director-General of the World Trade Organization, was inexplicably dismissed from office by Obasanjo in 2006, and the

EFCC was manipulated by Obasanjo to selectively target his political opponents (Lawson 2009: 86)—hence its label as "Obasanjo's errand dogs" (Akinnola 2008).[7] The International Crisis Group (ICG) reports that Obasanjo wielded the EFCC as "a political weapon to whip political foes, especially state governor likely to stand for the presidency and their supporters, into line" (ICG 2007: 3). By way of illustration, five state governors, some of whom were top contenders for the PDP's presidential nomination, were impeached in 2005–2006 on barely substantiated allegations of corruption. Kaushik Basu (2019: 417), writing about a similar situation in India, calls this political witch-hunting process "a manifestation of a political-economic trap in which nations tend to get caught."

Obasanjo's botched attempt to change the Nigerian Constitution in April 2006 to afford him the opportunity of running for a third presidential term substantially hurt his much-touted democratic credentials. He offered bribes of more than USD400,000 to Nigerian senators and representatives, had armed police officers break up a meeting of legislators and governors in Abuja who opposed his third term bid, and threatened governors who failed to support his bid with impeachment. Obasanjo's legacy was further soiled by an ugly spat with his vice-president, Atiku Abubakar, which saw both politically exposed men publicly accusing each other of corruption involving the government's Petroleum Technology Development Fund (BBC 2006).[8] Under Obasanjo, who acted as his own oil minster throughout his eight years in office, Nigeria staged the most fraudulent elections in its democratic history in 2007. Ballot boxes were stuffed and stolen, voters intimidated, and results magically appeared in areas where voting had not taken place. The Transition Monitoring Group, Nigeria's own independent election observer, called the 2007 election a "sham" and a "charade," while Nigeria's *This Day* newspaper dubbed it a "rigging and killing extravaganza" (Laurence 2007: 8).

As was the case under IBB and Abacha, Obasanjo's government openly supported corrupt politicians. One high-profile case was that of Chief Olabode ("Bode") George, a powerful figure within the ruling PDP and a former chairman

---

[7] Ribadu has dismissed allegations of "selective enforcement," noting that some of Obasanjo's friends were investigated and, in some cases, prosecuted. These include: "the Inspector General of Police, Tafa Balogun (accused by opposition elements as having used the police to help the president's party to rig the elections in 2003), Chief Bode George, the deputy chairman (south-west) of the ruling People's Democratic Party and the president's 'Man Friday' (who was eventually jailed after Obasanjo left power, based on the investigations and report submitted by Ribadu to the president), Governor Peter Odili of Rivers State (whom Obasanjo had anointed as his successor, until dissuaded by a report submitted by Ribadu to the president on allegations of corruption against him), and even Obasanjo's daughter, Senator Iyabo Obasanjo-Bello, and his successor, Umaru Yar'Adua (who, as state governor, was investigated by the EFCC and some of his commissioners arrested)" (Adebanwi & Obadare 2011: 196).

[8] Obasanjo attempted to use the EFCC to prevent Atiku from contesting the 2007 presidential elections on grounds of corruption, declaring a public holiday to hold up the seating of the country's Supreme Court, which eventually—barely a week before the polls—ruled that Atiku could run for the presidency.

of the Nigerian Ports Authority (NPA). In 2008, Bode was charged with contract-related offenses of close to N100 billion dating back to his time at the NPA. In 2009, Bode was convicted and sentenced to two-and-a-half years in prison after a surprisingly efficient trial. However, when Bode emerged from prison in 2011, he was welcomed rapturously by Nigeria's political elite, led by none other than President Obasanjo and his former defense minister, Ademola Adetokunbo. This brazen display sent an unmistakable message to all Nigerians: "proven criminality is no bar to the highest echelons of politics in Nigeria" (HRW 2011). Reacting to the lavish reception, former anti-corruption czar Nuhu Ribadu said: "It is really a shameful thing that has happened. Instead of hiding their heads in shame they have the effrontery to celebrate corruption, in fact it is a national shame" (*Vanguard* 2011a). The Action Congress of Nigeria was even more emphatic in its criticism: "The PDP's action sends a wrong signal to Nigerian youths that it is alright to steal or mismanage public funds, since it can even turn them into a 'hero' like Olabode George" (*Vanguard* 2011b).

Nuhu Ribadu may have been untouchable under Obasanjo, but not after him. Under President Umar Yar'Adua (2007–2010), Obasanjo's northern successor, Ribadu was demoted within the Force and formally dismissed in the middle of his guaranteed term. He was replaced by Farida Waziri, a retired police chief who was ostensibly backed by the very corrupt politicians that Ribadu had either indicted or was planning to indict. Waziri was openly critical of the EFCC's aggressive style under Ribadu, noting in one case that: "We will not embrace the Gestapo approach where if you want to arrest one person, you go with 40 mobile policemen. You go to newspapers and radio calling people thieves. But the rule of law is the difference" (Sa'idu 2009: 1). In the end, corruption fought back against Ribadu. As Said Adejumobi puts it: "Ribadu underestimated the strength and resilience of the forces he was fighting. Corruption... is like an octopus. It changes its shape and size; it contracts, expands, lowers itself and blows out differently. More than an octopus, corruption is a wild animal—a beast, which if you do not fight and tame it well, would fight you back. Today, corruption is fighting Nuhu Ribadu back" (cited in Adebanwi & Obadare, 2011: 202). Ribadu's experience is hardly unique. John Gitongo, the respected anti-corruption chief under Kenyan President Kibaki, suffered a backlash after exposing large-scale graft among the highest echelons of elected officials in Kenya. Following death threats to his life from the "big men" he had exposed, Githongo was forced to resign and flee into self-imposed exile (BBC 2005; Wrong 2009).

In the end, Obasanjo embodied the dilemmas and chronic contradictions that threaten Nigeria's democratic experiment. His anti-corruption reform agenda ended up promoting what it sought to eradicate—more political corruption and greater instability. His eight-year rule proved a mixed bag. Seen as an indispensable force for pulling Nigeria away from the difficult years of "blunt ethnomilitary rule" (Suberu 2001) into the halcyon era of national unity, Obasanjo instead presided over a country that arguably became more divided under his watch than at any time in its history. Seen as a force for national salvation, he instead watched from the sidelines as the country was nearly torn apart by sectarian violence (Adebajo 2008: 7). While much of the decay in Nigeria had set in under the previous era of military misrule, the situation deepened under Obasanjo's administration, after some early promise. Under Obasanjo, the powers of the presidency were (ab)used "to micromanage the country" (*Economist* 2000). In his 2006 memoirs, Wole Soyinka noted the deep flaws in Obasanjo's character:

> [He] is a man of restless energies… A bullish personality, calculating and devious, yet capable of disarming spontaneity, affecting an exaggerated country yokel act to cover up the interior actuality of the same, occasionally self-deprecatory yet intolerant of criticism, this general remains a study in the outer limits of compulsive rivalry, even where the fields of competence or striving are miles apart. (Soyinka 2006: 219)

President Goodluck Jonathan, 2010–2015

President Goodluck Jonathan is what some may call an "accidental president," due to the manner in which he inherited power after the untimely death of President Yar'Adua (2007–2010) in May 2010, apparently from a chronic kidney illness. At his inauguration, The Economist (2010) noted that, "Mr. Jonathan is taking over the leadership of one of the world's least governable countries in the least promising circumstances." Far from heeding the clarion call to "Be Focused, Be Bold" (ibid.), Jonathan embraced Nigeria's "soft, forgiving culture"[9] toward elite corruption. In a controversial case, he pardoned[10] the former Bayelsa State Governor and close ally, Diepreye Alamieyeseigha (1999–2005), who was convicted of stealing millions of dollars during his time in office and reportedly made his escape from the UK clad as a woman. Notably, Alamieyeseigha's release came just two days after he was handed a two-year prison sentence. Remarkably, Alamieyeseigha was also declared free to run for elections again because he had been "remorseful" (BBC 2013). Following this pardon, Wole Soyinka, warned: "What is going on right now gives the picture of a government that is floundering and justifying the unjustifiable. It amounts to encouragement of corruption" (The Herald 2013).

---

[9] To borrow the words of the former Singapore Leader Lee Kuan Yew, directed at the kleptocratic regime of Ferdinand Marcos, the tenth president of the Philippines from 1965 to 1986: "It is a soft, forgiving culture. Only in the Philippines could a leader like Ferdinand Marcus, who pillaged his country for over 20 years, still be considered for a national burial. Insignificant amounts of the loot have been recovered, yet his wife and children were allowed to return and engage in politics" (Farolan 2011).

[10] Before a presidential pardon can be granted in Nigeria, a proposal from the president's office must be reviewed and recommendations made by the Presidential Advisory Committee on the Prerogative of Mercy. However, Jonathan sidestepped this due process and went directly to the National Council of State, which simply approved his request.

In 2012, the US yearly Country Reports on Human Rights Practices (which are submitted to Congress by the State Department) noted that, "Massive, widespread, and pervasive corruption affected all levels of [the Jonathan] government and the security forces in Nigeria." The report scored the judiciary system low as it noted, "there was a widespread perception judges were easily bribed and litigants could not rely on the courts to render impartial judgements. Citizens encountered long delays and alleged requests from judicial officials for bribes to expedite cases or obtain favorable rulings" (United States Department of State 2012). The report concluded that while the law provides criminal penalties for official corruption, the government did not enforce the law effectively, and officials often engaged in corruption with impunity. An ICPC study of 55 high-profile cases of corruption in Nigeria from 2006 through 2013 shows that N1.35 trillion was stolen under Yar'Adua and Jonathan. Diezani Alison-Madueke, who served as minister of petroleum resources under President Jonathan from 2010 to 2015, allegedly stole a staggering USD90 billion (Watts 2019: 551). Based on World Bank calculations, one-third of this stolen sum (N451.377 billion) could have provided 635.18 km of roads, built 36 ultra-modern hospitals (one per state), built and furnished 183 schools, educated 3,974 children from primary level to their tertiary education (Owasanoye 2019). In December 2008, Jonathan proposed that the National Assembly amend the constitution to remove the immunity clause which prevents presidents, vice presidents, governors, and deputy governors from being prosecuted for corruption while in office (Ploch 2010: 10). This explains why Moses Ochonu (2008) argues that corruption and infrastructural voids are intertwined:

> The embezzlement, mismanagement, or misapplication of public funds often leads to a cessation of certain social services, or the non-completion of a road, school, or hospital project. The deterioration and scarcity of infrastructure and social services have worsened in direct proportion to the corruption problem. The loss of public funds to corruption translates inevitably to a lack of medicine in a rural hospital; a lack of access to education for millions of African children; a lack of potable drinking water and electricity for millions of Africans; and a lack of good transportation infrastructure.

Jonathan's War against Boko Haram: Misappropriation and Outright Corruption

A missing point here is the impact of corruption on the Nigerian "war on terror" and civilian protection. Under Jonathan, funds earmarked to buy arms to combat Islamist Boko Haram insurgents in northeast Nigeria were siphoned off by political leaders. Since 2009, Nigeria has been in throes of a violent insurgency by Boko Haram, which has killed thousands of citizens and displaced millions of others. The problem of deficient arms has hindered military ability to defeat Boko

Haram. This, in turn, contributed to Jonathan's loss at the polls. The problem of poor military arsenals is closely related to the culture of corruption that flourished under President Jonathan. Dambo Dasuki, the former National Security Adviser appointed by Jonathan from 2012 through 2015, allegedly masterminded the arms procurement deal ("Dasukigate") that resulted in the embezzlement of over USD2 billion through the office of the National Security Adviser. Reports have suggested that part of the stolen fund was diverted for the sponsoring of the re-election campaign of Jonathan. Dasuki is accused of awarding phantom contracts to buy 12 helicopters, 4 fighter jets, and ammunition (BBC 2015a). A quick look at the Nigerian defense budget since 2011, when the federal Joint Task Force under Jonathan was first deployed to fight Boko Haram, tells its own story. From USD1.4 billion and USD2.4 billion respectively in 2010 and 2011, the defense budget was increased to USD5.7 billion in 2012. In 2014, the defense sector received USD6 billion, constituting 20 percent of the entire budget that year (Cocodia 2016). The increases in defense spending under President Jonathan were premised on the need to equip the Nigerian military to defeat Boko Haram. Yet from 2013 until early 2015, Boko Haram had the upper hand in many clashes because soldiers were often ill-equipped. Indeed, many soldiers have complained of been outgunned by the insurgents during battle. Describing his experience of fighting Boko Haram, a former Nigerian soldier said: "They overpowered us and many died. Our mortars and rocket-propelled grenades wouldn't even explode. They were so old" (BBC 2015b).

President Muhammadu Buhari, who took over power from Jonathan in 2015, noted that corruption and misappropriation hindered the Nigerian army's ability to defeat Boko Haram under President Jonathan. "The system collapsed under [Jonathan's] leadership," said Buhari, adding that "It was the incompetence of the police initially and the soldiers later that led to the situation as it now is. Boko Haram was taken for granted and allowed to grow. It's a slide into anarchy. The soldiers don't have ammunition, so they abandon their posts and run away" (York 2015). Buhari, of course, made the "war against corruption" the cornerstone of his 2015 election campaign and administration,[11] announcing his commitment to "killing corruption before it kills Nigeria" (Buhari 2016: 40). Following his inauguration in May 2015, Buhari confirmed that in the preceding decade, illicit financial flows (IFFs) from Nigeria totaled USD182 billion, which translates into 15 percent of the total value of Nigeria's trade over the period of 2005 to 2014 (USD1.21 trillion). In the last year of Jonathan's rule alone, IFFs from Nigeria were estimated at USD12.5 billion, representing 9 percent of the total trade (Watts 2019: 551). This generalized "kleptomania" may have prompted British Prime Minister David Cameron's description of Nigeria as "fantastically corrupt" (BBC 2016).

---

[11] The assessment of Buhari's record against corruption is beyond the scope of this chapter or book. For a perceptive analysis on this, see Rotimi Suberu (2018).

2

The Language of Corruption

Corruption probably ranks with culture as one of the two or three most complicated words in the English language to define (Williams 1983: 87). Studying the relationship between corruption and culture in the Pacific Islands, anthropologist Peter Lamour (2012: 165) found that what is deemed corrupt often depends on language and involves social discussions or an internal kind of dialogue with family and friends. If, as Fela once observed, "You cannot sing African music in proper English" (The New York Times 1997), it follows that it must be even more difficult to try to articulate corruption in Africa in proper English. In his *English in Africa*, Josef Schmied (1991: 53) called attention to the complexity and considerable variation of the English language in Africa. While English is considered an official language in many African countries, only an esoteric few—the educated class—speak and use it. The vast majority of Africans speak African languages. When they speak English, it is frequently as a form of pidgin ("broken") English (Kirkpatrick 2007: 101).

Against this backdrop, eminent Africanist writers, among them Chinua Achebe, Amos Tutuola, and Gabriel Okara, have called for English to be adapted to more closely reflect the vernacular style of local languages in Africa. In his *World Englishes*, Andy Kirkpatrick tells us that the use of the vernacular in an African English "captures the essence of a culture even at a more mundane level" (2007: 113).

Africa is a continent of linguistic complexity and diversity, with speakers of over 1,300 languages. In Nigeria alone, Africa's most populous country, at least 520 languages are spoken. In Ghana, over 50 languages are spoken. In Cameroon, the co-official European languages of English and French heighten the linguistic complexity of the country. In South Africa, there are up to 11 official languages (Kirkpatrick 2007: 101). This linguistic complexity and unique sociolinguistic environment are central to any understanding of corruption in Africa. As far as I know, among the 520 languages spoken in Nigeria, there is no direct translation for the word corruption. Among the Hausa people of northern Nigeria, for instance, no single word fits corruption *sensu stricto*. In fact, as M.G. Smith found in the early 1960s, Hausa people use various phrases to explain a range of political conditions related to corruption, ranging from *zalunchi/zamba* (oppression/swindling) and *yi gaisuwa* (making greetings or gifts) to *manafunci* (treachery and breaking of political agreements), and *wayo* (tricks) (Smith 1964: 164). In the same vein,

They Eat Our Sweat. Daniel E. Agbiboa, Oxford University Press.
© Daniel E. Agbiboa (2022). DOI: 10.1093/oso/9780198861546.003.0003

in East Africa, three meanings of corruption can be identified: corruption (*n. uozi, ubovu, uchafu*); bribery (*rushwa, upenyezi*); alteration (*mageuzi, makosa*).

Beyond Africa, in India, terms such as *ghush* (Bengali for "bribe") and *bhrastachar* (Hindi for "corruption") are generally applied to describe illicit transgressions by public officials (Ruud 2000: 283). On Thailand, anthropologist Niels Mulder (1996: 174) argues that the conventional meaning of corruption as the misuse of entrusted power for private benefits is baffling to many Thais, who do not necessarily view corruption as an erosion of public interest. In fact, the closest equivalent for corruption in Thai is *choo rat bang luang*, "to defraud the state," or to steal from the king. Similar to the Hausa people of northern Nigeria who view corruption as oppression (*zalunchi*), that is, acts that were wrong but that were nevertheless not unexpected of people in government (Pierce 2016: 5–6), Thais "expect their leaders to be corrupt too, and accept the fact as part of life" (Kulick & Wilson 1992: 36). In fact, in Thailand, gifts to government officials in return for services rendered are either seen as *sin nam jai* (gifts of good will/tolerable/positive) or corruption (criticized), based on the particular cultural lens through which you interpret them. In a modern bureaucracy, such gifts undoubtedly constitute corruption. However, in a more traditional Thai context of relations between citizens and public officials, they may be seen as *sin nam jai* (Pasuk & Sungsidh 1996: 166). Similarly, in South Korea *chonji* ("bribe money") is a way of life that binds citizens and public servants together. So widespread and systemic is *chonji* that "mothers hand them out to ensure their kids get good marks at school; young lecturers to get jobs at colleges; and drivers to avoid speeding tickets. Small businesses constantly give *chonji* to public servants seeking money in exchange for every stage of administrative action related to their trade" (Kim 1998: 53, cited in Quah 2011: 322). In Mexico, bribery is generally seen as a way of life (DW 2013). However, unlike the situation in Thailand and South Korea, in Mexico there is a subtle difference in meaning between two common expressions for bribery: *soborno* and *mordida*. While the former is presumed to be a serious crime (involving large sums of money), the latter describes the more widespread forms of petty corruption, evoking what Covarrubias Gonzalez (2003) describes as the "folklore of corruption" pervading popular culture in Mexico. In this latter understanding, *mordida* constitutes part of the tactics of everyday survival, that is, an "informal strategy" used by average Mexicans to negotiate an undemocratic and repressive state (Baez-Camargo 2019). This applies well to Uganda, where everyday bribing is not necessarily perceived by local people as negative but instead as an instrumental strategy deployed to meet basic needs. In fact, many ordinary Ugandans expect government officials to enrich themselves through (il)legal channels since "man eats where he works" (Baez-Camargo et al. 2017: 11). This adds weight to empirical studies that have emphasized the pragmatics of the use of corruption (Muir 2016: 132; Mazzarella 2006), showing that corrupt practices may have their own morality, at least when seen through the actor's eyes (Bocarejo 2018: S49).

In the second part of Chapter 1, I focused mainly on the evolution of elite corruption in Nigeria since 1960 and the emergence of a crisis of value in the country. Although necessary, this top-down analysis is not quite sufficient to do justice to the corruption complex. To comprehend the full range of political ideas about corruption, we must go beyond "sterile, static and narrowly exegetical Afro-Saxon tradition" of analysis to account for "the diverse means by which people voice political ideas indirectly… [including in this account] the works of novelists, dramatists, poets, musicians, journalists, theologians, philosophers, and social scientists, as well as proverbs, fables and oral literature" (Schatzberg 2001: 3). This view aligns with growing calls for empirically grounded studies of the manner in which the state is made real and tangible through "symbols, texts, and iconography… but also to move beyond the state's own prose" and interrogate "how it appears in everyday and localized forms" (Hansen & Stepputat 2001: 5).

So, what can the study of language and idioms tell us about the shapes and contours of corruption? Following the call to root concepts in an analysis of their meaning in a particular language (Fearon & Laitin 2000: 4), this chapter grounds corruption in its local discourses and "moral imaginations," understood here as the "art by which individuals struggle to transform their social baggage into gear that suits urgent situational needs in terms of meanings and moral judgements" (Biedelman 1986: 203). By examining how ordinary people imagine and *talk* about corruption, we gain a better understanding of the polyvalence of corruption, the popular reactions to it, and the "political work" (Pierce 2016) that the discourse of corruption does. Moreover, paying careful attention to the sociolinguistics of corruption can expand our knowledge of its susceptibility to "slippage" (Keller 1992: 10), which happens when a term's meaning shifts back and forth between its technical (reconstructed) and ordinary meanings (Schaffer 2012: 2).

By exploring the local discourses of corruption in a way that strips it of its ordinariness, this chapter moves us beyond the rather narrow focus on "impartiality, impersonality and, above all, the strict separation of the incumbent and office" (Theobald 1990: 2). Situating corruption in the social and linguistic contexts in which it occurs entails looking closely at how corrupt practices are routinely discussed, how they are morally evaluated by the social actors involved, and how they are culturally constructed and rationalized (Smith 2007; Bocarejo 2018; Ruud 2000). The objective here is for the social mechanisms of corruption to be understood not only through the *point of view* of people who "come into contact with it, exploit it, or become its victims, on a daily basis" (Olivier de Sardan 1999: 25, 28; Smith 2007: 56), but also from their *point of talk*. By seriously considering the popular semiology of corruption (Blundo & Olivier de Sardan 2006: 98), this chapter reclaims the neglected but vital role of language and idioms in shaping the meaning of corruption. In so doing, it sheds fresh light on what counts as corruption in the value acceptances of locals and contributes to our limited understanding of the meanings that people everywhere ascribe to corruption or its rough equivalents in other languages.

Critical Discourse Analysis

This chapter is inspired by a critical discourse analysis, which describes a sociolinguistic approach that conceptualizes language as a form of social practice (Fairclough 1989) whose analysis can uncover hidden or implied meanings. Critical discourse analysis involves "studying and analyzing written texts and spoken words to reveal the discursive sources of power, dominance, inequality and bias and how these sources are initiated, maintained, reproduced and transformed within specific social, economic, political and historical contexts (...) it tries to illuminate ways in which the dominant forces in a society construct versions of reality that favors their interests" (McGregor 2003: 1). This approach is employed here, given that we still know remarkably little about how or the extent to which the idioms of corruption can become a weapon wielded by both the weak and the strong to critique, mislead, and manipulate. As Paul Eschholz and colleagues note in *Language Awareness*, "Few of us are really conscious of the way, subtle or not subtle, in which our use of language may affect others... Language is used to classify, dehumanize, deceive, and control human beings" (Escholtz, Rosa, & Clark 1978: v–vii).

This chapter examines the language and idioms of corruption, because they are the very categories through which local populations construct meaning out of lived realities. The rest of this chapter proceeds on the basis of a linguistic anthropology, which operates from the major premise that language is a symbolic form and, therefore, that discerning the meanings of local symbolic forms is a worthwhile endeavor (Basso 1992: xii), especially in light of the polyvalence and contested nature of corruption. Like any other word, corruption has no special claim to neutrality. As Mikhail Bakhtin points out, "All words have the 'taste' of a profession, a genre, a tendency, a party, a particular work, a particular person, a generation, an age group, the day and hour. Each word tastes of the context and contexts in which it has lived its socially charged life..." (Bakhtin 1981: 293). It is to this socially charged life of corruption that I now turn.

"Goats Eat Where They Are Tethered": The Politics of the Belly

The meaning and force of language derive from the sociocultural contexts in which they are embedded. It is for this reason that the linguistic anthropologist Keith Basso has argued that language "exhibit[s] a fundamental character—a genius, a spirit, an underlying personality—which is very much its own" (1992: 172). The genius of African speech communities lies in their resourcefulness and astute capacity to tersely capture the corruption complex by fusing elements of language and culture. Similar to the Western Apache language described in Basso's *Western Apache Language and Culture* (1992: 172), a few uttered words in African languages can do great amounts of "communicative work." Perhaps nowhere is this more evident than in the very vivid and visceral images of corruption as food in Africa, a continent where eating itself is an act of sociality and self-identification. As the adage goes: "You are what you eat" (Shapin 2014: 377).

Accounts of the state in Africa often revolve around a cannibalistic metaphor, the vampiric potential of the postcolony. Jean-François Bayart used the concept of "politics of the belly" to articulate a political rationality in postcolonial Africa where material wealth and physical corpulence are generally seen as political virtues, and where the state is said to coerce and consume its own citizens (1993: 242–43). At its core, politics of the belly embodies a complex array of cultural representations, most notably those of the invisible world of sorcery. In Africa, eating is often tied to the dark arts of witchcraft and sorcery as firmly rooted in local cosmogonies (Schatzberg 2001: 50). In Cameroon, sorcerers are said to "eat" (*kfuru*) their victims, tear them, and draw blood (Rowlands & Warnier 1988: 122). In the African political realm, "to eat" refers not only to the nourishment of self but also to accumulation, exploitation, defeat, attack, and killing by witchcraft (Bayart 1993: 270). In this perspective, the cupidity of African politicians in Africa evokes the witch's craving for human flesh. As Bayart puts it:

> This theme of the belly is based on two original cultural registers which are, moreover, closely linked: that of munificence which, for example, makes physical corpulence into a political quality and, above all, that of the invisible, i.e. the nocturnal world of the ancestors, of the dream, of divination and magic, of which the gut is the actual center. When the Africans assert that their leaders are "eating" them economically through excessive extortion they lend this assertion a disturbing connotation which haunts them from infancy and obsesses them until their death: that of the specter of an attack of witchcraft which generates prosperity for the aggressor and failure, illness and misfortune for the victim. (1993: 69)

Africanist scholars have long explored the interface between political actions, witchcraft, and occult economies in postcolonial Africa (Geschiere 1997; Comaroff & Comaroff 1999). In Malawi, corruption and witchcraft share a number of characteristics on account of the former's "paradoxical relationship between the legal and illegal, secrecy and publicity, condemnation and fascination" (Nuijten & Anders 2007: 19). In postcolonial Nigeria and post-apartheid South

Africa, "witchcraft persists as a practical discourse of hidden agency because eco-nomic development in the larger sense has failed" (Apter 1993: 124; Comaroff & Comaroff 1999). In Cameroon, sorcery is not only a mode of popular political action but is at the very heart of the state-building process from the past to the postcolony (Rowland & Warnier 1988: 121). It is in this sense that Bayart identi-fies belly politics as a fundamental feature of the African state as manifested in the "kleptomania" of its rulers. Thus, the politics of the belly is, first and foremost, a form of governmentality that constitutes the African state as a "rush for spoils," operationalized through "competitive patrimonial networks" (Hasty 2005a: 275). This perspective adds weight to the observation that, for a civil servant, positions of power offer the only realistic route for acquiring any kind of wealth. For this reason, refusing to avail oneself of bribes and "gifts" is tantamount to making "a simultaneous show of ingratitude, egoism, pride, naivete and even stupidity..." (Olivier de Sardan 1999: 43). Belly politics in Africa is exemplified by the popular African saying, "Goats eat where they are tethered," which tersely and ingeniously captures the "rush for spoils" that binds the rich and the poor, the ruler and the ruled, together (Bayart 1993: 235).[1]

The Spatial Vernaculars of Corruption in Africa

"The life of any language resides in the welter of its myriad particulars" (Basso 1992: xi). African languages are no exception. The continent boasts a kaleidoscope of evocative idioms for thinking and talking about corruption (Nuijten & Anders 2007; Isichei 2004; Schatzberg 2001), and they pervade political and social dis-course. None is more evocative than the corporeal metaphor of food and eating through which Africans have historically imagined and articulated the corruption complex. Before exploring the relationship between corruption and images of eat-ing in Africa, it is important to dissect, if briefly, the multiple meanings of eating. Like the concept of corruption, the verb "to eat" in Africa is inherently polyvalent. In northern Ghana, food (*dia*) and eating (*di*) intertwine with systems of exchange, building relationships, and sexuality. The meaning of the verb *di* (to eat) goes well beyond its English understanding. *Di* can mean "to obtain or use something," "to destroy," "to experience something fully," and "to marry" (Denham 2017: 95). Bantu Africa uses the word for "eating" to express a variety of meanings linked to power and property. In Busoga, a traditional Bantu Kingdom, when a ruler or

---

[1] In Cameroon, the supposed opposition between Beti and Bamileke ethnic groups often revolves around belly politics: "The latter, seen as dominant in the national economy, are supposed to be experts in accumulation, even at the cost of their own kin. In contrast, the Beti are supposed to be unable to keep their money: this is why they have to 'eat' the state in order to be able to satisfy the unrelenting demands of their own family. Such stereotypes will be invariably accompanied by the general comment: *Ah oui, la chevre broute ou elle est attachée* (Well, the goat eats where it is tethered)" (Oestermann & Geschiere 2017: 109).

leader conquers a neighboring territory, he is said to "eat it." Nowadays, "a man who secures for himself an appointment to chieftainship 'eats' the office and an embezzler 'eats' the money he misappropriates" (Fallers 1969: 83). In the early eighteenth century, a visitor to northern Nigeria warned the local elites of voracious European invaders. "By God," he said, "they *eat* the whole country—they are no friends: these are the words of truth" (Denham 1826: 279).

Clearly, then, Africa is fecund with discursive linkages between corruption and eating. In East Africa, a political faction is called *kula* ("eating"), and corruption is known as *chai* ("tea"). In northern Nigeria, solicitations of bribes by the police are coded in images of heat and water: *Shan rana* ("The sun is scorching us"), *gari yayi zafi* ("The town is hot"), *akwai ruwa?* ("Is there water?"), and *a zuba mana ruwa* ("Pour us some water"). In northeast Nigeria, truck drivers think of security checkpoints as a famished apparatus that *shàakudi* ("drink money") and *shàa-jini* ("drink blood"). Among the Hausa of northern Nigeria, bribery or involuntary giving is generally disparaged as *hanci* ("eating of nose") or *toshiyar baki* ("plugging of mouths") (Auwal 1987: 293).[2] In southwestern Nigeria, public office is seen by many as an "eatery" or "fast food" of sorts (Adebanwi & Obadare 2011: 186). In francophone African countries such as Niger, Senegal, and Benin, corruption is commonly registered as *manger* ("to eat") or *bouffer* ("to devour"). In these societies, the embezzler is said to have *mange la caisse oul'argent* ("eaten the till or the money") or that he is *un mangeur d'argent d'autrui* ("the devourer of other people's money"). In Niger, predatory rulers are often labelled *le clan des bouffeurs* ("the clan of the gluttons") (Masquelier 2001: 268). Among the Luba of eastern Zaire, chieftaincy is symbolized by the elephant "because it eats more than other animals" (Isichei 2004: 236). After the decline of the Ugandan formal economy under the despot President Idi Amin Dada Oumee (1971–79),[3] the *magendo* (black-market economy) flourished as a source of everyday survival (Titeca 2012: 50), involving the smuggling of goods such as cigarettes, fuel, batteries, coffee, paraffin, sugar, and gold. The Ugandan state was unable or unwilling to regulate the *magendo*, since it served the material and political purposes of the ruling class (Green 1981). Notably, operators in the *magendo* were called *mafutamingi*, "the fat ones." In Benin, the common Dendi[4] expression *dii ka dan me* literally means "take that and put in your mouth," implying, "that's your share."

In DR Congo, phrases such as *kukata milomo* ("to cut the lips") or *ya sucre, ya cayi* ("for lemonade, for tea") are common idioms of corruption. In Lubumbashi, the image of eating labels the embezzling of funds: *ll a tout bouffe* ("he has eaten it all"). So rife is corruption in this city that people call it *madesu ya bana*

---

[2] The Hausa people distinguishes between voluntary gifts (*dash*) and involuntary giving (*hanci*). The latter is often frowned upon while the former is generally tolerated.

[3] Nicknamed the "Butcher of Uganda," Idi Amin is considered one of the cruelest dictators in African history.

[4] A Songhay language used as a trade language across northern Benin.

("beans for the children") and *un petit quelque chose a manger* ("a little some-thing to eat"). Here, a person who fails to cash in on his (government) position is regarded as a fool (*akili*). Yet, anyone who eats too much is considered to be stupid because *ekonahribisha kazi* ("he spoils his job"), meaning he or she will soon be sacked. Addressing his party delegates in 1984, President Mobutu Sese Seko of Zaire, warned: "If you steal, do not steal too much at a time. You may be arrested. *Yi ba mayele* [steal cleverly], little by little." This underscores the point that "preda-tion finds the right tune in moderation" in DR Congo (Petit 2005: 477). Or, as the Congolese proverb goes, *kula ndambo, kwaca ndambo* ("eat some, leave some"). In Tanzania, Rwandan (Hutu) refugees lament of public officials: "They eat our sweat." In Dar es Salam, *daladala* drivers use the expression *Kula Tutakula Lakini Tutachelewa* ("we'll eat, but we'll eat late") to condemn their exploitative labor, especially the extortionate power of policemen en route. In West Africa, police extortion at checkpoints is generally coded as "cold water" to quench a thirsty of-ficer. Consider the following excerpts from mobile interactions between drivers and officers in Liberia and Nigeria:

Excerpt One (Liberia):

When the traffic finally moved forward, Opah drove right to the police officer at the junction. "I'm very thirsty," the police officer said standing between the cars. "I want some cold water today in this heat." Opah rolled down the window slowly and held out his hand. Sundayimah and Sundaygar both noticed the clean 100 Liberian dollar bill, which the police officer put in his pocket quickly. He waved Opah's car through the traffic in a lane that was not there before.

—Robtel Pailey, *Gbabga* (cited in Agbiboa 2016: 7)[5]

Excerpt Two (Nigeria):

OFFICER: *kai yaya kana gudu kamar zaka tashi sama?* (Hey, why are you speeding as if you were going to fly?)
DRIVER: *Ranka ya dade, yaya aiki?* (May you live long [literally, actually "Sir"]—how's work?)
OFFICER: *Gamu nan muna shan rana.* (Here we are, scorching in the sun).
DRIVER: *To ga na ruwan sanyi.* (Right, here's something for water [iced/cold water]).

Excerpt Three (Nigeria)

---

[5] *Gbagba* is a local Bassa word used by parents to warn their children against "lying, cheating, and stealing." Liberian academic Robtel Pailey tells me that the term describes "a facet of everyday interactions... it happens in every single sector of Liberia."

OFFICER: Alhaji, *gari yayi zafi* (Sir, the town is hot)
DRIVER: *To yaya za a yi* (So, what can be done?)
OFFICER: *A zuba mana ruwa* (Pour us some water)

(Mele & Bello 2007: 442).

In the above exchanges, there is intentional use of symbolic references to demand a bribe. And, as is true everywhere, symbols can be ambiguous and multivocal (Schatzberg 2001: 50). Water, for instance, signifies a bribe, and to say *gari yayi zafi* (the town is hot) is to suggest that one is in dire financial strait. Aside from protecting the police officer against accusations of corruption, symbolic references such as water and heat are also culturally embedded. "It is considered bad manners not to offer water to any visitor even if he/she does not ask for it. The fact that security personnel have to ask for water places the driver on the defensive morally, even though they know literal water is not what is demanded from them. Thus, in place of water they give what can buy water, which is what the security personnel were actually after in the first place" (Mele & Bello 2007: 445). As in Liberia and Nigeria, Uganda has a wide range of symbolic language for everyday bribe solicitation, including *lac kalam* (to be paid for the "writing pen"), *kintu kidogo* ("something small"), "give me my cut," "do you have brick?", "We're out of fuel," "give me airtime/transport," "I don't have a stamp," "put a stone on your paper," or "I need a pen to sign" (Baez-Camargo et al. 2017: 16). These verbal expressions are only matched by a range of bodily languages, including rubbing one's stomach to demonstrate that one is hungry and need something to eat; scratching one's throat suggesting that one is thirsty hence in need of something to drink; or a woman may deliberately expose her thighs to suggest she is offering sex in return for a favor (ibid.). In Ghana, people tend to express corruption in bodily fluids of "blood flow and circulation." When corruption is too much, it is seen as a "hemorrhage" (Hasty 2005a: 276).

In the next section, I draw on the example of Kenya to briefly illustrate how the logic of corruption as eating ("our time to eat") binds the ruler and the ruled together.

It's Our Time to Eat

In Kenya, a country with a reputation as the homeland of the bribe, *nchi ya kitu kidogo* ("land of the little something"), national politics has long been colored by rabid ethnicity. At election time, a common phrase is used: "Our time to eat" (*wakati wetu wa kula*), which refers to the politicization of ethnic identities and the pressures on politicians to feed their ethnic kinsmen after electoral victory. In Kenya, a politician who is considered to be "one of ours" is warned by his people that "we can't eat bones when others are eating meat." He is reminded of the steadfast loyalty of his people in times of difficulty: *meno ya mbwa hayaumani* ("The teeth of the dog do not bite [harm] each other") or *mchuma janga hula na wakwao* ("He [who] earns calamity, eats [it] with his people"). While the astute politician is not oblivious to the fact that, *chawa akuumao mbwa Nguni mwako* ("[The] louse that bites you is inside your clothing"), he also knows the meaning of *Zimwi likujualo halikuli likakwisha* ("A ghost that knows you will not devour you completely"). In short, political survival in Kenya rests on nourishing one's ethnic kinsmen.[6] As Wrong writes, "The various forms of graft cannot be separated from the people's vision of existence as a merciless contest, in which only ethnic preference offers hope of survival" (2009: 41–42). This zero-sum contest is neatly captured by the saying in francophone Africa: *Ote-toi de la, que je m'y mette*, which literally means: "Shift yourself, so I can take your place."

Wrong (2009: 27) argues that President Daniel Arap Moi's accession to power upon the death of President Jomo Kenyatta in 1978 meant that the Kalenjins' turn had finally come to "eat" the state. While the Kikuyus still flourished, "they now did so in spite of government patronage rather than because of it" (ibid.). Like most African leaders, President Mwai Kibaki (2002–2013), who took over power from Moi, came to office on an anti-corruption ticket. While Kibaki managed to curb the grabbing of public land for which the Kenyatta and Moi eras were notorious, he was less successful in taming Kenya's corruption problem. In a speech delivered to the British Business Association of Kenya, Edward Clay, Britain's former high commissioner in Kenya, said about the transition from Moi to Kibaki: "We hoped it would not be rammed in our faces. But it has... They may expect we shall not see, or notice, or will forgive them a bit of gluttony, but they can hardly expect us not to care when their gluttony causes them to vomit all over our shoes." So popular was this speech that shoeshine boys on the streets of Kenya cheered Clay: "Five shillings for shoeshine, 10 for vomit" (Bonner 2009). In many ways, the Kibaki government bears a semblance to Obasanjo's administration, specifically in regard to its checkered corruption cleanup campaign. On 4 March 2013, Kenya's *Daily Nation* published a piece entitled "End of a decade of highs and lows for Mwai Kibaki" that neatly summarizes the contradictions of Kibaki's government:

> For a leader who was popularly swept into power in 2002 on an anti-corruption platform, Kibaki's tenure saw graft scandals where hundreds of millions of shillings were siphoned from public coffers. Kibaki's National Rainbow Coalition—which took power from the authoritarian rule of Daniel Arap Moi—was welcomed for its promises of change and economic growth, but soon showed

---

[6] This is hardly specific to Kenyan. In Nigeria, many believe that if you don't have one of your own in a position of authority, you get nothing. This explains why there is so much discrimination against non-indigenes since many Nigerians view politics as a "zero-sum game" (HRW 2006: 13).

that it was better suited to treading established paths. "The initial response to corruption was very solid... but it became clear after a while that these scams reached all the way to the president himself," said Kenya's former anti-corruption chief John Githongo. Most notorious of a raft of graft scandals was the multi-billion-shilling Anglo Leasing case, which emerged in 2004 and involved public cash being paid to a complicated web of foreign companies for a range of services—including naval ships and passports—that never materialized (Daily Nation 2013).

Beyond Africa: Corruption as Eating

Lest one begins to think that the "politics of the belly" is unique to Africa, anthropologist A.F. Robertson (2006: 10) reminds us that, "Feeding is the universal metaphor for bribery and peculation." In nineteenth-century Siberian Russia, the term *kormlenie* ("feeding") referred to a corrupt practice in which government-appointed tax collectors "fed" off customary gratuities and fees from the poor people they administered (Humphrey & Sneath 2004: 86; Halperin 2019). In Mexico, bribe or *mordida* ("bite") portrays predatory policemen as "dogs" always on the lookout for innocent people to "bite." In India, a common refrain in election speeches is, *Na khaunga, na khaane doonga* ("Neither will I eat, nor will I let others eat"). The refrain is an anti-corruption declaration used by politicians to promise the common people a zero-tolerance for corruption (Mathur 2017: 1796). In the Hindu-speaking belt of India, the phrase *paisa khaoya* ("eating of money") is used in everyday talk to describe practices that are glossed together as "corrupt" as well as in discursive critique of a "leaky" Indian state, especially in the context of development programs. *Paisa khaoya* represents a powerful means through which popular discontents about the malfunctioning Indian state are voiced. India's poor showing in various development indicators—health, education, and employment—are commonly blamed on the state's predilection to "eat" money (Mathur 2017: 1796).

The use of metaphors of "eating" in everyday corruption discourses in India has a long history. From a fourth century BCE treatise on corruption and public administration in India, entitled *Arthashastra*: "Just as it is impossible not to taste the honey that finds itself at the tip of the tongue, so it is impossible for a government servant not to eat up, at least, a bit of the King's revenue" (Kangle 1972: 91). This imagery nurtures in India a sense of powerlessness in the face of corruption (Basu 2019: 415; Das 2015: 325). In a classic book on the corruption of local-level bureaucrats in South India under colonial rule in the nineteenth century, Robert Frykenberg (1965: 231) repeatedly employs the metaphor of white ants eating out the umbrella of the state:

The white ant is a tiny creature of tremendous energy and silence which, by combining its efforts with countless other tiny brothers, can make a hollow shell or empty crust out of the stoutest wooden structure—as many a person has discovered to his sorrow upon sitting in a chair long left in some neglected *dak* (traveler's) bungalow. The ant typifies what happens when energetic and silent local leadership, in combination, makes a hollow mockery out of the stoutest administrative structure. (cited in Price 1999: 326)

The corporeal metaphor of corruption as eating extends beyond the global South. For a long time, debates around police corruption in the United States pivoted on the few "rotten" apples theory, which generally viewed corruption as an individual pathological issue rather than an institutional problem (Sherman 1978: xxvii; Tankebe 2010). In 1970, however, the Knapp Commission hearings dismissed this theory, arguing that "a high command unwilling to acknowledge that the problem of corruption is extensive cannot very well argue that drastic changes are necessary to deal with the problem" (Knapp 1972: 6–7). Following an in-depth investigation into corruption in the New York Police Department (NYPD), the Commission developed the food-related terms "meat eaters" and "grass eaters" to distinguish between two sets of corrupt police officers. On the one hand, meat eating officers aggressively use their position of power to gain personal profit or acquire favors. On the other, grass eating officers do not seek out personal benefits—but also do not wave them off with a "no thanks" (Knapp 1972).

Eating the State: The Imagery and Discourse of Corruption in Nigeria

There is a popular joke that where two or more Nigerians are gathered, lamentations of corruption have a way of overshadowing the conversation. While this is probably a gross exaggeration, it nonetheless highlights corruption as *semper et ubique* in Nigeria, so much so that people tend to burst into laughter whenever the subject surfaces. As Michael Peel observes, "Nigeria's situation has turned many of its people into connoisseurs of the ridiculous, who have made self-deprecation a national pastime" (2010: 98). During my fieldwork in Lagos, I was struck by how often corruption constituted the essential lubricant of rumors, stories, myths, and discursive production, entangling every sphere of everyday life like an octopus does it prey. The ubiquitous nature of corruption, arguably, makes it a staple food of some sort, and as such it is easily taken for granted in its routineness. In what follows, I explore the politics of corruption and survival in urban Nigeria through the idiom of eating.

Vote-Buying: National Cake, Stomach Infrastructure, and Godfathers

In the words of President Muhammadu Buhari if we do not kill corruption, corruption will kill us (Nigeria). While thinking out what I would title this Convocation Lecture my mind kept going to the termite. We all know that the termite is such a small harmless looking insect. Yet they are the nightmare of any house owner as they can bring down the roof of your house if you don't respect them and provide radical and sustainable prevention processes where they coexist with you. Termites are so well adapted and have been in existence for over 120 million years. They have generally survived all attempts to eradicate them using pesticides, insecticides and other means. Builders routinely use steel struts or hardwood treated with solignum as roof members. To survive, the wood termite feeds tenaciously on its hosts so long as they are wooden: doors, floors, furniture, until it destroys or defaces the host medium. When the host is destroyed the termite self-destructs or moves on to a new host. Is Nigeria's corruption problem like a termite infestation? Having taken root, it has defied all known process to eliminate it doggedly eating off our roof and compromising the foundations of our institutions. To kill the termite, you must study and research it thoroughly. [...] I have learnt the ways of the termite and have applied it as a sure way of eradicating and curbing entrenched corruption in Nigeria in order to build a new national identity like Singapore did. (Nta 2017: 17–18)

The above is an extract from a convocation speech—entitled *Ethical Deficit, Corruption and Crisis of National Identity: Integrity of Termites*—delivered by Ekpo Nta, the chairman of the Independent Corrupt Practices Commission (ICPC) in Nigeria. Nta's reflections speak to the resilient and entrenched nature of corruption in Nigeria, and the need for all hands on deck to overcome it. In the extract, Mr. Nta draws upon vivid images of termites, food, and eating in a manner that throws into bold relief the gluttonous avarice of corrupt potentates and public officials who treat their offices as an "eatery" or "fast food" of sorts. In Nigeria today, politics revolves around battling for and sharing the shrinking "national cake," a form of belly politics in which the national resources are expected to be divided among political officeholders, party leaders, or partisans—an "arrangement and settlement system," as one astute Lagosian puts it. Nigerians have a common saying for this: "You chop, me self I chop, palaver finish." This saying reclaims political life in Nigeria as prebendal, that is, a system in which state power is treated as "congeries of offices which can be competed for, appropriated and then

administered for the benefit of individual occupants and their support groups"
(Joseph 1987: 63). What is particularly toxic about prebendal politics,

> is the virtual absence of any constraints at all on the use of office; the spectacularly
> voracious and predatory scale of the corruption that results; the narrowness of the
> circles that share in this fabulous accumulation; and the depth of the economic
> disarray, political chaos and popular anger and alienation that result. (Diamond,
> 1989: 285)

In an article on "Democracy, Credibility and Clientelism," economists Philip
Keefer and Razvan Vlaicu (2008) argued that newly democratic countries have
low to non-existent standing and thus no means of making credible promises to
the people. As a result, local politicians tend to rely on local patronage networks,
providing targeted goods to their supporters in direct exchange for votes (cf. Rothstein 2018: 37). In Nigeria, the poor reputation of politicians is traceable to the
colonial legacy, according to Claud Ake:

> The distinguishing characteristics of the state in Africa, however, is that it has lit-
> tle autonomy. This is a legacy of colonialism [...]. Colonial politics was not about
> good governance but about the resolution of two exclusive claims to rulership; it
> was a struggle to capture the state and press it into the service of the captor. [...]
> The [postcolonial] state is in effect privatized: it remains an enormous force but
> *no longer a public force*: no longer a reassuring presence guaranteeing the rule of
> law but a formidable threat to all except the few who control it, actually encour-
> aging lawlessness and with little capacity to mediate conflicts in society. Politics
> in Africa has been shaped by this character of the African state. It is mainly about
> access to state power and the goals of political struggle are the capture of an all-
> powerful state, which the winner can use as he or she pleases. The spoils, and the
> losses, are total. African politics therefore puts a very high premium on power.
> [...] In this type of politics, violence and instability are endemic, with anarchy
> lurking just below the surface. Despite the enormous power of the state, a political
> order does not emerge. (Ake 1995: 73)

In the past, Nigerian politicians enticed voters by promising them a piece of the
"national cake" when they assume office. Today, however, the national cake is
more and more a here-and-now reality rather than a lip service. Nigerian politicians increasingly distribute money and food items to citizens as an affective
political strategy to buy their votes. This increasingly common practice articulates
with "clientelistic accountability," which represents "a transaction, the direct exchange of a citizen's vote in return for direct payments or continuing access to
employment, goods and services" (Kitschelt & Wilkinson 2007: 2). In Nigeria,

clientelistic accountability is refracted through what is locally known as "stomach infrastructure," a term which reclaims the logic of "wealth in people" that underpins the politics of bigmanity in Africa (Bledsoe 1990; Utas 2012). Stomach infrastructure is illustrative of Mushtaq Khan's analysis of the ways in which existing politicians and the state in the developing world often buy off the opposition of organized groups, particularly the most vociferous opponents, in an effort to "purchase" support or legitimacy. Khan (1998: 28) describes this strategy as "an ongoing process of accommodation and incorporation." Under military rule in Nigeria, for instance, a form of political patronage—the politics of settlement—was established, where rulers lavishly deployed state funds to buy off (or silence) political sycophants and potential opponents (Yagboyaju 2020).

In the buildup to the 2015 General Elections in Nigeria, a period which coincided with my fieldwork in Lagos, I observed as political candidates invested substantial time and resources in distributing essential stomach infrastructural items (e.g. bags of rice, kerosene, milk, and chicken wings) to their potential supporters. In Ekiti state, former Governor Ayo Fayose (who coined the phrase) distributed an estimated 80,000 chickens, 100,000 bags of rice, and numerous cash gifts to lowly people in Ekiti under his "Stomach Infrastructure" program. Other Nigerian states, some of which were initially averse to Fayose's stomach infrastructure program (e.g. Lagos state), soon followed suit (Vanguard 2014b). The former PDP secretary in Ekiti state even lambasted the Lagos state governor for copying, rather hypocritically, Fayose's stomach infrastructure agenda:

> Tinubu distributed 2,000 bags of rice, vegetable oil, sugar and little cash to people from various parts of Lagos State. They abused us for providing immediate succor for our people. They described stomach infrastructure as an insult to Ekiti people. They said it does not add value to the people; that it diminishes their self-esteem, self-worth and that it denigrates what politics ought to be about. However, their party leader in Lagos has adopted the same concept of stomach infrastructure by personally sharing food items to people. After condemning the concept, isn't it rather too late that the APC [political party] people are just realizing that poverty should be addressed by providing immediate succor? (Vanguard 2015).

The politics of stomach infrastructure predates the 2015 elections. In Ibadan, Oyo state, the political influence of the late Chief Lamidi Adedibu—a powerful political patron variously described as the "godfather of Ibadan," "father of the PDP," and "strong man of Ibadan politics"—has long flowed from his specific belly politics that blended populism and raw thuggery (Lawal et al. 2008). Adedidu often distributed cash and food to various supplicants on a daily basis from his home in Ibadan, a brand of patronage called *amala* politics, after a traditional dish particular to Nigeria's southwest. In the face of severe hardship, it is not difficult to see why Nigerians seek instant gratifications, selling their votes like the biblical figure of Esau who sold his birthright for a bowl of soup.

The electoral politics of stomach infrastructure is neither new nor specific to Nigeria(ns). In Uganda, the electoral strategy of the ruling political party, the National Resistance Movement (NRM), is powered by stomach infrastructure. As one analyst notes:

> It's a game of money. The way it usually works is a candidate gathers people in a village for a speech and afterwards provides what everyone in Uganda calls "refreshment": a table filled plentifully with alcohol, food and a candidate's message to vote for him or her. Other times candidates will have their agents distribute money for "transportation" so people can get back to their homes. Another popular move is to have agents direct people behind a mango tree around the corner—somewhere out of sight—where they hand them a crisp 5000 shilling bill or maybe a little salt, sugar and soap. All they ask for in return is a simple tick on the ballot on election day. (Tabachnik, 2011: 15)

I want to briefly return to the image of "(god)father," through which political legitimacy is often established in Nigeria and much of Africa. The idea of "godfather" describes the process by which a person makes connections with a senior within a given institutional hierarchy in the expectation of favored treatment (Joseph 1987: 207). In much of Africa, fathers (not necessarily biological) are expected to nourish, protect, and provide for their children. The concept of godfather reclaims this "father-children" relation that is culturally embedded and evokes images of the political father as the one who protects and provides for his political children. As such, the father is entitled to "eat" part of his children's labor. Godfathers can enhance their political legitimacy by seeing to it that their children are well fed (*chop belleful*), both literally and figuratively (Schatzburg 2001: 24–25). By way of illustration, Tanzanians widely see Julius Nyerere as the "Father of the Nation." His political legitimacy was enhanced after the 1967 Arusha Declaration, which committed Tanzania to "socialism and self-reliance" in response to widespread poverty. In 1970, a Swahili praise poem appeared in the *Uhuru* newspaper praising Nyerere and the Arusha Declaration. The poet used images of eating/hunger to contrast the pre- and post-Arusha era, noting that average people in the pre-Arusha era could only afford to eat porridge and greens (*ugali na sukuma wiki*) because their greedy leaders had "eaten" too much and spoiled their legitimacy in the process. But now, in the post-Arusha era, ordinary Tanzanians are said to be fatter than before, eating rice and fish (*wali na samaki*) (Schatzburg 2001: 24). Occasionally, the political godfather disciplines his "children" who stray from his path, but he is generally pardoning and forgiving, as evidenced by the culture of presidential pardoning of convicted political allies in Nigeria.

Against this backdrop, the politics of stomach infrastructure establishes the familial or intimate ties that link politicians to the people. To turn down the opportunity to eat from the same bowl is tantamount to rejecting family membership (Denham 2017: 96). This explains why, in accusing his colleague Bola Ige, the Minister of Power and Steel, of not "eating" (stealing) in peace, a former Nigerian Minister for Internal Affairs said: "Look at somebody we have called to *come and eat…*" (Adebanwi & Obadare 2011: 186).

Cashivorous Elites: You Chop, Me Self I Chop (Eat-and-Let-Eat)

Ordinary language in Nigeria is replete with talk of "chopping [eating] money." But what exactly does it mean to chop? Similar to Bantu Africa (Fallers 1969: 83), chopping is a profoundly ambiguous notion that is deeply entrenched in Nigerian phraseology. At the most basic level, to chop is to eat, to express hunger. However, in Nigeria, "chop" is a common prefix for a multitude of slang phrases: "chop beans" is failing at something, "chop burger" means one has put on weight, "chop cockroach" is getting pregnant, "chop mouth" means kissing, "chop liver" is to be courageous, and "chopping money" means amassing wealth illegally (Bell 2019). In his piece titled "Bingeing on our National Cake," Jon Okafor criticizes the "national cake" mindset of Nigerian politicians who treats state funds as food to be "furiously eaten." The political mentality in Nigeria today is simple: "Let us grab as much as possible and go home to belch" (Okafor 2011). In its draft constitution of 1976, Nigeria notably defined political power as "the opportunity to acquire wealth and prestige, to be able to distribute benefits in the form of jobs, contracts, scholarship, and gifts of money and so on to one's relatives and political allies" (cited in Isichei 2004: 238). One of the political parties that contested the 1979 elections campaigned under the rallying slogan, *"You chop, me self I chop."*

Chopping is a powerful idiom through which average Nigerians criticize and hold their "cashivorous" elites[7] accountable for their precarious existence and lack of upward mobility. According to World Bank estimates, about 80 percent of Nigeria's oil and natural gas revenues accrue to 1 percent of the country's population (Afiekhena 2005: 15). At the height of the Nigerian oil boom in the 1970s, the ruling elites gobbled the resources of the state, while the rest of the nation wallowed in poverty. Indeed, "Of all the lessons Nigerians have had to learn since the oil started flowing, perhaps the hardest and most important is that government will give them almost nothing in terms of services… No road, no water, no light—no difference" (Peel 2010: 96). A poem composed in the 1980s best captures the plight of average Nigerians in the face of oil glut: *Our Father who art in heaven/Give us this day/Rice/Yams/Bananas/For/We are dying/All of Hunger/And*

---

[7] To borrow a term from the late Nigerian satirist, Pius Adesanmi.

my God/we haven't even/The right/To say/That we are dying/Of hunger (Schatzberg 2001: 49). In 2012, a leaked investigative report on Nigeria's oil and gas industry by the chairman of the Petroleum Revenue Task Force, Nuhu Ribadu, showed that an estimated USD30 billion was lost in the last decade in an apparent gas price-fixing scam implicating government officials and foreign energy firms (Idemudia et al. 2019). On the first day of January 2012, Nigerian President Goodluck Jonathan suddenly announced the removal of the fuel subsidy provided to citizens by the government. The fuel subsidy was one of the few benefits that average Nigerians received from a government widely perceived as corrupt and inept. Its sudden removal prompted widespread protest ("Occupy Nigeria") from January 1 through 16, 2012, which resulted in a partial reinstatement of the subsidy (Global Nonviolent Action Database 2015; Houeland 2018). The comments of the CNN in the aftermath of "Occupy Nigeria" reflect the paradox of prosperity of Africa's largest oil-producer:

> Nigerians are worn down by inherent corruption. The harsh reality is that despite being in the big league of oil producers with reserves of 36 billion barrels, the country's rank, according to the IMF, is 133rd in the world when it comes to per capita income—the lowest performance of a country with this level of natural resources. That per capita income ranking is just above its poor status in Transparency International's corruption index where Nigeria took the 143rd position in 2011 alongside Belarus, Togo, Russia, and Mauritania… This is a tale of two Nigerias—one that has garnered $67 billion of foreign direct investment, growing at 7–8 percent a year, and being singled out by Goldman Sachs as being one of the "Next-11" economies… According to the World Bank, 80 percent of the oil wealth has really only benefitted 1 percent of the population." (Defterios 2012)

Nowhere are the above oil-related corruption and attendant injustices more palpable that in Nigeria's Niger Delta region. Home to most of Nigeria's southern minority groups, the Niger Delta harbors crude oil reserves to the tune of 33 billion barrels and natural gas reserves of 160 trillion cubic feet (Omotola 2006: 4). From oil alone, Nigeria generated USD300 billion between 1970 and 2002, yet the Niger Delta people remain among the most deprived oil communities in the world, with 70 percent living on less than USD1 a day, the standard economic measure of absolute poverty (Amnesty International 2005). This paradox of prosperity is traceable to the First Republic, when corruption first became a "Nigerian factor." In his novel *A Man of the People*, Achebe turned to the image of eating to criticize officials of the First Republic who grew fat off bribes and graft, but also the apathy of "the People" who legitimized it:

> The people themselves, as we have seen, had become even more cynical than their leaders and were apathetic into the bargain. "Let them eat," was the people's opinion, "after all, when white men used to do all the eating did we commit suicide?

Of course not. And where is the all-powerful white man today? He came, he ate, and he went. But we are still around."

[T]he fat-dripping, gummy, eat-and-let-eat regime just ended—a regime which inspired the common saying that a man could only be sure of what he has put away safely in his gut or in language ever more suited to the times: "You chop, me self I chop, palaver finish." (Achebe, cited in Isichei 2004: 237)

Achebe's novel was written in 1966, the same year that the First Republic succumbed to a military putsch. At the time, newspapers in Nigeria celebrated the coup using idioms of eating: *Bribe? E Don Die. Chop-Chop—E no Dey* (literally, "Bribe? It is Dead. Eat-Eat—It does not exist anymore") (*The Morning Post*, Isichei 2004: 237). In retrospect, this elation proved premature, as the Nigerian military proceeded to cripple the economy by looting the state blind, violating the Congolese saying *kula ndambo, kwaca ndambo* ("eat some, leave some"). Like the colonial state, military juntas and their civilian minions entrenched corruption and left behind what I have described elsewhere as a "political economy of state robbery" (Agbiboa 2012). The frenetic looting of the state under the First Republic is captured in Cyprian Ekwensi's *Survive the Peace*, set in post-Civil War (1967–1970) Igboland. A village elder, Pa Ukoha, laments the gluttony of rulers:

When some black men begin to rule they become too greedy. They eat and fill their stomachs and the stomachs of their brothers. That is not enough for them. They continue till their throats are filled. And that too is not enough. They have food in their stomachs and in their throats and they go on till their mouths are full and then proceed to fill their bags. But no one else outside their families or their tribe must partake of this food... this is what brings trouble in Africa. (Ekwensi 1976: 77)

Ekwensi's *Survive the Peace* speaks to the frustration and anger felt by many ordinary Africans who continue to feel excluded from the rewards of political independence and freedom. For these marginalized Africans, Kwame Nkrumah's call to "Seek ye first the political kingdom and all else shall be added onto you" rings hollow.

"Monkey De Work, Baboon De Chop"

Road transport workers in Lagos routinely use idioms of consumption to denounce their exploitative labor, especially the predatory activities of mobile police officers. Two interrelated sayings are particularly instructive here. The first is in pidgin: *Monkey de work, baboon de chop* [literally, "monkey is working, baboon is doing the eating"] is a common saying which means that police officers (and transport union touts) are putting in less work but eating off the hard day's labor of drivers and conductors. The second saying is in Yorùbá: *Osisewa l'orun, eni maaje wa ni iboji*, [literally, "the worker toils in the full heat of the sun but the one who eats sits in a restful place"]. Police officers in Nigeria routinely stops transport operators to ostensibly check for vehicle particulars. A few squeezed naira note into the officer's hands and the check is complete before it started. In the often unlikely event that a driver has all his particulars intact, the officer will ask him, "Na particulars I go chop?", which means "Will I eat particulars?" This implies that the police officer is not really interested in the vehicle particulars but in "chop money" ("food money"). At this point, a driver would "drop something" (bribe) for the officer. However, if the driver is still reluctant, the officer will employ a delay-tactics by insisting on inspecting the entire car as part of "doing my job." This often requires passengers disembarking for inspection, a tactics geared at frustrating the driver into giving bribes. For this reason, passengers tend to urge their driver to *fun olopa lonje kia* ("feed the policeman quickly") because *asiko laiye* ("time is life"). Consider the following checkpoint exchanges between commercial drivers and police officers:

Exchange I:

OFFICER: What are you carrying?
DRIVER: Nothing, sir.
OFFICER: Come down and open your boot
DRIVER: (*Opens boot*) Here oga.
OFFICER: [*Sees bags inside*] I thought you said "nothing?"
DRIVER: Namy passenger's own (They belong to my passengers)
OFFICER: (*points out a bag*) who owns this bag?
PASSENGER 1: Oga, it is my bag
OFFICER: (*points out another*) what of this?
PASSENGER 2: Na my own (It is mine)
OFFICER: Let's see what is inside
PASSENGER 2: (*opens bag*) Na my clothes (They are my clothes)
PASSENGERS: Driver you no no what is happening? Make you clear am and save our time now (Driver, you don't know what's happening? [i.e. how things are done] Clear him [give him some money] and save our time]
DRIVER: (Supplies the bribe as he grumbles inaudibly and withdraws into the safety of his vehicle).

(Mele & Bello 2007: 450)

Occasionally, informal transport workers in Nigeria are able to negotiate their way out of police extortion by either claiming to have only just began work for the day (and, thus, have no money to pay the bribe-demanding officer) or complaining about carrying a small number of passengers. In the former sense, the driver is not saying that he won't "settle" (bribe) the police officer but, instead, that he needs more time to *jeun soke* ("eat upwards," to make money). The latter sense is evident in the following exchange:

Exchange II:

OFFICER: Slow down, my friend
DRIVER: Abeg oga, no vex. Sorry [I implore you sir, don't be annoyed]
OFFICER: Wey your *kola*[8] [Where is your kola?]
DRIVER: Oga my passengers no plenty. No full load [The passengers are not many, sir. There are still more empty seats]
OFFICER: So these ones no be passengers? [So, the ones here are not passengers?]
DRIVER: But oga, dem no plenty [But, sir, they aren't many]
OFFICER: Oya, de go! [Ok, go on your way]

(Mele & Bello 2007: 447)

Exchange II illustrates how corruption opens up, if briefly, a "space of negotiation" for people on the margins of society, such as drivers and street hawkers (Anjaria 2011). Scholars have long cast police corruption in the developing world in light of "just remuneration" or "compensatory allowance" for poor police wages in developing countries (Blundo & Olivier de Sardan 2006: 112; Bayley 1974: 93). One policeman in Lagos sums it up: "The Police is suffering, look at our barracks, or children. We receive meagre salaries and are often not paid on time. That is why you see some of our people on the road collecting illegal money from road users. They just want to survive…" (UNODC 2017: 35). However, this rationale has been challenged in a study of corruption in Ghana. In 2010, the Ghanaian government doubled the salaries of police officers in an effort to reduce road-related bribery. Far from decreasing petty corruption on the road, the study found that the Ghanaian salary policy "significantly increased the police efforts to collect bribes, the value of bribes and the amounts given by truck drivers to policemen in total." The authors adduced two reasons for this surprising result. First, that salary increases enhance the status and esteem of the officers, which in turn indirectly drive demand for higher bribes. Second, that demands from extended family to share the monetary bribes put pressure on those whose status had increased in line with higher salaries (Foltz & Opoku-Agyemang 2015: 27). This key finding tells us three important things. First, it exposes the limitations of theories of corruption based on the political economy of goods and monetary exchanges (Tankebe, Karstedt, & Adu-Poku 2019: 5). Second, it reflects an "economy of esteem" (Brennan &

---

[8] Kola nut in full, *kola* is the fruit of the kola tree, indigenous to West Africa. It is often offered to visitors as a sign of the host's gratification. It is also, however, often a synonym for bribe.

Pettit 2004) that facilitates corruption. Third, it underscores the need to emphasize the adjective over the noun in *moral* economy (Fassin 2009).

The mobile exchanges between drivers and police officers in Nigeria add weight to the point that an encounter with the police in the developing world is often an encounter with corruption: "In developing countries, bribery [is] a transaction fee for doing business with the police. It afflicts everyone, not just criminals, and it implicates all police officers" (Bayley & Perito 2011: 5–6). In Nigeria, the police uniform is a license for legitimate income generation. The widespread practice of police corruption is institutionalized through an organized scheme under which senior officers approve and profit from extortion committed by junior officers (Agbiboa 2015: 113; OSJI 2010: 82–83). The fact that police officers make little attempt to conceal the extortion of money from motorists not only erodes the rule of law but points to a lack of political will in Nigeria to hold officers accountable for their gross misconduct (UNODC 2017). Everyday road users in Nigeria, especially transport workers, have come to accept police corruption as a sacrifice they have to make to avoid higher penalties or substantial delays, since operators who refuse to pay are delayed for any number of hours or taken to the police station, where they may face trumped-up charges (OSJI 2010: 86). As one driver in Lagos explains, "We don't waste time in giving them the money. When you don't bring out the money in time, they will tell you at gunpoint to park, and then you might be required to pay more than the regular bribe. They won't collect anything less than N500" (Omotola 2007: 627). In some parts of Lagos, roadside extortion by the police has become so widespread and systemic that it is now standardized. In Oshodi, for example, *danfo* drivers who pass through state-controlled checkpoints on more than one occasion each day complained about having to bribe the same policeman repeatedly. In response, the police set up a creative system in which drivers are given a "password"—for example, a number on their license plate—to identify those that had already made the daily *egunje* (bribes). While survey evidence shows that eight of ten Nigerians (78 percent) perceive the Nigeria Police Force to be extremely corrupt (Afrobarometer 2015), some police officers have fired back that corruption is not specific to the Nigeria Police Force but permeates every institution in Nigeria. As a senior police officer in Lagos responded, "How can people say that the police are the most corrupt agency in Nigeria? What about Immigrations? As far as I am concerned, every sector [in Nigeria today] is corrupt, including the most important decision-making institutions in the country" (Oluwaniyi 2011: 74). This statement reinforces the generalization and banalization of corruption in Nigeria, which is best exemplified by the informal road transport sector.

3

The Politics of Informal Transport

By 2030, about half of all Africans will be urban dwellers. Yet, African cities have some of the world's worst cases of transport poverty. For instance, the continent has one of the lowest rates of car ownership in the world. Survey evidence from Lagos, Kampala, and Douala (the largest cities in Nigeria, Uganda, and Cameroon, respectively) suggests that there are only between thirty and seventy vehicles per one thousand people—far below the global average of 180 vehicles per thousand. An estimated three-fourths of daily commuters in African cities walk to and from wherever they need to go, by necessity (Agbiboa 2020a: 175; Olvera et al. 2016: 166). This reality has amplified calls for more efficient, environmentally friendly, and affordable rapid-transit bus lines and light rail systems (*Medium* 2018). For now, though, African cities generally run on informal modes of transport—typically minibuses, but also motorbikes, tricycles, and shared taxis. These are ground-level responses to the growing demand for mobility in the face of absent or inadequate formal public transportation services. For many African urbanites, it is impossible to imagine city life without its ubiquitous minibuses. They are the subject of news, gossip, rumors, and urban myths (Quayson 2018).

Minibus taxis account for an estimated 80 percent of Africa's total motorized trips (*Medium* 2018), constituting half of all motorized traffic in some corridors (Kumar & Barrett 2008: 5). They go by various appellations: *danfo* in Lagos, *trotro* in Accra, *daladala* in Dar es Salaam, *poda-poda* in Freetown, *matatu* in Nairobi, *otobis* in Cairo, *car rapides* in Dakar, *condongueiros* in Luanda, *gbaka* in Abidjan, *kamuny* in Kampala, *magbana* in Conakry, *esprit de mort* in Kinshaha, *sotrama* in Bamako, *songa kidogo* in Kigali, and *kombi* in Cape Town. The failure of state-owned mass transportation services has occasioned the growth and popularity of these informal and ostensibly unregulated services. They are also known as "paratransit," to indicate an alternate mode of flexible passenger transport services that caters to the poor in the developing world. Unlike modern mass transit systems with fixed stops, fares, routes, and timetables, paratransit services run flexible, even extralegal, schedules. Paratransit services "follow no particular schedule—they depart when they have reached maximum capacity and they arrive when they have successfully passed through all the checkpoints, paid all necessary fees and bribes, and fixed all

They Eat Our Sweat. Daniel E. Agbiboa, Oxford University Press.
© Daniel E. Agbiboa (2022). DOI: 10.1093/oso/9780198861546.003.0004

parts that have broken down during the journey" (Green-Simms 2009: 31). One *kombi*-taxi slogan in Cape Town sums it up: "This Is A Taxi! It Can Stop Anywhere, Anytime, Anyplace."

Paratransit vehicles are notorious for their squealing breaks, bald tires, and rattling exhaust pipes emitting thick, black smoke. And the practice of overloading has long been common in many African cities. Nigerian Nobel Prize winner Wole Soyinka describes paratransit taxis as a form of "transportation torture on four wheels," not simply because of the famished roads they ply daily. He describes "humans crushed against one another and against market produce, sheep, and other livestock suffocated by the stench of rotting food and anonymous farts" (1988: 251). On his 1977 album *Shuffering and Shmiling*, Fela Kuti sang about the discomfort of paratransit services in Lagos, particularly the iconic *molues* (midibuses): "*Everyday my people dey inside bus. Forty-four seating and ninety-nine standing. Them go pack themselves like sardine.*" Across African cities, informal transport services continue to vex vehicle inspection officers. "You wonder how these buses secured roadworthiness certificates in the first place," one officer in Lagos told me. "And when you ban these buses from the roads, they still find a way of returning to them."

Although paratransit services are commonly associated with chaos, criminality, and death, they nonetheless offer more than cheap transportation for multitudes of city dwellers in Africa. They also provide employment opportunities for many jobless youths from both urban and rural areas, which partly explains their influence on politics and popular culture. In Lagos, there are more than 20,0000 *okada* (motorbike-taxi) drivers; overall, the industry provides jobs to approximately 500,000 young men as drivers, renters, mechanics, and spare parts dealers. The popularity of *okadas* stems from their relatively low start-up capital and maintenance costs, and the feeling of economic freedom and autonomy that motorcycles afford. In Nairobi, the ubiquitous *matatus* embody "the era of cosmopolitanism, multiparty politics, neoliberalism and global hip-hop" (Mutongi 2017). In South African cities such as Durban, *kombi*-taxi vans became a powerful symbol of post-apartheid freedom and an important arena for black economic empowerment, even as they retained their underworld associations (Hansen 2006). Whatever their symbolism, paratransit vehicles provide the primary form of mobility for average Africans, who otherwise rely on walking to navigate the city, especially those eking out a living on the margins of society.

Multiple Impacts

Considering that the informal transport sector has manifold impacts on the political economy of everyday life in Africa, it is remarkable how little research has been done to understand its contributions to African cities. First, informal transport essentially serves the African poor, who typically make up the large majority of the population—in many cases these services account for over 80 percent of urban mobility needs. In Africa, owning a vehicle is a key marker of wealth, power, and privilege. One study finds that 99 out of 100 households in Africa's poorest cities do not own or have access to a private car, and thus are wholly reliant on paratransit services (Agbiboa 2020a: 176). This low motorization rate in Africa is not a new development. Whereas by 1966 one in four people owned cars in most industrialized countries, in West Africa, the rate was about 1 percent in the more well-off countries, with one in eighty people owning vehicles in Cameroon, Senegal, and Ivory Coast. Even then, most of these vehicles were likely to be second-hand (used) cars often purchased at auctions in Europe. Yet, Africans are still eight to ten times more likely to be in a fatal car accident than those in developed countries (Green-Simms 2009: 3). Other studies show that the average household in African cities can afford just one round trip daily; for the poorest, even that is out of reach. In Lagos, the average passenger spends about 40 percent of their income on bus fares (Adinde 2020). But walking is the primary way of getting around town for lower-income people who do not own a car. In Nairobi, only an estimated 12 percent of the population uses private vehicles (Pandey & Paul 2019), while the rest use paratransit services such as *matatus* or simply "leg it." Although paratransit services are widely available, they do not appeal to higher-income groups, because they are seen as dangerous and unreliable.

Second, informal transport provides opportunities for interaction and a means of economic survival, shaping circulation patterns for people, resources, and information in urban space (Mutongi 2006; Hansen 2006). The automobiles themselves do not simply express political, social, and economic relations, but rather shape and produce them. They are in effect meeting points for daily conversations in which humor alternates with pathos and dreams coexist with existential angst about bribery and extortion, endless road delays, dysfunctional services, moribund infrastructure, hard work and marginal gains, poverty, and relative deprivation. Third, the informal transport sector provides a unique window onto the political and social conditions of African cities. Operators and unions are key factors in party politics, often playing a decisive role in determining election outcomes.

Despite the chaos and disorder for which Africa's informal transport sector is deservedly notorious, there is an understudied "logic of practice" (to borrow a term from the French sociologist Pierre Bourdieu) that organizes and animates the sector. African cities do work amid the chaos, and we can gain a better understanding of how they work by studying how an apparently chaotic sector such as informal transport "reinvent order" (Trefon 2004). As Mbembe (2001a: 20) tells us, "fluctuations, volatility and indeterminacy do not necessarily amount to disorder, and any representation of an unstable world cannot be subsumed under the appellation of chaos."

Dirty Work

The state of informal transport in African cities mirrors the harsh lived experiences of its workers—mostly marginal men without status. Like many informal workers in Africa, transport operators have no fixed income, no days off, and no social protection. The sociologist Everett Hughes used the phrase "dirty work" to describe occupations and labor conditions that are perceived as disgusting or degrading (Hughes 1958). This term well describes the workaday world of informal transport workers in African cities, from Lagos to Nairobi. Despite lengthy workdays averaging around twenty hours, informal transport workers take home meager incomes due to the culture of corruption among police and other street-level bureaucrats, the exacting demands of vehicle owners, and the extortionate powers of mafia-like transport union touts who roam bus stations and junctions, collecting onerous fees from operators with impunity. "At the end of the day you check the money you have earned and you see it is nothing. You ask yourself if this is all I have worked for since day break," said one driver in Lagos (Adetayo, 2020). *Ise ko lowo* ("hard work does not guarantee money") was how one *danfo* slogan puts it. "*Okada* [motorbike taxi] is just daily income," said another driver. "What you get today you use today, and tomorrow you start again from scratch." One driver in Lomé, Togo, noted that, "If you are a *zem* [motorbike] driver, you can eat. You can't have any projects, but at least you can eat" (Olvera et al. 2016: 169).

There are four basic figures involved in running a paratransit business in African cities: the fleet owner (also known as taxi baron), the owner-driver, the taxi driver, and the bus conductor. In most cities, minibus-taxi drivers often have to remit a specific target income to the taxi owner each day; they are paid according to how much they bring in. The driver is responsible for all overhead costs, including fines frequently imposed by touts and police. In Freetown, Sierra Leone, taxi drivers are employed on a day-to-day basis. Owners expect drivers to pay 50,000 Le (USD10) "master money" per day, as well as to cover their fuel allowance and other small repairs out of their daily takings (Lipton 2017: 104). For motorbike-taxis, the arrangement is slightly different. Drivers often acquire their motorbikes through a process of hire purchase; they run their bikes for owners to whom they must make daily payments. Drivers are under immense daily pressures to meet the financial targets set by owners or forfeit their vehicles—their primary source of survival and social status—at the expiration of the twelve-month agreement. This pressure results in long working hours, high accident rates, and poor health. In this sense, then, Africa's informal transport workers are the "precariat" par excellence. A product of the global liberalization of labor in the post-Fordist phase, the precariat is a multitude of people united by common fears and insecurities, a new dangerous class "living bits-and-pieces lives, in and out of short-term jobs, without a narrative of occupational development" (Standing 2011: 1).

To meet their daily targets, drivers must race between the two end points of their chosen routes in a survival of the fastest, weaving in and out of traffic without regard for life. These drivers "do not race to experience sensations since they are not in it for a sport. They speed to meet deadlines if they are to keep their jobs" (Mutongi 2006: 564). For some urban workers, "speeding up [is] the essential criterion for the ability to keep one's head above water, to eke out minimal profit in sectors inundated with competition and seemingly infinite layers of subcontracting" (Simone 2016a: 14). For paratransit drivers, navigating the African city demands constant improvisation and experimentation. However, with this improvisation comes danger. International survey evidence shows that Africa has the highest number of road traffic fatalities. Of a total of 1.2 million annual deaths globally, over 225,000, or 19 percent, occur on African roads (*Medium* 2018). Aside from speed and experimentation, fatigue is a major cause of road accidents, commonly caused by long hours of work and inadequate sleep, which alter the body's circadian rhythms. In Lagos, according to the State Ministry of Transportation, 99 percent of *danfo* drivers suffer from hypertension (*PM News* 2015), a health challenge directly related to the demanding and dangerous nature of their work. Survey evidence from the Lagos State Drivers' Institute shows that 22 percent of *danfo* drivers are "partially blind" (*Vanguard* 2013a). The poor condition of the roads, especially the dust and piles of roadside debris, mainly accounts for this problem (though many *danfo* drivers have never had to undergo a vision test since they work without a license). In Nairobi, a study by the International Transport Worker's Federation (ITWF) found that *matatu* workers regularly reported "respiratory problems [resulting from] long hours of exposure to air pollution… [as well as] back pain, aching joints, swollen and painful legs, eye conditions, dust related issues, sore throats, headaches, and ulcers" (cited in Agbiboa 2020a: 177). In Lomé, Togo, nine out of every ten motor-bike taxi (*oleyia*, meaning "take me quickly") drivers suffers from back pain due to a potent mixture of long working hours and poor road conditions. "Look at the roads, they are so bumpy," said one *oleyia* operator. "Every time I get home I have to apply our renowned Victago ointment" (Olvera et al. 2016: 170). Between one and two in every five drivers complained of vision problems, fatigue, headaches, and sexual weakness. "What bothers me most is the dust," said one driver, adding, "Although I have a scarf, I can't use it much because I'm not used to it. So I often suffer from coughs and colds. Or, if I stay for long in the sun, I get headaches." (ibid.). All this explains why many transport operators in African cities view their workaday world as a struggle: "Life is War" (Rizzo 2011: 179). "Long hours, ruthless police and gang harassment, and susceptibility to deadly traffic accidents all render the work of operators one of the most dangerous jobs [in Africa]" (Mutongi 2006: 564).

The struggle to get by and get ahead forces many paratransit operators to reproduce the transgressive system that they condemn. Behavior such as overloading passengers, speeding dangerously, engaging in arbitrary pricing, failing to comply with the rules of the road, and feuding contributes to the criminalization and stigmatization of Africa's informal transport sector and workers. Driving work in Accra, Ghana, is referred to as "death work" and is dominated by young men routinely framed as "criminals, cheats, and bad citizens" (Hart 2016: 183). In Nairobi, *matatu* drivers are commonly viewed by the public as "political thugs who exploited and mistreated passengers and participated in gang or mafia-like violence" (Mutongi 2006: 549). In Tanzania, Matteo Rizzo alludes to the static discourse that "criminalizes the informal transport workforce and attributes the many accidents and chronic tensions of the transport system to the hooliganism and greed of its workforce" (2011: 1187). In Senegambia, cross-border drivers were subjected to social stereotypes, epitomized by the Wollof saying, "the chauffeur [driver] is not dependable" (Khan 2017: 113). In African cities that have endured civil wars, such as Monrovia and Freetown, motorcycle taxis serve as a source of income for unskilled ex-combatants, without calming "the fears of a resurgence of past violence" (Olvera et al. 2016: 166). In the capital city of Lomé in Togo, for example, there is a certain social stigma linked to driving motorbike-taxis. This explains why it is commonly seen as a temporary way of making ends meet, while "making savings in order to return to one's initial occupation under better conditions" (Olvera et al. 2016: 172). Often, the problem is not so much about the income as it is about issues of social status and respectability.

Against this backdrop, many operators struggle to construct a positive self-image. They see their work not as a real trade, but as a temporary occupation to which they resort *faute de mieux*. But many still derive pride from their vehicles—the material symbols of their survival, manhood, and respectability. Across Nigerian cities, it is common to see tricycle-taxi (*keke napep*) drivers using dusters to wipe dirt from their vehicles at the slightest opportunity, especially while stuck in traffic for any number of hours. In northern Nigeria, where a man's social and marital status are inextricably connected, *okada* work is a way out of "social death" for unmarried men: it enables them to pay the oft-inflated bride price, marry, and acquire the status of *masu gida* (household heads) and *homi completo* (complete men).

Indigenous Entrepreneurship

Across Africa, the informal transport sector is a site of indigenous entrepreneurship and creative adaptation. Nigerian transport entrepreneurs, such as Dawodu and Obasa, pioneered the importation and adaptation of cars to fill voids in mass mobility:

As early as 1913, Dawodu was operating transport services in northern Nigeria around Kano, and a few years later Obasa was running the only bus and van service in Lagos. In 1915 Dawodu imported the first Ford cars into Nigeria and was converting light Model T. Fords into commercial vans by building stronger bodies onto the chassis. That same year Dawodu's firm established an agency in Lagos where cars, mainly Fords, could be bought, sold, and repaired. By 1920 his firm was one of the largest vehicle importers, general mechanics, and builders of car and truck bodies in Nigeria. (Green-Simms 2009: 56–57)

Nowhere is this versatility more evident than in the building of Lagos' trademark *molues*, locally known as "flying coffins" and "moving morgues." They are built locally on chassis derived from second-hand (*tokumbo*) trucks and engines imported from Europe. This process of "hybridization" (Osinulu 2008: 49) is the stuff of cultural production and globalization in postcolonial Africa. In cities like Durban and Nairobi, minibus-taxis fiercely compete to attract passengers with music and airbrushed portraits of everyone from Kanye West to Barack Obama and Osama Bin Laden. In Lagos, *danfo* slogans shape the mood and choice of commuters on a daily basis.

The Corruption Trap

Corruption and violence are prevalent in the informal transport sectors of African cities. Union touts, urban street gangs, and law enforcement officials run riot. Paratransit workers say that corruption has eaten deep into the fabric of their workday world. In Nairobi, criminal gangs (so-called "cartels") such as the *Mungiki* use violence to control *matatu* terminals and routinely demand "security" fees to allow operators to ply a specific route. The *mungiki* typically work in small units at bus stations and report to a lieutenant or *munene* (LeBas 2013: 50). In the Lake Chad Basin, a volatile region where the violent insurgency of *Jama'atu Ahlis Suna Lidda'awati Wal Jihad*, commonly known as Boko Haram, has killed thousands and displaced millions, long-haul truckers and bus drivers often complain about the violent extortion and delay tactics of trigger-happy security personnel. For every 100 km traveled in West Africa, truckers transporting goods often lose an hour due to illegal checkpoints en route. "At some checkpoints if you don't *dash* [bribe] them, they can delay you for up to four hours before you will be released," said a trucker in Maiduguri. "Due to all the delays, a two-hour journey will take you ten hours." A tricycle-taxi driver in Yola complained to me about the choking presence of security checkpoints in the wake of Boko Haram: "If one is going out of town through *Haying Gida* [across the bridge], there is checkpoint in and out. If you're going out to Federal Government Girls College, there is checkpoint in and out. If you're going to Yola, as you live Bama going to Fufore, there is another checkpoint. The whole town is surrounded by checkpoints." "Before, if I leave from Gire to Jabbi Lamba, I will meet three checkpoints, said another driver in Damaturu. "Now, the checkpoints have increased to ten and, anywhere you go, soldiers will just stretch their hands in your direction to collect 'water money' [bribe] from you as if it is their right. If you complain that you don't have lower denomination of money, they will tell you they have change up to N1,000. If you refuse, they order you to 'park your car' and subject you to a time-wasting search. It is always best for you to submit to them and report to God." So rife is checkpoint extortion in Maiduguri that one checkpoint was known as *ko ruwa ka dauko* (literally, "even if it's water you are carrying"). Armed security personnel manning *ko ruwa ka dauko* insist that even if you are transporting water, you must "settle" (bribe) them to gain passage. "Forget Boko Haram," said one trucker in Maiduguri, "soldier corruption at checkpoints is our main concern here." This reinforces recent comparative surveys which have shown that, among some populations, corruption is perceived as a more serious problem than unemployment, poverty, and terrorism (Rothstein 2018: 36; Holmes 2015).

In Nairobi, *matatu* drivers often leave 50- or 100-shilling notes hidden under the handle of the trunk to avoid any delays, since "time is money." Traffic police inspectors know just where to reach for the bribe as they "inspect" the vehicle. In Lagos, it is not uncommon for a *danfo* driver to drive right to the traffic police inspector and squeeze a 50-naira note into his hands, saying, "Officer, for beer." The inspector will quickly put the bill in his pocket and wave the driver through an illegal "one-way" lane, a source of many head-on collisions on Lagos roads. Showing any reluctance to pay the required bribe can be a costly mistake that results in lengthy delays at roadblocks, detention in a police station, vehicle impoundment, or tire deflation. "We just pay them and go our way. What else can we do?" asked one *danfo* driver. It is not uncommon for policeman to open fire on paratransit vehicles when drivers refuse to surrender a portion of their hard-earned cash. During military rule in Nigeria, road checkpoints emerged as powerful symbols of corruption and lack of discipline. In the public consciousness, they have come to signify "the capriciousness with which the military resorted to violence but also the notion that violence could be an acceptable way to solve problems" (Smith 2004: 437). Stanislav Andreski's observation about police behavior in Africa in 1969 rings true today:

> The Police are among the worst offenders against the law: they levy illegal tolls on vehicles, especially the so-called mammy-wagons (heavy lorries with benches and roofs), which usually carry many more passengers than they are allowed and transgress a variety of minor regulations. [These vehicles] are allowed to proceed regardless of the infractions of the law if they pay the policeman's private toll. (Okereke 1995: 281)

Networks of Solidarity

Africa's informal transport workers are hardly passive in the face of constant police abuses, passenger insults, or other trouble (Agbiboa 2020a: 178–9; Olvera et al. 2016: 171). Despite their bottom-of-society status, paratransit operators draw power from their sheer numbers and capacity for collective organizing, or what Sara Ahmed (2014: 36) calls "feeling-in-common." In Lagos, accidents involving cars and motorbike-taxis (*okadas*) often draw scores of supportive *okada* drivers in a matter of minutes: "I have seen instances when they [*okada* drivers] gang up in support of their colleague, even if it is he who is at fault," one Nigerian street vendor told me. Informal transport workers often belong to neighborhood associations that provide networks of solidarity, financial support, and protection to drivers. In Lagos, this is known as *ajo* (from informal cooperatives known in Nigeria as thrift collections); in Freetown, as *esusu* (rotating credit association), and in Johannesburg as *stokvels* (informal saving clubs). Such associations are characterized by relationships of trust, mutual dependence, and a powerful sense of belonging (James 2014). Given the risk and radical uncertainty of city life, a transport operator will think twice before rejecting associational support, which he is sure to need one day. Operators are forced to pay one-time union membership fees, as well as "ticket fees" assessed on a daily basis. These fees tend to be exorbitant, and many operators complain that they cannot afford them. But failure to pay exposes them to violent attacks by union touts. "If people don't pay their union fees, their *okadas* are taken from them," said one *okada* unionist in Lagos. "If they still don't pay, the drivers are taken to the nearest police station to face the 'wrath of law'" (Peel 2010: 93). This explains why some drivers see their union as self-appointed extortionists. As one operator in Peel's study said: "If your wife dies, they will not give you anything. No welfare—it's just a group of people working for themselves" (2010: 95). This, of course, runs contrary to how unionists in Lagos see themselves. A leader of a tricycle-taxi (*keke napep*) union in Nigeria explained:

> If one of us is involved in an accident, it is our job to look after him in the hospital and take care of his bill and to take him home. If there is any problem between our member and mobile police, you know this job involves a lot of youth bound to make mistakes, it's our job to resolve the problem amicably. Also, if your vehicle got damaged or malfunctions, the association will give you N2000 [approximately USD5.50] on credit for you to repair the damage and pay back N1,000. If your wife delivers a baby and you can't afford a ram for the naming ceremony, the association will help you out.

This sense of solidarity and conviviality among informal transport operators (particularly motorbike-taxi drivers) is often conveyed by vehicle inscriptions such as "Marry One, Marry All," "Mourn One, Mourn All," "Family," "Brotherhood," and so on. In a risky and unpredictable urban environment where material infrastructures are absent, people themselves become infrastructures that suture the city and keeps it on the go.

Union Clout

Across large parts of Africa, transport trade unions are politicized organizations that engage in collective action to protect the socio-economic rights and interests of their workers, even as they are also mobilized by profit at the expense of workers. The ambivalent role of unions as protectors and predators is partly a product of their embeddedness within "gray practices" (Routley 2016) and a politically captured environment where disorder is politically instrumentalized (Chabal & Daloz 1999). As Jean and John Comaroff remind us, "Vastly lucrative returns inhere in actively sustaining zones of ambiguity between the presence and absence of the law: returns made from controlling uncertainty, terror, even life itself" (Comaroff & Comaroff 2006: 5). The political power exercised by transport trade unions at the state and national levels is facilitated by their capacity to impose large externalities on society, including through regular strikes and violent protests. By dint of their sheer size, concentration in cities, and violent potential, transport unions are potentially capable of paralyzing the economy and threatening the ruling political party (Konings 2000: 168–9). As a result, transport unions have become key targets for political capture and voter mobilization, often being (ab)used as "political machines where their members act as political brokers who deliver votes through their mobilization and influence on voters" (Larreguy, Olea, & Querubin 2014: 2). Despite their centrality to the political materiality of African cities, the activities of transport trade unions are surprisingly muted in studies of real governance and practical norms in Africa (de Herdt & Olivier de Sardan 2015). By governance here, I mean the complex networks and multiple arenas within which power dynamics and practices of governance are expressed, deployed, and contested (Healey 2000: 919; Lindell 2008: 1880).

Transport trade unions in postcolonial Africa tend to oscillate between autonomy and political affiliation, cooperation and conflict. They are both agents of order and specialists in violence (Agbiboa 2020b; LeBas 2013: 243). Across African cities, transport unions typically double as reservoirs of thugs for politicians (HRW 2007: 26), especially during election season. In return, these unions are allowed by the state to appropriate transit spaces such as terminals and exploit transport operators with impunity. Motor parks, bus stops, and junctions in African cities are sites of activity in a gray area between the legal and the illegal (Roitman 2006; Routley 2016). Consider the NURTW branch in Lagos. Founded in 1978, the NURTW constitutes the primary support base for the Lagos state governor during election campaigns. The state is often unwilling or unable to rein in the union's predatory treatment of its workers. The union routinely engages in patronage politics and voter mobilization in return for permission to levy taxes on transport operators in public spaces. "The NURTW is a law onto itself," said a *danfo* driver. In South African cities, *kombi*-taxi operators "enjoy a very substantial *de facto* autonomy in terms of regulation and police intervention" as a result of their "politically well-connected bosses....The sheer size and quasi-legality of the taxi industry have made it an important source of corruption" (Hansen 2006: 188). In his study of the politics of order and chaos in the informal transport sectors of Kampala in Uganda and Kigali in Rwanda, Tom Goodfellow (2012: 210) found that *bayaye* touts constituted "both an important voting block and a potential source of violence [that] could be mobilized" by unions.

Modernizing Ambitions

Although paratransit services fill an import void in African cities, they also contribute to urban insecurity through endless traffic congestion, road accidents, air and noise pollution, and violent skirmishes among rival union touts (Olvera et al. 2016). A study by the Stockholm Environmental Institute estimates that Africa has less than 3 percent of the world's motor vehicles, but it suffers 11 percent of global road fatalities. In Nairobi alone, the notorious *matatus* account for an estimated 95 percent of car-related fatalities; as many as 13,000 people die in road accidents every year (Agbiboa 2020a: 179). In many African cities, it can take up to three hours to cover 15 kilometers because of jammed roads at rush hour. In Nairobi, the daily productivity lost to traffic congestion is estimated at KSh 58 million (USD550,000) (Pandey & Paul 2019). South Africans reportedly lose about 90 working hours per year stuck in traffic. One study found that Lagosians spend an average of 30 hours in traffic each week, or 1,560 hours annually. Compare this with drivers in Los Angeles and Moscow traffic, who averaged only 128 and 210 hours in traffic, respectively, in the whole of 2018 (CNN 2019). This inefficiency explains why Africa's informal transport sector has increasingly been treated by policymakers and city planners as disposable, as a problem to be solved.

Today, urban megaprojects and megacity planning in Africa threatens to dislodge thousands of paratransit operators and reshape their spaces of maneuver, provoking shock, anger, and resistance from below and collectively reinforcing informal urban workers' fears about state caprice and coercion. Such large-scale projects, generally couched in the language of urban renewal, are shaped by ways of seeing and reading African cities that are still dictated by Western planning and logic. Such thinking activates state-led interventions and public-private partnerships aimed at modernizing and ordering the African city and transforming it into a clear text that is "planned and readable" (De Certeau 1984).

Driven more by the logic of the market than by the needs of their inhabitants, urban authorities in Africa increasingly exercise power through their capacity to construct and reconstruct categories of legitimacy and illegitimacy (Roy 2005: 149; Agbiboa 2018: 6). From Lagos to Johannesburg and Dar es Salaam, elite-driven modernizing ambitions have led to support for measures aimed at homogenizing and partitioning urban space, exemplified by the disruption of informal markets, the demolition of illegal structures, the deportation of street beggars, the violent eviction of dumpsite dwellers, and other measures aimed at purging African cities of supposedly undesirable elements. In 2017, former Lagos state governor Akinwunmi Ambode hinted of a plan to ban yellow *danfos* from the city's roads: "When I wake up in the morning and see all these yellow buses and see *okada* and all kinds of tricycles and then we claim we are a megacity, that is not true and we must acknowledge that that is a faulty connectivity that we are running" (Ladelokun 2017: 18). Ambode's comments highlight popular perceptions of the informal transport sector as a chaotic and violent embarrassment that needs to be replaced. The favored substitutes are bus rapid transit systems (BRTs), generally deemed more befitting of a "modernizing" city with world-class ambitions. BRTs, typically operated by public-private partnerships, feature dedicated lanes and right-of-way infrastructure to facilitate rapid and frequent service (Klopp, Harber, & Quarshie 2019). In February 2020, Ambode announced a ban on motorbike- and tricycle-taxis, including burgeoning motorbike-hailing startups (e.g. Gokada and O'Ride) that offer a much safer alternative to the notorious *okadas*. Given the limited reach of the state-endorsed BRTs, motorbikes and tricycle-taxis have bridged enduring mobility gaps. The ban has caused widespread disruption and discontent in Lagos, leaving many drivers and passengers without options. A leader of one bike-hailing startup in Lagos believes that the ban reflects long-term state urban planning, which has no place for paratransit services. "They have a master plan," he said, "but *okadas* are not in it."

Over the past decade or so, major African cities—such as Lagos, Accra, Johannesburg, and Dar es Salaam—have increasingly turned to BRT projects in their quest for a safer, more efficient, and cost-effective solution to the need for mass transportation and the chaos of paratransit services (Klopp, Harber, & Quarshie 2019; Rizzo 2017). In 2008, Lagos introduced Africa's first BRT-Lite corridor, with technical support from the World Bank. BRTs undoubtedly can make a positive contribution to urban lives and productivity. Johannesburg's *Rea Vaya* system—arguably the first true BRT in Africa—carries an estimated 16,000 passengers daily. According to a New Climate Economy, *Rea Vaya* has saved South Africa as much as USD890 million thus far by reducing travel time, improving road safety, and cutting carbon emissions. In Dar es Salaam, the rapid transit system (DART) has dramatically reduced commute times for city dwellers, who previously faced upwards of four hours stuck in traffic each day (ITDP 2016).

But BRT systems present serious challenges. For one thing, their rise has spotlighted the struggles of Africa's paratransit workers for survival, recognition, and inclusion in decision-making processes that affect their livelihoods. In Lagos, Nigeria's commercial capital, initial plans to restructure key public transport routes and introduce a BRT system were undercut by opposition from the politically powerful NURTW, which feared that it would be forced out of the market if bus routes were reconfigured and sold off to the highest bidder. Similarly, in South Africa, efforts to develop BRT corridors and to phase out paratransit services met with stiff resistance from transport operators. In Johannesburg, the arrival of BRTs set off strikes and violent clashes between transport workers in the informal and public sectors. In Kenya, a BRT system launched in 2015 by President Uhuru Kenyatta has remained on hold due to inadequate funding as well as protests by private *matatu* owners, who fear that the new system will relegate them to the margins of city (Pandey & Paul 2019). In Dar es Salaam, the recent rapid growth of Rapid Transit (DART) system has given rise to similar tensions (Rizzo 2014; 2017).

Transport Culture

AbdouMalique Simone has argued that, "no form of regulation can keep the city 'in line'" (2010: 3). Paratransit services in urban Africa are, above all, a way of life, an organizing urban logic that cannot simply be banned or wished away. At issue here is not just the informal sector but the entire transport culture of African cities. As an "everyday technology" (Foucault 1988) and a vital element of mass mobility, paratransit services are embedded in human and material infrastructures that are integral to the functioning of African cities—"a platform providing for and reproducing life in the city" (Simone 2004b: 7–8). Africa's informal transport sector is likely to continue to drive mass mobility well into the future and remain central to the sociality of urban life and materiality of urban economies. This reality is slowly sinking in; rapid-transit bus lines in African cities such as Lagos and Dar es Salaam are beginning to change from an ineffective paradigm of displacement and replacement to a promising strategy of upgrading paratransit services and involving transport unions in the ownership and operation of new BRT systems (Klopp, Harber, & Quarshie 2019). In Lagos, for example, the state government sponsored visits for NURTW officials to see how BRTs have been successfully integrated with existing bus services in other cities such as Curitiba (Brazil) and Bogota (Colombia). This encouraged buy-in from the NURTW and persuaded its officials to engage with the new system (Otunola, Harman, & Kriticos 2019: 12). This points to a gradual drive toward "forging collaborative initiatives between the formal and informal process" (Kombe & Kreibich 2000: 148). A hybrid transport governance—one that not only absorbs paratransit services but allows them to coexist with new forms of public transport such as BRTs, light rail systems, and e-ridesharing—would be the most sustainable way of moving commuter journeys in African cities onward and upward.

4

The Art of Urban Survival

Despite the centrality of paratransit vehicles to the aesthetic characteristics of cities and their profound effect on the multitude who navigate them on a daily basis, there are remarkably few studies of the slogans inscribed on those vehicles as a window onto modern urban life, especially its social, economic, and physical characteristics (Williams 1954: 97). Foregrounding space as a social construction (Lefebvre 1996) and spatial practices as imbued with tactics (De Certeau 1984), this chapter explores what the slogans inscribed on minibus-taxis (*danfos*) in Lagos can tell us about the megacity in which they weave their routiine existence, especially the hopes, fears, and actual material circumstances which may have informed the operators' choice of slogans. Using an interpretative approach to vehicle slogans, this chapter shows how informal transport workers in Lagos actively translate their dangerous lifeworlds into "scenes and actions that convey symbolic meaning" (Low 1996: 861–62). Vehicle slogans not only reflect the *danfo* workers' lived experiences and precarious labor, but they also are themselves fundamental ways through which these marginal men get by and get ahead. Vehicle slogans embody not only the power of the unforeseen and the unfolding, but are the very window into people's determination to impose order and predictability on their lives (Mbembe & Nuttall 2004: 349). I want to interrogate how popular culture manifests itself through vehicle slogans, as a means to interpret the social experiences of informal transport workers in Lagos as well as an expression of their "social theory" (Akyeampong, 1996; Meyer, 2001). By popular culture, I mean the unofficial, expressive culture of ordinary people (Barber 2018: 1). Through an analysis of *danfo* slogans, we are able to relate to the precarious lifeworlds and inventive responses of *danfo* operators and owners.

This chapter builds upon new approaches to contemporary African urbanism that sees and reads the city as lively archives of expression and aesthetic vision (Mbembe and Nuttall 2008; Quayson 2014; Green-Simms 2017). Specifically, the chapter answers the call to defamiliarize commonsense thinking of urban Africa by engaging "new critical pedagogies—pedagogies of writing, talking, seeing, walking, telling, hearing, drawing, and making—each of which pairs the subject and object in novel ways to enliven the relationship between them and to better express life in motion" (Mbembe 2004: 352). The invitation here is to explore how mobile subjects translate the daily challenges of the city into arts, using

They Eat Our Sweat. Daniel E. Agbiboa, Oxford University Press.
© Daniel E. Agbiboa (2022). DOI: 10.1093/oso/9780198861546.003.0005

danfo slogans as a veritable window into the "ordered chaos" that marks Lagos as both familiar and strange. In so doing, my goal is to contribute to knowledge on the relationship between texts, persons and publics in the contemporary African city.

In the course of my fieldwork in Lagos, I collected and analyzed a total of 312 eclectic slogans from the mobile and stationary bodies of *danfos* on bottlenecked roads. The analysis of these slogans was informed by unstructured interviews and informal interactions with drivers, owners, and passengers. These were then supported by cumulative observations drawn from my long residence in Lagos and my experience as a regular *danfo* user. Some of the vehicle slogans were so cryptic in meaning that it was only by questioning the owners that I was able to apprehend the context of the text, or the "text within the text" (Lotman 1988), thereby forestalling potential bias in textual interpretation. In this sense, vehicle slogans may be imagined as part of the "hyperreal space" of African cities (Masquelier 2001: 288), that is, spaces where "things no longer exist without their parallel" (Mbembe & Roitman 1995: 340). It is not uncommon for many *danfos* in Lagos to change hands several times during their lifecycle, with subsequent owners very keen to impose their own slogans, their personal identity, and self-identification, on their newly acquired or hire-purchased *danfos*. Inquiring about slogans from owners helped to reduce the "misleading one-sidedness of textual interpretation" (Jaworski & Thurlow 2010: 1). However, occasionally, I was unable to question the owners directly, since I jotted down the slogans from the back of *danfos* in motion. Despite this limitation, it is worth noting that lexico-semantic meanings are fluid and never entirely under the owner's control. Texts often generate surplus meanings that transcend, even subvert, the purported intentions of the author (Barber 1987: 4).

Taking a cue from the Yoruba philosopher Olabiyi Yai's argument that art (visual or verbal) has *ashe* (or life force) and is both "unfinished and generative" (1995: 107), I derived the slogan's essential character (*iwa*) from the insights offered by other transport operators and Lagosians who often commented on the slogans, joked about them or expressed their preferences for one over another. For those who may question the relevance of slogans to the lived experiences and aspirations of mobile operators in Lagos, Karin Barber has an apt response: "The views that ordinary people express may be 'false consciousness' (a concept not without its own problems) but they are also their consciousness: the people's arts represent what people do in fact think, believe, and aspire to. Their ideology is forged in specific socio-historical circumstances and takes specific forms" (1987: 8).

Theorizing Everyday Life: Beyond the Routine

Lest one begin to wonder how a study of painted slogans fits with the thematic concern of this book, this chapter operates from the overarching premise that paying attention to the "doing, being and experiencing of the everyday" (Hallisey

2015: 307) can shed new light on how everyday people experience, articulate, and respond to corruption and coercion. Everyday life is an extremely difficult problem to interrogate empirically because "it asks us to render visible not what is hidden but what is right before our eyes" (Das 2015: 323). The everyday is at once the most self-evident and the most puzzling of all concepts (Agbiboa 2019: 837). Some see it as that time when nothing happens. Others view it as essentially unknown because the time of the everyday escapes us; it eludes our grasp. Still others identify it with the repetitive, the negative, the residual, the taken-for-granted continuum of mundane activities (Felski 2000: 78). If by every-day we mean that which happens day after day, it follows that it is a temporal (time-based) term whose essence is in the relentless cycle of repetition, that is, its "fleeting, ungraspable" nature which accounts for its unintelligibility (Lefebvre 2004: 51). For this reason, therefore, it has become received wisdom to deprive everyday life of critical reflection or the capacity for transcendence (Schutz & Luckmann 1983). As Henri Lefebvre (1987: 10) puts it, "In the study of everyday, we discover the great problem of repetition, one of the most difficult problems facing us."

Relatively recently, ethnographic studies of the state have reclaimed the concept of the everyday in their attempt to challenge conventional ideas of a monolithic state standing apart from society. These studies reconfigure the state as constituted through quotidian encounters, practices, and contingent interactions between citizens and public officials (Titeca & De Herdt 2011; Olivier de Sardan 2008; Gould, Sherman, & Ansari 2013: 241; Masquelier 2001; Gupta 1995; Mitchell 1999; Piliavsky 2014; Ruud 2000). Joel Migdal and Klaus Schlichte (2005: 15), for example, have called our attention to "doing the state," which entails paying an-alytic attention to the unstable and shifting interactions and responses between state officials and non-state actors. In this perspective, the state is nothing but a site of "competition or dispute amongst different interest groups... a repository of power that can be subverted and appropriated for particularistic interests" (Gould, Sherman, & Ansari 2013: 242). This chapter sees everyday life as "the site in which the life of the other is engaged" (Das 2010). In other words, at its core, the study of everyday life encompasses:

> the ordinary, recurring, trivial or crucial actions, struggles, engagements, interac-tions, enactments, performances, exchanges, needs, communications, and other manifold forms of deeds or acts that define and condition human existence. These deeds or acts involving ordinary people are often geared toward attempts to man-age, cope with, suffer through, struggle with and/or improve the terms of human existence and human viability in relation to, or in the context of, various agencies, structures, institutions, rules and regulations that enable or circumscribe living."
> (Adebanwi, forthcoming)

Far from a world devoid of politics, the everyday is reimagined here as indissolubly linked to the political economy, often in "unnoticed and pervasive ways" (Moran 2005). In light of de Certeau's important warning against seeing practices of daily life as mere "obscure background of social activity" (1984: xi), this chapter elevates the everyday *danfo* slogan to the status of a critical concept in an effort to understand and explain the corruption and precarity that surrounds transport work in Lagos.

Space, Place, Practice: The Tactics of Everyday Life

This chapter is partly informed by Henri Lefebvre's spatial theory outlined in *The Production of Space* (1992). In this work, Lefebvre develops a sophisticated account of how space is relentlessly constructed at the intersection of "representations of space" (by architects, planners, and developers), "spaces of representation" (which denote the vast symbolic associations we associate with specific kind of spaces), and "spatial practice," that is, the material, concrete, tangible dimensions of social activity and interactions. Lefebvre's spatial theorizing sheds important light onto how cities embody immense heterogeneity, especially in terms of "their density as concentrations of people, things, institutions and architectural forms; the heterogeneity of life they juxtapose in close proximity; and their siting of various networks of communication and flows across and beyond the city" (Amin & Thrift 2002: 2). The reproduction of social relations is vital to the production of space: "The spatial practice of a society secrets that society's space; it propounds and presupposes it in a dialectical interaction; it produces it slowly as surely as it masters and appropriates it, i.e., through the network of roads, motorways and the politics of transport" (Lefebvre 1992: 38). Lefebvre's conception of space as socially produced rests on a recognition that space constitutes an integral part of all social life, both affecting and affected by social action. Perhaps nowhere is this more evident than in the writings of Doreen Massey, who contends that space is "one of the axes along which we experience and conceptualize the world." Massey calls for space to be conceptualized as a product of simultaneous social interrelations and interactions at multiple scales, from local to global (1993: 141; 1994: 265).

Lefebvre's spatial insights are complemented by Michel de Certeau who, in *The Practice of Everyday Life*, defines space as nothing but a "practiced place." In other words, the way a place is practiced (or used) essentially produces its space (1984: 117). For de Certeau, practice comprises the entire repertoire of "dispersed, tactical and makeshift" procedures by which people socially navigate daily life. In other words, practice involves a method of "textual poaching," whereby city dwellers manipulate and conform the commands of a disciplinary power to their own interests and rules (1984: xiv). Given the fluid nature of practice, space is always ambiguous, unstable, and mutable (Magee 2007: 112). While acknowledging that space and domination are intertwined (Massey 1994: 81), de Certeau nonetheless maintains that the dominated are not passive consumers but rather active interpreters of the dominant order who create opportunities out of the very conditions of their domination. By way of illustration, de Certeau points to the manner in which the stunning victory of Spanish colonization over the indigenous Indian cultures in the Americas was diverted from its intended aim by the use made of it:

> [E]ven when they were subjected, indeed even when they accepted their subjection, the Indians often used the laws, practices, and representations that were imposed on them by force or by fascination to ends other than those of their conquerors; they made something else out of them; they subverted them from within—not by rejecting them or by transforming them (though that occurred as well), but by many different ways of using them in the service of rules, customs or convictions foreign to the colonization which they could not escape. They metaphorized the dominant order: they made it function in another register. They remained other within the system which they assimilated and which assimilated them externally. They diverted it without leaving it. Procedures of consumption maintained their differences in the very space that the occupier was organizing. (de Certeau 1984: 32)

Against the above background, de Certeau argues that everyday practices (including but not limited to talking, reading, moving about, or shopping) are tactical in nature. By tactics,[1] he means "a calculated action determined by the absence of a proper locus. No delimitation of an exteriority, then, provides it with the condition necessary for autonomy. The space of a tactic is the space of the other... It operates in isolated actions blow by blow... In short, a tactic is an art of the weak" (de Certeau 1984: 37). The tactic is time-dependent: "It is always on the watch for opportunities that must be seized on the wing... it must constantly manipulate events in order to turn them into opportunities." In Panama, corruption is commonly known as *juega vivo*, a phrase which describes someone who manipulates the system to his or her own benefit (Dougherty 2002: 199). De Certeau's concept of the tactics is an apt description of *juega vivo*.

The theoretical insights of Lefebvre and de Certeau are central to our discussions in this chapter because they usefully attribute to urban spatial practice a form of active agency or capacity for action. In other words, they offer us theories with significant explanatory power with regard to the agency of people struggling

---

[1] "[A tactic] takes advantage of 'opportunities' and depends on them, being without any base where it could stockpile its winnings, build up its own position and plan raids. What it wins it cannot keep. This nowhere gives a tactic mobility, to be sure, but a mobility that must accept the chance of offerings of the moment, and seize on the wing the possibilities that offer themselves at any moment. It must vigilantly make use of the cracks that particular conjunctions open in the surveillance of the proprietary powers. It poaches them. It creates surprises in them. It can be where it is least expected. It is a guileful ruse" (de Certeau 1984: 37).

to survive under the shadow of the modern world system (Shipley, Comaroff, & Mbembe 2010: 654). At the same time, both authors acknowledge that space is not a neutral spectator but an active protagonist in urban lives and livelihoods. This chapter starts from the major premise that Lagos is not "a series of policies gone wrong" (Simone 2005: 1) but rather a system of inventive responses and sheer grit. As Mbembe notes: "Those of us who live and work in Africa know firsthand that the ways in which societies compose and invent themselves in the present—what we could call the creativity of practice—is always ahead of the knowledge we can ever produce about them" (Shipley, Comaroff, & Mbembe 2010: 654). It is to this creativity of practice on the dangerous roads of Lagos that I now turn.

Automobile Cultures and the Creativity of Practice

Automobiles have a history of neglect as objects of ethnographic research. In a seminal essay on "The Cultural Biography of Things: Commoditization as Process," Igor Kopytoff invites us to track the "cultural biography" of cars because of what they can tell us about our cultural landscape. Using Africa as an example, Kopytoff argues:

> The biography of the car in Africa would reveal a wealth of cultural data: the way it was acquired, how and from whom the money was assembled to pay for it, the relationship of the seller to the buyer, the uses to which the car is regularly put, the identity of its most frequent passengers and of those who borrow it, the frequency of borrowing, the garages to which it is taken and the owner's relation to the mechanics, the movement of the car from hand to hand over the years, and in the end, when the car collapses, the final disposition of its remains. All of these details would reveal an entirely different biography from that of a middle-class American, or Navajo, or French peasant car. (1986: 67)

Since Kopytoff's call, researchers have explored various aspects of automobile cultures in Africa, including vehicles as instruments of African colonization (Gewald, Luning, & Walraven 2009), expressions of popular culture and political imagination (Miller 2001; Mutongi 2006; Green-Simms 2017), hybrid environments for the discourse of identity, faith, and social vision (Klaeger 2009), cars in their symbolical, material-technological as well as spiritual dimensions (Verripps & Meyer 2001), and the politics of car importation and allocation as a window onto the shifting contours of state authority (Chalfin 2008). In Lagos, as in many other African cities, vehicles constitute not only the *axis mundi* of modernity, but they are also powerful symbols of class differentiation (Mbembe & Roitman 1995: 330; Adichie 2014: 544). The car you drive tends to determine your social status, whether you're *olowo* (rich) or *talaka* (poor). Over and over again, Nigerian and

Ghanaian home videos and music industry emphasize that "beautiful cars are much cherished and figure as ultimate icons of modernity" (Verripps & Meyer 2001: 159). In these West African societies, owning or driving a car, even if rented or old, bestows on the driver a certain importance (*eniyan pataki*). By contrast, the expression "legedisbenz" (a parody of Mercedes Benz) is typically used to taunt poor urbanites who commute on foot. *Tie da?* ("Where is yours?") is a common *danfo* slogan in Lagos (directed as an insult from a driver to a passenger) reflecting the pride in owning a vehicle. A certain power inheres in the driver's control of the car and in a sense confers on him a privileged citizen status (Lawuyi 1988: 5). The import of automobiles is also evident in the fact that when a *danfo* driver is reluctant to "settle" (bribe) union touts (*agberos*) on the way, the first action taken by these touts is to inflict damage on the body of the *danfo*: they will pull out windshield wipers, remove fuel covers, detach seats, or smash side-view mirrors.

Danfos are typically fashioned out of Mercedes 911, Bedford, or Volkswagen chassis and engines derived from second-hand buses (*tokumbos*) imported from Europe, around which the steel frame is constructed. Constructing the outer body of a *danfo* is very much a hybrid process; local craftsmen build a new body around an imported chassis, which is then creatively decorated by local painters with the state-authorized yellow and black colors. The crafting of the *danfo* points to how African city dwellers carve out their own mechanisms and forms of production and urbanism by dint of a hybrid mix of modernist and non-modernist rationalitities (Myers 2010: 10). Most *danfos* have lost the padding that is placed in the ceiling to insulate passengers from heat. Their windows are also permanently sealed off, creating a stuffy atmosphere inside the *danfo*. Passengers often must sit on bare planks, which are crudely attached to iron bars. Apart from the steering wheel, the dashboards of most *danfos* are without any functioning gadgets. Thus, the *danfo* driver relies on his conductor (or sometimes on his passengers) to marshal the roads and bark instructions to him regularly: *O wa legbe o* (there is vehicle by your side), *wole wa* (enter this side of the road), and *o nbo le o* (a passenger is dropping).

The form of *danfos* generally conforms to their slogans. Rickety *danfos* are driven by older men and often bear slogans such as *E still dey go* ("It is still going"), "God is in Control," "Slow but Steady," "No Shaking," "Tested and Trusted," "Experience is the Best Teacher," and "All that Glitters is not Gold." In contrast, newer-looking *danfos* driven by younger men bear slogans such as "Lagos to Las Vegas," "Fresh Boy," "Obama," "Land Cruiser," "Voda Foam" (a very comfortable local mattress), and "Paradise." This echoes Olatunde Lawuyi's point that taxi slogans express social stratification. He identifies three stages of self/business growth among Yorùbá taxi drivers. Young ones adopt optimistic slogans, those over thirty are more realistic/stoic, and some over forty tend to celebrate or flaunt their success (Lawuyi 1988).

Danfos are also vibrant spaces for petty trading and religious conversion of souls. Inside the *danfo*, itinerant traders and preachers typically secure a seat at the front. As the *danfo* makes its way out of the garage (bus station), the trader gets up, clears his throat, and begins to peddle his goods to passengers who are typically crowded together, as sardines in cans ("full loading," as they say in Lagos). A passenger entering an overloaded *danfo* will ask the other passengers to "abeg dress small," which means please move over a little. Sometimes, *danfo* drivers refuse to start the journey until passengers in a four-seater row have "dressed small" to allow space for the fifth person to squeeze in. When there is a pregnant woman or an elderly person entering the *danfo*, the conductor will shout to his driver *o loyun oponmo o* (she is pregnant and has a child on her back). On hearing this, the driver will often come to a full stop. Otherwise, drivers slow down at bus stops but never quite halt, leaving passengers to judge the best time to jump off or jump on. Apart from saving time, the slow-down-without-halting tactic is meant to reduce the time bribe-eating policemen and touts have to climb aboard and demand cash bribes from the conductor. As passengers jostle to enter barely stopped buses, they leave themselves exposed to pickpockets. In Nairobi, *matatu* operators often insist that incoming passengers *kaa kibiashara* (squeeze in more tightly) or *tafadhali songa mbele* (please move forward and create space for others) in order to maximize profits. On the other hand, passengers exiting the *matatus* are ordered by the operator to *ruka kama sitima* ("jump out with the speed of electricity"), with little regard for safety. The *matatu* logic is simple: "jump in, squeeze, jump out—quickly!" (Mutongi 2017: 93). In other capital cities in Africa, such as Kinshasa and Dar es Salaam, commuters may "hang out of the bus or even sit on the roof" (Kumar & Barrett 2008: xv). There are usually more passengers than seats in Kinshasa, and lines are awfully long. "Without knowing exactly where the minibus-taxi is heading, people try to squeeze in, even before the arriving passengers have succeeded in making their way out" (Trefon 2004: 30). In Kinshasa, the minibus is called *esprit de mort* ("spirit of the dead"), because of its propensity for fatal accidents.

Virtually all of daily life's necessities are for sale inside the *danfo*, from health care products (*agbo jedi*—medicine for piles) to household items (e.g. *ogun ekute*—rat poison). There is often plenty of time for the trader to peddle his goods, since commuter journeys in Lagos are often dotted with *go-slows*—a journey of twenty minutes can take up to two hours! This is not only due to the poor road conditions which compel slow driving but also the omnipresence of money-eating police officers and violent union tax collectors (*agberos*) at almost every bus stop and junction. Despite their relatively affordable prices, these goods are touted as working (like) magic: "touch and go." The sales gimmicks and "sweet mouth" of most traders, combined with their unbeatable comedian wit, ensure that several passengers will exchange their money for goods before their bus stop. As the trader takes his seat, a preacher seizes the moment. "My people, God has sent me to you with good news. This is year is your year of financial breakthrough! I command the curse of poverty in your life to die." The chorus of "Amen" are often emphatic. In a megacity dominated by poverty and scarcity, a doctrine of prosperity sells.

Vehicle Slogans as Mimesis of Everyday Life

> Life in the city today is a process of constant negotiation of the visible and in-visible. Increasingly, what one cannot see, or cannot see clearly, determines one's fortunes. An ability to see the otherwise invisible is a strategy not only for survival but for profit. And one is always subject to a gaze, whether it is the gaze of jealous rivals or lovers, witches, international NGOs or media, or the postcolonial state. (Hoffman 2011: 959; see also Mbembe 1992)

Given the intense visuality of the African cityscape, it is surprising that many studies still overlook the visual materiality of the city, by which I mean, "the ocular as well as the tactile and emotional qualities of the urban" (Clammer 2014: 66). The visuality of the African city can tell us something about the nature of space, how it is socially navigated, and the bodies that occupy it. To understand how informal transport workers in Lagos imagine and traverse dangerous roads, I looked interpretatively at the painted slogans that are prominently displayed on the rickety bodies of their *danfos*. The prevalence of vehicle slogans across African cities makes them a part of the occupational subculture of passenger transport and the intense visual qualities of the city (Date-Bah 1980; Lawuyi 1988; Rizzo 2011). *Danfo* slogans in Lagos tend to reflect the life histories, expectations, fears, and principles guiding the workaday world of transport operators. As part of the artwork and archive of popular urban wisdom, *danfo* slogans generally provide "insights into human beings and social relations that are not readily accommodated within science and scholarship" (Theodore Adorno, cited in Green-Simms 2009: 22). They embody and mirror not only national narratives (Guseh 2008) but also the simultaneous threat, resource, and possibility of city life (Simone 2010: 3). In short, they involve everyday Lagosians in the "operations of the productive imaginations" (Mbembe 2001a: 159). A vehicle slogan is not only that thing that is present to us because we see it but constitutes the very thing of our experience (Deleuze and Guattari 1980: 145). Slogans thus possess powers of enchantment and symbolization which enable the owner "to think of his existence not in a purely politico-instrumental way, but also as an artistic gesture and an aesthetic project open as much to action as to meditation and contemplation" (Mbembe 2002: 629). Slogans are not only abstract and discursive but also embodied and affective entities (Morgan 2008: 228; Stewart 2007).

Vehicle slogans are part of the urban expressive and stylistic forms that "offers the narrative structure—and the mood that underpins it—into which lifeworlds and experiences can be inserted; this structure enables audiences to give a place to experiences, hopes, and anxieties that cannot be easily anchored in a state-driven imagination" (Meyer 2004: 105). Across African cities, from Accra to Lomé and Nairobi, vehicle slogans reflect a wide range of sentiments, to wit: apprehension, pride, personal identities, role models, dreams and dreads, financial anxiety, praise of generous benefactors or patrons, fear of disappointment, joy about success, spiritual (in)security, pious platitudes, and waggish quips (Mutongi 2006). These vehicle slogans "sometimes relate to some personal experience of the driver or the owner of the truck, such as for instance a happy turn in his life, events or happenings on the road; they may derive from the fact of a gift (Good Mother or Good Uncle); or they may relate to a personal idol (like 'Samson'); or they may be an expression of the driver's relationship to God" (Kyei & Schreckenbach 1975: 1). In this light, an interpretative approach to vehicle slogans can tell us something about the oft-ignored precarious and affective dimension of car cultures. Slogans may be imagined as conduits for making our sensibility known to the wider world (Hepworth 1996: 376). Yet, slogans may contradict the very sensibility they project. For example, with all its risks and chaos, I was often struck by the wry slogans on rickety *danfos* in Lagos, such as, "No Cause for Alarm," "Life is Good," or "Just Relax." These slogans mirror the contradictory scene of commuter journeys in which meanings are "simultaneously represented, contested, and invested" (Foucault 1984: 3). Moreover, slogans furnish us with an entextualised language to represent urban experiences in Africa. Barber uses "entextualisation" as a way of describing the close relations between texts, persons, and publics in urban Africa. (2007: 22; see also Quayson 2014: 144). In terms of structure, most *danfo* slogans that I recorded during fieldwork were short and pithy ("Let them Say" or "Mind Your Business") and embedded in traditional aphorisms ("*Ise loo-gun ise*"—work cures poverty), religious texts ("Blood of Jesus"), or local slangs ("Chop Liver"—show courage).

Danfo slogans are integral to Lagos life, imbuing it with meaning, purpose, and humor. A commuter once told me, "I can't even imagine Lagos without its yellow *danfos* and their very funny slogans. Sometimes I am in a bad mood and I see a slogan that makes me burst into laughter and cheer me up instantly. My two favorite slogans of all time are 'No Time to Die' and 'Time is Money Don't Waste it on Bargaining.'" Other commuters in Lagos described how vehicle slogans and mottos shape their decision on which *danfo* to take to work on a daily basis. An analysis of slogans therefore offers real insights into how *danfo* workers develop and communicate a unique competitive edge through their textual choices and artistic preferences. The expressions of individual identity through slogans may be seen as a tactical means of resisting the many (meta)physical forces against which transport operators struggle on a daily basis. For example, whenever the term *aiye* (life or world) is used in slogans, it is usually in recognition of malignant forces or enemies (*ota*) of one's progress (*aiye nreti eleya mi*—"The world awaits my failure").

For this reason, *aiye* is a superior that must be supplicated (*aiye e ma binuwa*—"World have mercy on us") and respected (*aiye mojuba*—"I respect the world") lest our destiny be altered (*aiye e ma pa kadara*—"World, don't alter our fate"). For these transport operators, "everyday life has come to be defined by the paradigm of threat, danger and uncertainty. A social world has gradually taken form where general distrust and suspicion go hand in hand with the need for protection against increasingly invisible enemies" (Mbembe 2006: 310).

Many *danfo* owners believe that forces, named or unknown, are constantly conspiring against their success. Their fears are not surprising if we consider that vehicle ownership represents wealth, which gives rise to envy from one's enemies. One slogan reminds people that "God Condemns Envy," while another notes "Don't Envy Me, Work." During the course of my fieldwork, owners expressed fears of being struck by *juju* (sorcery) orchestrated by enemies envious of their success. As one *danfo* slogan puts it, *ota po* ("enemies galore"). Hence, to protect themselves, owners use their vehicle slogans as a talisman, a defense against *ota aiye* ("enemies of life"), or a constant supplication for "No Loss, No Lack, No Limitation," as one slogan put it. *Danfo* slogans such as "Back to Sender" expresses the owner's prayer that any bad wish toward his business should backfire on those who wish them. Others like "Sea never dry" reflect the owner's wish that his *danfo*, his only source of income, never leaves the road. Implicit in slogans such as "No Weapon Fashioned Against Me," "Do my Prophet No Harm," "Heaven's Gate," "Blood of Jesus," or "Any Attempt!" is a warning of the source of the *danfo* owner's power. In this instance, the message to the enemy is unequivocal: If you want to take me on, then you must take on God himself, who is regarded as superior to *awon aiye* ("the wicked world").

The above specter of danger is neither unique to road life in Lagos nor a recent development. In her study of the social lives of Ghanaian commercial drivers, Eugenia Date-Bah (1980: 525) found that owners of passenger vehicles were often "supplicants at shrines because of a paranoiac fear of failure, perceiving themselves as the objects of envy of those who wanted them to have financial disaster." An even earlier study of everyday security in Ghana by M.J. Field (1960: 134) found that the lorry owner is "acutely conscious of himself as an object of envy, and has much anxiety lest those seeking his humiliation should bring it about by bad magic designed either to wreck his lorry or to bring it financial disaster. Therefore, he seldom neglects to take his lorry to a shrine for protection."

Urban Representational Economy

Since Walter Benjamin's celebrated *Arcades Project*, it has been evident that cityscapes are subjects of the *gaze*. In other words, the city not only constructs itself to be seen, but also speaks to its residents through what it makes them see, that is, through its visual culture (Hooper-Greenhill 2000; Oha 2001; Magee 2007). From the position of urban citizens, the city is "a continuum of sensory experience, in which sounds, sights and smells, caused by all kinds of things, are blended into a composite and constantly changing whole" (Williams 1954: 98). Of particular interest in this chapter are the intensely visual and expressive culture of Lagos, most palpable in the proliferation of a kaleidoscope of slogans, mottos, stickers, and images. It is "impossible to move through [the streets of Lagos] without being bombarded by a multitude of posters, billboards and banners advertising churches, services, prayer meetings, revivals, miracles..." (Marshall 2015: 2).

As a site of popular resistance, urban expressive forms such as slogans embody the "quiet encroachment of the ordinary" (Bayat 2009: 45). This is not dissimilar to Mbembe's (1992: 25) description of how ordinary Africans tend to "guide, deceive, and actually toy with power instead of confronting it directly." Consider, for instance, the creative resistance associated with *danfo* slogans. Although drivers generally stick to the official requirements of yellow and black paint for intracity transport by the Lagos State Government, they are constantly finding ways to elaborate on this system through a process of "subversion by reinterpretation" (Osinulu 2008) or "textual poaching" (de Certeau 1984: 166). Of the midibuses (*molues*) in Lagos, Adedamola Osinulu writes: "One might find that one of the required black strips is thinner and shorter than the other and that the painter has made inscriptions within the black strip... The state has legislated conformity and anonymity, but the [informal transport] painters have carved out an identity for themselves within the interstitial spaces of the legislation" (2008: 50). By cleverly superimposing their own unofficial interpretation on formal city regulations, transport operators have found a way of "avoiding, taunting, attacking, undermining, enduring, hindering and mocking the everyday exercise of power" (Pile 1997: 14). The Lagos State Road Traffic Law 2012 stipulates that "Except as prescribed by the Motor Vehicle Administration Agency and the Lagos State Signage and Advert Agency, the use of marks, slogans, stickers, painting, photos etc. on commercial vehicles is prohibited" (Lagos State Government 2012). By implication, the stylistic *danfo* slogans marks the rise and flourishing of an unstable and shifting public sphere that can resist confinement to the place assigned it by the urban government (Meyer 2004: 92, 95). In this light, then, slogans signal a dominant representational economy[2] and semiotic ideology in Lagos, one that is characterized by a strong emphasis on the assertion of power through a dialectics of presence.

---

[2] A term used by Webb Keane (2002: 95) to "capture the ways in which practices and ideologies put words, things, and actions into complex articulation with one another."

Desconstructing Lagos

Before analyzing the *danfo* slogans, it is important to assess academic narratives of the spatial context from which these texts emerge and of which they speak. Similar to many African cities such as Johannesburg, Lagos typically emerge in the extant literature as extreme or exceptional, hopeless or hopeful. On the one hand, Lagos is represented as a bastion of expanding slums, biting poverty, rising unemployment, and surplus humanity; in short, as a place that falls well short of the expectations of modernity, which is said to have its *fons et origo* in the West (Comaroff and Comaroff 2012; Robinson 2013; Ferguson 1999). This dystopian reading reclaims colonial images of Lagos as a wasteland dotted with crime, disease, and "dirty natives" (Newell 2020). Far from being passé, this tendency towards homogeneous and binarized representations of African cities is alive and well in today's dominant analytical frames that closely aligns Western cities with modernity and non-Western cities with developmentalism. African cities thus enter urban studies as not-quite-cities, as problems to be solved, as cities struggling to acquire "world class" status – Lagos, for instance, brands itself as "Africa's Big Apple" (Agbiboa 2018b), while Johannesburg promotes itself as a "world class African city" (Sihlongonyane 2016). "To the degree that, from a Western perspective, the Global South is embraced by modernity at all," argues Jean and John Comaroff (2012: 114), "then, it is an outside that requires translation, conversation, catch-up." Relaxing this parochial practice of gazing at non-Western cities through Western lenses would require treating Africa as people (Achebe 1999) and "people as infrastructure" (Simone 2004b), that is to say, as products of social networks and inventive responses that animates the city.

Growing calls to move beyond Afropessimist discourses that view the African city as a basket case of multiple pathologies have opened a hopeful door for exceptional readings of the African city, what Matthew Gandy (2005), learning from Lagos, calls the "aesthetic of chaos." This approach underscores the coping mechanisms, improvisations, and inventiveness of city dwellers in Lagos, whose daily and defiant struggle for economic survival and social recognition is interpreted as defying commonsense logic and constricted Western notions of order. This viewpoint is exemplified by Rem Koolhaas, who sees the congestion and chaos of Lagos as revealing a hidden order.

> What is now fascinating is how, with some level of self-organization, there is a strange combination of extreme underdevelopment and development. And what particularly amazes me is how the kinds of infrastructure of modernity in the city trigger off all sorts of unpredictable improvised conditions, so that there is a kind of mutual dependency that I've never seen anywhere else. (Koolhaas 2001)

Far from been a backward situation, says Koolhaas (2007), Lagos is at the "forefront of a globalizing modernity." While this aesthetic, if depoliticized and dehistoricized, framing usefully underscores the emergence of new forms of urbanism in contemporary Africa, it overlooks the dire realities facing its informal workforce, especially extortion, dispossession, and displacement. Koolhaas seems to underestimate the ongoing criticism by Lagosians of their own city, especially the corruption of ruling elites and the *daku daji* (epileptic) of the nature of automobile infrastructure. In his fascination with a Lagos that works, Koolhaas overlooked the fact that this kind of city works mainly for those who are able to extract resources, in particular resources from the violent appropriation of its public spaces. This becomes all the more evident when we consider the ways in which ordinary Lagosians come to think about their own city. Themes of insecurity ("Remember Ur Six Feet"), precarity ("Life is War"), exploitation of labor ("Monkey de work, Baboon de chop"—one person works and another person reaps the fruit of his labor), tactics (the use of *juju* or road charms), abjection (*I dey like deadibody*—"I exist like a deadbody"), and hope ("No condition is Permanent") are used to piece together a phenomenology of Lagos life that is pervasive but rarely codified.

"This is Lagos"

"This is Lagos" is a popular saying and sign directed at naïve newcomers to Nigeria's commercial capital (also known as JJC—short for "Johnny Just Come") to warn them that *Eko lo wa* ("you are in Lagos")—a place where you must *shine your eyes* (be street smart) to get by, or risk falling easy prey to everyday deception. The need to always *shine your eyes* in Lagos reclaims the true essence of African cities which "often appear to act in an incessant state of preparedness. They keep residents in an almost permanent state of changing gears and focus, if not location" (Simone 2001: 18). Anecdotal evidence in Lagos suggests that "This is Lagos" is an expression from an old Nigerian joke:

> It used to be said that whereas other Nigerian cities receive visitors convivially with signs such as "Welcome to Jos" or "Welcome to Kaduna," visitors are not welcome to Lagos. Instead a terse notice informs you ominously, "This is Lagos." To confirm that you are now in a different clime, the familiar but unwelcome stench of refuse wafts in through open windows to assail the nostrils of those coming in by road... This is clearly not a city for the faint hearted. (Ngwodo 2005)

During my fieldwork, I asked a group of *danfo* drivers about what "This is Lagos" meant to them, as this was commonly painted on the sides of *danfos*. Their responses (quoted below) reinforce dominant narratives of the African city as a bastion of the brutal and the abject (Mbembe 2006: 153). The agency that the drivers below attribute to Lagos tells us that cities are not inert or neutral back-drops but "commonly talked about as actors: more anthropos than topos" (Gandhi & Hoek 2012: 3).

"This is Lagos" means that everybody has to be careful. Because in this Lagos brothers don't know brothers, sisters don't know sisters, uncle don't know uncle. Anything you can do and get money you will do it. That's why they say "This is Lagos." No one cares whether you are dying or living. Everybody is angry. Everybody is frustrated. Even though you are from the same mother or father, they don't care. If you like you live, if you like you die, that is all your business.

"This is Lagos" means that this is a land of nobody, a land of no mercy, a land of no trust. It is a jungle where anything can happen. You have to be vigilant all the time. No dulling (be sharp) my brother. This is Lagos is not a language of love but of cheating. At times I start to cry when I look at the situation because we are living in a loveless place.

"Remember Ur Six Feet"

A great many *danfos* ply for hire without licenses and brazenly flout traffic rules. These *danfos* are often overloaded, perilously speeding, and notorious for causing noise and air pollution. Due to their regular involvement in fatal road accidents, some Lagosians now refer to *danfos* as "flying coffins." The slogans painted on the sides of these *danfos* often ironically alert passengers to the strong possibility of death: "Carrying me Home," "See you in Heaven," "Heaven Could be Nearer than Home," "Home Sweet Home," *Orun Ile* ("Heaven, my Home"), "Free at Last," "Safety is of the Lord," "Remember Now Thy Creator," and so on. At a junction in Alimosho local government area, I asked one *danfo* driver about his choice of the slogan: "Remember Ur Six Feet" (Figure 6). He responded, "You see, in this Lagos anything [can] happen. Even the bible warns us to number our days. This is why I like to prepare my passengers for the worst. The road is an evil spirit that is very thirsty for blood." In Lagos, *danfo* accidents are so common that newspaper headlines announce them with a shrugging resignation: "At least nine killed in Agege train accident caused by *Danfo* driver"; "*Danfo* driver crushes *okada* driver to death in Lagos"; "*Danfo* Conductor falls to his death"; "Seven escape death as *Danfo* driving against traffic rams into another on highway." According to one commuter whom I spoke to in Oshodi: "Many of us know most of the *danfos* are death traps but since we can't afford the high taxi fares, we have no choice but to use them. What else can we do?"

The "human factor" is often blamed for the fatality of road accidents in Lagos, with 75 percent of crashes attributed to "human errors" (Akoni 2013). The Lagos State Driver's Institute ran a test on some 65,000 *danfo* drivers in Lagos in 2013

Fig. 6. *Ranti ese mefa*
(Remember ur six feet)
Photo credit: Author

and found that 22 percent, or 14,300, were "partially blind," while 99 percent were "hypertensive." The former is particularly alarming considering that about 95 percent of sensory input to the brain needed for driving comes from vision (Isawunmi et al. 2011). The regular consumption of *paraga* (locally brewed mixture of spirit and herbs) and hard drug (*igbo*), sometimes before 7:30 am each day, is part of the problem of Lagos's accident-prone roads. Drivers have easy access to *paraga* due to the location of *paraga*-selling vendors and drinking parlors inside or within 100 meters of motor parks, reinforcing the blurred boundaries between trade and transit.[3] All sorts of locally-brewed alcoholic beverages are sold here, from *alomo bitters* (herbal-based liquor) to *ogogoro* (a distilled spirit from the raffia palm tree). Rollups of different brands are also available, from marijuana (*igbo*) to cocaine and heroin. "Fuel the bike, fuel the driver," one *okada* driver wryly said (Peel 2010: 93).

Paraga vendors (mostly women and young girls) told me that their most reliable customers were *danfo* drivers. Said one vendor: "*Danfo* drivers and their conductors throng to my kiosk first thing in the morning to drink and smoke before work. Some of them come as early as 5 am and want me to put some *igbo*

---

[3] In an interview I had with one senior vehicle inspection officer in Alimosho, he alluded to Governor Babatunde Fashola's clearing of *paraga* kiosks in Lagos as a factor in the reduction of accidents and misconduct in and around motor parks and bus terminals. In his words, "Many operators think when they take *paraga* they become invincible."

inside their *ogogoro*." "There are no state guidelines on alcohol consumption especially for commercial drivers in this country," lamented a commuter in Lagos. "Police should crack down on the patrons and the bars around motor parks who sell alcohol indiscriminately. We don't have restrictive time for sale of drinks and it's particularly wrong for drivers to be under the influence of alcohol while driving. By this, they are putting the lives of passengers in grave danger" (Vanguard 2013b). The dangers of driving in Lagos are evidenced by road safety slogans such as: "Drive Carefully. Your Life in Your Hands," "Are you Following Jesus this Close" (a sticker on the rear of a *danfo*), "Choose – Home or Mortuary?" "Drive to Stay Alive," "Be easy, Life No Get Part 2." Many drivers, however, justified their drinking activities by claiming that the herbs blended into *paraga* boosts their performance (driving as well as sexual), while providing much-needed relief for work-related hazards such as backache. As one *danfo* driver noted, "I can't do without taking the one that is meant for back pain before embarking on any journey or that day would be miserable for me." Another driver insists, "I drink it for preventive measures because I find it to be very effective and I have observed that it boosts my immune system for my sex life as well" (Vanguard 2013d). This experience is similar to that of *matatu* operators in Nairobi, many of whom drive under the influence since "they habitually chewed *khat* or *miraa*, an addictive tobacco leaf with an amphetamine effect. It was the only way they could stay alert during their overlong shifts" (Mutongi 2017: 94).

"To Live is To Struggle"

For many *danfo* workers, survival is the ultimate concern. One *danfo* driver—whose vehicle had the inscriptions "To Live is To Struggle"—told me, "To survive in Lagos, you need to hustle 24/7 because our stomach has no holidays. Man must *chop* [eat], Man must survive." Another driver with the slogan "Time *na* [is] Money" told me that time in Lagos is a productive but very scarce resource that requires prudent management for maximum achievement of livelihood. In this light, time expenditure equips a framework for making sense of the dynamics of poverty management among the urban poor, especially their efforts to increase profit in a city of innumerable risks and possibilities (Agbiboa 2019). A *danfo* owner with the inscription "No Time to Check Time," who goes by the nickname "No Time," explained why he chose this slogan:

> I like this slogan because it describes my condition of living from hand to mouth. I begin work around 5 am in the morning and come home after midnight. In between, I live and eat on the road, inside *danfo*, during go-slows. Sometimes I don't get to see my little daughter for two or three days because when I am at home she is already sleeping. Such is life. My *oga* [his employer] is constantly on my neck to

deliver N4,000 [USD12] to his house or he will sack me. He warns me that there are people queuing up to take my job. So my brother, *time na money*. I need to speed as fast as possible between Ikotun Egbe and Cele Express if I am to make extra-cash for myself. Sometimes I bribe the *askari* [police] to take one-way so I can reach the motor-park faster and get ahead of the queue to load "next turn." I decided against a conductor to save money and because many are not trustworthy. I beg the passengers to collect the money for me and pass it forward. Life is hard, my brother, but we are managing. There is God.

Given the few gainful jobs in Lagos, and Nigeria in general, informal transport workers often attract plenty of labor in form of jobless youth, including university graduates. Consequently, owners/drivers (some drivers are owners) are usually in a strong position to dictate the conditions of labor on a person-by-person basis. In fact, the common practice is that most drivers operate on a daily franchise basis, earning income only after an agreed fee is paid to the owner, and petrol cost and other expenses (including road bribes) are covered from the driver's daily takings. The situation in Kampala is similar; *matatus* are run based on a system whereby the driver pays UGX 60-80,000 (USD30-40) per day to the owner for use of the *matatu*. Most of what the drivers make in excess of this they use for fuel, maintenance, and the payment of union fees (Goodfellow 2012: 205). In Nairobi's *matatu* industry, "wealthy owners hired drivers whom they ruthlessly fired if they did not collect a minimum of money each day" (Mutongi 2006: 554). In Dar es Salaam, a driver is cited as saying: "they [bus owners] can ask you whatever [daily sales or fees] they want and you have to accept it" (Rizzo 2011: 1186). In most studies, informal vehicle owners are represented as "government officials, businessmen, or professionals for whom involvement in public transport provides a way to supplement income without incurring much, if any, tax liability." These rich owners often exploit their position and influence to protect their interests in the transport industry; for instance, by ensuring preferential route access for their *matatus* (Kumar & Barrett 2008: 8). In Kampala, taxi ownership is a highly secretive space. This is partly because owners of fleets of *matatus* are commonly politically exposed persons with ill-gotten wealth (Goodfellow 2012: 203).

In Lagos, most *danfo* owners are not necessarily wealthy; in fact, many are in a precarious position themselves, a dimension which is often missing in analyses of labor precarity in urban Africa. The level of pressure and precariousness faced by workers is not the same as that faced by owners (the former, of course, experience greater pressure and precarity). However, owners experience a level of precarity about which little research has been conducted. For many owners, some of whom are low-salaried civil servants, the *danfo* business is their main source of income. This is because government jobs are often unrewarding and not as secure as popularly imagined. The *danfo* business in Lagos is fragmented and small-scale, with 80 percent of owners holding just one *danfo*. Owners are typically former *danfo* workers or civil servants who have invested their gratuity in the *danfo* business.

In the face of newly amended traffic rules in Lagos, owners are increasingly responsible for vehicle conditions and, like the *matatu* owners in Kenya, find themselves having to "buy wipers, give their vehicles a coat of paint, have them panel beaten, fix breaks, have the engine overhauled and fix new tires before taking their vehicle for inspection" (Mutongi 2006: 555) to secure a road worthiness certificate. The amended Lagos State Road Traffic Law (2012: A89) clearly stipulates: "Where a person is convicted of an offense relating to the condition of a commercial motor vehicle then in addition to the person convicted, the owner, if such person is not the owner, shall also be guilty of the offence unless he can prove to the satisfaction of the Court that he was not aware and could not by reasonably inquiry have been aware that the vehicle did not comply with the requirements of the law relating to the condition of the vehicle." A similar situation applies in Cape Town's taxi industry, where state rules and tight control over the past three decades or so have increased the financial burdens on *kombi* owners, forcing them to "incur huge debts for 'safe' new vehicles and obligating them to purchase broad insurance coverage, while this wide range of fees and taxes has made taxi owners increasingly vulnerable to the solicitation of bribes by the police" (Bähre 2014: 591).

One owner that I spoke to in Lagos acquired his *danfo* for N750,000 (USD3,770) and spent an additional N150,000 (USD753) on vehicle inspection, registration, and painting of the *danfo* to the state authorized yellow and black colors. The price of *danfos* fluctuate between N500,000 and N850,000, based on their age and condition. Like drivers, all *danfo* owners encounter the problem of how to minimize risk and maximize profit. In Lagos, owners without prior (insider) knowledge of how the *danfo* business works (i.e. they were not former *danfo* drivers) often opt for a "hire purchase" business arrangement. This involves leasing your *danfo* to a trusted driver with the agreement that he would use the *danfo* for passenger and goods haulage and pay an agreed daily sum of money (usually N4000, or USD20) until he covers the cost stipulated in the agreement (usually within six but no later than twelve months). Upon successful completion of payment, the driver assumes ownership of the *danfo*. Failure to meet the target amount at the end of the agreement means that the driver forfeits ownership of the hire purchased *danfo*. This explains why *danfos* are typically overloaded and dangerously speeding, and why *danfo* drivers often suffer from hypertension (PM News 2015). According to one report, a significant number of *danfo* drivers have died from depression due to debt burden linked to their inability to pay back the money borrowed to hire purchase their vehicles in instalments (Lawal 2015).

"Because of Money, No Truth"

The role of money as a major catalyst for the transformation of social life and relations is indexed in the field of anthropology of money (Simmel 1978). Here, money is seen as driving a wedge between person and things, and spoiling the relationships between producers and their produce (Parry & Bloch 1989: 5). Nowhere is this truer than in the highly monetized and precarious relationship between the *danfo* owner and his driver(s), as well as between the driver and his conductor. A vehicle in reasonable condition and with a reliable driver has the potential to yield a decent income (Kumar & Barrett 2008: xii). The key word here, however, is *reliable*. Many *danfo* owners complained about the scarcity of reliable drivers in Lagos. From the vantage point of these owners, drivers will always be inclined to filch from the owner's share in order to supplement their wages. Thus, one owner had the *danfo* inscription: "Because of Money, No Truth." This slogan reflects the owner's lived experience of being forced on many occasions to dismiss his driver who "played" him *wayo* ("419"), that is, the driver plotted with the owner's mechanic to "eat" his money. Another "419" tactic less visible but no less present in Lagos is the employment of "second" or "third" drivers:

> Needless to say, drivers had their own ways of "taking advantage of" their employers. This often occurred through arrangements made illicitly and unbeknownst to the taxi owners. For example, taxi drivers routinely recruit fellow taxi drivers, mainly friends from the neighborhood, to take over the operation of the car—effectively inserting themselves as intermediary bosses. These "second" or in some cases "third drivers" would be expected to provide a larger "master money" [daily payment to the owner] rate. This was sometimes achieved by creating an additional shift in the day, undertaken by a different driver. Sometimes drivers would take several cars in a single day, and find other drivers to drive them simultaneously. The result was that drivers had the potential to make more money than the taxi owners themselves, as well as to effectively become "bosses" ("owners" of the means of production), even if they were in reality gatekeepers who did not legally own the taxis they were "managing." (Lipton 2017: 105–6)

The above imposes fluidity on rigid, Marxian-style divisions between workers and owners, supply and demand. Owners in Lagos expressed a preference for a matured driver who is married (preferably with children) to run their *danfo* business. The rationale is simple: married drivers are presumed to have more *bukata* (responsibilities) and, therefore, likely to take the *danfo* business, their job, more seriously than most youth, who are seen as carefree in their approach to life. As one owner in Alimosho told me:

> I personally prefer a family man with children because I know he will try to be responsible to his family. If he defaults, I don't ask questions, I just collect the *danfo* and show him the door. No *abeg* [please] sir in this matter. I hate stories because I have a family to feed. I have my own mechanic. If my driver repairs the car, it is on his own account, unless I gave him the order to go ahead.

Absent a binding "legal contract" between owner and driver, owners turn to informal social networks to vouch for the background and character of drivers prior to hiring them. Some owners told me they will only consider a driver who presents a character reference from the pastor/imam of his church/mosque or was highly recommended by a trusted friend. Other owners reported that they prefer members of their own family or ethnic group to run their business. For these owners, "blood is thicker than water." But this is not always the case. One owner in Oshodi described how his nephew, to whom he entrusted his *danfo* business, stole all his money and "vanished into thin air" along with his *danfo*. "Till today, I haven't heard anything from him. I don't know whether he is alive or dead. The thing is like magic. My own nephew whom I thought will be honest with me. It shook me to be frank with you." This experience reinforces the argument that "[a] sense of vulnerability applies even to intimate social relations despite the security these relations appear to offer" (Bledsoe 2002: 21). Other owners shared personal stories of drivers who had absconded with their *danfos* and resettled in the southeast or sold the *danfo* and changed their contact address. Said one former *danfo* owner in Oshodi:

> Running a *danfo* business is like digging your early grave. The drivers always have one problem. Yesterday police, tomorrow gear problem, next tomorrow radiator or silencer or tout *wahala* [trouble]. Everyday same story. One excuse after another. I bought a *danfo* and within 3 months I was left penniless! The problem is that my driver was bringing in about N4000 every day. But he was arrested twice in two weeks and given ticket of N27,000. Each time he brought the ticket to me to settle [bribe] the authorities.

A commuter in Lagos narrated the distresses her husband endured when he tried his luck as a *danfo* owner following his retirement from civil service:

> My husband ran this business for a while. So I'm talking from experience. We nearly died of hypertension I tell you. Every week I had high BP [Blood Pressure]. The driver would work full day, after which he would lie that he was with mechanic the whole day. He would have pre-arranged with a mechanic who will testify on his behalf and share your money. Let me tell you, drivers would take even the money you think you made. Our driver would collude with the mechanic to remove a spare part that is working and replace it with *daku daji* [epileptic spare parts]. When he tells you about the spare part you have to buy, he will inflate the cost and try to eat your money. I got so vexed that one day I insisted on following him around. That day, the useless driver kept telling the *agberos* that I was the *danfo* owner, which made them inflate the illegal dues.

The above statement resonates with Tim Gibb's research into the taxi-industry in South Africa. Gibbs notes that during his interviews with migrant factory workers in Johannesburg's shack settlements, he was frequently "struck by the number of men who had dabbled unsuccessfully in the taxi [owning] business and could tell bitter stories of failure" (2014: 437). But one may ask: If the *danfo* business is so unprofitable, how do we explain the fact that nearly 100,000 *danfos* still provide public transport in Lagos? The answer to this partly lies in the fact that many *danfo* owners have stopped searching for reliable drivers and, instead, assumed the role of driver-owners. For these driver-owners, driving the *danfo* yourself is the best way to overcome the trust factor. As one owner in Alimosho told me: "There is money in this business but the problem is that you can never find an honest driver who would not suck you dry. The best thing you can do is to drive it yourself." This is in marked contrast to other African cities like Dar es Salaam, where less than ten percent of owners are said to operate their own bus (Rizzo 2017: 66).

So much for the precarious relationship between *danfo* owners and drivers. What about the relationship between drivers and their conductors? If, for the owners, the goal is to minimize risks and maximize profits in their pursuit of upward mobility, for drivers and especially conductors, precarity refers to tactics deployed in the attempt to survive at the margins of society. This distinction is important, since no matter the uncertainties experienced by *danfo* owners in Lagos, they are still owners. That is to say, in the popular imagination car ownership still epitomizes wealth and prestige—the owner remains a "privileged citizen" (Lawuyi 1988). The driver is generally responsible for hiring and paying his conductor from the day's takings. The conductor occupies a subordinate role as an apprentice to the driver and therefore has a lesser say in how much he gets each day. The conductor's dream is to become a *danfo* driver someday. In Lagos, conductors have a bad reputation for shortchanging their drivers by pilfering from the day's takings and from bus fares while the driver is busy driving. One way in which conductors cash in on bus fares is through delay tactics, that is, hanging on to the passenger's change for as long as possible in the hope that (s)he will forget to ask for it. For any *danfo* user in Lagos, "Conductor, *shenji mi da*? ("conductor, where is my change?") is a familiar expression. To which the conductor retorts: *Eni suru* (exercise patience), an ironic response since conductors are the very epitome of impatience, especially in money matters. As is sometimes the case, passengers end up forgetting their change in the mad rush to exit the bus and catch another one. *Ere te mi ni yen* ("That is my own gain"), said one mischievious *danfo* conductor in Oshodi.

Just as owners find it challenging to find a reliable driver, a major challenge for drivers is to find a reliable conductor. The Yorùbá concept of work is captured by the maxim "Whoever works at the altar must eat at the altar" (Lawuyi 1988). In this light, *danfo* drivers expect conductors to appropriate some of the fare. At the same time, stealing must be done in moderation. As one *danfo* driver/owner in Oshodi told me: "All conductors will eat some of the bus fares. You cannot really prevent that from happening since they hold the money and you cannot keep tab of all the passengers that enter or exit the bus while you have your eyes on the road. You're lucky if you find a conductor that at least eats you with love." Increasingly, *danfo* drivers are choosing to run their business alone, with passengers filling in the gaps. For example, drivers often invite passengers to help them collect the money row-by-row during the journey. The total money is then passed on to him. This is where the multi-tasking skills of the driver is put to the test. While weaving from slow to fast and fast to faster lanes, and avoiding potholes and piles of debris that have started competing with motorists for rights of way, the driver counts the money to make sure that it is complete, responds to demands for change by passengers in undue haste, and settles the violent touts shouting *owo da* (where is your money?) Amid all these distractions, the driver still finds time to take an incoming call and spot passengers heading in his direction, even from far off in the streets. Multitasking while driving is a dangerous practice that has resulted in several fatal accidents. To avoid this, drivers now collect their fares and distribute change before they embark on the journey.

"Police is Your Friend"

A *danfo* with the slogan "birds of the same feather" told me about how touts (*agberos*) and traffic police officers routinely combine to create a predatory economy at checkpoints and junctions. Another *danfo* slogan in Lagos conveys the same meaning in a more ironic manner: "Police is Your Friend" (Figure 7).

Many *danfo* slogans in Lagos speak to the relentless corruption and deceptions on the road. One *danfo* slogan reads "*Jeun [Eat], Kin Jeun [I eat]*," which suggests that the benefits of corruption should be distributed rather than hoarded since, as another slogan implies, "eating together makes the exercise enjoyable". Yet another vehicle slogan says, "Shine Your Eyes," which is a warning to always be vigilant to swindlers ("419ers"), who are never far away in Lagos. Explaining his choice of the slogan "Life is War," Wahid, a *danfo* driver in Alimosho, said: "This business is what I use to feed my family. I don't have any other source of money. I have four children, and three are in school. I thank God for my life." For Wahid, daily demand for bribes by *agberos*, in collusion with the police, presents the greatest threat to his survival:

> NURTW now put their touts at every bus stop in the city. Once you make a stop, you pay them just to pick a passenger or two from the bus station. Some of them say they are collecting booking fee (*owo booking*) others say it is for security (*owo security*), some say they are collecting afternoon cash (*owo osan*), when it is night, some say they are collecting night money (*owo ale*). It's something that is very irritating. My wife and children advise me that if *agberos* or police ask me for

Fig. 7. Police is your friend
Photo credit: Author

money, I should give it to them without story, so that they will not hurt me. I believe that leaving my home in good health and coming back home in good health, there is no greater happiness than that.

"No Pain, No Gain"

Despite their precarious existence, many operators believe that hard work and hustle is key to survival and altering their bad fortunes. As one *danfo* driver said, "*Eko o gba gbere* ("Lagos holds nothing for lazy individuals"). Steeped in Yorùbá culture, the view of hard work as the antidote for success emerged in various *danfo* slogans: "No Pain, No Gain" (Figure 8), "Work and Pray," "2day's Struggles, 2morrow's Success." Other *danfo* slogans draw upon the traditional Yorùbá worldview that links laziness or idleness to theft or the propensity to steal: *Alapa ma sise ole ni da* ("The one with hands yet refuses to work will turn a thief"), *Eni o sise a ma jale* ("The one who refuses to work will steal"), *Ole o raye wa* ("The thief has no place in this life"), *Ole sun o daso iya bora* ("The thief sleeps, cloaks himself in suffering"), *Ole darun* ("Laziness is a disease"), *Mura si ise ore mi, ise la fi deni giga* ("Focus on work my friend, work helps you to become a big man"), *Eni tio bi ole koromo bi rara* ("The one who gives birth to a thief has no child"), *Ewo aiye ole, o ma se o* ("Look at the life of a thief. O what a pity"). Slogans such as *Ise loogun ise* ("Work is the cure for

Fig. 8. No pain no gain
Photo credit: Author

poverty") point to the belief that each person is spiritually bestowed with the capacity for success, but he has to make that success by himself. All this supports the point that "although the poor are powerless, nevertheless they do not sit around waiting for their fate to determine their lives. Rather they are active in their own way to ensure their survival" (Bayat 2000: 539). For many operators, *agberos* are the ultimate example of laziness, of thieves who reap where they have not sown. The foregoing gives a nod to a recent ethnographic study of an informal settlement in South Africa, which shows how "surplus populations" often connect labor and income together within "a bidirectional logic that posits both that income must be deserved through work, and that the hard-working deserve income" (Dawson & Fouksman 2020: 230). Within this logic of practice, there is "No Food 4 Lazy Man" and there is "No Success without Struggle," to string two *danfo* slogans in Lagos together.

"Monkey De Work, Baboon De Chop"

There is an ever-growing presence of semi-formal actors on the interface between public service and citizens in all aspects of public administration in Africa (Bierschenk 2008: 130). In Oshodi and Alimosho, these oft-violent intermediaries can be seen at various junctions, a lucrative spot where miscreants, marauders, beggars, fraudsters, and union touts converge to exploit moneymaking opportunities (Ismail 2009, 2013). Junctions are typically located at *orita*—intersections of three roads. In the mythologies of Yorùbá cultures, *orita* is a sacred place where people offer sacrifices (*ebo*) to two Yorùbá *orishas* (gods): *ogun* and *eshu*. The former is much feared for his propensity to induce violence and death at the slightest provocation, while the latter is the trickster and messenger of the gods whose shrines are found at the entrances of compounds (*esuona*), crossroads (*eshuorita*), and markets (*eshuoja*) across Lagos. In his seminal work *The Signifying Monkey*, Henry Louis Gates, Jr. presents a partial list of *eshu's* qualities, including:

> individuality, satire, irony, magic, indeterminacy, open-endedness, ambiguity, sexuality, chance,… disruption and reconciliation, betrayal and loyalty, closure and disclosure… all of these characteristics… taken together, only begin to present an idea of the complexity of this classic figure of mediation and of the unity of opposed forces. (1988: 6)

Orita activities are never seen as good ventures deserving of *omoluabi*—a hardworking person of good character. Unlike drivers who are seen as involved in "Honest Labor," as one *danfo* slogan puts it, owners of the junction, such as touts, are seen as *omo orita* (children of the junction) who take on the very identity of *eshu* and see moneymaking opportunities at *orita* as part of the repertoires of *ebo* on offer. The illegal taxes collected by touts are seen as *owo eru* ("money that enslaves") that brings death (*owo ree! iku ree!* "behold Money! behold Death!"). Thus, in Lagos, junctions represent a "micro-economic self-organizing system that embodies the spirit of *eshu*" (Weate & Bakare-Yusuf 2003).

During my fieldwork, I watched from a newspaper stand as touts were hired by traffic police inspectors and positioned each day at junctions (*oritas*) to extort illegal *owo askari* ("police money") from transport operators (Figure 9). At the junction, the police officer wields a gun, while the uniformed and un-uniformed tout holds a horse whip (*koboko*) and a felt marker to mark the vehicles that have "settled" (bribed) them. At the junction, "functional compromises are negotiated and renegotiated" (Simone 2005: 5) between touts, officers, and drivers, as all three parties find "zones of interactions and cooperation in endless search for opportunity" (Pieterse 2011: 19). At the close of day, the motor park tout receives a "fee commission" from the traffic inspector that hired him. The role of union touts as *aja olopa* ("police dogs") emerged during an interview with a driver whose *danfo* displayed the slogan: "Monkey de work Baboon de Chop."

> I originally inherited the slogan "Cool Boy" from the previous owner. After working in this business for one year, I took the *danfo* to the painters and decided to change it to *Monkey de work, Baboon de Chop*. Why? Because there is no

Fig. 9. A traffic police officer and "her tout" collecting "police fees" (*owo olopa*) from a tricycle-taxi (*keke napep*) driver in a junction in Alimosho local government area.
Photo credit: Author

"Cool Boy" in this business. I chose this slogan because it really captures the meagre profits that I make after a hard day's work due to these *agberos*. I work tirelessly each day, while the baboons [touts & police] stand in the roundabout and just *chop* [eat] my sweat. The police officer cannot call them to order because they are their dogs. Many policemen hire touts to collect money from us. So, you see different touts collecting money for different police. Sometimes even MOPOL (mobile police) will fight themselves over junctions where they can put their touts. Junctions bring more income because every vehicle must pass through it; you can't avoid it.

The organizing logic that underpins the tout-police mutuality challenges the common tendency in the existent urban literature to depict city governance regimes as mutually exclusive.[4] Thus, it complicates the conventional formal/informal divide that has long characterized urban studies and challenges us to look beyond the idea of the state to "recognize multiple systems of governance, multiple forms of political community, and the less formal, everyday interactions and enactments through which governance and political belonging take shape"

---

[4] A prime example is AbdouMaliq Simone's (2010: 4) account of how two governance regimes (formal and informal) in Lagos can alternate in the course of a single day. Simone argues that Ojuelegba, a busy area in Lagos, undergoes a nightly alteration in which "the assemblage of discrepant activities seems to pile up on each other," only to give way to a regime of formal governance during the day. Far from this, my own study of the tout-police alliance in Lagos suggests that multiple urban governance regimes often co-exist and work together to govern urban space and economies (cf. Mbembe & Nuttall 2008: 8). For a more complex treatment of Ojuelegba, see Weate & Bakare-Yusuf 2003.

(Jaffe 2018: 1099). If anything, the tout-police cooperation suggests that collusions and collisions between state and non-state actors play a fundamental role in the politics of order and disorder in contemporary African cities. Given their close ties with law enforcement agents, NURTW touts are emboldened to conduct their predatory activities without fear of arrest from members of the police. The alliance between touts and mobile police shows how illegal and violent activities are developed in close connection with formal procedures and actors (Nuijten 2003: 3; Ismail 2010: 37). According to James Tyner (2012: vii), "violence can become so pervasive, so prevalent, that we don't always 'see' violence." This is true of Lagos, where the driver or conductor's refusal to pay bribes can result in severe physical harm, even violent death. A passenger recalled his harrowing experience of tout violence on a conductor and the "I don't care" attitude of a nearby police officer:

> The other day, a set of NURTW touts beat one conductor to death at Cele bus stop. They shoved him down from the *danfo* in motion and descended on him with sticks and heavy blows to his face and head. Blood was pouring from his head, his mouth, everywhere. All because he refused to pay N200 (USD1). Can you imagine that? The traffic inspector simply watched from a distance and did nothing. But I'm not surprised. The touts are their boys; they collect bribes on their behalf. It's so painful to see.

"One Chance"

The inscription of "One Chance" on a *danfo* offers a window onto a dangerous tactic that *danfo* operators in Lagos often deploy to evade police and touts inside the motor parks and bus stops and make the most of their hard day's labor. One chance *danfos* typically load passengers along major routes rather than at designated bus stations. These *danfos* are called "one chance" because they usually have one or two spaces left, which is ideal for Lagosians who are generally in haste. One chance was initially a catchword deployed by *danfo* conductors to inform prospective passengers travelling toward their direction that there is only one seat left. For instance, a conductor could say "Ikotun one chance!" However, the catchphrase has created an opportunity for robbers and money-ritualists in Lagos to execute their nefarious activities in the city. These dark forces have usurped the "one chance" tactic to rob, sexually assault, and kill many Lagosians, thus making the term one of the most feared expressions in daily life. Operating under the façade of *danfo* drivers, one chance robbers tend to position their own members inside their fake *danfo*, acting as *bona fide* passengers. This tactic makes their victims—the true passengers—unsuspicious. "One chancers" generally reserve two or three seats for unwary passengers, whom they intend to rob, rape, and/or kill for money ritual purposes. They drive their victims to a remote part of Lagos, strip them of their valuables (such as money, handsets, jewelries) at gun point, and throw them out of the *danfo* while it is still in motion, causing them to sustain severe injuries in addition to losing their personal belongings.

Media reporting in Lagos suggests that "one chance" has become a constant feature of a Lagosian's life. One report notes that nearly two out of ten Lagosians have been victims of "one chance" at one time or the other. In a megacity of roughly 22 million residents, the report adds, this amounts to five million victims (Nigerian Tribune 2018). Another report claims that one of every three Lagosians has had a one chance encounter (Medium 2019). So common is "one chance" that it is often the subject of movies and songs in Lagos. During the course of my fieldwork, I heard stories about the ordeals of "one chance" victims. One story has stayed with me, that of a young man who was robbed and had a four-inch nail driven into his skull because he refused to hand over his wedding ring. Stories also abound of women raped by "one-chance" gangs before being dumped along the way. "One-chance" gangs tend to operate at times of the day when police presence is thin on the ground, particularly during the early hours of the morning when passengers are looking to catch the cheapest buses, before nightfall when people are in haste to beat traffic, and in the late night. At the start of my fieldwork in 2014, the Lagos State Special Anti-Robbery Squad arrested a gang of "one-chance" robbers operating under the guise of *danfo* drivers. One member of the gang described the gang's modus operandi:

> We don't go out until 9 pm. I was a *danfo* driver and I was plying the Oshodi and Mushin routes. I have been in the once-chance robbery for about 10 years, and we were able to escape police arrest on several occasions. When we go out for an operation, I usually drive while another gang member will stand at the door. Some of our guys will also be at some bus stops. When our bus is full we then drive to an isolated point, and rob all of them. We collect money, jewellery, gold, phones, and other valuables. We drop them at areas that we know will be hard for them to get another bus, thereby preventing them from calling the police. We made an average of N50,000 [USD128] from each outing. Although we were rough, we never molested any woman during operation. We did not have guns, but we were many and we had objects like car jack to deal with any stubborn passenger. The jack actually looks like a gun, and then in the dark, no passenger wants to risk finding out if the gun is real or not. (Babajide 2014)

One commuter in Alimosho told me, "At a point, one chance robbery died down in the state, but unfortunately, the menace is very much on the rise again." To address the resurgence of "one chance," the Lagos State Government established a new Road Traffic Law in 2012, with a section that required all commercial transport operators to wear registered uniforms and badges for proper identification, as well as to ply only the routes boldly written on their buses. Section 44 of the Road Traffic Law also bars commuter bus drivers from driving for more than eight hours at a stretch. The hope, according to one state official, is that these changes will result in better surveillance and stem the problem of "one chance" in passenger transport. According to the former Lagos State Commissioner for Transportation Kayode Opeifa, "With these moves, we want to curtail kidnapping, robberies and other forms of crimes perpetrated by the continuous usage of unregistered vehicles for commercial purposes. We are out to tackle the issue of 'one chance' headlong" (Ibekwe 2013).

"Trust No Body"

The presence of "one chancers" and violent extortionists, combined with bad roads, compels drivers in Lagos to turn to some form of spiritual protection against an urban life where "Anything Can Happen," as one *danfo* slogan puts it. For many transport operators in Lagos, roads symbolize their lifeblood, but they are also fraught with malicious forces that crave blood, human blood. This underscores the contradictory nature of roads in Africa as objects of fear and desire (Masquelier 2002: 831). The road is a liminal space that embodies the contradictions of modernity, particularly "its inescapable enticements, its self-consuming passions, its discriminatory tactics, its devastating social costs" (Comaroff & Comaroff 1993: xxix). In Lagos, *danfo* drivers tend to embrace *juju* (charms) as a defense against accidents and bad luck, as well as to attract passengers, and reduce contact with touts and police on the way. The *jujus*, which are indicative of the power that inheres in social relations, usually come in various forms: the shape of a lock, a dry head of a rat tied to a cowrie, or a dry animal skin twisted into a rope and tied around the arm. These symbols—typically hidden under the dashboard, tied to the rear-view mirror, or placed under the *danfo* driver's seat—display "a form of empowerment which expresses 'the fact of powerlessness'" (Gelder & Thornton 1997: 375). One study of Yorùbá taxi drivers found that 80 percent of Muslims and 60 percent of Christians had protective charms in their vehicles (Lawuyi 1988: 4). The *juju* in the *danfos* mainly serves to remind drivers of their power to escape from any danger on the road. At the same time, the *juju* brings wealth by attracting passengers to the *danfo*.

During my fieldwork, I interviewed a group of *danfo* drivers in Oshodi who related to me their habitual offering of weekly food sacrifices to *eshuona* (the Yorùbá god of the road) before work commences. These sacrifices, they say, are intended to propitiate *eshuona* so as to fortify themselves against his malevolent tricks and to implore him to *fi wa le* ("leave us alone"). These sacrifices tell us that "local reality itself has become impossible without a 'knowledge of the hidden' and of the spiritual worlds beyond the physical reality of everyday life" (De Boeck, Cassiman & Van Wolputte 2009: 36). These repetitive placations of *eshuona* help drivers to avert accidents in the nick of time. In this light, repetition indicates "resistance through rituals" (Hall & Jefferson 1993) as well as "symbolic opposition to a dominant order" (Highmore 2002: 12). As Rita Felski notes, "repetition is one of the ways in which we organise the world, make sense of our environment and stave off the threat of chaos" (2000: 21).

I was often struck by the *danfo* owner's "pervasive sense of insecurity in the face of unseen powers and invisible forces capable of causing real, palpable, material, physical effects in the here and now" (Ashforth 1998: 62). The owners that I spoke to in Oshodi and Alimosho often fell prey to fears that forces, both known and especially unknown, are working against their success when it may very well be "[their] powerlessness and estrangement that produces this erosion of self-confidence" (Jackson 2008: 71). The sense of insecurity among transport workers in Lagos is best exemplified by their abiding awareness of the *ota*, that is, "persons or entities that have malignant feelings towards the individual" (Osinulu 2008: 52). The concept of *ota* chimes with occult economies, which is underpinned by the assumption that power operates in two distinct but connected realms, one visible, the other invisible (Sanders & West 2003: 6–7). The fear of *ota*, especially among owners, evokes hypervigilance and apprehension, as embodied by the *danfo* slogan "Trust No Body."

"No More Person"

Available studies show that the poor often build relationships with big men who can advocate for them and boost their navigational capacity (Utas 2005a: 405). In this perspective, patrimonialism is seen as fulfilling "the need for mechanisms of 'social insurance' in the risky and uncertain environment of low-income societies" (van de Walle 2001: 118). From Lagos to Accra and Freetown, urban big men are vital to personal security, including finding employment (Paller 2014: 127). In patronage politics, we learn that "things work more by influence than by bureaucratic fiat. People do not seek a dangerous state of independence. Rather they seek ever-more powerful mediators who can use personal influence to get them jobs and scholarships, and protect them from heavy-handed government bureaucrats or jealous neighbors who might trump up destructive court cases against them. In fact, the more desperately individuals need something, the more they need patrons with contacts and resources, and the more they grow vulnerable to demands of recompense" (Bledsoe 1990: 75). For their part, big men amass political power by accumulating followers in urban life—urban big men are friends, entrepreneurs, parents, and preachers (Paller 2014: 123–4; cf. Sahlins 1963).

In Lagos, *danfo* drivers often align themselves with big men who provide them with physical and/or material security, often in exchange for their loyalty translated into votes during elections. In this way, patron-client relations serve to bridge "functional gaps" in the social fabric and protect individuals against insecurity (Wolf 1977: 175–6). In order to win elections and maintain the grip on power, big men are increasingly under pressure to distribute largesse to their lowly followers, which in turn raises the stakes for control over state resources. Such logic of solidarity networks sheds light onto the forms of social capital of commercial drivers in the building of social networks that will protect them in times of trouble (*wahala*). Sasha Newell, writing about street crime, consumption, and citizenship in Abidjan, calls this "the productivity of social networks" (2012: 85).

While some big men may assist transport workers when they run into trouble, others may not. Patrons who have the resources to help and do so are fondly remembered in *danfo* slogans such as "Givers Never Lack," *Ola oga mi l'eko* ("The benevolence of my Big Man in Lagos"), *Oga nla fans* ("Big Man fans"), *Oga Oga* ("Big Man, Big Man"), *Oga mi* ("My Big Man"), *Oga tie da* ("Where is your Big Man"), *Ere oga mi* ("The benefits of my Big Man"), and *Kiku ma pa alanu mi* ("May death not befall my helper"). Vehicle slogans such as *Ola Iya* ("mother's benevolence") or *Ola Egbon* ("brother's benevolence") express gratitude to one's relative who provided financial support in acquiring the *danfo*. In a Lagos context where auto loans from banks or even loan sharks are scarce ("No Credit, Come Tomorrow," as one *danfo* slogan put it), for many drivers, family members become the most promising avenues for obtaining start-up capital. Patrons (including relatives) who have the means to help but fail to do so are labeled *Awon Aiye* (the wicked world), confirming the beneficial as well as deleterious possibilities that flow from social/familial relationships. When patrons disappoint, it is time for *danfo* workers to ponder on the frailty of human behavior (*iwa eda*) and the cruelty of Lagos life (*aiye ika*). This mood is often exemplified by *danfo* slogans such as: "Such is Life," "Helpers are Scarce," "If Men were God," *eyi a lo* ("This will pass"), "Delay is not Denial," "No More Person" (Figure 10), and "No One Knows Tomorrow." These slogans undercore the relatively low level of trust that marks the social structure of clientelistic societies (Eisenstadt & Roniger 1984: 211). The slogan "No More Person" mourns the lack of the normative notions of personhood emerging from traditional African cultures and couched in terms of a dominant communitarian ethic (Oyowe 2015).

To reduce or manage the chances of disappointment, *danfo* workers tend to keep many big men simultaneously. Yet, the ultimate lesson for these transport workers is that *igbekele omo araye, asan ni* ("reliance on people of the world leads to disappointment") because *olowo kin se olorun* ("the rich man is not God"), to string two slogans together. Thus, transport workers are compelled to turn to God—*Oga pata pata* (the "Biggest Man")—to negotiate everyday setbacks. As one *danfo* slogan

Fig. 10. No more person
Photo credit: Author

puts it: "Jesus Na Biggy Man" [Jesus is a Big Man]. "In an uncertain and competitive world where fortunes are seen to be made and lost and one's own fortune often appears to be beyond one's control, God, fate and luck are common (and not unwarranted) categories for the explanation of success or lack of it" (Williams 1980: 114).

"Man No Die, Man No Rotten"

To my social question about how they are doing, *danfo* drivers typically responded: *I dey like deadi body* (literally, "I exist like a dead body/corpse"). According to Julia Kristeva (1982: 3), the corpse is "the most sickening of all wastes, is a border that has encroached upon everything…" In like vein, drivers see themselves as sickening wastes waiting for decomposition. Although the waiting may lead to ennui, it is not entirely unproductive. The very act of waiting denotes an "active state of the mind" (Cooper & Pratten 2015: 11) which is always on the watch for opportunities that must be "seized on the wings" (de Certeau 1984: 37). In this light, then, transport operators are best studied as people who are "conscious actors and participants in their own lives, struggling to some extent to stay in control, and therefore continuously busy to seize and capture the moment and the opportunity to reinvent and re-imagine their lives in different ways" (De Boeck, Cassiman, &

Van Wolputte 2009: 38). One *danfo* slogan puts it well: *Man No Die, Man No Rotten*. On the one hand, this *danfo* slogan implies that as long as there is life, one's hope is always alive. This cautious optimism inspires operators to "wait out the crisis" and experience the "heroism of the stuck" (Hage 2009). One is reminded here of Joshua Grace's (2013) description of mobile operators in Tanzania as "heroes of the road." On the other hand, *Man No Die, Man No Rotten* reclaims the view of operators as statusless men, whose daily struggle against anonymity has become a precondition of their urban life (Le Pape 1997: 47). Anonymity, according to Marc Le Pape, "menaces the weak" and "permits anybody to accuse you of doing anything, or of doing anything to you" (1997: 47). *Man No Die* is neatly précised in Mbembe's articulation of the common man eking out a living on the famished roads of Africa:

> Vulgarly carved from day to day by the harshness of the times, brutalized by the police, the search for subsistence, the fear of having nothing and the obsessive dread of famine… *Life itself is nothing but a permanent struggle.* That is the reason why, here, the ordinary man defines himself as a "fighter." *To the question: "what is your occupation?" he will reply: "I get by."* (Mbembe 1997: 157; my emphasis)

Imaginations of city life as a permanent struggle are commonplace in Nigeria and, broadly, Africa. In southeast Nigeria, Annang people often appropriate the idea of "the rugged life" (Pratten 2006) when describing their lived experience—in Annang language, the life of *ntime ntime* ("trouble") and of anything can happen (*akeme itipe*). In Dar es Salaam, Rizzo (2011) found that *daladala* minibus-taxi operators were preoccupied with the daily struggle for economic survival. He points to the example of *daladalas* with eye-catching inscriptions such as *kazi mbaya; ukiwanayo!* ("Bad job; if you have one"), "Money Torture," *maisha ni kuhangaika* ("Life is Suffering"), *kula tutakula lakini tutachelewa* ("We'll eat, but we'll eat late"), and "So Many Tears."

"Lagos Will Not Spoil" (*Eko o ni baje o*)

This chapter has explored the ways in which *danfo* slogans shape, and are shaped by, the mobile subject's lived experience of, and struggle for survival in, Lagos. The slogans, and the stories behind them, account for the manifold ways in which informal transport workers inhabit the world and give expression to it. They also point to spaces of hope that lie beyond the shadows of the state. The *danfo* slogans provide us with a unique entry point into not only the precarious labor of informal transport workers but also their instrumentalities of survival. During my fieldwork in Lagos, I was often struck by the capacity to aspire of poor transport workers, which enabled them to project themselves into the future, form aspirations, and commit themselves to their realization. Informal transport workers construed the realization of the good life as a genuine possibility beyond their chronic state of abjection. Several operators that I spoke to aspired toward owning a *danfo* or fleets of *danfos* (so that they could become their own boss), acquiring a university degree, wining the American Visa Lottery, becoming *eni olokiki* (a famous person), *olowo* (a rich person), *eniyan giga* (a high person), or *eniyan pataki* (an important person). These aspirations are epitomized by the official slogan of Lagos itself, *Eko o ni baje o* ("Lagos will not spoil").

There is a temptation to dismiss the above hopes and aspirations as mere utopianism, in other words, to smother the *danfo* driver's hopes analytically with our own "wet-blanket 'realism'" (Clifford 2009: 241). Yet, these aspirations are not mere fantasies woven from sleep but rather a technique for navigating the corruption and dangers of the present in hope of a better tomorrow. "Dreams," according to Kenelm Burridge, "tend to pull a future into current sensible reality; they give definity to hope, adding faith, thereby putting the dreamer in touch with a verity shortly to be manifest" (1995: 180). The positive expectancy of operators in the face of extortion, violence, and spiritual insecurities, is exemplified by future-oriented slogans such as: "One Day," "Keep Keeping On," "Never You Give Up," "God's Time is Best," "Who Knows?" "Time will Tell," and "No Competition in Destiny."

Through the repetitive/replicative power and unclosed possibility of vehicle slogans, *danfo* drivers reclaim "a positive orientation to the near future" (Guyer 2017; see also Crapanzano 2003: 6), which is steeped in Yoruba worldview. For these mobile subjects, hope is at once temporal and eternal. As Jane Guyer (2017) puts it, "Hope endures as a kind of daily promise that there is, indeed, an eternity, and it lies more in the recurrence by which it 'springs' than in any confident comprehension of an ultimate horizon." In this light, then, daily uncertainty becomes a vital resource that transport operators draw upon not just to carve out a pathway in the here and now, but also to *carry on* in the near future. As Marco Di Nuncio's ethnography of street life in urban Ethiopia shows, "living contain[s] the seeds of open-endedness, possibility, and reversibility" (2019: 4). What emerges from this is a greater appreciation for ways of reading, representing, and socially navigating the African city that focus less on the product(ion) of uncertainty (crisis as context) and more on the productivity of uncertainty (crisis as possibility).

5

Nigeria's Transport Mafia

The nomenclature *agbero* is a euphemism for a cohort of dreaded urban youths who survive through their parasitic dependence on the spatial regulation of public transport in Lagos. Predominantly male, *agberos* appropriate the spaces of motor parks, bus stops, and junctions across Lagos, which they use as an operational base from which to extort cash bribes from *danfo* operators in the name of the politicized and violent National Union of Road Transport Workers (NURTW) (Albert 2007; Agbiboa 2020b). According to Jimoh, a *danfo* driver plying the Oshodi-Ikotun route, "*agberos* have converted all motor parks, bus stops, junctions/roundabouts in Lagos into ATMs for collecting money from us each day to the extent of physically assaulting us if we refuse to surrender our hard-earned income. They break screen wipers, fuel tank cover, side-view mirror, or a passenger seat from our *danfo* and say that is their share." Such routinization of extortion illustrates the predatory micropolitics that embeds many informal sector provisions in African cities and precludes any aesthetic framing of Africa's informal urban sector (e.g. Koolhaas 2001). Yet, the violent appropriation of contested public transit spaces, and the creation of parallel modes of governance and taxation by the NURTW, constitute a usurpation of the constitutional function of local governments in Nigeria. For example, Section 7, Schedule 4, of the Nigerian Constitution of 1999 clearly states that the control of motor parks in the federation is the domain of local governments. Indeed, on 21 February 1992, in the case of *The Road Transport Employers Association of Nigeria (RTEAN) v. The NURTW,* Nigeria's Supreme Court ruled that the NURTW has no right to collect fees from operators: "The defendant has no right to control or operate by way of collection of dues, levies and fees or otherwise at any motor parks in Nigeria other than to load and offload goods and passengers at such motor parks" (Supreme Court 1992).

Common to every single *agbero* that I encountered in Lagos, there was the same no-nonsense mien, the hair-trigger temper, the scarred face, and the willingness to get into any fight. The ruggedness of *agberos* is described by one *danfo* driver: "If them give am blow for mouth, *agbero* go buy *ogogoro* use wash am down tell you say na treatment be that. *Agbero* get plenty action. *Agbero* no get fear. *Agbero*

They Eat Our Sweat. Daniel E. Agbiboa, Oxford University Press.
© Daniel E. Agbiboa (2022). DOI: 10.1093/oso/9780198861546.003.0006

no be person."[1] Frequently acting under the influence of *paraga* (locally brewed alcohol) and *morocco* (Indian hemp, also known as *igbo*), *agberos* are liable to attack operators who delay in responding to their shouts of *owoo da?* (Where is your money?), *efumi owoo joor!* (Give me your money without hesitation), *ma se 'in lese o!* (I will injure you), *Sho fe ku* (Do you want to die?). The *agberos* are deeply feared by *danfo* operators and commuters in Lagos because of their violent extortionary tactics and the impunity they enjoy due to the NURTW-state mutualities. As one *danfo* driver warned me at the start of my fieldwork: "The fear of *agbero* is the beginning of wisdom."

Despite their centrality to the everyday (mal) functioning of public transport in Lagos, the figure of the *agbero* has so far escaped scholarly attention. While the NURTW has been described as the most politicized and violent trade union in Nigeria (Albert 2007), its intraorganizational dynamics and relationship with the state and workers are still poorly understood. Yet, "analyses of urban governance ought to consider not only how civil groups relate to the (local) state, but also the relations within these groups as they exercise governance" (Lindell 2008: 1884). In this chapter, I draw on empirically grounded research in Lagos (Oshodi and Alimosho local government areas) to explain the changing role of *agberos* in urban public transport. Locating their emergence within the widespread crisis of the IMF-led structural adjustment program (SAP) of the 1980s in Nigeria, this chapter explains the transformation of *agberos* (from passenger callers [*a gba ero*] to violent extortionists) in light of their tacit incorporation into the NURTW as tax collectors and foot soldiers for the union's "dirty work." The unionization of *agberos* had the twin effect of politicizing and expanding their role and designation in urban transport. Furthermore, state efforts to rid motor parks of *agberos* are compelled by the post-1999 urban renewal ambition of the Lagos State Government, which seeks to order the chaos and clean the dirt of Lagos, transforming it into a "world class" megacity. Yet, the ingrained role of patronage politics (e.g. the strategic alliance between the NURTW and the Lagos State Government) in the management and control of urban transport explains the difficulty, if not impossibility, of doing away with *agberos*.

By focusing on their changing role in the Lagos passenger transport sector, this chapter foregrounds the critical and mediating role of *agberos* in the routine control of public transportation, while illuminating the politics of violent patronage and extortion rackets in which they are popularly implicated. Far from the conventional tendency to separate informal/formal, official/unofficial, legal/illegal, the study of the NURTW in relation to the Lagos State Government underscores two points. First, that the informal economy is neither residual nor unregulated.

---

[1] When you punch an *agbero* in the mouth, he would buy *ogogoro* (local gin) and wash down the blood with it, saying that it is a form of treatment. An *agbero* has plenty of action. An *agbero* has no fear. An *agbero* is not a person (author's translation).

Second, that formal and informal economy are, in practice, connected and constitute one another. Understanding statehood in Africa requires careful attention not only to state institutions but also to "the whole spectrum of formal and informal actors in the 'field of power' around state institutions" (Titeca & De Herdt 2011: 216).

The material for this chapter was gathered from fieldwork conducted in two major local government areas in Lagos: Oshodi and Alimosho. My key informants from these sites were *agberos*, *danfo* drivers and conductors, and commuters. In total, I interviewed thirty *agberos* and sixty *danfo* operators. Occasionally, interviews were recorded with audio equipment (a device not without its drawbacks, see Introduction), and later transcribed and analyzed. But in most cases, I simply hung out with drivers, operationalizing the "go-along" method that engages the informants' daily stream of practices *in situ* as they move (Kusenbach 2003: 458). In addition, I repeatedly visited newspaper kiosks by the roadsides,[2] where I searched for news involving the activities of *agberos* in Lagos. For the most part, I spent my time at checkpoints and junctions, where daily encounters between *danfo* drivers, motor park touts, and law enforcement agents were often tense affairs marked by extortion and complicity. Checkpoints represent "governmental or para/shadow governmental apparatus that blocks passage between two points, while imposing criteria—often the checking of 'identity' through the examination of documents and bodies—for passage through the checkpoints" (Jeganathan 2018: 403). More than just sites through which arrays of governmentality operate, checkpoints in Lagos are predatory infrastructures that serve to keep transport operators stuck in traffic, which makes it easier to extort bribes from them. Extortion, violence, and substantial delays have become a normal part of the everyday that drivers in Lagos learn to live with, to navigate. "There are loses from bad roads," a *danfo* driver told me, "but losses from checkpoints are higher than losses from bad roads."

The Politics of Transporting: Mutualities and Double Capture

This chapter is located within an emergent body of works that critically examines how seemingly representative organizational forms expected to be conducive to Africa's democratization process can end up breeding "authoritarian pseudo-organizations" (Goodfellow 2017) that reproduce rather than challenge predatory and unaccountable modes of governance (Meagher 2012). In analyzing the interface between the NURTW and the Lagos State Government, I build on a new and emergent body of works that moves us beyond the pervasiveness of "state thought" (Bourdieu 1994: 1), that is, the state as an *idea*, and invites us to engage the state as practice, as a "translocal institution" (Gupta 1995). This literature criticizes

---

[2] These are discursively vibrant sites where Lagosians gather to share their views on pressing issues.

simplistic renderings of the state and civil society as distinctly separate entities with clearly defined boundaries. Instead, it calls attention to the blurred boundaries of the state, specifically the manner in which it is localized in the politics of transporting.

I draw insights from two compelling works on the politics of transporting in urban Africa. The first is Erik Bähre's (2014) analysis of "violent and shifting mutualities" as the organizing logic of Cape Town's mafia-like taxi industry, particularly the collusion and collisions between taxi associations and urban government. Mutuality describes "a form of sociability forged in participation in each other's existence despite and because of radical difference, where people partially hold some ground together, by virtue of the circumstances in which they find themselves" (Golomski 2020: 286). Bähre's study sheds light on how political capture is often disguised as popular legitimacy and how the government tends to cooperate with criminal taxi associations out of convenience, corruption, or fear (2014: 590; see also Meagher 2012: 1073). Mutualities, for Bähre, produce particular moral economies that cannot exist without social networks of trust, reciprocity, and protection that impose some predictability on unstable urban settings (2014: 577). The concept of mutuality is critical in light of the manifold risks and uncertainties of everyday, urban life which exposes "the fragile and necessary dimensions of our interdependency" (Butler 2012: 148). In Lagos, for instance, political life is governed by patron-client relations, which constitute a vital gateway for political participation and upward mobility (Forrest 1993). Here, mutualities serve as a social infrastructure of major importance for self-protection, economic survival, and social recognition (Lindell & Utas 2012; Newell 2012: 90). As Olivier de Sardan (1999: 41) bluntly puts it: "Woe betide the man who knows no one, either directly or indirectly."

The second work is Tom Goodfellow's (2017) account of the phenomenon of "double capture" in Uganda's Taxi Operators and Drivers Association (UTODA). Going beyond traditional notions of state capture as a unidirectional process in which societal interests are "captured" or appropriated by the state as a conduit for private accumulation, Goodfellow shows how the organizational power of UTODA evolved over two distinct phases (which he terms "double capture"): "First, the government infiltrated the informal transport sector, but subsequently the transport organization came to wield disproportionate influence over the government itself, with detrimental effects on both urban services and popular representation" (2017: 1568). Unsurprisingly, the relations between UTODA and the state government came to combine "collusion (primarily with national politicians) alongside the threat of mobilizing opposition if the state (especially at the city level) attempted to exert control over the industry" (Goodfellow 2017: 1578), with both order and disorder resulting from the shifting relations and scales (Moncada 2013: 242). The phenomenon of double capture is particularly salient in light of the sparseness of literature on how formal governance regimes in "state space" are linked to informal associational activity that occupies "shadow state space" (Schindler 2014: 404).

The rest of this chapter is divided into three parts. I begin with a review of the extant literature and the void that this chapter fills. I then situate the coming of the *agbero* within the widespread crisis, insecurity, and uncertainty wrought by the SAP years, clarifying, along the way, the misleading conflation of the history of *agberos* with that of *area boys* in Nigeria. This is followed by an analysis of how the role and designation of the *agberos* has developed and changed over time, with particular attention to their incorporation into the NURTW as tax collectors and foot soldiers. The final section explores the difficulty of removing *agberos* from the roads and motor parks (bus stations) of Lagos.

Transport, Labor, and Everyday Survival

Several studies have interrogated thematic issues of the history and chaotic politics of informal transportation in African cities (Peace 1988; Rasmussen 2012; Heinze 2018; Mutongi 2017), tactics and strategies used by operators to navigate everyday risks and uncertainties (Date-Bah 1980; Lawuyi 1988; Agbiboa 2018a), struggles for survival amid abysmal labor conditions (Rizzo 2011; Mutongi 2006; Agbiboa 2018b), and the role of masculinities and becoming in Africa's informal transport sector (Gibbs 2014). These key works provide a useful "port of entry" for understanding how African cities work without extensive "formal" infrastructures. More recent accounts have pivoted on contemporary neo-liberal reforms (such as the rapid growth of Bus Rapid Transits [BRTs] across African cities) and the reproduction of precarious livelihoods (e.g. the displacement of informal transport operators) (Rizzo 2017; Klopp, Harber, & Quarshie 2019).[3] In a study of Dar es Salaam, Matteo Rizzo demonstrates how *daladala* minibus operators get by under the harsh conditions of flexible labor markets and economic liberalization (2011: 55 Rizzo 2017). A related literature examines the micropolitics of relations between informal transport owners, operators, passengers, and infrastructures (Mutongi 2006; Xiao and Adebayo 2020), as well as the widespread problem of political patronage and protection rackets implicating powerful unions and vested government interests (Agbiboa 2019). Combined, these works have advanced our understanding of the harsh conditions of labor and everyday challenges facing Africa's informal transport operators and, perhaps more importantly, how these operators are negotiating these challenges to make the most of their time.

Important as these insights are, we still know surprisingly little about the intermediary role and micro-level dynamics of semi-formal transport unionists

---

[3] Since 2002 the World Bank-funded Lagos Urban Transport Project (LUTP) has supported a Bus Rapid Transit (BRT) system which has coincided with the crowding out of informal midibuses (*molues*), and the restriction of motorbike taxis (*okadas*) on major Lagos routes, resulting in a massive loss of jobs in the informal transport sector (Klopp, Harber, & Quarshie 2019).

(e.g. motor park touts) forcefully collecting taxes in motor parks and bus stops in virtually every African city with a vibrant informal transport sector. In some studies, the tendency has been to conflate these actors with existing social categories (such as the frequent confusion of *agberos* with *area boys* in Lagos). Such confusion reinforces homogenizing and de-historicized tropes that haunt many studies on youth politics and urban informality in Africa. The situation is complicated by the absence of the voices and activities of these intermediaries in studies of urban transport and city governance, precluding a nuanced understanding of their changing role in the city, and how that role is perceived by those (i.e. transport operators and commuters) who come into contact with them, negotiate with them, resist them, or become their victims daily.

Africanist scholars, among them Thomas Bierschenk (2008), Blundo and Olivier de Sardan (2006), and Mahaman Alou (2006), have recently articulated a new research agenda on the phenomenon of a "gray area" of intermediaries on the interface between the public service and citizens in all areas of public administration in West Africa. These intermediaries come under various epithets: "fixers," "brokers," "middlemen," "auxiliaries," "go-betweens," "captains," and "bosses" (Mbembe 2001a; Price & Ruud 2009). Intermediaries also surface in many studies on how youth carve out meaningful temporalities and spaces of maneuver in urban Africa, including Tatiana Thieme (2013) and Jeremy Jones' (2010) account of "hustle" economies in Kenya and Zimbabwe, respectively, Janet Roitman's (2006) work on road bandits, unregulated economic activities, and the "ethics of illegality" in the Chad Basin, and Sasha Newell's (2006) study of a "moral economy of theft" in Abidjan. A key quality of intermediaries is their local knowledge (even appropriation) of how things really work on the ground, making their services indispensable to the daily functioning of African public service and to navigating popular urban culture (Bierschenk, Chaveau, & Olivier de Sardan 2002: 17; Gopfert 2016). Intermediaries often portray themselves as those who "make things happen" and they demand a "commission" or "donation" for their role or services (Bierschenk, Chaveau, & Olivier de Sardan 2002: 16). Located within this growing body of work on real governance and the political economy of everyday life in Africa, this chapter focuses attention on the role of intermediaries in the daily management of urban transport in Lagos. In particular, it seeks to explain the dynamic role of *agberos*—the most visible and violent face of the NURTW—as intermediaries at the interface between the union and the state and between *danfo* operators and the union. The analysis sheds new light on the embedding of corruption (in particular, extortion) in the "normal" regulation and functioning of informal transport in Lagos, and the centrality of *agberos* to this process. In this way, the chapter goes beyond the usual tendency to portray Africa's informal transport sector as ungoverned and chaotic, without any engagement with the contours of networks that organize and galvanize the sector.

The Emergence of the Agbero from the Era of SAP

Under the SAP of the 1980s, the prices of food items spiraled upward, transport costs increased, and education became the prerogative of the rich. In Lagos, the incomes of the working class became so devalued that it was difficult for salary earners and those on marginal and inelastic incomes to survive on their official earnings, forcing many hard-pressed civil servants into multiple modes of urban social livelihoods (Mustapha 1992) and "occult economies" (Comaroff & Comaroff 1999). With the dwindling socio-economic and traditional support base occasioned by the "SAP-ed" years, youths in Lagos were pushed to the limits of survival on the fringes, becoming "victims and agents" (Momoh 2000; Osoba 1996). Meanwhile, the sustained withdrawal of the state from social provisioning made it extremely difficult for young Nigerians to attend, or even remain in, school. The situation was further complicated by the lack of gainful employment after graduation. Such disempowering circumstances revived (colonial) tropes of youth as "a smoldering fire ready to burn African urban areas" (Bay & Donham 2007: 10).

With this market fundamentalism in Nigeria emerged an increased blurring of the putative boundaries between the "informal and the illegal, regulation and irregularity, order and organized lawlessness" (Comaroff & Comaroff 2006: 5; Roitman 2006). These blurred boundaries are most evident in the case of Lagos, where the SAP years contributed to the institutionalization of organized street gangs as a means for youth to negotiate economic distress and social exclusion. One of the main results of the SAP was the impact it had on the identity of *area boys*—the precursors of *agberos* in Lagos. Identities undergo constant change in situations of significant socio-economic flux (Mustapha 2000: 86). This is true in the case of *area boys*—that is, youths who identify themselves with the area in which they live and seek to control the flow of goods and services in that area to their advantage. To be called an *area boy* "used to be a thing of pride," said an elderly resident and former *area boy* in Lagos. The meaning of *area boys* had its origins in *omo eko* ("child of Lagos") or *omo area/omo adugbo* ("a child of the community or street"). Thus, youth in Lagos were ordinarily identified with the streets where they lived, and once you belonged to a particular street, the youth of that street protected you from abuse from youth from other streets (Omitoogun 1994).

Historically, the designation of *area boy* was perceived as a form of identity and social control. As one informant in Olawale Ismail's study recounted, "Back then, youth are known by two ways… their family name and their area. From your area, people will know the *area boy* group you belong to… so if you do anything bad like fight, steal or cause trouble anyplace, you are easily traced to your *area boy* group" (Ismail 2009: 470). Prominent figures in Lagos—including Dr. Wahab Dosunmu (former Nigerian Minister of Works and Housing), Bola Ahmed Tinubu (former Governor of Lagos), and Prince Demola Adeniji Adele (former Chairman of Lagos Island Local Government)—all claim to have belonged at some point to *omo area* which they recall as made up of "responsible, respectable and well-to-do" indigenes of Lagos Island (Momoh 2000: 188). While this category is seen as the "real" *area boys*, counterfeit *area boys* are identified with the influx of post-SAP migrants, which altered the identity and respectability of *omo area* as a social category in Lagos. This view emerged in an interview with a government official in Lagos:

> When we were much younger, *area boys* meant youth of the area. It was mainly to do with various pockets of youth in various locations, hanging out together, living life, and just generally being boys and girls. But gradually with SAP and urban migration, youth increasingly coming into Lagos from villages and the other areas around Lagos, the term now soon degenerated to include undescribed miscreants, confused young men and women, tax collectors, and political thugs.

While urban scholars have studied *area boys* and organized street violence in Lagos (Momoh 2000; Ismail 2009), the related phenomenon of *agberos* has received scant attention. This dearth of literature on the figure of the *agbero* is partly due to the regular conflation of *agberos* with *area boys,* as if both social categories were interchangeable. Yet, from my interviews with veteran operators and unionists in Lagos, it seems that *agberos* came into existence during the socio-economic flux from the mid-1970s onward, when the material and mental insecurities of the Nigerian urban and rural economies generated a range of everyday practices for youth to get by. To ward off the "specter of nothingness" (Mbembe & Roitman 1995: 324) and cope with "a world that seem to be falling apart before their very eyes" (De Boeck 1998: 25), a cohort of dispossessed and desperate youth turned to urban transport in droves—touting at motor parks and riding *okadas*. It was during this economic crisis that the figure of the *agbero* emerged as a mode of survival and making do, a "trickster who survives and can 'eat' without 'handiwork'" (Pratten 2013: 246–47). While the notion of *area boys* is tied to a particular area (*omo area*—area child), *agberos* are identified with *omo garage* (child of the garage).[4] This nomenclature clearly marks out the primary operational base of the *agbero*. According to one *danfo* driver in Alimosho, "*omo garage* is superior to *omo area*. To move from *omo area* to *omo garage* is to step up big time." Yet, *agberos* may be said to have carved out their identity from *area boys* with a longer history of "juvenile delinquency," dating back to the colonial period (Heap 2010; Fourchard 2006).

In contrast to *area boys*, *agberos* are institutionally embedded within the daily management of public transport by the NURTW. Unlike *area boys*, who are frequently seen as deprived street urchins surviving on the social margins of the megacity (Omitoogun 1994), "real *agberos*"—by this, I mean those *agberos* who are

---

[4] In Lagos, garage and motor-parks are used interchangeably to mean the same thing.

able to appropriate the union's name to legitimize their extortionary activities—are seen as moneyed (*olowo*) and powerful (*alagbara*), with strong multiple connections to big men (*ogas*) at the top. As one *danfo* driver said to me: "Some of these *agberos* have been doing this work for over ten years now. They won't leave it because it is very lucrative. Where else in this Nigeria can you *chop* [eat] over N10,000 in one day without really working for it? Where else can this happen?" In 2019, *Premium Times* (Nigeria) estimated that a minimum of N200 billion (USD514,163 million) is generated annually from dues collected by NURTW *agberos* in Lagos, representing about one half of the state's internally generated revenue in 2018. "With an average of 150,000 buses paying N2,000 daily, the union generates about N300 million daily from buses, if all dues are collected. 100,000 motorcycles and 100,000 tricycles also pay N1,000, respectively, averaging a minimum of N200 million from these sources daily" (Olawoyin 2019). Thus, unlike the marginalized and excluded *area boys*, *agberos* are, in fact, the "included" youth who play a central role as conduits for the daily extortion rackets of the NURTW. As one *danfo* driver told me:

> *Agberos* have mouth [connections in high places] and money. Put *agbero* in prison and his *ogas* will bail him within 24 hours. Put *area boy* there, he will rot there. You will always see police arrest *area boys* but not *agberos* because they are well connected. They are dropouts who live better than many university graduates. And you wonder why more youth nowadays are trying to become *agberos*.

According to one *agbero* I spoke to in Oshodi:

> We are not like *area boys* who are hungry people and have no mouth [connections]. They beg and steal money in addition to their *owo ita* [street money]. We are not like that. Let me tell you, we *agberos*, we no dey hungry. We work for our *ogas* [big men] and they feed us well. That is why we are loyal. Anywhere they send us, any job they ask us, we just go there and conquer for them. They treat us like humans. They nourish their boys.

In fact, my understanding during fieldwork in Lagos was that to call an *agbero* an *area boy* was an insult, because it implied that you were debasing them by implying that they were *talakas*—that is, a person without an official position; a common man or woman in the street. While *area boys* occasionally solicit tolls from operators under duress, this ordinarily happens when, in a bid to avoid the extreme traffic gridlock or "go-slow," *danfo* drivers use alternative street routes. When this happens, *area boys*—boys from that area—will block the streets with sticks that have open nails, and demand *owo ita* [street money] from the drivers. *Owo ita* is not to be confused with *owo garage* ("garage money") collected by *agberos*. Furthermore, many *agberos* made a distinction between themselves (*awa*—we) who

represent the interests of the NURTW, and "other touts" (*awon*—they) who collect taxes from operators pretending to belong to the NURTW. The *agberos* that I
spoke to in Oshodi, for instance, saw themselves as the "official" and "rightly connected" *agberos* (in Yorùbá, *awon to lenu nbe*—"those who have a voice") because
they work every day for the NURTW on a commission-only basis; the "others" are
renounced as "unofficial" (*awon ti o lenu nbe*—those who have no say or belong
to rival unions). These are seen as the "fake" *agberos* who collect money from operators by (ab)using the NURTW's name for criminal purposes. "These people are
spoiling our name," said one *agbero* in Ikotun.

During fieldwork in Oshodi and Alimosho, many operators complained to
me about the confusion between "real" and "fake" *agberos*. Drivers regularly bemoaned the fact that they ended up paying triple of the charges imposed on them,
since different sets of *agberos* claim to be representing the NURTW and threaten
to unleash violence (at the slightest provocation) if their demand for money is not
met there and then. In fact, during the course of my fieldwork, some *danfo* drivers
in Oshodi went on strike, not because they had to pay taxes to *agberos* for each
trip, but because of the confusion surrounding how much is to be paid, where they
should be collected, and, crucially, who should collect it. Reinforcing this point,
one *danfo* driver in Oshodi told me:

> It is total confusion. You don't know who is who, my brother. The more you look
> the less you see. Every tout claims to represent the union and threatens to un-
> leash violence if you don't pay them. Maybe it's a moneymaking strategy that
> they use to extort more money from us. I really don't know. With this people
> anything can happen. I don't trust them from here to there. Some of them now
> wear uniform but these are all re-packaged *agberos*. Lagos should be a place for
> well-mannered and educated people just like the civilized countries like America
> and Great Britain. Then we can call it the "center of excellence." At the moment,
> it is the center of confusion.

This confusion partly explains why "official" NURTW *agberos* in Lagos now increasingly wear a green and white uniform and carry with them a union identity
card to determine those who really "belong" from fakes (Newell 2006: 179). Many
agberos whom I encountered in Oshodi and Alimosho were quick to claim legitimacy through the proud show of their union card. Key officials in the transport
sector see those without uniforms and/or form of identity as "hoodlums" who constitute a nuisance to the free flow of traffic in Lagos. According to an official in the
Ministry of Transport: "It is because the system has become so fluid that a lot of
people have decided to take advantage of it. Some hoodlums have taken that opportunity to terrorize these motorists, because nobody will ask them who they are."
The confusion between real and fake *agberos* is hardly surprising when we consider
that even within the NURTW, there are various rival fractions (each with their

own loyal sets of *agberos* and unit chairmen) jostling for ascendancy and control of public transit spaces (Albert 2007). This confusion partly explains why many Lagosians tend to lump *all* transport workers together as criminals. One commuter in Alimosho stated, "They are all looking for where they will get easy money and satisfaction. I don't care if they are drivers or *agberos*. They are all the same thing. They reap where they have not sown." Yet, many *agberos* insisted that they are not "thieves" but responsible citizens doing all it takes to survive (like any other hard-working Lagosian) and getting a just reward for their hard labor. *Ise wa lan se* ("We are only doing our work") or *E se nidi pepe a je nidi pepe* ("Whoever works at the altar eats there"), meaning you make your wealth from where you work, were re-current responses from *agberos*. The wisdom of the motor parks, junctions, and bus stops is that resisting *agberos* may be penny-wise but pound-foolish. Many de-fiant operators end up being beaten (to death) and/or their vehicles, their main source of livelihood, vandalized beyond recognition.[5] In Oshodi and Alimosho, transport operators explained to me that daily demands for "donations" (bribes) by *agberos* remains the biggest threat to their pursuit of survival. To be sure, the lists of settlements demanded by *agberos* are endless and borders on farcical:

Booking fee (*owo booking*), loading fee (*owo loading*), dropping fee (*owo drop-ping*), money for weekend (*owo weekend*), money for sanitation (*owo sanitation*), security fee (*owo security*), Chairman's meal (*onje Chairman*), LASTMA's money (*owo LASTMA*)), police money (*owo olopa* or *owo askari*), money for parking (*owo parking*), money for the morning (*owo aro*), money for afternoon (*owo osan*), money for evening (*owo irole*), money for the night (*owo ale*), money for party (*owo faji*).

These fees of various sorts imposed on drivers are "designed to tire out the bodies of those under it, to disempower them not so much to increase their productivity as to ensure the maximum docility" (Mbembe 2001a: 110). Any hesitation to pay any of the above fees spells *wahala* (trouble) for the *danfo* driver and his conductor. As one *danfo* driver explained: "*Agberos* and police are the kings. We serve them. We do the work while they eat the food. More than half of my takings goes into their pockets. We are at their mercy. What can we do when they violently attack us in broad daylight without fear? This tells you that they have political backing. If they don't, they will not be terrorizing us like this." This view reinforces the collective action thesis, which states that in a context where corruption is the rule rather than

---

[5] This is mainly based on anecdotal evidence and the author's first-hand experience in the motor parks, junctions, and bus stops of Lagos, specifically Oshodi and Alimosho local government ar-eas. There are no "official" figures of operators killed in a year/over years by *agberos* in Lagos. Many deaths/injuries by *agberos* go undocumented or are simply ignored by security personnel who are of-ten complicit in the violent extortion of the NURTW. This helps to conceal the internal politics that surrounds mutualities in Nigeria's transport industry.

the exception, individuals often see little option but to participate or be punished. Yet, the association of *agberos* with the union and its violent patronage was not always the case during its early years.

The Changing Role of Agberos

From the onset, *agberos* assumed the self-imposed role and responsibility of re-cruiting and organizing passengers who wished to travel by road, and for this work they earned a fee or a "commission" that was usually paid by the *danfo* drivers shortly before departure from the motor parks or bus stops. Hence, in Yorùbá, *agbero* means "caller of passengers." My interview with Ibikunle, a veteran *danfo* driver plying the Oshodi-Ikotun route, suggests two kinds of *agberos* that have emerged in light of the increased association of *agberos* with the NURTW's dirty work (illegal tax collection and political thuggery): "The *agberos* at the top they are somehow closer to the government. And the ones below they are the *eruku*—they are the ones dying for the ones up. The ones up they can travel abroad, have big investments, but the one dying for them they have but not much. They are very loyal to those at the top who reward them handsomely for their loyalty. The *erukus* aspire to rise through the ranks one day, to become patrons to other *erukus*."

Most *agberos* are recruited from a large, ready pool of unemployed "area boys" roaming the streets of Lagos. Many young men who became *agberos* migrated to Lagos from neighboring states with the goal of "becoming somebody in life." The majority of *agberos* are from extended families, with a mother in one place and a father in another. The *agbero* dreams of one day becoming an *oga agbero* (head of *agberos*, an NURTW boss) and leading a motor park. *Oga agberos* have scores of *agberos* who deliver money to them on a daily basis. Many *oga agberos* take home about N60,000 (USD190) each day, according to one *agbero* whom I spoke to in Oshodi. They also own and/or control choice properties across Lagos, send their children abroad for schooling, wear the most expensive accessories (such as gold chains and gold teeth), and generally "eat very well." "It is not out of place to see transport union leaders around with bundles of cash when attending parties particularly during weekend. A union chairman could stand before a Fuji musician for several minutes spraying N1,000 notes to the consternation of spectators and the more an artiste showers encomium on them, the heavier they rain cash on the singer" (Hanafi 2020). The *agberos* are encouraged by the fact that most *oga agberos* started out as *erukus* in one of the many bus stops across Lagos. In fact, there were many "grass to grace" stories in circulation in motor parks during the course of my fieldwork.

But to become an *agbero*, it is not enough to be unemployed; you must also be feared. As one veteran *danfo* driver in Oshodi said to me in no uncertain words: "If you're in your street or area and you can create a scene, cut somebody's head, do whatever. They [the NURTW] will find a motor park for you immediately as an *agbero*. You're born to kill." Another driver told me that he used to be an *agbero* until the day he saw another *agbero* detach a person's head with a cutlass in a motor park clash in Oshodi. According to him, "*Na dat day I run comot for agbero*" [that was the day I quit *agbero* work]. These gory accounts reinforce the point that "the streets have become the arena for what is learned and expected by others to gain recognition and approval" (Vigil 2003: 230). In a BBC documentary entitled "Law and Disorder in Lagos" by the noted documentary filmmaker Louis Theroux, one of the *agberos* interviewed claimed that "when you want to be an NURTW member, you have to control some part of your area. You have to be a tough guy. When you want to be a tough guy, you have to go through scarring things in your streets. You get caught several times in violence and life goes on after the wounds have healed" (BBC 2010). Thus, violence, along with its visible scars, are critical to the making of an *agbero* in Lagos. Indeed, nearly all *agberos* that I spoke to in Oshodi and Alimosho had multiple cuts on their faces sustained from street brawls. Whenever I asked them how the wound came about, they simply said, "It comes with the territory." In fact, my sense from interacting with *agberos* was that the more scars one has, the more respect one garners inside the motor parks. As such, scars were a powerful signifier of belonging, something to be proud of, something to be displayed.

My fieldwork interviews and analyses of media reporting suggest that the practice of collecting dues from transport operators at motor parks and bus terminals used to be a non-intimidating survival strategy for many young boys who fled to Lagos because of their parents' inability to provide for their basic economic needs (obviously made worse by the SAP). However, with the establishment of the NURTW in 1978, the *agberos* morphed into a serious menace and became increasingly connected to violent party politics (Agbiboa 2018; Albert 2007). As the following quote from a *danfo* driver in Alimosho elucidates:

Agberos were historically poor and hopeless people among us. They were the youth without food to eat or shelter to lay their head. The drivers who were once in business but suffered a great misfortune because their vehicles were destroyed in an accident or because they lost their jobs. And we their colleagues often helped them out of pity by asking them to load passengers for us so we can pay them a token for food. But with the coming of the union, agberos have become more powerful and bolder. They have seen that they can make more from the business, especially during election, and have organized themselves into a strong union to oppress us, to bite the fingers that once fed them. Nowadays, the table is turned. *Agberos* are now the rich and influential ones with power and connections in high places. But right from the start agberos were the wretched ones, the unfortunate ones among us. Nobody wanted to be an *agbero* back then.

The coming of the NURTW gave *agberos* "a new kind of independent aura of invincibility, and [they] slowly became more of a nuisance to the transport industry" (*Newswatch* 2013). There is a widespread perception among Lagosians that the NURTW is a major supplier of political thugs recruited among its battle-ready *agberos* to advance the Lagos State Governor's electoral campaigns and interests (through voter intimidation and the billions of naira generated at the motor parks, junctions, and bus stops), in exchange for the full autonomy to control and exploit motor parks and bus stops across the state (Fourchard 2010: 51). The NURTW is generally viewed in Lagos as a mafia-like union that is home to "a bunch of illiterate thugs, extortionists, murderers, and highway robbers" (Adejumo 2016). Explaining how the NURTW works, one driver in Lagos said: "They can beat you, beat the conductor, just for 50 naira (18p). They are not a union, they are a group. You can say they are a kind of gang, really" (*The Guardian* 2016). Ironically, on its official website, the NURTW defines itself as a trade union that "represents employees' interests to management on such issues as wages, work hours, and working conditions" and that was formed to "protect, defend and promote the rights, well-being, and the interests of all workers in the union against discrimination and unfair labor practices." In reality, however, the union engages in patronage politics and systematic voter mobilization to support the state government and ruling political party with whom it forges mutualities over time in return for uninterrupted control of motor parks and bus stops and the extortion of monies from road transport workers.

The close relations between *agberos* and the NURTW illuminate a model of urban youth clientelism, that is, "the social production of dependency on patronage when local and national structures fail to provide for the social and economic needs of youth" (Murphy 2003: 62). Many *agberos* in Lagos told me they became dependent on the patronage of their NURTW bosses as a way of escaping economic despair and becoming somebody. This view reinforces the *youth clientelism model*, which sees patronage as providing youth with a response to the political marginalization and economic destitution enforced by the corrupt regimes of the nation state (Murphy 2003). The menace of *agberos* in Lagos has been explained in light of a nationwide unemployment crisis, where youth with few opportunities see politicians as a "meal ticket." As Adewale Maja-Pearce writes, "there [are] too many young men hanging around, waiting for some action. All you have to do is go and meet them and pay them and they will do what you want... you can't blame the youths... they want to eat" (AFP 2015). While this is generally true, Maja-Pearce omits the fact that youth in Lagos are not simply pawns in a political game of chess, but active agents capable of manipulating just as they are able to be manipulated. Like the tactical but "ordinary practitioners of the city" described in de Certeau's *The Practice of Everyday Life* (1984: xix), *agberos* can see and seize opportunities "on the wing." In Oshodi, for instance, a set of *agberos* bragged about how they would organize themselves into small groups and meet with local politicians on their own turf to broker a deal, which involved eliminating or warning a political rival. In this light, the relationship of interdependence between *agberos* and NURTW bosses is best understood according to Anthony Giddens' (1979: 76, 93) association of autonomy and dependence in his dialectic of control, or Jean-François Bayart's (1989: xiii) view that "subjection can constitute a form of action."

Interviews with *danfo* drivers confirmed that the intensity of NURTW violence increases during election seasons, when *agberos* are generally under immense pressure from their union superiors to raise enough money to fund the expensive electoral campaigns of the ruling political party (Agbiboa 2018). As one *danfo* driver said, "Agberos have become political. They can determine who becomes the commissioner or governor. During elections, who will be used to snatch ballot boxes and disrupt the electoral process? They are now political tools, the instrument of winning elections. That is the problem" (Adetayo, 2020). Nigeria is not unique in this respect. In a study of the politics of order in the informal transport sector of Kampala and Kigali, Goodfellow (2012: 210) found that *bayayes* (*matatu* touts) constituted an important "voting bloc" and a "potential source of violence" that was mobilized by their respective unions, whose affair with local politicians involved "collusion alongside the threat of opposition." In Lagos, NURTW leaders are connected to state politicians and local government officials according to a deal that satisfies the vested interests of the actors involved and which has little to do with urban planning or the smooth running of the transportation system (Fourchard 2010: 51).

Since the 1950s, local government councils in Nigeria have been statutorily charged with the task of establishing, maintaining, and collecting fares at motor parks. During the Second Republic (1979–1983), however, the control and management of motor parks and bus stops, especially in Lagos, became the epicenter of political antagonism when transport unions usurped their management.

> The politicization of the management of motor-parks started in Lagos as the capital was the place of two concurrent powers: The Federal government, the president Shehu Shagari, and his party, the National Party of Nigeria (NPN) on the one hand, and the governor of Lagos State, Lateef Jakande and the UPN on the other hand. NPN decided to enlist the support of members of a new union,the NURTW created a year before, in 1978 under the leadership of Adebayo Ogundare, known as Bayo Success who was given the assignment of winning all the motor parks in Lagos over the UPN [Unity Party of Nigeria]. He did so in mobilizing his large clientele of drivers during the 1979 electoral campaign and in resorting to violence and killing of his potential opponents in most of motor parks in Lagos. (Fourchard 2010: 40–56)

It was during this time that *agberos* were instrumentally mobilized and incorporated into the NURTW (both adversely and/or willingly) as tax collectors and foot soldiers to do the union's bidding. Ever since, *agberos* have continued to be potent weapons in the hands of local politicians as thugs to kill or threaten political opponents, settle political scores, intimidate legitimate voters, disrupt political rallies, rig elections, and disseminate fear throughout the state (Fourchard 2010; Albert 2007; Uyieh 2018). In both the 2003 and 2007 general elections, the then-ruling People's Democratic Party (PDP) in Lagos hired the services of *agberos* as thugs to chase away would-be voters in order to stuff ballot boxes and rig elections in favor of their candidates. The need for "hard men" who can deliver votes during elections fosters the patron-client relationship between political god-fathers, office holders, and political candidates in Nigeria (Pratten 2013). To my question of why most *agberos* are so feared, a *danfo* driver in Alimosho replied: "It is not about them, it is the big men around them that protects them, so they must show loyalty at all cost. Even if you arrest the *agbero*, before you treat the wound they inflicted on you, they are back to their duty post. The NURTW chiefs ensures they are freed. That is how the system works. They're all like mafias." In return for their services, *agberos* are offered cash rewards, which they often spend lavishly on hard drugs (*igbo*), alcohol (*paraga*), and casual sex with prostitutes (*ashewo*).

The NURTW's practice of providing thugs recruited among its workers to assist the state governor during elections (Fourchard 2010: 51) is neither new nor specific to Lagos state. In Gombe state, a group of violent touts known as *Kalare boys* have proven "easy prey for politicians who offer them small amounts of money, drugs, alcohol, and weapons in exchange for engaging in acts of intimidation and assaults or simply to accompany their campaigns in a demonstration of muscle" (Aniekwe & Agbiboa 2014: 12). The activities of the *Kalare boys* have included assault, rape, and extortion of ordinary Nigerians. Many of the *Kalare boys* worked for the PDP as political loyalists during the 2003 and 2007 elections. As Ma'azu, the PDP youth leader in Gombe state puts it, "thank God we have more boys than the opposition" (HRW 2007: 94). Gombe aside, in the 2003 elections in the Niger Delta region, one astute commentator observed:

> Politicians from the major political parties mobilized and surreptitiously armed groups of unemployed and disenchanted youths, and deployed them to cause mayhem and manipulate the electoral process. In this contestation and competitive arming of young groups, the party, which controlled the state government, got the upper hand. These political elite rivalries, coupled with a struggle for turf, contributed immensely to the rise of armed militancy and inter-militant armed violence, which preceded the 2003 elections and became consolidated in the period between the 2003 and 2007 general elections in the Niger Delta. (Ayoade & Akinsanya 2013: 295)

In light of the 2003 and 2007 elections, Human Rights Watch (HRW 2007) concluded that the NURTW was "largely converted into reservoirs of thugs for local politicians." A prime illustration is the political fallout of Rashidi Ladoja, former governor of Oyo State (2003 to 2007), with the late Chief Lamidu Adedibu, the political "godfather" of Oyo state (whom we briefly encountered in Chapter 2). Adedibu had endorsed Ladoja as the ruling PDP (Peoples Democratic Party) candidate in the 2003 elections, using his ability to mobilize violence and money to rig the elections in Ladoja's favour. Once in office, however, Ladoja attempted to break free of Adedibu's influence, neither granting him access to "eat" the treasury nor allowing him to handpick the Commissioners who would serve in his cabinet. The tensions between Adedibu and Ladoja caused the State House of Assembly to split into two and played out in motor parks, streets, and bus stops across the state (such as Ibadan) through regular battles between proxy union gangs. This illustrates the ways in which urban politics and the state are located across diverse sites, from official government buildings to the space of the street (Pilo & Jaffe 2020; Gupta 1995). The political instrumentality of the NURTW in the violent clash between Adedibu and Ladoja led an Oyo state senator, Lekan Balogun, to call for the total ban of the NURTW, noting that "They do not have any purpose. They are available for negative activities including thuggery and they [politicians] draw their thugs from there" (HRW 2007: 56).

Due to the association of *agberos* with party politics in Lagos through the powerful NURTW, there is a widespread perception among transport operators and Lagosians that the *agberos* have become "undisputed kings of Lagos roads." "The relationship is parasitic," said one *danfo* driver, "each component is taking advantage of the other with the drivers at the base. The government takes advantage of the union and uses them for what they want, like using them to challenge political opponents during elections; the union takes advantage of the drivers" (Adetayo, 2020). The mutuality between union leaders and state officials is evident in the observed ways in which *agberos* join forces with law enforcement agents to unleash a predatory economy on Lagos roads, especially at checkpoints and junctions. Since its creation in the 1970s, the political party in power in Lagos state (whether PDP or APC) has tended to give the NURTW leadership, who supported their candidature, the freedom "to do and undo" within the motor parks. In fact, during the 1980s, NURTW played a central role in the Second Republic (1979–83) elections. This gave them enormous political power to run bus terminals across Lagos. NURTW chiefs took the liberty to create more illegal motor parks and bus stops from where they violently extort fees from operators through their battle-ready *agberos*.[6] This instrumental NURTW-state mutuality mirrors discussions of "patronage democracy" in India, where political choice is often "an ongoing calculation

---

[6] A similar alliance was found among taxi associations in Cape Town, South Africa, where "the state cooperates with criminal taxi associations sometimes out of convenience, sometimes as part of corruption, and sometimes out of fear. Equally, businesses rely on violent association leaders. Banks, insurers, car manufacturers and car dealers cooperate with suspicious taxi association leaders in order to sell their products to the thousands of members they represent" (Bähre 2014: 590).

of loss and profit" (Piliavsky 2014: 15). The NURTW's autonomy is thus protected by "big politics"—most union chiefs remain loyal and supportive of the ruling All Progressives Congress (APC) party, others to the People's Democratic Party (PDP), or other fringe political parties. In such a politically charged environment, violent clashes between rival unions and their *agberos* are the rule of the game (Albert 2007). As one editorial observes, "50 percent of the violent activities in Lagos is because of the activities of the *agberos*. Their frequent clashes with rival groups constitute about 50 percent of the spate of insecurities experienced in the state" (AutoJosh 2018). Given their lucrative and politicized nature, motorparks, bus terminals, and junctions across Lagos are some of the most insecure and fractionalized spaces, and their control has become purely a matter of life and death.

The NURTW generates its funds through the numerous levies it imposes on its members and enforces through its feared *agberos*. Each day, *agberos* brutally collect and make returns to their respective unit chairman, who reports to the state chairman, who is the direct link to the national chairman. Along this chain, financial returns must be remitted daily. As earlier noted, the NURTW in Lagos generates an average of N200 million daily (Olawoyin 2019). According to one senior *agbero* in Oshodi, "The NURTW chair for Oshodi pockets up to N5 million [USD31,250] daily from the different units under him." Upon receiving this sum, the chairman is expected to "declare surplus"—that is, to circulate the returns among other higher union executives, police inspectors, local council chairmen, and party officials. This everyday system of redistribution is in tune with the NURTW's guiding slogan: "Eat Alone, Die Alone." This political settlement echoes the depiction of a "trickle-up economy" in Cape Town's taxi industry, which relies on mutualities to distribute cash to the state, to transport trade association leaders, and to officers (Bähre 2014: 590). It also resonates with a study of corruption in Latvia, which shows that corruption is generally considered morally acceptable—and the money associated with it as "fertile"—when it benefits the social community. However, it is considered "barren money" when it benefits only the individual (Sedlenieks 2004). The huge revenue collected by the NURTW and the high social mobility this facilitates explain why the union remains the most politicized, factionalized, and violent in Nigeria.

Every member of the union aspires to become a chairman—whether at branch, city, state, zonal or national level. This partly explains why the members regularly engage one another in bloody skirmishes. It explains why NURTW members and members of other transport unions kill each other in defense of their position in most Nigerian cities. (Albert 2007: 154)

Modernization and the Drive to Eliminate Agberos

Until 1999, Lagos was largely regarded as an "urban jungle,"[7] a prime example of Third World urban dysfunction, crime, and corruption. However, during his time in office, the civilian government of Bola Ahmed Tinubu (1999 to 2007) envisaged a radical change to the status quo, announcing a rescue operation "to make Lagos the reference point of harmonious physical development in Nigeria through best practices and physical planning and development." Building on Tinubu's legacy, Governor Babatunde Fashola (2007 to 2015) started his term in office by announcing his plans for "a new and beautiful Lagos that would become a reference point for best practices found anywhere in the world" (Basinski 2009: 6). Fashola sought to realize his megacity vision and "aesthetic governmentality" (Ghertner 2011) through the elimination of the violent extortion by *agberos* in transit spaces like motor parks and junctions. As one commuter in Oshodi told me: "We have been complaining about *agberos* for many years but nothing happened. But now that Governor Fashola want to attract investors to Lagos and create this model megacity of his dreams, they have decided that *agberos* are no longer needed in this new and beautiful Lagos. They don't make the city beautiful. But it's too late. *Agberos* have become institution."

In February 2008, Fashola inaugurated a twelve-member Tribunal of Inquiry, headed by Justice Dolapo Akinsanya, to investigate the role and operations of the NURTW and their *agberos* in motor parks and bus terminals across the state. The expectation was that the "instant inquiry" would help the Lagos State Government to identify "a unique opportunity to unravel the circumstances which might have precipitated violent clashes in the past and the challenges confronting passenger transport system, in order to avert future re-occurrence" (Agbiboa 2018c: 77-78). The Tribunal's findings included "(f)ighting and misuse of motor-parks, collecting money on the roads indiscriminately, stopping passengers, abusing alcohol, among others" (*Punch* 2012). The Tribunal found that *agberos* have morphed into a "complete menace that must be immediately addressed; what we considered needed to check the menace is the total enforcement of the existing laws on the NURTW because if enforcement takes hold, Lagos will become the real and desired megacity" (*The Nation* 2008). Citing the Nigerian Constitution of 1999, which empowers local governments to collect tolls at motor parks, Justice Akinsanya lamented the fact that, "[*agberos*] have taken over; they now collect tolls at these places with impunity; they even rape innocent victims after taking hard drugs" (*The Nation* 2008).

The Tribunal's recommendations inspired the enactment of the Road Traffic Law of 2012 in Lagos, which prohibited *agberos* from collecting taxes inside motor parks, bus stops, and junctions. Thus, to address the ubiquitous problem of

---

[7] A term used by President Olusegun Obasanjo, on the occasion of his first official visit to Lagos.

agberos, the Lagos State Government, under the Fashola administration, resorted to interventions within the framework of spatial governmentality—a principle that gathers "new mechanisms of social ordering based on spatial regulation" (Merry 2001: 16). This concept focuses essentially on space in lieu of networks and institutions. The fundamental aim is, therefore, to regulate people's behavior by (lawfully) prohibiting particular conduct in particular places (Geenen 2009: 350). As former Commissioner for Transport Kayode Opeifa declared:

> Henceforth, union activities are no longer allowed at our parks. They are to relocate to offices from where they will operate just like the National Union of Teachers and the National Union of Journalists. Also, no union member must be seen collecting money on the road. We recognize the right for them to associate but we believe that the motor-parks should be made easy for those who want to carry out their legitimate business of commuting in the state... no union member should be seen on the road collecting money from transport operators as it is *illegal*. (*The Guardian* 2015)[8]

There was early evidence of a determination to succeed when the local authorities attempted to enforce the ban by targeting the physical presence of *agberos* in public spaces such as motor parks and bus stops across the state. In June 2013, for instance, the Task Force on Environment and Special Offences arrested forty-six *agberos* who were collecting illegal taxes from *danfo* operators, intimidating road users during heavy traffic hours, and causing extreme traffic congestion on most routes in Lagos. The Special Offences Court in Lagos later sentenced these *agberos* to fifty hours of community service for "constituting nuisance to the public peace," noting that "we are simply telling them to repent" (*National Mirror* 2013). In an interview with the *National Mirror* in June 2013, Bayo Sulaimon, Chairman of the Lagos State Task Force, stated:

> We have declared war against *agberos* again; we will not allow them to take over the state. We have flushed them out and they are coming back and we will flush them out again. In the next few hours now, more of them will be arrested. We are moving to different places to arrest more of them. Soon, we will move to other areas in the state. With this arrest, we are passing a message to others. Their leaders should call them to order. (*National Mirror* 2013)

---

[8] This is not the first time that the Lagos State Government has banned the activities of *agberos* in motor-parks, or that the question of control of motor-parks has surfaced. Fed up with the violent activities and internal clashes of the NURTW, Fashola's predecessor Governor Bola Ahmed Tinubu (1999–2007), made a landmark decision in 2002 by banning NURTW from operating in motor-parks across Lagos. Tinubu's government argued that the NURTW does not have the constitutional backing for some of the powers they arrogate to themselves (Albert 2007: 135).

However, the authorities failed to sustain the ban against *agberos*, mainly because of their connection to the politically influential NURTW. This reinforces not only the selective enforcement of laws in Lagos, but also intensifies public perception that the NURTW is a "sacred cow" that operates in realms above the law. As one commuter in a motor park in Oshodi remarked:

> The government themselves know that it is impossible to remove *agberos* from the roads where they eat and gain respect and recognition. *They created a monster from beggars and now they can't tame it.* Instead, they are now trying to rebrand *agberos* as responsible union workers by giving them green and white uniforms— the colour of our own national flag. You can't change who an *agbero* is by changing what they wear. You need to change the space they occupy and cut off the connections that give them power and confidence to do and talk anyhow. You need to create better jobs that give them other options.

Other *danfo* operators and commuters were very sure that government interventions have *intentionally* proven ineffective so far, since the billions routinely extracted by *agberos* finds its way into coffers of the ruling political party in Lagos—the All Progressives Congress (APC). To my question about what they think about their ban, some *agberos* in Oshodi boasted: *Ta lo fe dan wo? ni bo? Oga Fashola gon ko to be. Ti won ba dan wo, a ma dagboru* (Who can try it? Where? Even Fashola cannot ban us. If they try it, we will make this city ungovernable). To the same question, another *agbero* taunted the lip service of the Lagos State Government: *Enu ni'joba ni, won'ni action. Nah we get Lagos. ti be.* (The government has mouth without action. We own Lagos). Governor Fashola, widely applauded in international circles as an "action governor" who "tamed Nigeria's most lawless city" (Ekundayo 2013: 201; *The Telegraph* 2014), failed to show his action against *agberos* represented by one local newspaper as "untamed monsters" (*The Guardian* 2015). This failure only served to deepen the fear of *agberos* among Lagosians, fueling the view that *agberos* are *omo ijoba* (state children), *omo oba* (child of a king), or *omo onile* (owner of the land) and, thus, "untouchable." Today, *agberos* cash in on their much-dreaded status on Lagos roads to solicit various "settlements" (bribes) from transport operators and street hawkers. As one "pure water" hawker in Alimosho said to me: "There is *agbero* for everything. Their code is simply tax anybody taxable." Mr. Ibrahim, the Area Commander of the Vehicle Inspection Service in Alimosho, tells me that the blame for extortion and chaos in Lagos should not be heaped entirely on *agberos* but also on operators and commuters who facilitate their anti-social activities and complicate the free flow of traffic:

> *Agberos* are supposed to generate their funds inside motor parks. They are not supposed to come to the main roads to collect tolls. When you see them go on the main roads to collect their money, it is because most of these vehicles do not

want to enter motor parks. You're not supposed to pick or drop passengers along the road. You're supposed to get to the designated parts of garages to board ve-hicles. Because even members of the public too, we are a very serious problem to the society. Why do I want to stand by the side of a road and board a bus when there are bus stations? These are the issues. Because most of these vehicles due to their menace, due to their socio-economic problem the minibus operator wants to meet up his target and he feels going into the motor park to queue up for his turn will delay him since he can readily see people to pick on the road and make quick, good money. In this way, they boycott the standard and that's why you see those boys [*agberos*] coming out to collect money. So the two parties are very wrong. Even the three parties: the commuters, the vehicle operator and the unionists [*sic*].

Mr. Ibrahim's statement echoes the analysis of poor people in Mexico, which pre-cipitated a "culture of poverty" in which the habits, values, and behaviors of the poor were appropriated to explain their daily predicament (Lewis 1966). This, in turn, gives rise to myopic state-instituted solutions that end up "treating the phe-nomenal forms rather than the essential relations behind the problem" (Lugalla 1995: 178–79). Such a representation is often couched in a neoliberal ethos that attributes equal agency to all, including those who are struggling daily to survive (Scheper-Hughes 2006: 155). The problem with Mr. Ibrahim's statement is that it obscures or downplays the role of government failure in the emergence and in-fluence of *agberos*, especially the ineptitude of law enforcement agents. As Mike Ozekhome, a Senior Advocate of Nigeria, notes:

How can any serious and responsible government say it cannot control forcible collection of dues by motor park touts from drivers that are plying the routes on legitimate business? Why should innocent drivers and vehicle owners be subjected to multiple taxation in the presence of a government whose first and primary duty is the security and welfare of its citizen in accordance with Section 14 of the 1999 constitution? There is freedom of association and also free-dom of movement. No one can be forced to belong to a union it does not want to belong to. Any exertion of force to actualize such by a union borders on criminal-ity, for which the culprits should be brought to book. We cannot afford to have a government within a government. (*The Guardian* 2017)

Reinventing Order

This chapter has interrogated the changing role of *agberos* in the informal trans-port sector of Lagos. While the figure of the *agbero* emerged during the difficult years of the SAP as a means of getting by, it gradually transformed into a menace in urban transport as a result of its association with the politicized and violent NURTW. This interdependent association between *agberos* and the NURTW illustrates the routine instantiation of violent extortion within networks of patronage that have become an endemic feature of electoral and informal politics in African cities (Bähre 2014: 409). The mutuality between the NURTW and the Lagos State Government has had the double effect of weakening formal state capacity while emboldening the union to gain a much stronger foothold, even legitimacy, over the control of lucrative motor parks across Lagos. This, in turn, has resulted in more violent and predatory forms of interaction between (and among rival) unions and operators, eroding the moral and epistemological certainties of operators who are increasingly unsure about who stands for what. Indeed, there is a sense in which both violence and order result from the shifting interactions among these multiple territorial and institutional scales in Lagos road transport. For example, efforts by some local governments to reclaim their authority over the control of motor parks have frequently triggered violent resistance from *agberos* controlling that area. In one case during my fieldwork, Oshodi saw a violent eruption when the local council secretary ordered the immediate cessation of extra-legal tax collection by *agberos* in motor parks and bus terminals across the local government. Expectedly, the decision did not go down well with *agberos* and their unit chairman in Oshodi. In a matter of days, *agberos* brutally attacked motor parks en masse, razing any *danfo* in sight. Worried about the threat to lives and properties in the densely populated area, the council secretary was compelled to rescind his order within the same week of its issue. Violence, in this case, functions as a tactical means of re-establishing "order" (business as usual), social control, and everyday profiteering in contested urban spaces.

The analysis presented here contributes to a grounded, place-based understanding of corruption, informal governance, and labor precarity in African cities, especially its dynamic, predatory, and seemingly chaotic functioning. In particular, the focus on the changing role of *agberos* reveals an "organizing urban logic" (Roy & Alsayyad 2004) that underpins the perception and practice of informal public transport in Lagos and, more broadly, the politics of urban informality in Africa (Meagher 2010; Khayesi, Nafukho, & Kemuma 2015). Beneath the appearance of menace and chaos in Lagos's informal transport sector exist webs of relationships (between the union and the state) that structure its everyday functioning. As intermediaries, *agberos* play a critical role in managing these transport mutualities through running the NURTW's extortion rackets. Thus, a study of *agberos* enhances our understanding of how the blurred boundaries between the state and non-state play out on the ground in the informal urban sector of Africa (Blundo & Le Meur 2009). This chapter also provides us with a deepened knowledge of the micropolitics of elections and the precarious nature of patronage politics in Nigeria. Elections are times of uncertainty that highlight the precariousness of both transport union leaders and state officials, who struggle to remain relevant and influential. Through a case study of the *agberos*, this chapter affirms the critical observation that the dynamics and lines between state and non-state actors are less straightforward than commonly assumed.

6

The Paradox of Urban Reform

As engines of growth and livelihood opportunities, but at the same time spaces of poverty and deprivation, African cities are fast becoming "rebel cities" (Harvey 2013), characterized by discontents and contestations. This chapter focuses on the disconnect and resulting tensions between, on the one hand, the elite-driven ambitions to make Lagos a "model megacity for the twenty-first century" and, on the other hand, the practical consequences of the application of these goals to the everyday and lived experiences of the ordinary inhabitants of Lagos in general and operators of informal motorbike-taxis (*okadas*) in particular. The chapter delves into the violent and predatory manner in which the Lagos State Road Traffic Law of 2012 was adapted by the state to restrict the space and mobility of *okada* drivers as a function of making Lagos a "world class" megacity. This analysis extends to the manner in which *okada* associations are using legal channels to counter these neoliberal urban legislations that constrain their opportunities and their "right to the city." It illuminates our tenuous grasp on how informal urban workers in Africa exercise agency as they attempt to intervene in the corrupt, violent, and unequal processes of urban renewal as driven by elite interests and "public-private" partnerships (Myers 2011).

This chapter draws on the legal case (Suit No. ID/713M.2012) filed by Lagos state *okada* drivers and their associations against the Lagos State Government over the wanton violation of their right to the city, particularly their restriction from plying major routes in Lagos. In analyzing this dispute, I draw insights from scholars who argue that the process of dispute opens a window into "the socio-cultural order at large" (Comaroff & Roberts 1981: 249) while also foregrounding "contested meanings and conflicting interpretations" (Caplan 1995; Roy 2013: 3). The data presented here were gleaned from several pages of court records (comprising originating summons, affidavits, and counter-affidavits) obtained from the Lagos State High Court. Obtaining access to these records proved a complex, lengthy, and costly process. This is partly because "gatekeepers" at various levels control access and brazenly demand bribes before allowing access. Court records were triangulated using in-depth interviews with *okada* drivers and their associational leaders, officials of the National Union of Road Transport Workers (NURTW) and Road Transport Employers Association of Nigeria (RTEAN), passengers, legal representatives (Bamidele Aturu & Co), as well as press materials. The chapter is inspired, in part, by an analysis of how the urban poor use state laws to negotiate their rights:

They Eat Our Sweat. Daniel E. Agbiboa, Oxford University Press.
© Daniel E. Agbiboa (2022). DOI: 10.1093/oso/9780198861546.003.0007

While citizens might often not act according to state law themselves and also make strategic use of the extra-legal practices of state agents, they are at the same time engaged in a protest that uses legal terms against the transgressions of law by state agents and other bodies of governmental authority. This is evident in their efforts against a misuse of state powers and their fight against corruption. In this we see a shift towards state law as a means of resistance as well as a parameter of the "good order." (Eckert 2006: 45)

During my fieldwork in Lagos, I used *okadas* as a primary means of transport; I seized the moment to ask questions during the ride. This "go along" method gave me access into the transcendental and reflexive experiences of daily mobility *in situ*, especially "an array of dispositions and arts of negotiation that are constitutive of subjectivities of conflict" (Mbembe & Roitman 1995: 329). By viewing the *okada* as a field site, my attention was constantly drawn to the *okada* driver's daily struggles to make the most of their time and assert themselves as valuable and rights-bearing members of Lagos. Further insights were derived from attending meetings of *okada* associations, specifically in the Oshodi and Alimosho local government areas, where I was primarily based. Oshodi is the key terminus for commercial road transportation in Lagos. It is commonly ranked among the worst urban conditions on the planet (Probst 2012; Aradeon 1997). Alimosho, on the other hand, is the largest local government area in Lagos, with more than two million residents. Both Alimosho and Oshodi can be said to be positioned at the interstices between "the real and abstract, official and unofficial, local and international, and the legal and illegal identity and manifestation of the Nigerian state" (Ismail 2010: 30).

Following this introduction, the rest of the chapter is divided into four parts. The first part explores the post-1999 urban renewal campaign in Lagos and its mixed-bag results. The second part focuses on the displacement of the Lagos poor by the urban megacity plan. The third part examines the controversial Road Traffic Law of 2012 and its malcontents. The fourth part focuses on Henri Lefebvre's concept of "right to the city" and how it applies to and helps us to understand the *okada* struggle in Lagos. The chapter concludes with a discussion of the culture of legality that is emerging in Lagos.

A "World Class City" for Whom?

African cities are all too often seen as spaces of rapid urban growth, marginalization, unemployment, expanding slums, where around 60 percent of city dwellers live in, and an intensifying informal economy that accounts for about 87 percent of employment. Far from being the exception to these sobering realities, Lagos is the quintessential example. Until 1999, Lagos, Nigeria's commercial capital and

Africa's largest city,[1] was widely considered "the armpit of Africa." The rottenness of Lagos life is taken to be a microcosm of Nigeria, which at the time held the unenviable record of being the second and first most corrupt country in the world, in 1999 and 2000 respectively. A fast-growing population (600,000 people added annually) without commensurate improvements in basic social services gave rise to nightmarish visions of a "coming anarchy" (Kaplan 1994). However, after nearly three decades of systematic neglect by successive Nigerian military governors and the Federal Government (Gandy 2005; Kuris 2014),[2] the new Lagos state government (starting in 1999) made great strides toward laying the foundations of a functional, livable, and sustainable megacity that, inter alia, can attract foreign investors. The civilian and technocratic[3] administrations of Bola Ahmed Tinubu (1999 to 2007) and his successor, Babatunde Raji Fashola (2007 to 2015), overhauled city governance, raised new revenues, improved security and sanitation, reduced traffic gridlock (go-slow), expanded infrastructure and public transit, and attracted global investment (Kuris 2014; Cheeseman & de Gramont 2017).

Breaking from the "business as usual" mentality in Lagos in particular and Nigerian politics in general, Tinubu promoted a ten-point agenda "to make Lagos the reference point of harmonious physical development in Nigeria through best practices and physical planning and development matters" (Basinski 2009). On the road to making Lagos a "world class" city, Tinubu's first priorities were to reform the civil service and set the state on a firm fiscal footing through taxation reform and new private investment (Kuris 2014: 7; De Gramont 2015). Tinubu's government notably initiated a project aimed at revitalizing the historical core of Lagos Island in an attempt to reverse the decline of previous decades. His efforts were inspired, in part, by a new urban policy in Nigeria, entitled the National Urban Development Policy, introduced by the Federal Government in 2002 with the central goal of developing "a dynamic system of urban settlements, which will foster sustainable economic growth, promote efficient urban and regional development, and ensure improved standard of living and wellbeing of all Nigerians" (Fajemirokun 2010: 268). The majority of Tinubu's reforms came to fruition under his successor, Babatunde Raji Fashola, who assumed office in 2007.

A New and Beautiful Lagos

Building on Tinubu's legacy, Fashola started his tenure by announcing his overarching vision of "a new and beautiful Lagos which would be a reference point

---

[1] Lagos is the eighth fastest-growing city in Africa and is home to some 21 million people.

[2] The deliberate punitive underdevelopment of Lagos under previous military governors "partly conditioned the chaotic environment that became stereotypical of [Lagos] in the global imagination" (Owen 2015: 655).

[3] For a detailed discussion of the politics of technocracy in Nigeria, see Alexander Thurston (2018).

for best practices that you can find anywhere in the world" (Basinski 2009: 6). His rallying cry was "Think Africa, Think Lagos." This world class megacity ambition coincided with growing interest in "Third World" megacities, exemplified by notable books such as Mike Davis's *Planet of Slums* (2006), Suketu Mehta's *Maximum City* (2004), and Robert Neuwirth's *Shadow Cities* (2006). In a government-endorsed YouTube documentary, titled "Lagos: Africa's Big Apple," the Fashola administration projected the brand new image of Lagos as follows: "Welcome to Lagos... [a] vibrant mega-city whose pulse is felt as wide as its influence reaches, a discovery of opportunities at the heart of Africa... a world of unique possibilities where untold opportunities are never far away... whatever it is you are looking for, Lagos has it all and is waiting for you" (YouTube 2013).

Fashola sought to realize his world class city aspirations through a number of channels, including the overhauling of the tax revenue systems in Lagos, reforming of waste collection systems, introducing high-capacity Bus Rapid Transits (BRTs)[4] funded by the World Bank, and efforts to address the culture of violent extortion on the road by *agberos* and police inspectors (Agbiboa 2018). The wheels of the urban renewal plan were set in motion with the radical and largely unannounced clearing of so-called illegal shops and sprawling slums, evictions of dumpsite dwellers, and beautification of parts of Lagos (Oshodi, for example) notorious for their clutter and criminality. This move was cast in media circles as a warning to Lagosians that Fashola means business, but not as usual. In light of his radical reforms, Fashola garnered global praise as the "action governor" who "tamed Nigeria's most lawless city" (The Telegraph 2014). *Al Jazeera* even produced a documentary entitled "Boom Time in Nigeria: Action Government Transforms Lagos." Seth Kaplan of the New York Times (2014) viewed Lagos as a "Model City" of effective governance in Africa, while The Economist (2015), in a piece titled "Learning from Lagos," claimed that Lagos was "a model for the rest of the country... a lesson in how one big city can sometimes kick-start wider change." Back home, the leading Vanguard (2014a) newspaper claimed that, "since the lofty days of [Governor Lateef] Jakande,[5] no other leader has filled us with such adulation as Fashola."

---

[4] The BRT was adopted to provide safe, affordable, and reliable transportation services to all Lagosians, while simultaneously formalizing the obstreperous transport industry. The post-1999 government in Lagos gave pride of place to transportation as the key engine of economic development.
[5] Lateef Jakande (nicknamed *Baba Kekere*—"small father") was the first elected governor of Lagos State from 1979 through 1983. During his time in office, Jakande advanced a strategic plan for Lagos and undertook large municipal investments in housing, schools, and transportation, including plans for an urban rail system which was later abandoned due to military incursion into politics in 1983 (LAMATA 2013: 13). In ten years, military governors (nominated by the government) in Lagos had managed to complete only one waterworks to serve the upper-class town of Festac (supplying four million gallons of water each day), whereas in four years, the Jakande government built ten waterworks in various poor and middle-class areas of Lagos (twenty million gallons per day). Also, in five years, Jakande's government built more primary schools than all the schools built by previous military governors combined (Fourchard 2010). Though Jakande was later criticized for accepting a ministerial post under Abacha's regime, his progressive political legacy from the early 1980s extended to education, housing, and sanitation (Godwin & Hopwood 2012).

Public perceptions that the Fashola-led government is delivering the goods is said to have enhanced tax compliance in Lagos (de Gramont, 2015). With 70 percent of its entire budget funded by taxpayers' money in 2014, Lagos was touted as the only state in Nigeria whose Internally Generated Revenue about doubled its federal allocation from oil earnings (The Guardian 2014b).

Yet, the success narratives of the Fashola government pale in the face of the adverse effects that the urban renewal project had on the lived realities of Lagosians, especially those surviving in the dark underbelly of the informal transport sector. Far from a state learning from informal service provisions (Banks et al. 2020), the Lagos State Government saw urban informality as a major threat to its urban renewal plan and conflated informality with illegality, in a manner similar to the reorganization of markets and the regular clearing of the streets by Zimbabwe's Harare Municipality (Chikolo, Hebinck, & Kinsey 2020: 8–9). Particularly striking about the Lagos megacity plan is the fact that it carried neither the promise nor the pretense of resettlement or alternative source of livelihoods for its victims, who were mostly informal urban workers. Instead, Fashola's government unleashed a systematic deportation program against street beggars, mobile hawkers, and the homeless poor, drawing widespread criticisms from poor Lagosians and human rights activists. As one astute observer decried: "Making Lagos a mega city does not mean that the poor will be banished from the state. The menaces of *area boys* and *agberos* are more inimical to making Lagos a [modern] megacity than the presence of beggars." Reacting to the partial demolition and discharge of thousands of Lagosians from their slum dwellings, one Lagos resident lamented: "[This government] want a Lagos that looks good, that feels good, that glitters. But they forget that Lagos is Lagos because of the people that live here. They're doing this without regard for people who live here" (The New York Times 2013). This reinforces the critique that to be a "World Class" city is "to 'look' new and cater to the needs of the elites seen as exclusive drivers of a modern city's future" (Bedi 2016: 393). As another Lagosian puts it, "Development is not about high-rise buildings and flyover bridges," but about the people and "how their basic needs are taken care of." These remarks constitute the real sinews of the influential idea of "people as infrastructure," which moves us beyond common understandings of infrastructure in physical terms and emphasizes "economic collaboration among residents seemingly marginalized from and immiserated by urban life" (Simone 2004b: 407).

A comparison, if cursory, may be drawn between the Lagos State megacity campaign and the Mumbai evictions in India—"Vision Mumbai"—where local authorities pulled down numerous slums in a matter of weeks, rendering an estimated 300,000 people homeless (Roy 2012: 7). As in Lagos, "Vision Mumbai" sought to transform Mumbai, a city famous for its enormous slums, terrible traffic congestion, and poor infrastructure, into a "world class" city—one that is globally competitive with other Asian successes (McKinsey & Company 2003). The municipality officer who led the demolitions declared that it was time to turn Mumbai into the "next Shanghai," and to do so "we want to put the fear of the consequences of migration into these people. We have to restrain them from coming to Mumbai" (Roy 2012: 8).

Tinubu and Fashola's bid to transform Lagos into a model megacity for the twenty-first century provides us with an account of the ways in which theatricality and performativity are increasingly dramatized in African metropolises, from Accra to Cape Town and Dar es Salaam. Painted street slogans—such as "For a better Mega-City, Pay Your Tax" (Figure 11)—have been used to significant effect by the Lagos Internal Revenue Service to raise tax consciousness in the city. Others like *Eko o ni baje* ("Lagos will not spoil," Figure 12) have been used not only to remind Lagosians of their duty to "Keep Lagos Clean" but also to sound a note of warning: "Don't Mess With Lagos" (Figure 13). These slogans, combined with emphasis on accountable governance, due process, and service delivery, plug into the "urban perfomativity" thesis which states that "good city planning demands an ethics of performance, whereby citizens become spectators and co-performers in the urban drama" (Makeham 2005: 150). Yet, performers and spectators often exist in a complex web of power that "heightens the drama of living" (Bacon 1974: 19). This urban drama begs uneasy questions: Who controls the performance space? Who has the right to it? And, importantly, whose interests are fostered by the performance?

Fig. 11. Lagos State public service announcement
Photo credit: Author

Fig. 12. The motto of Lagos
Photo credit: Author

Fig. 13. Public posting by the Lagos State Signage and
Advertisement Agency (LASAA)
Photo credit: Author

No Place for the Poor?

The Lagos urban renewal campaign reinforces the logic of the market that shapes
so-called "progressive" cities in contemporary Africa. The banning of roadside

vendors, the deportation of beggars, and the flattening of extra-legal structures are all external markers of the internal pains inflicted by the Fashola-led government on Lagosians, 60 percent of whom live below the poverty line. This pain was palpable in an interview I had with Abosede, a roadside *okro* seller in Oshodi, whose goods were destroyed by officers of the Kick Against Indiscipline (KAI), the paramilitary task force charged with enforcing the Lagos world-class city vision. Abosede tells her story:

> I am a roadside *okro* seller who was chased out of Oshodi by member of KAI [Kick against Indiscipline]. I used to earn my living from this *okro* selling but since *oga* [big man] Fashola's campaign, my source of livelihood has been taken away from me by force. Those with shops gloat at me because they think I am the one spoiling their market and preventing customers from coming to meet them in the shops. In less than one month, I became half of my body size. My children all quit school. I tried to go back to my village to start something. But those in my village chased me out of the market saying that there is no space for me. They mocked me that I have come from the big city to take their work. I cried.

Difficult experiences such as that of Abosede surfaced throughout my fieldwork in Lagos; they explain why many local newspapers have mocked Fashola's megacity vision by stating, "The true Lagosian is the rich man. The poor have been served quit notice. They are no longer wanted in Lagos… they can have no place in Lagos, if Lagos is to become the megacity of Fashola's lofty dreams!" (*Vanguard* 2013c). Other headlines are more explicit: "The Kidnapping of Poor Nigerians by Governor Babatunde Raji Fashola of Lagos" (*The Village Square* 2013), "WARNING: Poor People are not Wanted in Lagos Megacity" (Vanguard 2013c), "In Nigeria's City: Homeless are Paying the Price of Progress" (*The New York Times* 2013), "Can't the Poor Live in Lagos?" (NewswireNGR 2015). An editorial from the respected *Osun Defender* newspaper raised some critical questions about the impact of Fashola's megacity project on the Lagos poor in general and informal transport workers in particular:

> From mobile street hawkers consistently terrorized by KAI operatives to taxi drivers [increasingly] priced out of business by the government's decision to phase out the trademark yellow-and-black taxis in favour of brand-new cabs, to dumpsite dwellers at the mercy of a government that has no plans for them, to the multitudes forced out of the city into the hinterland under a puzzling "deportation" programme. Are we asking ourselves this troubling question: All these former *okada* drivers now out of work—where are they; what are they doing; how are they surviving? (Cited in Agbiboa 2017: 184)

In a similar vein, the Punch (2014a) newspaper noted:

> Today, the average Lagos commercial driver bears the burden of multiple levies.
> How can any business survive under such a draconian regime? With all its preten-
> tions to attaining mega-city status, Lagos has the worst transport extortion regime
> in Nigeria, Africa and perhaps the world… the different levies and impositions
> being heaped on commercial buses in Lagos State have become a disincentive to
> commercial bus operators. And the *danfo* [minibus-taxi] drivers ultimately pass
> on the heavy bill to the commuters, the common man, who will be forced to pay
> more for public transportation.

While the focus on Fashola's megacity project has been on multiple displacements
of slum dwellers and informal settlers, there is remarkably little work on its implications for informal transport workers in Lagos, and how these marginalized
and stigmatized "dirty workers" are experiencing and responding to this change.
Yet, there is no denying that reforming the transport sector forms the engine of
the Lagos world class city strategy. While the clearing of places such as Oshodi is
an oft-cited example of displacement by some observers (e.g. de Gramont 2015),
in reality it was a result of transport planning by Fashola's administration to ease
flows through the city and test the possibilities of clearing the railway corridor in
advance of a light railway planned to run along the existing rail tracks. Indeed, the
most important document to have emerged from the modernizing urban renewal
project was the Lagos State Road Traffic Law 2012, which, relegated *okada* drivers
from the city's lucrative center to its slow periphery. In what follows, I explore
the effects of, and resistance to, this law by *okada* drivers and their association.
But first, it is important to understand how and why an *okada* culture emerged in
Nigeria.

The Emergence of *Okadas* from the Era of SAP

Since the 1980s, the majority of urban Nigerians have relied on cheap, two-
stroke engine motorcycles for their daily commute, the common man being
too poor to own a car. Produced by foreign manufacturers, mainly Honda and
Yamaha, and imported secondhand, *okadas* emerged as a popular means of public transport for lowly Nigerians during a time of massive urban population
growth, when increased demand for mobility widened the gap between supply
and demand (Madugu 2018). By way of illustration, in northern cities such as
Kano, the population increased from 900,000 in 1983 to four million in 2012.
Prior to *okadas*, bicycles and donkeys constituted the primary forms of mobility for country dwellers (farmers) and poor inhabitants of outlying urban areas

in northern Nigeria (Udo 1970: 184). The emergence and reach of *okadas* revolutionized Nigeria's transport industry, positioning them as the number one means of movement and survival for people and off-road communities trapped in transport poverty. Although *okadas* have never been officially recognized as an income-generating activity in Nigeria, authorities have tolerated their operations. In this sense, *okadas* mirror the Nigerian society, where what is non-legal is not necessarily illicit.

The culture of *okada* in Nigeria is part of the broader informal transport industry that emerged in Africa around the 1980s as an indigenous response to government failure to provide adequate and affordable mass transportation services (Cervero & Golub 2007). In particular, the proliferation of *okadas* is traceable to the IMF-led Structural Adjustment Program (SAP) introduced by the IBB regime in mid-1986 to address the economic crisis that greeted the fall in oil prices. Nigeria's oil boom lasted from 1974 to the early 1980s, before being replaced by serious recession and debt crisis by the mid-1980s. The SAP was advanced by the IMF and World Bank as a panacea to the 1984 oil crisis in Nigeria, and its early phase saw the implementation of currency devaluation, elimination of subsidies, and reduction of state intervention in the economy. The SAP was meant to restructure and diversify the Nigerian economy, especially to reduce its dependence on oil and gas (Roy 2017: 10). However, these implementations led to the devaluation of the real incomes of the working class, so much that it became very difficult for salary earners to survive on their real earnings, forcing many struggling civil servants into multiple modes of livelihood, self-identification, and expression (Mustapha 1992).

Following an abrupt reversal in their living conditions, everyday life for many Nigerians became increasingly precarious. With the dwindling economic and traditional support base caused by the SAP, youth were pushed to the limits of survival; "many young men lost even the possibility to establish themselves as adults, by building a house or getting married—though they continued to become fathers, of children for whom they could not provide" (Utas 2005b: 150). In particular, the lack of social services along with the rising cost of education intensified by the withdrawal of the state from social provisioning made it difficult for Nigerian youth to attend, or remain in, school. The situation was not helped by the lack of available jobs after graduation, as was once the case. Such disempowering circumstances brought on frantic imaginings of the Nigerian youth as "a smoldering fire ready to burn African urban areas" (Bay and Donham 2007: 10). Nigerian newspapers of the 1990s and early 2000s painted a picture of the moral panic about the chronic crisis of youth in that era. In its piece "Nigerian Youths: What Hopes, What Future?", the *Post Express* of 1998 wrote: "Formerly a vibrant force for positive social changes, today's Nigerian youth has been clobbered by societal contradictions unto at best a supine state of schizophrenia and at worst unto a state of dare-devilry with increasing properties for anti-social activities… with its army of unemployed but qualified and able-bodied youth, Nigeria could be said to be sitting on a tinder-box" (Beekers, 2008).

The SAP introduced a mobility dimension to exclusion in Nigeria. By this I mean, "the process by which people are prevented from participating in the economic, political and social life of the community because of reduced accessibility to opportunities, services and social networks, due in whole or in part to insufficient mobility in a society and environment built around the assumption of high mobility" (Kenyon, Lyons, & Rafferty 2002: 210–11). Specifically, the withdrawal of the Nigerian state from social provisioning negatively impacted the public transport sector. "Roads deteriorated rapidly because of the shortage of funds for maintenance, vehicle purchases declined as a result of the escalating costs of imported vehicles, spare part supplies declined for the same reason, and much pressure was placed by the Bank to force cuts in fuel subsidies" (Porter 2012: 6). On top of this, Nigeria was hit hard by high inflation, which increased the cost of imported vehicles and made it difficult to replace worn-out vehicles with newer-looking ones. For instance, vehicle imports plummeted from 15,750 units in 1979 (during the oil boom) to only 2,729 units in 1986 when the SAP was implemented (Samaila 2015). The number of buses in circulation was severely affected. In Kano, for instance, the state official statistics show that in 1982, 5,000 buses were registered, but by 1986, that number fell remarkably to 565 (Kano State Motor Vehicle Statistics 1986: 4–5). This was a marked contrast to the halcyon years of the oil boom, when vehicle ownership was so high that even relatively poor farmers could afford an *okada* (Guyer 1997: 86). Official records show that the number of registered cars in Nigeria during the decade of oil boom doubled between 1976 and 1982 (Kumar & Barrett 2008). This unprecedented scale was largely due to the massive pay increases in the public and private sectors. Even those who could not afford a car of their own had the means to pay transportation fares (Porter 1995: 4).

Efforts by the federal government to address the problem of reduced mobility amid the economic crisis from the mid-1980s, most prominently the Urban Mass Transit program introduced in 1988, failed woefully (Madugu 2018: 45). To supplement their meagre wages, low-income workers increasingly converted their private cars to commercial use. But these car owners were reluctant to take their cars beyond paved roads because of the difficulties of obtaining spare parts and the soaring cost of pre-owned vehicles in Nigeria. As Gina Porter writes: "So long as sufficient business could be found on a motorable paved road, no transporter would risk his vehicle operating off-road routes" (2012: 16). As a result, people living in peripheral regions and off-road communities found it difficult to bridge spatial distance and improve their chances of upward mobility, giving rise to further exclusion and inequality. Women in particular were adversely impacted by poor roads and transport services, which impinged on their access to markets, services in health and education, agricultural extension services, and banking facilities and credit. This reinforces the point that "being mobile and immobile are important factors of social differentiation and a generator of patterns of inequality" (Ohnmacht, Maksim, & Bergman 2009: 20).

A combination of high population growth, desertification, moribund infrastructures, and shortage of investment stretched the carrying capacity of Nigeria's rural economy to its limits, provoking a hemorrhaging of young, jobless, and single men into urban areas in search of survival jobs and/or access to formal education (Meagher 2013: 170). The youth turn to urban centers as a survival strategy supports the argument that "for many people across the world, moving into the city from rural areas or smaller towns is a first step in achieving social mobility" (Jaffe, Klaufus, & Colombijn 2012: 644). Urban life, however, offered no guarantee of instant financial security for rural migrants. Once in the cities, many youths turned to *okada* work (Figure 14), reinforcing the argument that transport work in Africa often provides a route out of poverty and is central to attaining successful, sustainable livelihoods (Porter et al. 2017). *Okada* drivers soon became "men who have not been put to work in factories, or farms, who cannot enter the civil service, who in many cases are even denied the rights to full adulthood within a hierarchical society because many cannot marry. They are men without status" (Walker 2016: 137–38). This is particularly true of northern Nigerian cities, such as Maiduguri, where driving *okadas* became a way for single men to pay often inflated bride prices, marry a wife, and overcome shame by carving out new spaces of belonging. In short, "Bike riding is about building up one's personhood as a responsible and full member of society, an adult, in continuous check and balance with the environment… [by] riding a bike, young men had found a way to overcome at least partially the social inertia of not becoming adults, caused by the lack of resources" (Burge 2011: 60).

Okada drivers exploited an unmet need in Lagos, tapping a revenue stream that had not existed previously for timely transport (Ismail 2016: 148). The *okada* driver's time-saving tactics included driving on the wrong side of the road and ignoring traffic regulations. Because *okada* drivers could weave in and out of traffic gridlocks and take people to their destination in time (a rush hour commuter in Lagos can take three hours to cover fifteen kilometers), they became very popular among Lagosians of all walks of life, navigating both spaces of enormous wealth and privilege (such as Lekki, Victoria Island, Maryland, and Ikoyi) and "bastions of the uninhabitable" (Simone 2016b) (such as Ajegunle, Agege, and Amukoko). The time-space compression that *okadas* embody in Lagos meant that *okada* drivers were constantly exposed to, and reminded of, larger systems of exclusion and exploitation (cf. Sopranzetti 2014: 125; 2017). *Okadas* were soon nicknamed *Okada Air*, which, during the 1980s, was the most popular local airline in Nigeria. *Okadas* in Lagos serviced an estimated ten million commuters every day and provided jobs to more than 500,000 urban youth (including

Fig. 14. *Okada* drivers in Alimosho, waiting for passengers
Photo Credit: Author

graduates) as drivers, renters, mechanics, and spare-parts dealers. Taxes paid by *okada* drivers constitute an important source of revenue for the local government through the umbrella transport union, the National Union of Road Transport Workers (NURTW). During my fieldwork in Lagos, the roads were often bursting with young men carrying passengers on their *okadas* and weaving in and out of go-slowed traffic, often recklessly, their passengers holding on for dear life.

The popularity of *okadas* among marginal men in Lagos derives precisely from their relatively low start-up capital and maintenance costs (Ismail 2016), as well as the feeling of economic freedom and autonomy that *okadas* afford. As Thomas Hansen writes: "The promise of earning a fast buck in a job that does not require formal training, the cool style of the drivers, and the sheer promise of a world flush with quick cash and potential have made the industry a highly attractive place for many young men" (Hansen 2006: 187). For many *okada* drivers, the *okada* business is their primary source of income. "*Okada* business puts food on my table and change in my pocket. Otherwise, I will be on the streets," said a young driver in Alimosho. The *okada* business is made more attractive by relatively high daily takings. The majority of *okada* drivers that I spoke to have a net daily earning of between N3000 (USD9) and N5000 (USD13), a substantial pay, considering that Nigeria is home to the largest number of people living in extreme poverty, with around half of the country's population thought to be living on less than USD1.90 a day (CNN 2018).

To most Lagosians, *okada* drivers symbolize the precariousness and struggle economy of city life, but they also represent the "do-it-yourself" mentality of Lagosians in the face of crisis. Commuters who used *okada* did so because of their easy maneuverability on congested routes and poorly maintained roads. However, some commuters disliked *okadas* because of their propensity to cause accidents as well as their expensive nature compared to other means of public transport. Nearly all commuters accused *okada* drivers of being rude men, inclined to violence, law breaking, and criminally minded. "These *okada* men you see everywhere are good for nothing," said a commuter in Oshodi, adding that "They are foul-mouthed and violent." The *okada* experience is publicly humiliating for some women because of "the indignity of having to roll up your skirts past your knees, sometimes revealing your underwear. A respectable housewife, a corporate lady, a college principal, all having to sit behind a stinking dirty *okada* driver. Sometimes body hugging [to avoid falling off]. And the risk to limbs and arms" (Saheed n.d.; Animasawun 2017: 246). Despite their dangerous reputation, many Lagosians continue to use *okadas* for lack of a better option. Said one resident of Lagos: "When you're involved in *okada* accident, the fastest way to hospital is on the back of an *okada*. When your wife goes into labor, *okada* is the fastest way to the hospital. *Okada* is like water— it has no enemy." Herein lies the contradiction of *okadas*. "If you are in a car or bus, you will curse their incessant horn-blowing and gadfly dodging across lanes; if you are late for a meeting, you will silently cheer your *okada* driver as he rides roughshod over traffic laws to get you to your appointment in time" (Peel 2010: 91– 92). *Okadas* are symptomatic of government failure in Lagos and, more broadly, in Nigeria. "Why Exactly are Lagosians attracted to motorcycles? Why, despite the deaths and robberies, do they keep flying bikes on highways?", asks one Lagos-based journalist. "The answer is traffic—the maddening Lagos traffic that makes multi-car owners abandon their intimidating machines at home and fly bikes to work instead. Solving the traffic conundrum is what [the state] should be doing, not the self-confessed 'wielding the big stick'" (The Cable 2020). In their blatant flouting of the rules of the road, argues Michael Peel, *okadas* reflect and reinforce "an economic system in which a lack of regulation has allowed debatable charges, hidden taxes and extortion to flourish" (2010: 92).

"Na Condition Make Crayfish Bend:" Why Youths become *Okada* Drivers

At the outset, the work of *okada* is embedded in a "complex situation of disadvantage" (Mehretu, Pigozzi, & Sommers 2000: 14). Narratives of circumstances that pushed many young men to take up *okada* work are emblematic of the "tortuous paths and the complex trajectories" of motorbike-taxi drivers elsewhere (such as Bangkok; see Sopranzetti 2014: 124). During the course of my fieldwork in Lagos, many *okada* drivers adduced various circumstances of social disadvantage that had compelled them to do *okada* work, most commonly a lack of economic alternative, desire to achieve a personal ambition (such as acquiring a university degree), dreams of paying bride-price and marrying a wife, or simply the need to *chop* (eat). Nearly all *okada* drivers described some difficult experience in their life that made them "try their luck" in the *okada* sector. A common saying among *okada* drivers in Lagos was *"Na condition make crayfish bend,"* which suggests that poor conditions (such as the failure to find employment after graduation) forced many youths to join the *okada* business. For these young men, *okada* work was essentially a means to a desired end rather than an end unto itself. The personal narratives of Tayo, Akeem, and Akangbe—three *okada* drivers in Lagos—are particularly revealing.

Tayo, a twenth-eight-year-old university graduate, explained the frustrating experience that pushed him into the *okada* business:

I am a graduate of public administration from AAU [Ambrose Ali University]. I graduated with a second class upper. Upon graduation, I did the compulsory NYSC [National Youth Service Corp program] for one year. But I did not get a job after. For two years, I roamed the streets with my CV with nothing to show. Most of the money that I saved up from my *alawi* [a government stipend during NYSC] was spent in applying for jobs. I made it to several interviews but I was rejected. My brother, we both know that in Nigeria it is all about "long legs" [connections] and whom you know. If you don't have any Big Man like myself, it is almost impossible to make it. I saw candidates who had third class or even a pass. They were offered a job ahead of me because they had connections. Me, I don't know anyone but God. Sometimes, I was told to bring N50,000 or N25,00 to "settle" [bribe] those who will review my job application. But these were all "419" [fraud]. My money was eaten and there was no job. Seeing my plight, my poor mother took out a loan from her informal cooperatives, which I then used to purchase this *okada* to put food on the table for myself and daughter. I feel like I wasted my time and funds in the university because now I can't use my certificate to eat and thank my poor mother who worked hard to train me. I feel like the system has failed me and I am really sad. But since stealing is not an option for me, I have to continue in this *okada* work to survive. My wife used to assist me with some cash from her hair making business. But she died last year from appendix, which burst in her stomach because we did not have money to take her to the hospital on time for the operation. Life is really hard but I have to be strong, at least for my little daughter and my mother. Life goes on.

Tayo's case sums up the trouble with Nigeria, which compels many highly qualified but unemployed university graduates to turn to *okada* driving as a survival strategy or to avoid the shame that comes with unemployment. In Nigeria, most jobs for graduates offer meager salaries that are barely enough for basic survival. It is common for a university graduate to earn a monthly salary of N15,000 (USD75), out of which s/he must devote N10,000 (USD70) for the cost of bus fare. However, many graduates still accept such jobs partly to avoid the stigma associated with idleness in Nigeria. As one graduate told me, "I needed to get out of the house and search for job, any job. An idle mind is the devil's workshop." For such poorly paid graduates, a worthless job does not exist. To ensure their daily bread and avoid a life of shame, they would do anything (Mbembe 2001a: 157; cf. Trefon 2002: 487). On the poor salary situation in Nigeria, one retired traffic police officer in Alimosho told me, "Things are getting worse daily because there is [a] scarcity of jobs outside. Look at the turnout of students everyday in the university. There is no job for them. [It] is just the problem of this country. So, if it happens that I say I want to employ people for [a] traffic job and I ask them to pay N50,000 up front, they will bring it, because there are no jobs outside. And it fuels corruption. The Yorùbá adage says *eni ebi npa ko gbo wasu* ['You don't preach to a hungry person']. So, you find out that corruption increases."

The second story is that of Akeem, a thirty-year old man who migrated to Lagos from Osun state in search of a better life. Akeem's father sold his only plot of land to raise the money needed to acquire his *okada*. Through *okada* work, Akeem hopes to raise enough money in a few years to return his father's favor and acquire a college degree.

> I have always wanted to be a graduate of mechanical engineering—that's my dream. I desire it a lot. It is my passion. But my family is very poor. My dad is a farmer and my mum sell *okrika* [second-hand clothes]. My parents could not afford to send me to university. We are five in my family. I'm the last born and the only boy. My elder sisters had to sell bags of pure water on extremely dangerous highways so that I can raise money for my secondary school. One of them was even forced into early marriage to raise money for us. None of my sisters went to school as my parents felt they were girls and it was a waste of time. I came to Lagos and took this *okada* business to make something good of my life. It's not easy but I am coping by God's grace.

Then there is Akangbe, a forty-five-year-old "youthman" who became an *okada* driver to save up toward getting married and socially becoming a man.

> I joined *okada* to raise money to marry so that I can become somebody, a man. I will be 45 years old this year and I'm still not married and no children. Most

people laugh at me and call me a boy because I can't take care of a family. So, I took up *okada* work to raise money in order to marry a wife, to feel good about myself again. You know, it is not easy to marry a wife these days. The family of the woman wants so much and the list of things you have to buy is a lot for a poor man like me. My girlfriend of many years left me last year for another man because he had money to throw around and her family encouraged her to leave me, even though we have been together for more than five years. I know she love me more, but she was under pressure. Nowadays, girls their eyes are open. They like money and will go for comfort than love.

Okada Associations: Predators and Protectors

Okada driving in Lagos is embedded in strong support networks that put the notion of "people as infrastructure" (Simone 2004b) into practice. Ordinarily, all new *okada* drivers in Lagos must obtain drivers' cards and register their motorcycles with one of the several *okada* associations affiliated with the National Union of Road Transport Workers (NURTW) and the Road Transport Employers Association of Nigeria (RTEAN). These include the All Nigerians Auto Bike Commercial Owners and Workers' Association (ANACOWA), the largest *okada* association in Lagos with about 57 branches, the Amalgamated Commercial Motorcycle Owners and Riders Association of Nigeria (ACCOMORAN), the Motorcycle and Tricycle Operations Association of Nigeria (MOTOAN), and the Motorcycle Association of Lagos State (MOALS). These associations control the market through self-regulation; they provide protection to their members, represent their interests, and use their economic power and numerical strength to influence political or policy decisions. These associations emerged to fill the void left by government failure to regulate the public transport sector (Kumar 2011: 17). *Okada* associations are often highly organized into zones, with each zone controlled by a branch of the union.[6] In addition to the daily taxes collected by the local council—known as "tickets"—all *okada* drivers are required to pay a one-time NURTW membership fee in return for the right to operate and form an identity. Ticket collections constitute a primary source of revenue for the *agberos*, who purchase them in bulk from the local government and sell them to *okada* drivers at inflated prices.

In Lagos, the NURTW's control is enforced by the *agberos* who extract ticket payments from *okada* drivers, a day-to-day practice which can quickly turn violent should the driver be reluctant to pay the illegal ticket fee. The NURTW's

---

[6] Across Nigeria, *okada* associations have sometimes demonstrated themselves to be highly organized and politically engaged. For example, Smith recalls how *okada* drivers were among the most ardent supporters of the new Biafra movement: "They spent hours at newsstands in towns across southeastern Nigeria, discussing the country's ills, debating the best solutions to problems of corruption and inequality, and sharing the latest political rumors…" (Smith 2014: 796–97).

chain of command is generally well defined: the *agbero* is in charge of ticketing and collection of illegal dues, which he remits to his unit chairmen, who report to the zonal chairman, who reports to the local chairman, who, in turn, reports to the state chairman, who is the direct connection to the national Chairman and, along this chain, financial returns must be made on a daily basis. These burdensome ticket dues—a constant source of (violent) confrontation between drivers and *agberos*—are used to manage and oil the NURTW's operations by seeking favors from politicians and police chiefs. During my fieldwork in Oshodi and Alimosho, *okada* drivers shared harrowing stories of clashes over inflated taxes on the daily tickets issued by *agberos*, resulting in the death of, or injury to, fellow drivers. One *okada* man had this to say about the routine ticket extortion:

> Every morning we have to pay ticket money to agberos. On the ticket from the local government is written N100, but *agbero* will add one more zero to it to make N1,000. If you argue, they will beat you up, damage your *okada*, and stop you from working. Some of the union boys carry *juju* (charms) in form of a ring (*oruka*). When they slap you, you're gone! Because of their spiritual power, we don't waste time arguing with them. We settle them and get on with our work to avoid delay. What else can we do?

One *okada* driver who plies the Oshodi-Ikotun route told me that he pays N1,400 (USD3.58) daily (for booking and loading) to the *agberos*. Of this amount, he gets a receipt of only N300 (USD0.77). He pays another N100 (USD0.26) called *owo chairman* (money for the union chairman), bringing his daily total to N1,500 (about USD4). This largely unreceipted payment to the NURTW is separate from another N500 collected by a different set of *agberos* contracted by traffic police inspectors in complicity with members of the Lagos State Traffic Management Authority (LASTMA). Recently, NURTW-affiliated *okada* associations in Lagos, such as NNAMORAL Motorcycles Owners and Riders Association, have been embroiled in a negotiation with the new wave of bike-hailing startup companies (Gokada, Oride, and Max.ng), whose drivers are forced by *agberos* to part with five times the original price of union ticket fees on a daily basis (*Quartz Africa* 2019). On the front of most "official" tickets issued by the *agberos*, the sum of N100 is printed in bold. On the reverse side, however, the handwritten sum of N500 next to an official stamp is the real charge, according to many *okada* drivers whom I spoke to in Lagos. An NURTW official explained this apparent discrepancy: "For our collaboration with the companies and the government, we have allowed them to pay N500 (USD1.38) which is half of what the normal *okada* in Lagos pays. And then they will also get N100 (USD0.27) tickets from their local governments, that brings it up to N600 (USD1.66) daily per bike" (*Techpoint.africa* 2019). However, an executive of one of the bike-hailing companies dismissed this claim: "Except government taxes [N100], every other thing is extortion" (*Quartz Africa* 2019).

Resisting the *agberos* in Lagos is generally not recommended since "with these unions, matters ranging from takeover of motor parks, failure to pay for tickets and dues by drivers, conflict of interest, as well as minor arguments, could spiral into bloody wars within hours... innocent members of the public caught in the crossfire end up paying the ultimate price" (*Sunday Magazine* 2017). As a result of having to pay daily union tickets, many operators in Lagos have been forced out of work/contract. As one driver explains:

> Many people get their vehicles on hire purchase basis and they have had to deliver certain amount to their principals. But if you calculate how much goes into payments to union people in Lagos, it has forced many people out of this business. There are many people who got vehicles from people in the past but could not pay when it develops fault because of the huge number of tickets you have to purchase before you can be allowed to work. It is pathetic. It's a huge tax empire. (Olawoyin. 2019)

The complicity of the NURTW and the Lagos State Government reinforces the argument that "state agencies often do not act on their own interest. Non-state agencies of governance are implicated in the transgression of state law by state agencies" (Eckert 2006: 53). Despite popular perception of the NURTW in Lagos as aggressive protection rackets mobilized by profit at the expense of laboring workers, along with growing calls for their statewide ban (*Sunday Magazine* 2017), membership in *okada* associations remains a supportive network of personal protection and solidarity for poor, often migrant *okada* drivers. For these drivers, the *okada* association is a means through which their everyday interests are protected within the predatory and unpredictable roads of Lagos. At the neighborhood units, members of *okada* associations, such as ANACOWA, form close-knit groups with a strong sense of collective identity. Drivers in Lagos described their associations as "brothers" and "extended families" in which all members provided each other with unwavering support, especially in time of *wahala* (trouble). As one driver puts it: "When we are driving *okada*, we are one... we protect the interests of the *okada* driver—whether right or wrong." Said another driver: "It's a system you enter by force—force of the economy. That's what always bring our solidarity—people united by frustration. It's like particles attracted by magnet" (Peel 2010: 93).

Okada associations render financial support to needy members by keeping a common savings (*ajo*) that is allocated to members "turn-by-turn" or based on emergency needs such as accidents, funeral, or marriage expenses. Such conviviality is fostered by mutual need and the prospect of mutual gain. The sense of solidarity among *okada* drivers cuts across ethnic and religious lines and is popularly expressed in slogans such as "Family" or "Mourn One, Mourn All," "Come Rain, Come Sun." These solidarity slogans reclaim the traditional Yorùbá worldview that generally frowns upon working exclusively for one's own profit (Beekers & Gool 2012: 23). Beyond financial support, members of *okada* associations also display a strong (sometimes blind) sense of loyalty, evident in the swift mobilization of *okada* drivers against any threat to their individual or collective survival. Accidents involving cars and *okadas* often draw scores of supportive *okada* drivers in a few minutes. Even the police are careful in how they deal with *okada* drivers; the Nigerian press has carried many accounts of deadly clashes between the two groups (Smith 2014: 796). "When we are driving an *okada* we are one," said an *okada* associational leader in Lagos. "We protect the interests of the *okada* driver—whether wrong or right" (Peel 2010: 93). In 2005, *okada* drivers destroyed property to the tune of N4 million in solidarity with one of their members who was shot and killed by a military officer after he crashed his *okada* into the officer's car (ibid.). It is in this context of solidarity that we must understand why *okada* drivers and their associational leaders took to the streets en masse to protest the Lagos State Road Traffic Law of 2012, which they perceived as discriminatory and violating of their right to move freely in Lagos, and therefore, their chances of everyday survival.

Conforming to the Right Path? Motorcycles, Morality, and Marginality

The late geographer Doreen Massey (1994: 156) draws our attention to the politics of mobility and access, arguing that "some are more in charge of it than others; some initiate flows and movement, others don't; some are more on the receiving end of it than others; some are effectively imprisoned by it." Two points are noteworthy here: on the one hand, the close relationship between power relations and the production of space, and on the other, the embeddedness of automobility within the political. As Tim Cresswell reminds us, "Movement is rarely just movement; it carries with it the burden of meaning and it is this meaning that jumps scales" (Cresswell 2006: 6–7). To these, I add a third important point—the closely intertwined nature of mobility and morality. All discussions of mobility are underpinned by "moral overtones of one sort or another" (Morley 2000: 238). This is true of *okada* work in Nigeria which, has been all along a site of monitoring, enforcement, and protection of public morality and sanity, reinforcing the manner in which urban spaces tend to give rise to "attempts to separate and draw lines; to policies of order-making and securitization" (Christensen & Albrecht 2020: 389).

Nowhere is this more evident than in northern Nigeria (especially Kano and Zamfara states), where Sharia law has been used to exclude women from using *okadas* in the name of public morality, generating popular discontent and protests among poor *okada* drivers (Adamu 2008: 148). The popular practice of men and women sitting very close to each other on *okadas* or siting astride an *okada* was interpreted as an offense to public morality. A group of concerned husbands disapproved of such type of iniquitous mobility. As the Acting Director-General of the Sharia Commission in Kano commented: "Everyone knows the type or manner in which women sit on *okadas* and it looks quite adulterous because women sit quite close to *okada* drivers with their bodies touching each other. If mere looking can lead to adultery, then the manner in which women sit on *okadas* can increase the rate of adultery" (*Weekly Trust* 2006). Subsequently, authorities in Kano and Zamfara banned women from using *okadas* to get around town (Adamu 2008: 148).

In Kano, the State House of Assembly passed its Traffic Amendment Law in May 2004, which forbade women from using *okadas*. The state then imported some 1600 three-seater motorized rickshaws (known as *adaidaita sahu*, literally "conforming to the right path") which, unlike *okadas*, preserved the sexual segregation of men and women. The law punished defaulters with six-month imprisonment and a fine of N5000 (USD37). A 9000-strong *hisba* vigilante was set up to stop *okada* drivers from carrying as passengers women unrelated to them. The *hisba* was entrusted with the powers to fine drivers and confiscate their *okadas*. Over 2000 *okadas* were confiscated by the *hisba*, who often ordered women off of them. A report by the Human Rights Watch alleges widespread abuses by *hisba* groups, including extrajudicial arrests and floggings; stopping vehicles carrying men and women and forcing the women to disembark; disrupting conversations between men and women in public places on the grounds of alleged immorality; the seizure and destruction of alcoholic drink and the causing of damage to the vehicles transporting them; and the violation of the rights of people to privacy (Mustapha & Ismail 2016: 3). Excluded and enraged *okada* drivers took to the streets in protest, attacking members of the *hisba* group, and setting fire to the state-endorsed tricycle-taxis. The *okada* protests were largely economically driven, as drivers stood to lose substantial income if the law held. Women, for instance, made up the bulk of *okada* passengers. Also, in barring women from driving with men, the law deepened the inequality between men and women. Equal access to transportation must be understood as critical to ensuring social and spatial equality (Polk 1998: 208). In Kano, the law banning *okada* drivers from carrying female passengers met with such resistance that Governor Shekarau had to relax it in his second term in order to avoid alienating the large Muslim *okada* constituency, leaving it to each operator's conscience whether to carry women passengers or not (Meagher 2018: 193).

If the rationale for banning *okadas* in northern Nigeria was public morality and decency, in Lagos, the official ban on *okadas* was legitimized as part of making Lagos a "world class" megacity and restoring sanity to chaotic roads. While in the case of northern Nigeria, local authorities made some effort, if woefully inadequate, to provide an alternative to *okadas*, in Lagos, *okada* drivers were left to fend for themselves, reinforcing popular views that the post-1999 Lagos renewal campaign had "no place for the poor."

The Lagos State Road Traffic Law

No urban transport policy has elicited more heated debates in Nigeria than the Lagos State Road Traffic Law implemented in 2012 by the Fashola-led government as part of its efforts to make Lagos a "world class" megacity and a "center of excellence." The Road Traffic Law (Schedule II) restricted the activities of *okada* drivers on 475 major routes, claiming that *okadas* facilitate incidences of armed robberies and constitute a menace to urban lives and properties. To support this point, the government produced a documentary, entitled *Aye Olokada* ("Life of an *okada* driver"), aimed at demonizing *okada* drivers and discouraging millions from using them. Labeling *okada* drivers as criminals was part of an official process of "erosion of the claim of the poor to be legitimate urban citizens" in the neoliberal city (Bhan 2009: 140). In a speech titled "Freedom from Fear," Fashola challenged critics of the traffic law to visit the hospitals and emergency wards and observe the countless poor Lagosians who have lost limbs and arms; those who have lost children; or those who have become orphans due to the recklessness of *okada* drivers. In less than two decades, argues Fashola, *okadas* have gained such huge prominence that they have become a phenomenon that should not have been allowed in the first place: "The only way to stop the business from flourishing is by not patronizing them… If the income from *okada* business dwindles, the business proposition of those in it will change" (Vanguard 2012a). Subsequently, in 2008, the Fashola government set up a Tribunal of Inquiry into *okada* activities across Lagos state. The Tribunal recommended that:

> It is necessary to restrict *okada* operations to those Local Government Areas where they are needed and even then, to certain roads within those Local Government Areas. They should then be prohibited from inter-Local Government operations as well as operations on our major highways and bridges like Third Mainland Bridge, Eko Bridge and all Bus Rapid Transit (BRT) designated routes. (Report of the Tribunal of Inquiry 2012)

At issue here is not simply the future of *okadas*, but of the entire *okada* culture in Lagos. As a fundamental aspect of mobility for millions of Lagosians, *okada* driving is embedded in affective economies and support social networks that build the infrastructure of Lagos. This, of course, is not to glorify *okada* drivers, whose dangerous conduct on the road has caused the untimely deaths of many Lagosians, earning them the tag "murdercycles." One senior editor of the *Vanguard* describes Lagos as at the mercy of *okada* drivers:

> Almost on a daily basis, bus and truck loads of youths are being transported into Lagos. These young ones have no relations in Lagos and are basically illiterates. They have no jobs and hope to get menial jobs in Lagos. Many of these end up as mai-guards, cart pushers, load carriers and majority end up as *okada* drivers who learn to drive *okada* on the high ways. They learn on the job and the result is the increase in accident rate. These *okada* drivers are everywhere in Lagos. You will find them on Apapa, Mile-Two, Oshodi-Apapa Expressway, inside streets and roads in Lagos. There are no rules guiding them. They ply their *okada* against the traffic and are often the cause of major *okada* accidents in Lagos which have claimed the lives of many…. These *okada* drivers have worsened the already chaotic traffic situation [in Lagos] due to deplorable condition of the road. In many places they occupy more than half of the road and policemen are helpless. They park on the roads, causing heavy traffic and obstruction. (*Vanguard* 2018)

In northern Nigeria, *okadas* are also known as *dàfàa-dukà* taxi ("cook all") because of their reputation of being frequently involved in road accidents—where, metaphorically, all will be "cooked." General hospitals across Nigerian cities from Lagos to Maiduguri often have a dedicated "*Okada* ward" or "Jincheng ward" (after the *Jincheng* motorcycles manufactured in China), where only victims of *okada* accidents are treated. In some cities, hospital records show that 75 percent of corpses in the mortuary belonged to *okada* drivers or their passengers (Dan Borno 2011). It is no wonder that for many operators, *okada* work is "a last resort because of the high risk involved in it. You could collide with a car, bus, tipper or trailer, or even your fellow *okada* driver" (*Daily Trust* 2015). Yet, according to one *okada* driver in Lagos, "the danger of driving a motorcycle is much less than the danger of starving without a job" (Animasawun 2017: 243). While acknowledging the dangers of *okadas*, one driver in Alimosho lamented the lack of a viable alternative:

> *Okada* used to be a very serious problem on our road. Drivers won't use their *okadas* to carry passengers but to snatch people's handbags. Before the law, *okada* accidents were 24/7. Some *okada* dead bodies are pulled out under trucks and trailers in Lagos almost on a daily basis. But with the law, accidents have reduced. So, governor Fashola has tried. But the real problem is that he has not given us *okada* drivers another option for eating. As far as you don't have anything to do, you will do and undo. Anything you see you will do. If you don't have work at hand, hunger will beat you. A hungry man is an angry man.

A leader of one of the *okada* associations believes that the real threat to public safety lies in Nigeria's poor quality roads rather than in *okadas*: "Our problem here is that of roads. The roads the government built since 1982 have not been renewed. The roads used by motorists are the very same ones used by cart pushers, water vendors, wheelbarrow, and my members—the *okada* operators. And the roads are not wide enough to contain the vehicles. This is why you see this congestion. It is not caused by my members alone. This is why a lot of road accidents involving my members happen." This claim is not without merit. Roads in Nigeria and much of West Africa are in a state of decay and dilapidation: "Central avenues are as bad as streets in peripheral neighborhoods. Many roads that were paved a few years ago are now paths of beaten earth. They are broken up by sections that juxtapose efforts at resurfacing with potholes, crevices, and ditches which can be as wide as the road itself. Most traffic circles are nothing more than a heap of old tires or empty, rusted barrels" (Mbembe & Roitman 1995: 328). No wonder a Yorùbá adage describes roads in Nigeria as the "long coffin that holds 1400 corpses" (Isichei 2004: 213).

One columnist in the Nigerian *Osun Defender* compared the scale of deaths caused by bad quality roads in Lagos to Boko Haram—the violent extremist group in northeast Nigeria that kills innocent people on a daily basis. The columnist adduces the case of the Lagos-Badagry expressway, which in the past seven years has become a death trap:

> From Seme, the Nigerian-Benin Republic border to Volkswagen in Ojo local government area of Lagos State, there are over 10,000 potholes and several other valleys that are big enough to consume a car. Ordinarily, from Seme border to Mile 12 is not supposed to be more than 45 minutes for any vehicle speeding at the moderate of 80km per hour, but due to the horrible condition of the roads, commuters spend more than 4 to 5 hours lurking one another up in hundreds of the bad spots on the road. As a matter of fact, vehicles plying the road get spoilt so easy, thereby making owners spend lot of hard-earned money in repairing their vehicles (*Osun Defender* 2012).

Turning now to the Lagos Road Traffic Law, the bone of contention centers on Section 3(1) (5) and (8), which restricts the spatial and temporal activities of *okada* drivers in the city and imposes serious punishment on offenders (up to three years imprisonment):

> *3—(1) No person shall ride, drive or propel a cart, wheelbarrow, motorcycle or tricycle on any of the routes specified in Schedule II to this law.*[7]

[7] From the perspective of the Lagos State Government, Section 3(1) of the LSRTL is a deliberate legislative response to the growing public concern about the spate of avoidable deaths, crime, and high casualty rate directly associated with the commercial motorcycle operation in Lagos.

(5) Any person who fails to comply with any of the provisions of this Section commits an offence and shall be liable on conviction to—

    (i) Imprisonment for a term of three (3) years or render community service in accordance with the provisions of Section 347 of the Administration of Criminal Justice Law of Lagos State; and

    (ii) Have his vehicle forfeited to the State

(8) As from the Commencement of this Law Commercial motorcycles shall only operate between the hours of 6.00 am—8.00pm within the State
(Lagos State Road Traffic Law [LSRTL] 2012: A76–A77)

The law gave much discretionary power to officers of authority to ensure implementation and zero tolerance. Section 28 of the law states: "Any Police Officer or officer of the Authority may apprehend without warrant any person who commits within his view, or whom he reasonably suspects of having committed, an offence under this Law" (LSRTL 2012: A88). The public outcry among *okada* drivers over such powers is not unjustified, considering that the Nigeria Police Force has an unenviable legacy of corruption, brutality, and low accountability (Agbiboa 2015). For instance, the #EndSARS protests that erupted across Nigerian cities in October 2020 were the result of decades of brutal and unaccountable policing. In giving discretionary powers to police officers, therefore, the law, ostensibly enacted to protect lives and properties on Lagos road, paradoxically created a vicious circle where insecurity produces the very behavior that fosters corruption and further urban insecurity. What the Lagos State Government is being indicted for here is the commission of "lawfare," that is, "the resort to legal instruments, to the violence inherent in the law, to commit acts of discrimination, coercion, even erasure... reducing people to bare life" (Comaroff & Comaroff 2006: 144).

Despite these restrictions (Figure 15), many *okada* drivers remained defiant by continuing to ply the restricted routes, daring the government-run paramilitary task force known as Kick Against Indiscipline (KAI). During fieldwork, I watched as KAI officers impounded or crushed hundreds of *okadas* and arrested their drivers en masse. According to Tunde, an *okada* driver in Alimosho: "Anytime we hear that KAI is around, we will take cover because there is nothing you can do but run. If you drag the *okada* with them, they will carry you and the *okada* to Alausa [Lagos State headquarters], which is double *wahala* [trouble]. What can you do? So, we run for our dear lives."

For many *okada* drivers such as Tunde, the state is at fault because it has not provided drivers with an alternative source of livelihood while depriving them of the only means that they have managed to create for themselves. On the issue of *okada* restriction, Lagosians that I spoke to were generally torn between a legalistic and survivalist approach. For some Lagosians, *okada* drivers are lawbreakers

Fig. 15. A street posting restricting road access for commercial motorcyclists (*okadas*)
Photo credit: Author.

who constitute a nuisance to Lagos roads. As one commuter said: "If they [*okada* drivers] are violating the law, then whatever happens is good for them. No one is above the law."

Other residents in Lagos took a different approach. Having just witnessed a crackdown on *okadas* by KAI officials, one market woman in Lagos told me, "In Nigeria today, there is unemployment everywhere you look. Universities are churning out graduates without jobs. These *okada* men are trying to survive on their own. The state needs to provide jobs for them. You can't just limit their mobility or take away their only means of eating, something they use to feed their family, and you expect them to disappear just like that. They won't." Taking this survivalist view further, civil rights activists in Nigeria have generally criticized the state ban on *okadas* as lazy and "anti-people":

The restriction on *okadas* is not only a lazy approach to problem solving, but pedestrian, unjust, inhumane, callous and vicious. Taxis and buses are used for the famous "one chance" [theft and kidnapping], why weren't they banned? Militants and pirates use[d] speed boats to bunker oil and attack ships on the high sea. Were they banned even at the height of the Niger-Delta militancy? For years, Nigerian airlines have become flying coffins leading to the death of hundreds, not even the lives of prominent Nigerians were spared. Aircrafts and air travel should have been banned! It becomes glaring why *okada* drivers are singled out for ban, throwing their families and dependents deeper into the abyss of privation. For

Fig. 16. Vehicles involved in road accidents in Nigeria
Credit: Nigerian Bureau of Statistics (2018).

such an anti-people move to be taken somewhat hastily without due consultation with stakeholders, to a large extent, is an indication that these state Governors have lost touch with the common man (Ilevbare, 2013, cited in Animasawun, 2017: 247).

For their part, *okada* drivers and their associations felt expressly discriminated against by the Lagos State Government, since other forms of transportation in the megacity were not restricted. In his Sworn Affidavit against the Lagos State Government at the Federal High Court in Ikeja, Mr. Aliyu Wamba, Chairman of the ANACOWA, claimed that *okada* restrictions were imposed by the Lagos State Government, "[on] account of our being poor and underprivileged as some of the deadliest robberies and felonies are committed using cars, and there are more fatal car accidents than *okada* accidents. We all pay permit fees to the government as conditions for operating *okadas* from which they (the government) earn sizeable revenue for Lagos. We are not averse to regulations which are limited to speed limits, use of helmets and maximum number of passengers." Survey evidence from the Nigerian Bureau of Statistics on cars involved in road accidents in Nigeria in 2018 confirms part of Wamba's claim (Figure 16).

Wamba's statement should be interpreted as an attempt by *okada* drivers in Lagos to lay claim to equal rights of membership in a political urbanity that is not only spectacularly unequal but also highly uneven. In the wake of their restriction, *okada* drivers took to the streets to protest indiscriminate arrest of their members and forcible seizure of their *okadas* by corrupt and violent police and KAI officials. The protesters carried placards with inscriptions such as: "You gave us no job, we gave ourselves one and you are killing us for it." "People like *okada* pass motor. Allow us! Free us!!!" "They say *okada* drivers are robbers, who gave them the guns?" "Fashola, give me my vote back." According to one of the protesters, "We are here to tell the Lagos State Government that enough is enough of the humiliation of poor people. The law banning *okada* is a bad law. This is the start of the struggle to liberate the poor people in Nigeria and the struggle must continue until we win" (Izuekwe, Dedeigbo, & Toheeb 2012).

Some protesters took out their anger on the World Bank-funded BRTs, vandalizing them and pelting their uniformed operators with stones. For *okada* drivers, the BRTs are symbols of their marginalization and oppression in the city they call home *(Eko Ile)*. Of course, the introduction of the BRTs into parts of Lagos, along with the creation of dedicated bus lanes for them, coincided with the prohibition of *okada* drivers from plying major roads and bridges across Lagos. That restriction led to the disappearance of *okadas* from many parts of the coastal city, leaving many Lagosians with no way to get to and from work. In addition, transport fares tripled with the contraction in supply. As one editor notes:

> The [*okada*] ban has abruptly eviscerated the means of livelihood of tens of thousands of Lagosians, mainly the already poor or semi-poor. There are families just getting by before that will now truly struggle to eat three meals daily. With the crowds at bus stops and terminuses these days, Nigerians are technically fighting a bloodshed-less civil war to navigate the otherwise simple task of finding a bus to office. Those who aren't strong enough for the challenge, or those who aren't patient enough to wait endless minutes, end up enduring the arduous option of long treks to their office and back home. (*The Cable* 2020)

The politics of patronage surrounding the Lagos state urban renewal project is also noteworthy. Many *okada* drivers felt betrayed by the Fashola-led government and his ruling political party, the All Progressives Congress (APC). During the mass protest, one *okada* driver displayed a banner with the inscription: "Fashola Distributed Helmets in 2011. NOW Destroying OUR Bikes." The import of this banner emerged in an interview with the late Dr. Fredrick Fasheun, the founder of the Oodua Peoples Congress (OPC) and National Chairman of the Unity Party of Nigeria (UPN):

> Lagos citizens must remember that this [APC] party used and dumped *okada* drivers after harnessing their support and services in the elections of 1999, 2003, 2007 and 2011. During campaigns for those polls, APC politicians even donated to *okada* drivers branded helmets, motorcycles and reflective jackets. But no sooner did the Action Congress of Nigeria [now a part of the APC] come into power than they turned around to bite the finger that fed them, by banning *okada* all over Lagos. (*The Punch* 2014a)

During my fieldwork in Lagos, many *okada* drivers told me that they received their *okadas* and crash helmets from Fashola's aides in the run-up to the 2011 elections, in exchange for their votes and loyalty to the APC. Such political stratagem is neither new nor unique to electoral politics in Lagos. Orji Uzo Kalo, the former governor of Abia state, won substantial support in his state by pledging and then creating a program to provide *okada* drivers with new motorbikes on credit

(Smith 2007: 198). Similarly, in Borno state, buying thousands of motorcycles for supporters was key to Ali Modo Sheriff's re-election in 2007. In the run-up to the 2015 elections in Lagos, the enforcement of the ban on *okadas* was appreciably relaxed across Lagos state in what was a deliberate political ploy aimed at securing the votes of *okada* drivers. In offering instant reprieve to *okada* drivers, political elites in Lagos had mastered the art of "manipulat[ing] the mechanisms of discipline and conform[ing] to them only in order to evade them…" (de Certeau 1984: xiv).

De Certeau's *The Practice of Everyday Life* (1984) is often deployed to illustrate how social actors in structurally weak positions use tactics in the absence of the possibility for more enduring strategizing. Here, however, I ascribe these tactics to political elites, not the *okada* drivers. In the wake of the traffic law, politicians from other Nigerian states seized the opportunity offered by the sour relations between *okada* unions and the Lagos State Government to shore up their own patronage. In the build-up to the 2015 elections, the governor of Ekiti state, Ayodele Fayose, pledged not to ban *okadas* as they had done in Lagos, arguing, "If you cannot provide an alternative, you must not take away the only one that is available. I won't ban *okada* in Ekiti state." Instead, Governor Fayose challenged *okada* associations across Ekiti to partner with his administration in registering all its members, in view of the incessant robbery operations that plagued the state. Addressing *okada* drivers in Ado Ekiti, Fayose said: "If they cancel *okada* in every other state, that won't happen in Ekiti State. But what I want is disciplined and responsible motorcyclists' association that can partner with government for meaningful development. Government alone cannot maintain security; I have to partner with an organization like you. But I won't tolerate unruly behavior" (*The Sun* 2014). The former governor of Edo state, Adams Oshiomole, also expressed similar sentiments, saying "It is a class issue and I belong to the working class, so I cannot ban *okada*. First, I believe that *okada* is a response to certain deficit in our intra-urban transportation system" (Ilevbare 2013). In like vein, the former governor of Anambra state, Peter Obi, commented: "I agree that *okada* contributes to crime, but we must also accept that many of them are also good people and we cannot punish the multitude because of the sins of a few" (Animasawun 2017: 246).

Of interest in this chapter is the fact that *okada* drivers in Lagos articulated their grievances in the language of rights (e.g. to free movement), their everyday struggle for rights being the means of contesting the perceived injustices and violence of the government toward them. As one *okada* protest banner read: "Okada and Tricycle workers! They have Human and Constitutional Rights!" The open defiance of *okada* drivers against the Road Traffic Law resulted in violent clampdowns from the KAI and the mobile police. In his sworn affidavit in the Ikeja High Court, Mr. Wamba criticized the fact that "On a day-to-day basis officers of authority forcibly seize our *okadas* and detain our poor members at the Task Force Office in Alausa.

Law enforcement officials have arrested me on a couple of occasions along with my *okada* forcibly seized from me and detained." If dealing with informality requires recognizing the right to the city of informal urban workers (Roy 2005: 148), then it is vital to probe deeper into what that right entails and how it applies to the daily struggle of *okada* drivers for economic survival and recognition in Lagos.

Right to the City: The *Okada* Struggle for Survival

Henri Lefebvre's (1996) "right to the city" remains a *tour de force* on how we theorize the politics of urban space and the transformative possibilities and practices of city life. Here, "right" refers not just to a "legal claim enforceable through a judicial process" but essentially a "right to totality, a complexity, in which the parts are part of a single whole to which the right is demanded... a collectivity of rights, not individualistic rights" (Marcuse 2009: 193). Lefebvre's right to the city is based on two fundamental rights—appropriation and participation—which are both earned through meeting particular responsibilities and obligations, in which each person helps to create the city as artwork by performing one's everyday life in urban spaces (Lefebvre 1996). By blending appropriation (usage) and participation (decision-making) rights into the inhabitance of urban space, Lefebvre challenges the fictional division between the public and private, while simultaneously rethinking both liberal-democratic forms of citizenship (Purcell 2003: 565) and capitalist social relations (Butler 2012: 150).

Lefebvre's concept of right to the city has some limitations. To start with, right to the city is imbued with a diversity of often-contradictory meanings (Marcuse 2014: 8). Many analysts (mis)read Lefebvre's right to the city as one aimed specifically and literally at the city as a built environment, that is, a fixed physical space. This "collaborationist" spatial reading, as Marcuse (2014) calls it, tends to overlook the power relations that entrench patterns of exploitation and adverse incorporation in the city. Yet, using the context of Lefebvre's own reading, the right to the city suggests a political claim and a revolutionary call, in short, a refusal to let oneself be discharged from the city through forced dispersal to the peripheries, with attendant dearth of economic opportunities (Lefebvre 1996: 158). More directly: "The right to the city legitimates the refusal to allow oneself to be removed from urban reality by a discriminatory and segregative organization. This right of the citizens... proclaims the inevitable crisis of city centers based on segregation.... which reject towards peripheral spaces all those who do not participate in political privileges" (Lefevbre 1996: 34). Here, the use of segregation implies both market-driven processes that deepen social divisions and accentuate the polarization of cityscapes, as well as the re-location of marginal groups into ghettos by deliberate enforcement of state policies informed by neoliberal visions. Lefebvre (1996) understands the proliferation of capitalist forms of accumulation as intensifying the disenfranchisement of urban inhabitants. To address this situation, he argues that the right to the city must necessarily involve an urban spatial approach to political struggles, with the participation of all those who inhabit the city without discrimination (Dikeç 2001: 1730). In this light, the Traffic Law in Lagos State represents a prime example of segregation in its restriction of *okada* drivers from plying 475 routes, leaving a dent on their daily struggle for survival. During my fieldwork, many *okada* drivers complained that the law has "added salt to our injury." As Jimoh, a driver in Alimosho, recounted:

> Before, I used to run my *okada* in Apongbon area. It is a busy area, and in a day, I can make up to N4000. Sometimes, I could earn N200 for just one trip with a passenger. And if the passengers are two, that will be N350. The trip is quicker because I pass through tarred express roads. But now, with the government ban on us, I have been forced to relocate to Ikotun where business is very slow and I operate mainly in small streets and over short distances. The roads are so bad and every time I have to take my *okada* to mechanic for repair because of one fault or another. Local government has refused to do anything. For them, it is not important road. For each trip, I get only N30. In a day I am lucky if I make N1,500. Yet my family *bukata* [needs] keep increasing. My four children need to *chop* [eat] and go to school. My first child, Banke, is starting high school this year. Where do I go from here? What else can I do?

Jimoh's concluding questions gives a sense of how the need to maintain a dignified life underlies the poor's sense of justice (Bayat 1997: 61). For an impecunious head of a household such as Jimoh, not only would the failure to provide for his children impinge on the quality of their lives, it would inflict an excruciating blow to his pride as a complete man. Jimoh's predicament and fear of "social death" mirrors that of many drivers who have seen their daily income halved by the enactment of the Road Traffic Law. A significant number of *okada* drivers are now without identified work after the seizure and destruction of their *okada*s by law enforcement agents such as KAI and the police. According to Wamba:

> Many of (my *okada* members) have huge responsibilities. Some have more than one wife and two to three children in the university. I'm aware of one of my members whose first child is currently at 400 level while the younger one is 200 level at the university. This man uses proceeds generated from his *okada* business to pay their school fees, buy books and provide feeding allowance for them. Now, under this current situation how will the man cope? Government just wakes up one morning and say to hell with their problems.

Against this backdrop, the dragging of the Lagos State Government to court by *okada* drivers and their associations (ANACOWA) may be represented as an effort by the latter to reclaim their right to the city which, according to Lefebvre (1996: 158), implies "a cry and a demand... a transformed and renewed right to urban life." The demand, on the one hand, derives from "those directly in want, directly oppressed, those for whom even their most immediate needs are not fulfilled." The cry, on the other hand, comes from "the aspiration of those superficially integrated into the [capitalist] system and sharing in its material benefits, but constrained in their opportunities for creative activity, oppressed in their social relationships... unfulfilled in their lives' hopes" (Marcuse 2009: 190).

In its Originating Summons against the Lagos State Government and its security agencies, members of the Autobike Commercial Owners and Workers Association (ANACOWA) claimed, among other things, that the forcible possession of their *okada*s by the police and KAI violates not only their right to free movement but also their rights not to have their moveable property (their *okada*s) compulsorily possessed, as guaranteed by section 44(1) of the Nigerian Constitution. This claim is not unrelated to the grievances of drivers regarding the corrupt and coercive manner in which members of the police and KAI have enforced the law. During my interviews with *okada* drivers in Lagos, a recurrent source of anger and frustration was the manner in which the Traffic Law and the *okada* ban has created more room for *egunje* (bribery) by law enforcement agents. Drivers accused KAI officers of "eating" their hard-earned income in the guise of applying the law, even when they were not plying the restricted routes. Notably, in 2011, the Lagos State Government sacked ninety officials of the KAI over cases of stealing, extortion, and obtaining money from commercial drivers under false pretenses (*PM News* 2011). One commuter in Oshodi complained about how policemen and KAI officers aggressively pursue *okada* drivers right into the inner streets without regard for human life on the *okada*. Seun, an *okada* man in Alimosho, bemoaned the fact that,

> The traffic law has created plenty room for police and KAI officers to collect more money from us with license. Whenever and wherever they see us these days, they stop us. There is always one fault or the other, always one reason to stop us and demand *kola* [bribe] from us. Things have become worse since the law gave them plenty powers. They threaten us with taking our *okada*s to Alausa where it would be grounded. If you fail to give them N5000, *tie ti tan* [you're finished].

In the wake of the *okada* ban, the streets and highways of Lagos degenerated into a space of negotiated bribery between *okada* drivers and members of the police-*cum*-KAI. The latter often operated in an ambush-like manner,

> suddenly emerging from hidden places to pounce on the *okada* driver who usually have to stop suddenly, sometimes leading to accidents in which the passenger, the driver and the policeman would sustain injuries. If no injury is sustained,

the passenger is allowed to go while the negotiation between the policemen or LASTMA officials as the case may be, commences. If the *okada* driver has sufficient money ranging from 2,000 to 3,000 naira, the *okada* driver is released immediately. If the *okada* and/or the driver is taken to the Police Station, the driver or owner in some cases will have to pay a bribe as high as 5,000 naira to ensure release of the motorcycle, or risk permanent confiscation and/or trial and three years' imprisonment upon conviction. However, the bribe given to policemen is considered a milder option by many of the *okada* driver interviewed. This is because, according to them, if an *okada* is seized by a LASTMA official, rather than a police officer and it is taken to their office the chances of "negotiation" are close to zero because the official penalty which is "non-negotiable" is 20,000 naira and/or three years in jail. In instances of arrests where the *okada* driver feel they outnumber the policemen, they usually decide to resist the impounding of their motorcycles which often triggers clashes between them and the law enforcement agents, which can lead to fatalities and casualties. (Animasawun 2017: 258)

In Alimosho and Oshodi, where my fieldwork was conducted, *okada* drivers lamented the fact that the police and KAI men routinely abused the powers afforded them by the Traffic Law to confiscate *okadas* and use them for their own private purposes. Drivers shared experiences of how their colleagues who refused to surrender their *okadas* to KAI were badly beaten, some to death, by the security operatives. There was a story of how a police officer knocked down an *okada* driver while he was trying to escape. In the process, he fell off his bike and dislocated his left arm. While the driver was still struggling to get up, the policeman impounded his *okada*, leaving him lying in his own blood. There were other reported stories of an *okada* driver stripped naked and another who was shot in the chest by the police and died hours later from his wounds. Former *okada* drivers claimed that they saw policemen and KAI officials using their seized *okadas* to run errands and even driving them on the prohibited routes with impunity. ANACOWA Chairman Wamba condemned the predatory manner in which law enforcement agencies in Lagos interpreted the law:

The law states that when you are caught violating the prohibited routes, you will be charged to court. The minimum fine is N20,000 for first offender. If you commit the offence a second time, your *okada* will be impounded. But this is not what they are doing at the moment. Whether you ply the prohibited routes or not, wherever they set their eyes on you, your *okada* will be impounded. Even if you're fixing your deflated tire with a vulcanizer, the police or task force members will stop, and impound your *okada*. For now, the police are haunting *okada* drivers. It was in the newspapers that the Lagos State Government grinds about 3,000 *okadas* daily. We have firsthand information that some task force members and police officers were even selling the impounded *okadas* and sharing the proceeds among themselves.

At other times, some of them converted these *okadas* for personal use. (*Vanguard* 2012b)

For *okada* drivers in Lagos, the Road Traffic Law demonstrated the insensitivity of the Lagos State Government to the plight of informal workers who get by under extremely difficult circumstances. As one Lagosian told me, "The Lagos State Government clearly does not know the hard life and stories of these *okada* drivers. This is evident in the haste with which they rolled out the traffic law. For many of these drivers you see, life is a constant war." Consider the story of Kehinde, an *okada* driver in Alimosho who fell victim of the law. A university graduate of Banking and Finance, and formally account officer with WEMA Bank in Lagos, Kehinde's second shot at life ended abruptly with the forcible possession and destruction of his *okada* by the KAI:

> I was a Cashier with WEMA Bank until I was sacked in 2011 as fallout of the Central Bank of Nigeria's tough stand on the bank. I went around in search of jobs to no avail and I decided to gather what I have to buy *okada* so that I could make ends meet. This unfortunate event happened to me immediately after my wedding so I had to look for an alternative means of making a living pending when I get a better job. Rather than roaming the streets, I decided to become an *okada* driver carrying passengers from here to there. But now, my *okada* has been taken from me and destroyed. I am now out of frying pan into the fire.

Toward the Culture of Legality?

This chapter set out to interrogate the legal disputes resulting from the Lagos State Government's restriction of *okada* drivers from plying major routes in Lagos state as part of its modernizing ambition to make Lagos a world class megacity. We have seen how the enactment of the Road Traffic Law has had the effect of reproducing precarious existence for *okada* drivers, while creating more "legitimate" avenues for bribery and corruption by law enforcement agents. This perceived oppression of their poor drivers has inadvertently awakened the rights consciousness of *okada* associations, who have appealed to state laws to contest a law that erodes their livelihoods and renders them invisible in the city they call home, *Eko Ile* ("Lagos Home"). By reclaiming their right to the city, *okada* drivers legitimize their refusal to be relegated from the city's center to its periphery by a discriminatory and subjugative system of spatial legislation and restructuring. Beyond the usual narrative of Africa's urban marginals improvising survival tactics in subcultures outside hegemonic structures (Honwana 2012), the *okada* drivers and their associations in Lagos developed a fluency in the "language of stateness" (Hansen & Stepputat 2001), as exemplified by their frequent reference to the Nigerian Constitution to justify their claims for political inclusion, non-discrimination, and equal citizenship under the law. The legal disputes between *okada* drivers and the Lagos State Government highlight the need to adapt urban reform policies to the local context. This will require city planners and policymakers to develop a hybrid framework that not only engages African cities as socially and physically constituted spaces (Rakodi 2006: 312), but also integrates the voices of all those that would be affected by urban reform legislations, especially informal urban workers. As Vanessa Watson argues, "Unless planning approaches... are closely aligned to the strategies of survival of poor urban populations, there is little chance that they will make a positive difference" (2009: 187).

During my fieldwork in Lagos, the Road Traffic Law was frequently criticized by *okada* drivers and union leaders as "*wuru wuru* to the answer" (a sprint to the answer), meaning that the law was hastily drafted without due consultations with drivers and their associations, who remain the mainstay of mass transport in Lagos. As ANACOWA's Chairman, Wamba, stated in an interview: "We were not consulted when the bill to ban commercial motorcyclists was in the works... the *okada* operators were not carried along... What the government would have done was to distribute the complete document to all *okada* drivers' associations in Lagos for scrutiny before the eventual endorsement of it into law... Let the *okada* drivers make their own input. Perhaps, all these controversies would have been averted." Wamba's words allude to the idea of "adverse incorporation," which emphasizes the *terms* rather than the *fact* of urban inclusion. The call here is to move beyond popular narratives of mere "exclusion," towards a better understanding of how poverty often stems from the disadvantageous ways in which people are incorporated into social and economic life (Hickey & du Toit 2007: 31).

The above explains why *okada* drivers and their associations have resolutely resisted the Traffic Law to the point of suing the Lagos State Government over what they perceive to be a wanton violation of their right to the city. This legal action by informal *okada* associations indicates their collective refusal to be "imposed upon and resisting being fixed and bounded in place" (Blair 2019). At the same time, it adds weight to the argument that urban Africa is becoming saturated with legality as social conflicts, once articulated by popular means of street protests, increasingly find their way to the judiciary (Comaroff & Comaroff 2006: 143). Far from the conventional view that Africa is indifferent to constitutionalism, the legal action by *okada* drivers and their associations indicate that a culture of legality seems to be pervading everyday life. Africa's informal workers are increasingly appealing to the law as a viable way of contesting their exclusion from the city. By using the language of rights to express their grievances against their marginalization and oppression in the city, *okada* drivers come to imagine themselves as "rights-bearing-persons" (Eckert 2012). This suggests that turning to law is not simply a weapon of combat (Comaroff & Comaroff 2006), which evokes a winner-loser binary, but an act of "rightful resistance"[8] (O'Brien & Li 2006) in which the urban poor seek active involvement in decision-making processes that affect their lives. This explains why ordinary people invoke the law even when they have little to no chance of winning (Eckert 2012: 167). Such legalism from below sheds light on our rather limited understanding of the right that informal urban workers perceive themselves to own toward the state. For their part, city governments in Africa today find themselves increasingly under pressure to justify their public actions.

---

[8] The concept of rightful resistance describes a form of partially institutionalized popular contention against the state, whereby aggrieved citizens seek to legitimize their causes by making use of state's own laws, policies, or rhetoric in framing their protests (see O'Brien & Li 2006).

Conclusion
Learning from Corruption

Corruption is at once everywhere and nowhere. So elusive is the concept of corruption that some researchers see it as an "empty signifier" (Koechlin 2013). In spite of this—or perhaps because of it—the concept of corruption is frequently used throughout the social sciences. In this study, corruption was interrogated as a multi-faceted phenomenon, located in "gray zones" between the legal and the illegal, and shaped by the complex and shifting interactions between political, social, and economic actors and processes (formal and informal). Going beyond the conventional definition of corruption as "private regarding behavior of public officials for money or status gains" (Nye 1967: 420), a normative analysis that fastens upon self-interested individuals, this grounded, place-based study underscored the role of mutuality, that is, the ambivalence, ambiguity, and hybridity of corrupt discourses and practices (Routley 2016). At its core, mutuality is about how state (formal) and nonstate (informal) actors and logics overlap and imbricate themselves in each other's lives (Golomski 2020), with both actors situated in unequal and ambivalent "social relations that constitute and position desiring subjects" (Hasty 2005b: 365). Such mutualities call attention to the concept of "incompleteness" (Nyamnjoh 2017) as the main condition of African politics, of the powerful no less than of those whom they prey upon (Englund 2018: x; Mbembe 2001a). It also reinforces the observation that formal/informal division is not a useful distinction in Africa, since "illegal practices are also performed in the formal sector, while so-called informal economic networks operate with well-established hierarchies and are fully integrated into social life" (Hibou 1999: 80). Corruption, therefore, becomes a productive arena for exploring the intersections of the formal and the informal, the urban and the political, and the spatialization and materialization of power, exclusion, and inequality in cities.

This study problematized the essentialism, cultural determinism, and functionalist explanation that characterizes the dominant approaches to corruption in contemporary Africa, in the form of neopatrimonialism, which tend to obscure rather than clarify "important differences between many African countries and neopatrimonial regimes" (deGrassi 2008: 112; see also Pitcher, Moran, & Johnston 2009). One popular conclusion is that in the end "what all African states share is a generalized system of patrimonialism and an acute degree of apparent disorder" (Chabal & Daloz 1999: xix). A similar claim is that while neopatrimonial practices

They Eat Our Sweat. Daniel E. Agbiboa, Oxford University Press.
© Daniel E. Agbiboa (2022). DOI: 10.1093/oso/9780198861546.003.0008

exists in all polities; in Africa, it constitutes the core feature of politics (Bratton & van de Walle 1997: 62). This study took issue with such convenient claims that corruption in Africa is *sui generis* and an indigenous pathology. Seeing the state and political failings in Africa purely through the uncritical and de-historicized lens of neopatrimonialism is problematic in many ways:

> (1) It has established and naturalized a supposedly characteristic form of leadership and governance to the continent as a whole; (2) it has attributed to this form of governance both the failure of African states to operate according to the principles of liberal democracy and the "passivity" of African citizens in demanding accountability; and (3) it has located the poor economic performance of postcolonial Africa in the political chaos caused by "strong men" and "weak states." It thus makes historical, political, and economic claims about the continent as a whole, providing a neat and consistent explanation for violence, state collapse, petty to extreme corruption, irresponsible resource allocation, and a host of other ills. (Pitcher, Moran, & Johnston 2009: 141)

Against this backdrop, it becomes apparent that any critical understanding of corruption in Africa requires an empirically grounded approach that pays attention to the longue durée of corruption-talk (Pierce 2016) and the political and moral economies (Olivier de Sardan 1999) of formal and informal and elite and non-elite relationships in specific sectors, especially their ability to foster agency (Meagher & Lindell 2013: 62) and double capture (Goodfellow 2017). In so doing, the study has transcended the conventional *idea* of the state, inviting us to explore the multiple forms of governance and the less formal, everyday interactions that animate corruption. In a sense, then, this book is a response to the pertinent question raised by Obadare and Adebanwi: "How might street logic (say, the common roadblocking policeman's requesting query: 'wetin you carry'?) be linked to state logic (say, the 'national cake,' or the metaphor of 'a land flowing with milk and honey') in understanding the collusion and collision of the powerful and the powerless?" (2013: 13).

Corrupt practices are extremely difficult to extricate from other social behaviors because of their embeddedness in wider everyday practices that are not corrupt *sensu stricto* but tend to facilitate and legitimize corruption (DFID 2015: 25). In this light, corruption becomes a constitutive element of daily life, melding state politics with societal (urban) politics. This melding is most evident in the fluid and contradictory space of the road, which constitutes a fertile ground for understanding how the state and state agents are constructed and contested from below. Inside the tight spaces of the *danfos*, I observed that poor passengers were often more willing to parse their frustrations about government failures and the violent demands for bribes at countless roadblocks manned by police and/or NURTW touts. This willingness reflects the level of anonymity that the *danfo* guarantees:

passengers enter and exit en route. Like power, corruption is about politics, "not just in the formal sense, but also more broadly, about the politics of everyday life" (Clegg 1989: 149). To grasp corruption, therefore, one must attend to the underlying narrative and interpretative frames that ordinary people deploy to negotiate power relationships and make meaning of life's events.

Devoting sustained attention to the micro-dynamics of corruption in the road transport sector of Lagos, this study provides a detailed excursion into the way that corruption and coercive practices by officials of the NURTW (National Union of Road Transport Workers) and law enforcement agents impinge on the workaday world of transport workers. Going beyond celebratory narratives of Africa's informal economy as transformational, the evidence presented here reveals a predatory union-state alliance that criminalizes the hard work and "eats the sweat" of drivers, making their driving work a "Living Hell," as one *danfo* slogan puts it. An analysis of petty corruption sheds light onto the exchanges between drivers and bribe-eating officials at checkpoints, and how the latter "exercise claims to wealth through violent means" (Roitman 2004: 13).

At least three important points are raised here. First, given the vital role of social norms in the diffusion of corruption in Nigeria, the intertwining of street- and state-level corruption must be recognized and emphasized. This falls within what Mbembe calls the logic of conviviality, that is, "the dynamics of domesticity and familiarity, inscribing the dominant and the dominated within the same *episteme*" (2001a: 110). Second, a vital aspect of this book is its analysis of the language, idioms, and imageries of corruption, particularly the metaphorical connections between corruption and eating, or what Nyamnjoh (2018) calls "eating and being eaten." Rumors about greedy elites consuming the state illustrate a "quiet encroachment of the ordinary," described by Asef Bayat as "the silent, protracted but pervasive advancement of the ordinary people on the propertied and powerful in order to survive and improve their lives" (1997: 57). Third, average Nigerians are not necessarily innocent victims of corruption but often active participants who are compelled to participate in corruption by an urban spatiality where being an honest and law-abiding citizen no longer pays (Osoba 1996: 384). As one *danfo* slogan in Oshodi puts it: *"Naija No De Carry Last,"* implying that Nigerians strive to finish first, even in matters of fraud. Slogans such as this one point to how "state intuitions and economic precariousness are folded into people's intimate relations, commitments, and aspirations" (Han 2012: 17).

By locating corruption within the NURTW-state mutualities—as enacted at lucrative but contested transit sites such as bus stops, checkpoints, and junctions—this book demonstrates how and why centers and margins endlessly redefine each other. At the same time, it underscores the role of the state as a creator and regulator of inequalities (Mbembe 2001a: 44). State officials who were authorized to enforce the Lagos State Road Traffic Law became active participants in the illegal. In the wake of the *okada* ban, police and KAI officers instrumentalized the

Traffic Law to extort more money from marginalized *okada* drivers, showing how those in charge of enforcing the law in Africa today often (ab)use their privileged position to bend and break these rules for private gain (Titeca 2012: 49). Alejandro Portes calls this the "informalization of privilege" (Portes, Castells, & Benton 1989). Moreover, the government ban on unofficial but legitimate practical occupations such as *okada* driving, a fundamental source of daily survival for marginal men in Lagos, points to how the putative line between what is legal and what is illegal is increasingly "a political one, established by the dominant to maintain their power and control" (MacGaffey & Bazenguissa-Ganga 2000: 5).

The predatory way in which the Traffic Law was enforced on the roads of Lagos reinforces the law as a powerful arena for the exercise of biopower—becoming a potent weapon to legalize the criminalization of an entire way of life and to deprive many laboring subjects of the ability to have control over their daily life (Butler & Athanasiou, 2013: 6). The law in this case constitutes what Mbembe (2003: 38) calls "necropolitics" (or "letting die")—that is, contemporary forms of subjugation of life to the power of death. The Lagos ban on *okadas* denied many marginalized and stigmatized men of their only source of livelihood, thereby creating "death-worlds" that subject these dispossessed workers to the status of "living-dead" (Mbembe 2003: 39). Far from an outside-of-the-law site of economic survival and empowerment for disadvantaged sections of the city, informal road transport work is experienced as "a site of disempowerment, which further entrenches clientelist practices. In other words, rather than representing a disengagement of the state, the informal economy signifies an engagement with the state: rather than constituting an escape route from a corrupt state, it is intrinsically part of the corrupt state" (Titeca 2012: 49). Yet, by using state law as a weapon of combat, *okada* drivers and their close-knit associations demonstrate two things: first, that the informal urban sector is not only a space of "nonmovements," but a central site of "social movements" (Bayat 2009). Second, that this mobile sector is not only a site of strictly *economic* survival, but a more general *political* site of resistance and redress: "It is a reaction against the state and the domination of the political class, and their neglect of the concerns of the marginalized groups—the 'powerless'" (Titeca, 2012: 48).

"Margins are a necessary entailment of the state, much as the exception is a necessary component of the rule" (Das & Poole 2004:4). This statement is confirmed in how grand and petty forms of corruption are routinely intertwined at the motor parks, bus stops, and junctions of Lagos, particularly how the relationships of collusion and collisions between union leaders and state officials reflect a shared moral economy, which is as much about profit maximization (Thompson 1971; Scott 1976) as it is about "maintaining and accumulating social relations" (Newell 2012: 67). The avaricious and immoral politics of the NURTW in cahoots with the state, party politics, and law enforcement agents, have rendered both the union and the state "less a public good than a social relation of domination founded essentially on coercive exchanges, plunder and consumption" (Mbembe & Roitman 1995: 335).

Despite its centrality to everyday corruption, there is a dearth of research on the informal transport sector in Africa. This book foregrounds the road transport sector in how people routinely encounter the translocal state and come to think of and socially navigate its generalized informal functioning (Blundo & de Sardan 2006), which cuts deeply into the very structure of people's lives. The book's focus on the endemic crisis encountered by informal transport workers stresses the precarity that is involved in the everyday attempt by minibus- and motorbike-taxi drivers to reclaim economic agency and assert their right to a city they call *Eko Ile* ("Lagos home"). For every single driver that I encountered during my fieldwork in Lagos, transport infrastructures, in the form of checkpoints, bus stops, and junctions, constituted a locus for bribery and coercion, giving rise to fear, popular discontents and disillusionment with the NURTW-state mutuality. The vast bulk of transport workers in Lagos saw their driving work as a blessing and a curse, as both a space of agency and a source of limitation. The voices and lived experiences of commercial drivers in Lagos point to how informal workers in Africa are increasingly exploited and immobilized through infrastructures that "facilitate the flow of goods, people, or ideas and allow for their exchange over space..." (Larkin, 2013: 327–28).

Across African cities, transport infrastructures are key sites of corruption, coercion, and complicity that not only reveal the "negotiated nature of statehood" (Titeca & de Herdt, 2011), but also the symbiotic relationship between space and (in)justice. Mustafa Dikeç calls this "the spatiality of injustice and the injustice of spatiality" (2001: 1792). In *Mobility Justice*, Mimmi Sheller shows how the governance and control of movement are inherently shaped by power and inequality, and gives rise to unequal patterns of mobility (2018: 32). In a similar vein, Hagar Kotef and Merav Amir argue that "control over movement was always central to the ways in which subject positions are formed and by which different regimes establish and shape their particular political orders" (2011: 63). This argument is confirmed in the study of "roadblock politics" in the Central African Republic (CAR), which shows how control over roadblocks along strategic transit and trading routes constituted a fundamental source of "logistical power" and an "object of struggle" (Schouten 2019). That study found that armed predation at roadblocks in the CAR is central to the political and financial power of "entrepreneurs of imposition," to wit, rebel militia groups and state security operatives. The "politics of pillage" that governs roadblocks in the CAR makes it difficult for local people to go to farms and markets, thus eroding their livelihoods (Schouten & Kalessopo 2017: 12). If "a study of automobility is also necessarily an exploration of the complicated ways that consumption, mobility, stasis, scarcity, and excess all intersect along West Africa's bumpy and multidirectional roads" (Green-Simms 2017: 4), then localizing corruption within the "system" of transportation in Lagos, as this study has done, allows for both specialized and comprehensive analyses of the political economy of everyday life. Moreover, mobile ethnographers have long argued that being "on the move" is a powerful way to "venture into" people's lives and "to understand their social and cultural reality" (Neto 2017: 141). Therefore, this study has treated movement along the fast and slow lanes of Lagos as a privileged site of research and observation of corruption, complicity, precarity, and social navigation.

Evidence presented here suggests that it may be more constructive to reroute corruption as a "collective action-social trap" problem rather than the more conventional "principle-agent" mode of thinking. On the one hand, collective action argues that if corruption is the social norm in any society, individuals will opt to behave in corrupt ways, because the costs of acting in a more principled manner dwarfs the benefits, at least at the individual level. On the other hand, the principle-agent theory approaches corruption exclusively as an agent problem (Booth & Commack 2013). In this perspective, corruption is said to occur when principals are unable to monitor agents effectively, and the agent betrays the principal's interest in the pursuit of his or her own self-interest (DFID 2015: 15). In Lagos, a commercial driver who is reluctant to offer water (bribe) to quench a thirsty police officer when pulled over is commonly derided by his own passengers as *oponu* (an ignoramus or a very stupid person), a "Good Samaritan," or a "JJC," short for "Johnny Just Come" (a naïve newcomer to Lagos). As a result, almost every driver in Lagos has become fluent in the oft-coded "language of corruption" and skilled in bribe negotiation. These capabilities constitute a precondition of daily survival in Lagos, as the failure to decode the *rules* of corruption could result in substantial delays, trumped-up charges, vehicular and bodily harm, or even (social) death. These rules fall under what Elinor Ostrom (2005) calls "work rules" or "rules in use" and what Peter Hall (1993: 281) calls "standard operating procedures." Although these "work rules" are unwritten, ordinary practitioners of Lagos (e.g. road transport workers) are generally familiar with them; they know "how the system works and how to work the system" (Dougherty 2000).[1]

More than simply the pursuit of private gain, involvement in corruption in Lagos chimes with broader concerns or benefits that reinforce the struggle for

---

[1] While living in Panama, Elizabeth Dougherty describes her encounter with a policeman who pulled her over to give her a ticket. As the officer approached her car, she took all the money save USD5.00 out of her wallet and stuffed the rest under her car seat. After a lengthy interaction with the policeman during which she pretended not to speak Spanish and to not understand his demand for bribe. The frustrated policeman got into her car and "He told me to drive down the road to a largely abandoned parking lot in order to explain to me how to make this exchange. 'Look, *this is how it works*. I stop you and give you a ticket. Then you give me money so you do not have to waste your time going to the police station to pay a larger fine than the money you are paying me. Understand?' I told him I did and handed him the $5.00 in my wallet, saying how sorry I was that this was all the money that I had, whereupon he got out and walked away" (Dougherty 2002: 198; my emphasis).

survival. On the one hand, drivers and conductors are compelled to pay bribes at roadblocks—manned by violent motor park touts and gun-toting, woefully underpaid policemen—not simply to avoid physical harm, which is serious enough, but to prevent their family from dying of hunger. "I have mouths to feed," said an *okada* driver who had just paid his onerous N1000 ticket fee. "If I don't settle them [*agberos* and police officers], they won't let me work. My family will go hungry. Then what kind of a man am I?" So, in Lagos, drivers are not only "dying of corruption" (Holmberg & Rothstein 2011) but also performing corruption to avoid "social death." This equilibrium of mutual expectations—that is, the view that one disadvantages oneself by not engaging in corruption—supports the argument that, "Whoever practices corruption auto-legitimates his own behavior, by presenting himself, for example, as a victim of a system in which he is bound to this kind of practice to avoid wasting time and/or an insupportable amount of money, being penalized or condemned to inactivity" (Olivier de Sardan 1999: 29).

So, while road transport workers in Lagos resent corruption and are generally in favor of stamping it out, the pursuit of survival and the avoidance of shame force many to partake in the corrupt practices that they denounce.

Some African case studies (for example, the DRC) argue that commercial taxi drivers do not see corruption as "morally problematic" (Alexandre 2018: 570). Others (such as Ghana) claim that "many people do not see anything wrong with [petty corruption] and do not think about it as corruption" (Lindberg 2003: 135). In Lagos, nothing could be further from the truth. During my interviews, informal transport operators routinely lamented the "evil" of extortion, with many calling for a revolution to address this crisis of corruption that they see as endemic rather than episodic. A distinction, a necessary one, must be made between people's involvement in corruption as a survival tactic and their personal views about the system. As Bo Rothstein puts it, "cultural values and actual practices are not always consistent" (2018: 40). For example:

> Respondents in the Afrobarometer survey for eighteen sub-Saharan African countries were asked their views on scenarios in which an official either "decides to locate a development project in an area where his friends and supporters live"; "gives a job to someone from his family who does not have adequate qualifications"; and "demands a favor or an additional payment for some service that is part of his job." Between 60 and 76 percent of the 25,086 respondents considered all three examples of corruption to be "wrong and punishable," while only a small minority view such actions as "not wrong at all." Furthermore, only about 20 percent deem these actions "wrong but understandable." (Rothstein 2018: 39)

On the other hand, the cash bribes collected around the clock by the *agberos* are distributed along a convoluted financial chain that serves to keep the union-state coalitions winning. This cash distribution shows how the informal transport sector in Lagos has become a big business to all those who feed off it. An obvious but over-looked element of this mutually reinforcing union-state relationship is the fear and insecurity that compels both sides. Given this "ordered corruption" (Blundo 2006: 260), the issue of who is actually running things is often unclear, as "complicities of all kinds between supposed antagonists are often necessary in order to maintain any semblance of order" (Simone 2016b: 5). This reinforces the idea of the "corrup-tion complex," which involves practices that are often connected to corruption but may or may not be illegal as such. No wonder, then, that an evidence paper on cor-ruption by the UK Department for International Development (DFID) concluded that corruption is a collective (rather than purely individualized) challenge: "It in-volves a variety of interactions, dynamics and linkages between multiple actors, organizations and institutions at different levels" (DFID 2015: 79).

The Africanist scholar Giorgio Blundo (2006: 260) reached a similar conclu-sion from his ethnographic inquiry into the social world of public procurement in Senegal. He found that corruption functioned "across networks and alliances, which tend to structure themselves and become permanent." Commonplace cor-ruption, he notes, derives from a triangular and complicit system composed of "corrupting contractors, corrupted officers, and intermediaries, giving rise to real chains of complicities." In Lagos, we have seen that in return for helping rig elec-tions, the state government allows the NURTW to control the roads and motor parks. This suggests that instead of placing corruption *in* context, we need to see corruption *as* a context of action and meaning (Vigh 2009: 5). Unless corruption's real but perversely counterintuitive networks, pacts, and coalitions are taken se-riously, "success stories" will continue to be "depressingly thin on the ground" (Hough 2017). This study shows that anti-corruption policies have "hardly had an impact on levels of corruption 'on the ground'" (Rothstein 2018: 39), precisely because "on the ground" realities of corruption have never truly penetrated "top down" anti-corruption cleanups.

In sum, this book takes an empirically grounded approach—an anthropological approach if you like—to corruption, which grounds corruption in the daily formal and informal encounters of mobile subjects with the state and the union, and in the state-union mutuality. Drawing upon a combination of documentary sources, ethnographic interviews, and cumulative observations on the bottlenecked and dangerous roads of Lagos, the study argues that corruption is not embedded in Nigerian "culture" but is in fact shaped by popular efforts to manage precarious lives in transit by bending the rules. In place of a culturalist approach to corrup-tion, this study offers a more pluralist perspective that considers how informal transport workers have developed normative systems to fit their own needs rather than following the rules or breaking them. Challenging the conventional distinc-tion between grand and petty corruption, this study argues that both typologies are deeply intertwined and continually imbricated in the texture of everyday ur-ban life. Thus, it offers an approach to corruption "from below" that is not detached from but rather inextricably linked to corruption "from above" in the Lagos transport sector. Furthermore, it analyzes precarity and popular agency in the context of neoliberal urban reforms that reproduce rather than address corruption, insecurity, and radical uncertainty. This is not just a book about corruption but also about Lagos, its transport system, and the society surrounding it.

References

Abbas, Ackbar. 1999. "Dialectic of Deception." *Public Culture*, 11 (2): 29–45.

Abrams, Philip. 1988. "Notes on the Difficulty of Studying the State." *Journal of Historical Sociology* 1 (1); 58–89.

Achebe, Chinua. 1964. *Arrow of God*. London: Heinemann.

Achebe, Chinua. 1983. *The Trouble with Nigeria*. London: Heinemann.

Achebe, Chinua. 1999. "Africa is People." *The Massachusetts Review*, 40(3): 313–321.

Adamu, F.L. 2008. "Gender, *Hisba*, and the Enforcement of Morality in Northern Nigeria." *Africa* 78 (1): 136–52.

Adebajo, A. 2008. "Hegemony on a Shoestring: Nigeria's Post-Cold War Foreign Policy." In *Gulliver's Troubles: Nigeria's Foreign Policy after the Cold War*, edited by A. Adebajo & A.R. Mustapha, pp. 1–37. Pietermaritzburg: University of KwaZulu-Natal Press.

Adebanwi, Wale. 2017. *The Political Economy of Everyday Life in Africa: Beyond the Margins*. Rochester, New York: Boydell & Brewer.

Adebanwi, Wale and Obadare, Ebenezer. 2011. "When Corruption Fights Back: Democracy and Elite Interests in Nigeria's Anti-Corruption War." *The Journal of Modern African Studies*, 49 (2): 185–213.

Adebanwi, Wale, ed. Forthcoming. "Introduction: Everyday State and Democracy in Africa." In *Everyday State and Democracy in Africa: Ethnographic Encounters*, edited by Wale Adebanwi. Athens: Ohio University Press (forthcoming).

Adebanwi, Wale, and Ebenezer Obadare. 2011. "When Corruption Fights Back: Democracy and Elite Interest in Nigeria's Anti-Corruption War." *The Journal of Modern African Studies* 49 (2): 185–213.

Adejumo, A.A. 2016. "Our Politicians, the NURTW and Us." *Trumphet Media Group*, August 01.

Adekanye, B.J. 1993. "Military Occupation and Social Stratification." An Inaugural Lecture Delivered at the University of Ibadan. November 25.

Ademowo, A.J. 2010. "They are Poor and Violent: Stereotypes and the Ibadan Urban Motor Park Space." 197–220.

Adetayo, O. 2020. "Nigeria's Bus Drivers Battle Thugs, A Union and Police in Lagos." *Aljazeera*, October 14.

Adichie, C. 2014. *Americanah*. New York: Anchor Books.

Adinde, S. 2020. "The Implications of the Lagos Okada Ban." *Stears Business*, February 26.

Afikehena, J. 2005. "Managing Oil Rent for Sustainable Development and Poverty Reduction in Africa." Paper presented at the UNU-WIDER Jubilee Conference: "Thinking Ahead: The Future of Deveopment Economics." Helsinki, Finland.

AFP. 2015. "Gangs Threaten Election Peace in Nigeria's Key City." *Agence France Presse*, March 19.

Africa Confidential. 2000. "High Street Havens." October 27.

Afrobarometer 2018. "Public Perceptions of Nigerian Government's Fight Against Corruption Improves, Study Shows." Abuja, January 15.

Afrobarometer Data. 2006a. "Corruption in Kenya, 2005: Is NARC Fulfilling Its Campaign Promise." Afrobarometer Briefing Paper No. 26: 1–7.

Afrobarometer Data. 2006b. "Round 3, Questions 58a, 58 b, and 58c for: Benin, Botswana, Cape Verde, Ghana, Kenya, Lesotho, Madagascar, Malawi, Mali, Mozambique, Namibia, Nigeria, Senegal, South Africa, Tanzania, Uganda, Zambia, Zimbabwe. Retrieved from <https://microdata.worldbank.org/index.php/catalog/887>

Agamben, Giorgio. 2009. *What is an Apparatus? And Other Essays.* Palo Alto: Stanford University Press.

Agbaje, A. and Adisa, J. 1988. "Political Education and Public Policy in Nigeria: The War against Indiscipline (WAI)." *The Journal of Commonwealth & Comparative Politics* 26 (1): 22–37.

Agbese, P.O. 1992. "With Fingers on the Trigger: The Military as Custodian of Democracy in Nigeria." *Journal of Third World Studies* 9 (2): 220–53.

Agbiboa, Daniel E. 2011. "The Corruption-Underdevelopment Nexus in Africa: Which Way Nigeria?" *The Journal of Social, Political and Economic Studies* 35 (4): 474–509.

Agbiboa, Daniel E. 2012. "Between Corruption and Development: The Political Economy of State Robbery in Nigeria." *Journal of Business Ethics* 108: 325–45.

Agbiboa, Daniel E. 2015. "'Policing is not Work: It is Stealing by Force': Corrupt Policing and Related Abuses in Nigeria." *Africa Today,*62 (2): 95–126.

Agbiboa, Daniel E. 2016. "A Child's Eye View of Corruption." *Oxford Development Matters,* May 9.

Agbiboa, Daniel E. 2017. "The Rights Consciousness of Urban Resistance: Legalism from Below in an African Unofficial Sector." *The Journal of Legal Pluralism and Unofficial Law,* 49(2): 183–203.

Agbiboa, Daniel E., ed. 2018a. *Transport, Transgression and Politics in African Cities: The Rhythm of Chaos.* London: Routledge.

Agbiboa, Daniel E. 2018b. "Conflict Analysis in 'World Class' Cities: Urban Renewal, Informal Transport Workers, and Legal Disputes in Lagos." *International Journal of Urban and Regional Research,* 29: 1–18.

Agbiboa, Daniel E. 2018c. "Informal Urban Governance and Predatory Politics in Africa: The Role of Motor Park Touts in Lagos." *African Affairs,* 117 (466): 62-82.

Agbiboa, Daniel E. 2019. "The Manipulations of Time: On the Temporal Embeddedness of Urban Insecurity." *Urban Studies* 56 (4): 836–51.

Agbiboa, Daniel E. 2020a. "How Informal Transport Systems Drive African Cities." *Current History,* 119(817): 175–181.

Agbiboa, Daniel E. 2020b. "Between Cooperation and Conflict: The National Union of Road Transport Workers in Lagos, Nigeria." *Crime, Law and Social Change,* 73: 605–622.

Ahearn, L.M. 2001. "Language and Agency." *Annual Review of Anthropology* 30: 109–32.

Ahmed, S. 2014. *The Cultural Politics of Emotion.* Edinburgh: Edinburgh University Press

Aina, O. 2014. "How Corruption Contributes to Poverty." International Conference on Development of Social Enterprise and Social Business for Eradication of Extreme Poverty and Street Begging, holding at Chittagong," Bangladesh, December 19–20.

Aina, Tade. 2003. "Working People's Popular Culture in Lagos." In *Leisure in Urban Africa,* edited by T. Zeleza and R. Veney, pp. 175–92. Trenton, New Jersey: Africa World Press.

Ake, Claude. 1995. "Socio-political Approaches and Policies for Sustainable Development in Africa."In *African Development and Government Strategies,* edited by B. Onimode, pp. 5–19. London: Zed Books.

Akinnola, R. 2008. *The Politics of Corruption and the Corruption of Politics: The Atiku Abubakar Cases in Perspective.* Lagos: Rich Consult.

Akinwale, Anthony. 2017. "Let's Stop Talking About Corruption." *The Guardian,* December 04.

Akoni, O. 2013. "14,300 Lagos Drivers are Partially Blind—LASDRI Boss." *Vanguard*, September 17.

Akyeampong, E. 1996. *Drink, Power and Cultural Change: A Social History of Alcohol in Ghana, c. 1800 to Recent Times*. Oxford: James Currey.

Alam, M.S. 1989. "Anatomy of Corruption: An Approach to the Political Economy of Underdevelopment." *American Journal of Economics and Sociology* 48 (4): 441–56.

Alao, A. 2000. "Security Reform in Democratic Nigeria." Working Papers, The Conflict, Security and Development Group, 1–52.

Albert, Isaac Olawale. 2007. "Between the State and Transport Unions: NURTW and the Politics of Motor Parks in Lagos and Ibadan." In *Gouverner les villes d'Afrique: Etat Governement Local et acteurs Prives*, edited by L. Fourchard, pp. 125–38. Paris: Karthala.

Alexandre, A.B. 2018. "Perceptions of Corruption by Traffic Police and Taxi Drivers in Bukavu, DR Congo: The Limits of Moral Analysis." *Journal of Contemporary African Studies* 36 (4): 563–74.

allAfrica . 2007. "Nigeria: Corruption Fights Back." 18 April.

Alou, Mahaman T. 2006. "Corruption in the Legal System." In *Everyday Corruption and the State: Citizens and Public Officials in Africa*, edited by G. Blundo & J.-P. Olivier De Sardan with N.B. Arifari & M.T. Alou, pp. 137–76. London: Zed Books.

Amin, Ash, and Nigel Thrift. 2002. *Cities: Reimagining the Urban*. Oxford: Blackwell.

Amnesty International 2005.

Anders, Gerhard. 2009. *In the Shadow of Good Governance: An Ethnography of Civil Service Reform in Africa*. Leiden & Boston: Brill.

Andreski, Stanislav. 1968. *The African Predicament: A Study in the Pathology of Modernization*. London: Michael Joseph.

Andrews, Edmund, L. 1997. "Behind the Scams. Desperate People. Easily Duped." *New York Times*, January 29.

Andrews, M., and L. Bategeka. 2013. "The Role of the State in Economic Development: Employment Challenges in Uganda." EPRC Working Paper. Kampala: Economic Policy Research Center.

Aniekwe, Chika Charles and Agbiboa, Daniel E. 2014. "Civic Engagement and its Role in Mitigating Electoral Violence in Nigeria: Implications for the 2015 General Elections." Social Science Research Network, Working Paper, December 21.

Animasawun, Gbemisola. 2017. "Marginal Men and Urban Social Conflicts: *Okada* Riders in Lagos." In *The Political Economy of Everyday Life in Africa: Beyond the Margins*, edited by W. Adebanwi, pp. 239–63. Rochester, New York: Boydell & Brewer.

Anjaria, Jonathan Shapiro. 2011. "Ordinary States: Everyday Corruption and the Politics of Space in Mumbai." *American Ethnologist*, 38(1): 58–72.

Appadurai, Arjun. 2004. "The Capacity to Aspire: Culture and the Terms of Recognition." In *Culture and Public Action*, edited by V. Rao & M. Walton, pp. 59–84. Stanford: Stanford University Press.

Apter, Andrew. 1993. "Atinga Revisited: Yorùbá Witchcraft and the Cocoa Economy, 1950–1951." In *Modernity and its Malcontents: Ritual and Power in Postcolonial Africa*, edited by J. Comaroff & J.L. Comaroff, pp. 111–28. Chicago: University of Chicago Press.

Apter, Andrew. 2005. *The Pan-African Nation: Oil and the Spectacle of Culture in Nigeria*. Chicago: Chicago University Press.

Aradeon, D. 1997. "Oshodi: Replanners' Options for a Subcity." *Glendora Review: African Quarterly on the Arts* 2 (1): 51–58.

Ashforth, A. 1998. "Reflections on Spiritual Insecurity in a Modern African City (Soweto)." *African Studies Review* 41 (3): 39–67.

Assimeng, M. 1986. *Social Structure of Ghana*. Accra: Ghana Universities Press.

Austen, R. 1993. "The Moral Economy of Witchcraft: An Essay in Comparative History." In *Modernity and its Malcontents: Ritual and Power in Postcolonial Africa*, edited by J. Comaroff & J.L. Comaroff, pp. 89–110. Chicago & London: Chicago University Press.

AutoJosh. 2018. "Are the Agberos above the Law in Lagos State?" March 21.

Auwal, N. 1987. "A Housa Vocabulary on Corruption and Political Oppression." *Corruption and Reform*, 1(2): 293–96.

Ayoade, John A. & Akinsanya, Adeoye A. (ed.). 2013. *Nigeria's Critical Election*. New York: Lexington Books.

Babajide, O. 2014. "Nigeria: What is Happening to the Giant of Africa?" *Sahara Reporters*, January 16.

Bach, Daniel C. 2012. "Conclusion: Neopatrimonial and Developmental—The Emerging States' Syndrome." In *Neopatrimonialism in Africa and Beyond*, edited by Daniel C. Bach & Mamoudou Gazibo, pp. 221–24. Abingdon, UK: Routledge.

Bacon, Edmund. 1974. *Design of Cities*. London: Thames & Hudson.

Badru, Pade. 1998. *Imperialism and Ethnic Politics in Nigeria, 1960–1966*. Trenton, New Jersey: Africa World Press.

Baez-Camargo, Claudia. 2019. "Mordida (Mexico)." INF. 17 May.

Baez-Camargo, Claudia., P. Bukuluki, R. Lugolobi, C. Stahl, and S. Kassa. 2017. "Behavioral Influences on Attitudes Towards Petty Corruption: A Study of Social Norms and Mental Models in Uganda." Basel Institute of Governance, December.

Bagayoko, Niagale, Eboe Hutchful, and Robin Luckham. 2016. "Hybrid Security Governance in Africa: Rethinking the Foundations of Security, Justice and Legitimate Public Authority." *Conflict, Security & Development* 16 (1): 1–32.

Bähre, Eric. 2014. "A Trickle-Up Economy: Mutuality, Freedom and Violence in Cape Town's Taxi Associations." *Africa* 84 (4): 576–94.

Bakhtin, Mikhail M. 1981. *The Dialogic Imagination: Four Essays*. Translated by M. Holquist. Austin: University of Texas Press.

Banks, Nicola, M. Lombard, and D. Mitlin. 2020. "Urban Informality as a Site of Critical Analysis." *The Journal of Development Studies* 56 (2): 223–38.

Barber, Karin. 1981. "How Man Makes God in West Africa: Yorùbá Attitudes towards the Orisa." *Africa* 51 (3): 724–25.

Barber, Karin. 1987. "Popular Arts in Africa." *African Studies Review*, 30(3); 1–78.

Barber, Karin. 2007. *The Anthropology of Texts, Persons and Publics*. Cambridge: Cambridge University Press.

Barber, Karin. 2018. *A History of African Popular Culture*. Cambridge, UK: Cambridge University Press.

Bardhan, P. 2015. "Corruption and Development Policy." *Journal of Public Economic Theory* 17 (4): 472–79.

Basinski, Sean. 2009. "All Fingers are not Equal: A Report on Street Vendors in Lagos, Nigeria." CLEEN Foundation, July 16.

Basso, Keith. 1992. *Western Apache Language and Culture: Essays in Linguistic Anthropology*. Tucson: The University of Arizona Press.

Basso, Keith. 1996. *Wisdom Sits in Places: Landscapes and Language among the Western Apache*. Albuquerque: University of New Mexico Press.

Basu, Kaushika. 2019. "India." In *Asian Transformations: An Inquiry into the Development of Nations*, edited by D. Nayyar, pp. 401–23. Oxford: Oxford University Press.

Bauman, Zigmunt. 1992. *Mortality, Immortality and Other Life Strategies*. Cambridge: Polity Press.

Baviskar, Amita. 1995. *In the Belly of the River: Tribal Conflicts over Development in the Narmada Valley*. Oxford: Oxford University Press.

Bay, Edna and Donham, Donald (eds). 2007. *States of Violence: Politics, Youth, and Memory in Contemporary Africa*. Charlottesville: University of Virginia Press.

Bayart, Jean-François. 1989. *The State in Africa: The Politics of the Belly*. London: Longman.

Bayart, Jean-François. 1993. *The State in Africa: The Politics of the Belly*. London: Longman.

Bayart, Jean-François. 2000. "Africa in the World: A history of extraversion", *African Affairs*, 99: 217-267.

Bayart, Jean-François. 2005. *The Illusion of Cultural Identity*. London: Hurst & Co.

Bayart, Jean-François, S. Ellis, and B. Hibou. 1999. *The Criminalization of the State in Africa*. Oxford: James Currey.

Bayat, Asef. 1997. "Un-civil Society: The Politics of the 'Informal' People." *Third World Quarterly*, 18(1): 53-72.

Bayat, Asef. 2000. "From 'Dangerous Classes' to 'Quiet Rebels': Politics of the Urban Subaltern in the Global South." *International Sociology* 15 (3): 533-57.

Bayat, Asef. 2009. *Life as Politics: How Ordinary People Change in the Middle East*. Stanford: Stanford University Press.

Bayat, Asef, and K. Biekart. 2009. "Cities of Extremes." *Development & Change* 40 (5): 815-25.

Bayley, D. 1974. "Police Corruption in India." In *Police Corruption: A Sociological Perspective*, edited by L.W. Sherman, pp. 74-93. New York: Anchor Books.

Bayley, D., and R. Perito. 2011. "Police Corruption: What Past Scandals Teach about Current Challenges." United States Institute of Peace Special Report, 294. November.

BBC. 2005. "Kenya Graft Fighter 'Threatened.'" February 09.

BBC. 2006. "Nigeria Leader Denies Corruption." December 19.

BBC. 2010. "Law and Disorder in Lagos." By Louis Theroux. October 4.

BBC. 2012. "Former Nigeria governor James Ibori jailed for 13 years." April 17.

BBC. 2013. "Nigeria Pardons Goodluck Jonathan Ally, Alamieyeseigha." March 13.

BBC. 2015a. "Nigeria's Dasuki 'Arrested over $2bn Arms Fraud.'" December 01.

BBC. 2015b. "The Soldiers without Enough Weapons to Fight Jihadists." January 22.

BBC. 2016. "David Cameron Calls Nigeria and Afghanistan Fantastically Corrupt." May 10.

BBC. 2017. "Why Nigeria Wants to Remove Police Roadblocks." 26 September.

Beck, Kurt. 2013. "Roadside Comforts: Truck Stops on the Forty Days Road in Western Sudan." *Africa* 83 (3): 426-45.

Becker, Howard S. 1958. "Problems of Inference and Proof in Participant Observation." *American Sociological Review* 23 (2); 652-60.

Bedi, Tarini. 2016. "Taxi Drivers, Infrastructures, and Urban Change in Globalizing Mumbai." *City & Society*, 28(3): 387-410.

Beekers, D. 2008. "Children of a 'Fallen House': Lives and Livelihoods of Youth in Nigeria." Univeristy of Oxford (MPhil thesis).

Beekers, Daan, and Bas Van Gool. 2012. "From Patronage to Neopatrimonialism: Postcolonial Governance in Sub-Saharan Africa and Beyond." ASC Working Paper 101: 1-33.

Bell, Rosie. 2019. "You Speak the Language, But You May Get Lost Without This Guide to Nigerian English." Fodor's Travel, October 12.

Benjamin, Walter. 1985. "Moscow Diary." *Moscow Diary* 35: 9-136.

Bhan, G. 2009. "'This is No Longer the City I Once Knew': Evictions, the Urban Poor, and the Right to the City in Millennial Delhi." *Environment & Urbanization* 21 (1): 127-42.

Bicchieri, C., and H. Mercier. 2014. "Norms and Beliefs: How Change Occurs." In *The Complexity of Social Norms*, edited by M. Xenitidou and B. Edmonds, pp. 37–54. Cham: Springer International Publishing.

Biedelman, T.O. 1986. *Moral Imagination in Kaguru Modes of Thought*. Bloomington: Indiana University Press.

Bienen, H., and J. Herbst. 1996. "The Relationship between Political and Economic Reform in Africa." *Comparative Politics* 29 (1): 23–42.

Bierschenk, T. 2008. "The Everyday Functioning of an African Public Service: Informalization, Privatization and Corruption in Benin's Legal System." *The Journal of Legal Pluralism and Unofficial Law* 40 (57): 101–39.

Bierschenk, T., J.-P. Chauveau, and Jean-Pierre Olivier de Sardan. 2002. "Local Development Brokers in Africa: The Rise of a New Social Category." Working Paper, Institute for Ethnology and African Studies, Johannes Gutenberg University.

Blair, G. 2019. "The Sounds of Transgressive Geographies." *Echo: A Music-Centered Journal* 15 (1).

Bledsoe, Caroline H. 1990. "'No Success without Struggle': Social Mobility and Hardship Foster Children in Sierra Leone." *Man* 25: 70–88.

Bledsoe, Caroline H. 2002. *Contingent Lives: Fertility, Time, and Aging in West Africa*. Chicago: University of Chicago Press.

Blundo, Giorgio. 2006. "An Ordered Corruption? The Social World of Public Procurement." In *Everyday Corruption and the State: Citizens and Public Officials*, edited by G. Blundo & J.-P. Olivier de Sardan with N.B. Afrifari & M.T. Alou, pp. 225–62. London: Zed Books.

Blundo, Giorgio. 2007. "Hidden Acts, Open Talks: How Anthropology can 'Observe' and Describe Corruption." In *Corruption and the Secret of Law: A Legal Anthropological Perspective*, edited by M. Nuijten & G. Anders, pp. 27–52. Aldershot: Ashgate.

Blundo, G. & Olivier de Sardan, J.-P. (with N.B Arifari & M.T. Alou) (eds.). 2006. *Everyday Corruption and the State: Citizens and Public Officials in Africa*. London & New York: Zed Books.

Blundo, Giorgio, and P.-Y. Le Meur. 2009. *The Governance of Daily Life in Africa: Ethnographic Explorations of Public and Collective Services*. Leiden: Brill.

Bocarejo, Diana. 2018. "Thinking with (Il)legality: The Ethics of Living with Bonanzas." *Current Anthropology* 59 (18): S48–S59.

Bodruzic, D. 2016. "Vice or Coping Mechanism? Bridging Political Science and Anthropoligical Approaches to the Study of Corruption," *Critique of Anthropology* 36 (4): 363–79.

Bonner, R. 2009. "The Stink of Corruption." *The Guardian*, March 13.

Booth, D. 2012. "Development as a Collective Action Problem: Addressing the Real Challenge of African Governance." Synthesis Report of the Africa Power and Politics Program. London: Overseas Development Institute (ODI).

Booth, D., and D. Commack, eds. 2013. *Governance for Development in Africa: Solving Collective Action Problems*. London: Zed Books.

Bourdieu, Pierre. 1994. "Rethinking the State: Genesis and Structure of the Bureaucratic Field." *Sociological Theory* 12 (1): 1–19.

Brachet, Julien. 2012. "Geography of Movement, and Geography in Movement: Mobility as a Dimension of Fieldwork in Migration Research." *Annales de geographies* 687–88: 543–60.

Bratsis, P. 2003. "The Construction of Corruption, or Rules of Separation and Illusions of Purity in Bourgeois Societies." *Social Text* 21 (4): 9–33.

Bratton, M. 1989. "Beyond the State: Civil Society and Associational Life in Africa." *World Politics* 41 (3): 407–30.

Bratton, M., and N. van de Walle. 1994. "Neopatrimonal Regimes and Political Transition in Africa." *World Politics* 46 (4): 453–89.

Bratton, M., and N. van de Walle. 1997. *Democratic Experiments in Africa: Regime Transitions in Comparative Perspective.* Cambridge: Cambridge University Press.

Brennan, G., Eriksson, L., Goodin, R.E. & Southwood, N. 2013. *Explaining Norms.* Oxford: Oxford University Press.

Brennan, Geoffrey and Pettit, Philip. 2004. *The Economy of Esteem: An Essay on Civil and Political Society.* Oxford, UK: Oxford University Press.

Brown, K.P. 2020. "Rumor Has It: Strategies for Ethnographic Analysis in Authoritarian Regimes." *Ethnography*, 0(0): 1–22.

Brownsberger, William N. 1983. "Developmment and Government Corruption: Materialism and and Political Fragmentation in Nigeria." *Journal of Modern African Studies*, 21: 215–233.

Buck-Moss, S. 1989. *The Dialectics of Seeing: Walter Benjamin and the Arcades Project.* Cambridge: MIT Press.

Buescher, M. and J. Urry. 2009. "Mobile Methods and the Empirical." *European Journal of Social Theory* 129 (1); 99–116.

Buhari, M. 2016. "Special Guest of Honor's Remarks." Presidential Advisory Committee Against Corruption, International Workshop on the Role of Judges in the Fight Against Corruption: A Compendium of Papers. Abuja: Office of the President.

Bures, F. 2008. "A Mind Dismembered: In Search of the Magical Penis Thieves." *Harpers Magazine*, June.

Burge, M. 2011. "Riding the Narrow Tracks of Moral Life: Commercial Motorbike Riders in Makeni, Sierra Leone." *Africa Today* 58: 58–95.

Burridge, Kenelm. 1995. *Mambu: A Melenesian Millenium.* Princeton: Princeton University Press.

Butler, C. 2012. *Henri Lefebvre; Spatial Politics, Everyday Life, and the Right to the City.* London: Routledge.

Butler, J., and A. Athanasiou. 2013. *Dispossession: The Performative in the Political.* Cambridge: Polity.

Caiden, G.E. 1988. "Toward a General Theory of Official Corruption." *Asian Journal of Public Administration* 10 (1): 3–26.

Camic, C. 1986. "The Matter of Habit." *American Journal of Sociology* 91 (5); 1039–87.

Campbell, Robert. 1860. *A Few Facts Relating to Lagos, Abbeokuta, and other sections of Central Africa.* Philadelphia: King & Baird Printers.

Caplan, P. 1995. *Understanding Disputes: The Politics of Argument.* Michigan: Berg.

Carrier, J.G. 2018. "Moral Economy: What's in a Name?" *Anthropological Theory* 18 (1): 18–35.

Center for Global Development. 2017. "Nigerian Debt Relief." Retrieved from <https://cgdev.org/topics/nigerian-debt-relief>

Cervero, R. and A. Golub. 2007. "Informal Transport: Global Perspective." *Transport Policy* 14: 445–57.

Chabal, P., and J.-P. Daloz. 1999. *Africa Works: Disorder as Political Instrument.* Oxford: James Currey.

Chabal, P., and J.-P. Daloz. 2006. *Culture Troubles: Politics and the Interpretation of Meaning.* London: Hurst & Co.

Chalfin, B. 2008. "Sovereigns and Citizens in Close Encounter: Airport Anthropology and Custom Regimes in Neoliberal Ghana." *American Ethnologist* 35 (4): 519–38.

Chapman, O. 2013. "Sound Moves: Intersections of Popular Music Studies, Mobility Studies and Soundscape Studies." *Journal of Mobile Media* 7 (1).

Chatterji, R., R. Plariwala, and M. Thapan. 2005. "Ethnographies of the State: Report of a Workshop." *Economic and Political Weekly* 40 (40): 4312–16.

Cheeseman, N. and D. de Gramont. 2017. "Managing a Mega-city: Learning the Lessons from Lagos." *Oxford Review of Economic Policy* 33 (3): 457–77.

Chikolo, S., P. Hebinck, and B. Kinsey. 2020. "'Mbare Musika is Ours': An Analysis of a Fresh Produce Market in Zimbabwe." *African Affairs*, 1–27.

Christensen, M.M. and P. Albrecht. 2020. "Urban Borderwork: Ethnographies of Policing." *EPD: Society & Space* 38 (3): 385–98.

Clammer, J. 2014. *Vision and Society: Towards a Sociology and Anthropology from Art*. Oxon: Routledge.

Clapham, Christopher. 1985. *Third World Politics: An Introduction*. London: Croom Helm.

CLEEN. 2013. "Summary of Results: Afrobarometer Round 5 Survey in Nigeria, 2012." Lagos: CLEEN Foundation.

Clegg, S.R. 1989. *Frameworks of Power*. London: Sage.

Clifford, J. 2009. "Hau'ofa's Hope." *Oceania* 73: 238–49.

CNN. 2018. "Nigeria Overtakes India in Extreme Poverty Ranking." By Bukola Adebayo. June 26.

CNN. 2019. "Employees in Lagos are Stressed, Burned Out and Exhausted because of 'Hellish Traffic.'" August 02.

Cocodia, J. 2016. "Boko Haram: Cash Cow of the Sahel or Part of a Grand Strategy?" *Kujenga Amani*, September 07.

Collier, Paul. 2005. *The Bottom Billion: Why the Poorest Countries Are Failing and What Can be Done About It*. London: Oxford University Press.

Comaroff, Jean, and John L. Comaroff. 1993. *Modernity and its Malcontents: Ritual and Power in Postcolonial Africa*. Chicago: University of Chicago Press.

Comaroff, Jean, and John L. Comaroff. 1999. "Occult Economies and the Violence of Abstraction: Notes from the South African Postcolony." *American Ethnologist* 26 (2): 279–303.

Comaroff, Jean, and John L. Comaroff. 2000. "Millennial Capitalism: First Thoughts on a Second Coming." *Public Culture*, 12(2): 291–343.

Comaroff, Jean, and John L. Comaroff. 2006. *Law and Disorder in the Postcolony*. Chicago: University of Chicago Press.

Comaroff, Jean, and John L. Comaroff. 2012. "Theory from the South: Or, How Euro-America is Evolving toward Africa." *Anthropological Forum: A Journal of Social Anthropology and Comparative Sociology*, 2(2): 113–131.

Comaroff, Jean, and John L. Comaroff. 2015. *Theory from the South: Or, How Euro-America is Evolving Toward Africa*. London: Routledge.

Comaroff, John L. and S. Roberts. 1981. *Rules and Processes: The Cultural Logic of Dispute in an African Context*. Chicago: Chicago University Press.

Cooper, E., and D. Pratten, eds. 2015. *Ethnographies of Uncertainty in Africa*. New York: Palgrave.

Crapanzano, V. 2003. "Reflections on Hope as a Category of Social and Psychological Analysis." *Cultural Anthropology* 18 (1): 3–32.

Cresswell, T. 2006. *On the Move: Mobility in the Modern Western World*. London: Routledge.

Cruise O'Brien, Donal. 1996. "A Lost Generation? Youth Identity and State Decay in West Africa." In Werbner, R and Ranger, T. (eds), *Postcolonial Identities in Africa*. London: Zed Books, pp. 55–74.

Daily Nation 2013. "End of a decade of highs and lows for Mwai Kibaki." March 4.

Daily Trust. 2015. "Nigeria: Mpape's Kings of the Roads." By Uthman Abubakar. 05 December.

Dan Borno. 2011. "Bye Bye to Achaba." July 08. Available at https://danborno .blogspot.com/2011/07/bye-bye-to-achaba.html?view=flipcard.

Darmon, I. & Warde, A. 2018. "Habits and Orders of Everyday Life: Commensal Adjustment in Anglo-French Couples." *The British Journal of Sociology* 70 (3): 1025–42.

Das, Veena. 2010. "Engaging the Life of the Other: Love and Everyday Life." In Michael Lambek (ed.), *Ordinary Ethics: Anthropology, Language and Action*, pp. 376–99. New York: Fordham University Press.

Das, Veena. 2015. "Corruption and the Possibility of Life." *Contributions to Indian Sociology*, 49(3): 322–43.

Das, Veena, and D. Poole, eds. 2004. *Anthropology in the Margins of the State*. Santa Fe, NM: SAR Press.

Dasgupta, Sandipto. 2019. "The Power of Corrpution." *Comparative Studies of South Asia, Africa and the Middle East*, 39(3): 558–62.

Date-Bah, Eugenie. 1980. "The Inscriptions on the Vehicles of Ghanian Commercial Drivers: A Sociological Analysis." *Journal of Modern African Studies* 18 (3): 525–31.

Davis, Mike. 2006. *Planet of Slums*. London: Verso.

Dawson, H.J., and E. Fouksman. 2020. "Labor, Laziness and Distribution: Work Imaginaries among the South African Unemployed." *Africa* 90 (20): 229–51.

De Boeck, Filip. 1998. "Beyond the Grave: History, Memory, and Death in Postcolonial Congo/Zaire." In *Memory and the Postcolony: African Anthropology and the Critique of Power*, edited by R. Werbner, pp. 21–57. London: Zed Books

De Boeck, Filip and Baloji, Sammy. 2016. *Suturing the City: Living Together in Congo's Urban Worlds*. London: Autograph ABP.

De Boeck, Filip, A. Cassiman and S. Van Wolputte. 2009. "Recentering the City: An Anthropology of Secondary Cities in Africa." *African Perspectives* 1–10.

De Boeck, Filip, and Marie-Françoise Plissart. 2004. *Kinshasa: Tales of the Invisible City*. Tervuren: Ludion.

De Certeau, Michel. 1984. *The Practice of Everyday Life*. Berkeley: University of California Press.

De Gramont, D. 2015. "Governing Lagos: Unlocking the Politics of Reform." Carnegie Endowmenent for International Peace. January 12.

De Herdt, T., and Jean-Pierre Olivier de Sardan, eds. 2015. *Real Governance and Practical Norms in Sub-Saharan Africa: The Game of the Rules*. London: Routledge.

Defterios, J. 2012. "Nigeria's Oil Economics Fuel Deadly Protests." CNN, January 11.

DeGrassi, Aaron. 2008. "'Neopatrimonialism' and Agricultural Development in Africa: Contributions and Limitations of a Contested Concept." *African Studies Review* 51 (3): 107–33.

Deleuze, Gilles, and Félix Guattari. 1980. *Capitalisme et Schrizophrenie. Mille plateaux*. Paris: Minuit.

Denham, A. 2017. *Spirit Children: Illness, Poverty, and Infanticide in Northern Ghana*. Madison: University of Wisconsin Press.

Denham, D. 1826. *Narratives of Travels and Discoveries in Northern and Central Africa in the Years 1822, 1823, and 1824*. London: Thomas Davison Whitefriars.

Desjarlais, R. 1997. *Shelter Blues: Sanity and Selfhood Among the Homeless*. Philadelphia: University of Pennsylvania Press.

DFID (Department for International Development [UK]). 2015. "Why Corruption Matters: Understanding Causes, Effects and How to Address them." Evidence Paper on Corruption. January.

Di Nuncio, Marco. 2019. *The Act of Living: Street Life, Marginality, and Development in Urban Ethiopia*. Ithaca: Cornell University Press.

Diamond, Larry. 1987. "Class Formation in the Swollen African State." *The Journal of Modern African Studies* 25 (4): 567–96.

Diamond, Larry. 1989. "Book Review." *African Affairs* 88 (351): 284–86.

Diamond, Larry, A. Kirk-Greene, and O. Oyediran, eds. 1997. *Transition without End: Nigeria's Politics and Civil Society Under Babangida*. Boulder, Colorado: Lynne Rienner.

Dikeç, Mustafa. 2001. "Justice and the Spatial Imagination." *Environment and Planning A* 33 (10): 1785–1805.

Diouf, M. 2003. "Engaging Postcolonial Cultures: African Youth and Public Space." *African Studies Review* 46 (2): 1–12.

Dlakwa, H.D. 2015. "Peace Management Perspective of the North-Eastern Scenario." Al-Mahran, VII.

Dougherty, Elizabeth. 2000. "The Hegemony of Corruption." Paper presented at the AAA Meeting, San Francisco.

Dougherty, Elizabeth. 2002. "Politics of Environmental Conservation: A Study in Civil Society, Scales of Influence, and Corruption in Panama." University of Pennsylvania (PhD thesis).

Dowden, Richard. 2008. *Africa: Altered States, Ordinary Miracles*. New York: Public Affairs.

Downey, G., M. Dalidowicz, and P.H. Mason. 2015. "Apprenticeship as Method: Embodied Learning in Ethnographic Practice." *Qualitative Research* 15 (2): 183–200.

Du Toit, A., and D. Neves. 2007. "In Search of South Africa's Second Economy: Chronic Poverty, Economic Marginalization and Adverse Incorporation in Mt. Frere and Khayelitsha." CPRC Working Paper No. 102. Manchester, UK: Chronic Poverty Research Center, University of Manchester.

Dudley, Billy J. 1973. *Instability and Political Order: Politics and Crisis in Nigeria*. Ibadan: Ibadan University Press.

Duffield, M. 2002. "War as a Network Enterprise: The New Security Terrain and its Implications." *The Journal of Cultural Research* 6 (1-2): 153–66.

DW. 2013. "Mordida Remains Mexican Way of Life." 07 September.

Eckert, Julia. 2006. "From Subjects to Citizens: Legalism from Below and the Homogenization of the Legal Sphere." *Journal of Legal Pluralism and Unofficial Law* 38: 45–75.

Eckert, Julia. 2012. "Rumors of Rights." In *Law against the State: Ethnographic Forays into Law Transformations*, edited by J. Eckert, B. Donahoe, C. Stumpell, and Z. Ozlem-Biner, pp. 147–70. Cambridge: Cambridge University Press.

Eisenstadt, S.N. and L. Roniger. 1984. *Patrons, Clients and Friends: Interpersonal Relations and the Structure of Trust in Society*. Cambridge: Cambridge University Press.

Ekeh, Peter P. 1975. "Colonialism and the Two Publics in Africa: A Theoretical Statement." *Comparative Studies in Society and History* 17: 91–112.

Ekpo, M.V. 1979. "Gift-Giving and Bureaucratic Corruption in Nigeria." In *Bureaucratic Corruption in Sub-Saharan Africa: Toward a Search for Causes and Consequences*, edited by M.V. Ekpo, pp. 161–88. Washington DC: University Press of America.

Ekundayo, John M.O. 2013. *Out of Africa: Fashola Reinventing Servant Leadership to Engender Nigeria's Transformation*. Bloomington: Author House.

Ekwensi, Cyprian. 1961. *Jagua Nana*. London: Hutchinson.

Ekwensi, Cyprian. 1976. *Survive the Peace*. London: Heinemann Educational.

Ellis, Stephen. 2006. "The Roots of African Corruption." *Current History* 105 (691): 203–8.

Ellis, Stephen. 2016. *This Present Darkness: A History of Nigerian Organized Crime*. Oxford: Oxford University Press.

Englund, H. 2018. "Foreword." In *Eating and Being Eaten: Cannibalism as a Food for Thought*, edited by F.B. Nyamnjoh, p. ix. Mankon, Bamenda: Langaa Research & Publishing CIG.

Escholtz, P., A. Rosa, and V. Clark, eds. 1978. *Language Awareness*. New York: St. Martins.

Evans, P. 1995. *Embedded Autonomy: States and Industrial Transformation*. Princeton: Princeton University Press.

Fairclough, N. 1989. *Language and Power*. London: Longman.

Fajemirokun, M. 2010. "Policy and Legal Perspectives on Actualizing the Right to the City in Nigeria." In *Cities for All: Proposals and Experiences towards the Right to the City*, edited by A. Sugranyes & C. Mathivet, pp. 267–69. Santiago, Chile: Habitat International Coaltion.

Fallers, L. 1969. *Law Without Precedent: Legal Ideas in Action in the Courts of Colonial Busoga*. Chicago: Chicago University Press.

Falola, Toyin. 1998. *Violence in Nigeria: The Crisis of Religious Politics and Secular Ideologies*. Rochester: University of Rochester Press.

Farolan, R.J. 2011. "Lee Kuan Yew on Philippines." *Philippine Daily Inquirer*, September 26.

Fassin, Didier. 2005. "Compassion and Repression: The Moral Economy of Immigration Policies in France." *Cultural Anthropology* 20 (3): 362–87.

Fassin, Didier. 2009. "Moral Economies Revisited." *Annales: Histoire, Sciences Sociales* 6: 1237–66. Unpaginated English Translation.

Fearon, D., and D. Laitin. 2000. "Ordinary Language and External Validity: Specifying Concepts in the Study of Ethnicity." Presented at APSA Annual Meeting, Washington, DC.

Felski, R. 2000. "The Invention of Everyday life." *Cool Moves: A Journal of Culture, Theory and Politics* 39: 15–31.

Ferguson, James. 1999. *Expectations of Modernity: Myths and Meanings of Urban Life on the Zambian Copperbelt*. Berkeley: University of California Press.

Ferguson, James. 2006. *Global Shadows: Africa in the Neoliberal World Order*. Durham: Duke University Press.

Ferme, Mariane C. 2001. *The Underneath of Things: Violence, History, and the Everyday in Sierra Leone*. Berkeley: University of California Press.

Ferme, Mariane C. 2013. "Introduction: Localizing the State." *Anthropological Quarterly* 86 (4): 957–63.

Field, M.J. 1960. *Search for Security: An Ethno-Psychiatric Study of Rural Ghana*. Evanson: Northwestern University Press.

Foltz, J.D. and K.A. Opoku-Agyemang. 2015. "Do Higher Salaries Lower Petty Corruption? A Policy Experiment on West Africa's Highways." Working Paper, International Growth Center (IGC), June.

Forrest, T. 1993. *Politics and Economic Development in Nigeria*. Boulder, Colorado: Westview Press.

Foucault, Michel. 1976. *The Will to Knowledge: The History of Sexuality*. Volume 1. (trans. R. Hurley, 1998).

Foucault, Michel. 1978. *The History of Sexuality, Vols. 1, 2*. New York: Pantheon.

Foucault, Michel. 1980. *Power/Knowledge: Selected Interviews and Other Writings, 1972–1977*. London: Harvester Press.

Foucault, Michel. 1984. "Of Other Spaces: Utopias and Heterotopias." Available at: <https://web.mit.edu/allanmc/www/foucault1.pdf>

Foucault, Michel. 1988. "Technologies of the Self." In *Technologies of the Self*, edited by Luther H. Martin, Huck Gutman, and Patrick H. Hutton, pp. 16–49. London: Tavistock Publications.

Fourchard, Laurent. 2006. "Lagos and the Invention of Juvenile Delinquency in Nigeria." *Journal of African History*, 47(1): 115–37.

Fourchard, Laurent. 2010. "Lagos, Koolhaas and Partisan Politics in Nigeria." *International Journal of Urban and Regional Research* 35 (1): 40–56.

Fourchard, Laurent. 2012. "Lagos." In *Power and Powerlessness: Capital Cities in Africa*, edited by S. Bekker & G. Therborn, pp. 66–82. Pretoria: CODESRIA.

Friedrich, C. 1989. "Corruption Concepts in Historical Perspectives." In *Political Corruption: A Handbook*, edited by A.J. Heidenheimer, M. Johnston, and V.T. LeVine, pp. 149–64. New Brunswick: Transaction Publishers.

Frimpong-Ansah, J.H. 1992. *The Vampire State in Africa: The Political Economy of Decline in Ghana*. London: James Currey.

Frykenberg, Robert E. 1965. *Guntur District 1788–1848: A History of Local Influence and Central Authority in South India*. Oxford, UK: Oxford University Press.

Gandhi, Ajay, and Lotte Hoek. 2012. "Introduction to Crowds and Conviviality: Ethnographies of the South Asian City." *Ethnography* 13 (1): 3–11.

Gandy, M. 2005. "Learning from Lagos." *New Left Review* 33: 37–53.

Gates, Henry Louis. 1988. *The Signifying Monkey: A Theory of African-American Literary Criticism*. New York: Oxford University Press.

Gates, Henry Louis. 1995. "Powell and The Black Elite," *The New Yorker*, 25 September.

Gatt, L., and O. Owen. 2018. "Direct Taxation and State-Society Relations in Lagos, Nigeria." *Development and Change* 49 (5): 1195–222.

Geenen, K. 2009. "'Sleep Occupies No Space.': The Use of Public Space by Street Gangs in Kinshasha." *Africa* 79 (3): 347–68.

Geertz, Clifford. 1983. *Local Knowledge: Further Essays in Interpretive Anthropology*. New York: Basic Books.

Gelder, K., and S. Thornton, eds. 1997. *The Subcultures Reader*. London: Routledge.

Geschiere, Peter. 1997. *The Modernity of Witchraft: Politics and the Occult in Postcolonial Africa*. Charlottesville: University of Virginia Press.

Geschiere, Peter, and B. Meyer. 1998. "Globalization and Identity: Dialectics of Flow and Closure." *Development and Change* 29 (4): 601–15.

Geschiere, Peter, and M. Rowlands. 1996. "The Domestication of Modernity: Different Trajectories." *Africa* 66 (4); 552–54.

Gewald, J.B., S. Luning, and K.V. Walraven. 2009. *The Speed of Change: Motor Vehicles and People in Africa, 1890–2000*. Leiden: Brill.

Ghertner, A.D. 2011. "Rule by Aesthetics: World-Class City Making in Delhi." In *Worlding Cities: Asian Experiment and the Art of Being Global*, edited by Ananya Roy and Aihwa Ong, pp. 279–306. Malden: Wiley-Blackwell.

Gibbs, Tim. 2014. "Becoming a 'Big Man' in Neo-Liberal South Africa: Migrant Masculinities in the Minibus Taxi Industry." *African Affairs* 113 (452): 431–48.

Giddens, Anthony. 1979. *Central Problems in Social Theory: Action, Structure and Contradiction in Social Analysis*. Berkeley and Los Angeles: University of California Press.

Gill, N., J. Caletrio, and V. Mason. 2014. *Mobilities and Forced Migration*. New York: Routledge.

Gillmartin, D. 2014. "The Paradox of Patronage and the People's Sovereignty." In *Patronage as Politics in South Asia*, edited by A. Piliavsky, pp. 125–53. Cambridge: University of Cambridge Press.

Glaeser, Edward L. and Claudia Goldin, eds. 2006. *Corruption and Reform: Lessons from America's Economic History*. Chicago: University of Chicago Press.

Global Corruption Barometer. 2015. "People and Corruption: African Survey 2015." African Edition. Transparency International & Afrobarometer.

Global Nonviolent Action Database. 2015. "Nigerians Protest Removal of Fuel Subsidy, 2012." March 29.

Godwin, J., and G. Hopwood. 2012. *Sandbank City: Lagos at 150*. Lagos: Prestige.

Goffman, E. 1963. *Stigma: Notes on the Management of Spoiled Identity*. New York: Prentice-Hall.

Golomski, C. 2020. "Greying Mutuality: Race and Joking Relations in a South African Nursing Home." *Africa* 90 (2): 273–92.

Gonzalez, C. 2003. "El Impacto de La Corrupcion En El Proceso de Democratizacion de Mexico." *Revista Probidad* 24 (9): 1–14.

Goodfellow, Tom. 2012. "State Effectiveness and the Politics of Urban Development in East Africa: A Puzzle of Two Cities." London School of Economics, Unpublished PhD Dissertation.

Goodfellow, Tom. 2017. "'Double Capture' and De-Democratization: Interest Group Politics and Uganda's 'Transport Mafia.'" *The Journal of Development Studies* 53 (10): 1568–83.

Gopfert, M. 2016. "Surveillance in Niger: Gendarmes and the Problem of 'Seeing Things.'" *African Studies Review* 59 (2): 39–57.

Gore, Charles, and David Pratten. 2003. "The Politics of Plunder: The Rhetorics of Order and Disorder in Southern Nigeria." *African Affairs* 102: 211–40.

Gould, W., T. Sherman, and S. Ansari. 2013. "The Flux of the Matter: Loyalty, Corruption and the 'Everyday State' in the Post-Partition Government Services of India and Pakistan." *Past and Present* 219: 237–79.

Grace, Joshua. 2013. "Heroes of the Road: Race, Gender and the Politics of Mobility in Twentieth Century Tanzania." *Africa* 83(3): 403–25.

Graf, W.D. 1988. *The Nigerian State: Political Economy, State Class and Political System in the Post-Colonial Era*. London: James Currey.

Green-Simms, L. 2009. "Postcolonial Automobility: West Africa and the Road to Globalization." University of Minnesota (PhD thesis).

Green-Simms, L. 2017. *PostColonial Automobility: Car Cultures in West Africa*. Minnesota: University of Minnesota Press.

Green, Robert. 1981. "Magendo in the Political Economy of Uganda." *IDS Discussion Paper*, No. 164.

Guest, Robert. 2004. *The Shackled Continent: Africa's Past, Present and Future*. London: Macmillan.

Gupta, Akhil. 1995. "Blurred Boundaries: The Discourse of Corruption, the Culture of Politics, and the Imagined State." *American Ethnologist* 22: 375–402.

Gupta, Akhil. 2012. *Red Tape: Bureaucracy, Structural Violence, and Poverty in India*. Durham: Duke University Press.

Gupta, Akhil, and James Ferguson. 1997. "Discpline and Practice: 'The Field' as Site, Method, and Location in Anthropology." In *Anthropological Locations: Boundaries and Grounds of a Field Science*, edited by A. Gupta & J. Ferguson, pp. 1–46. Berkeley: University of California Press.

Guseh, J.S. 2008. "Slogans and Mottos on Commercial Vehicles: A Reflection of Liberian Philosophy and Culture." *Journal of Africa Cultural Studies* 20 (2): 159–71.

Guyer, Jane I. 1997. *An African Niche Economy: Farming to Feed Ibadan, 1968–88*. Edinburgh: Edinburgh University Press.

Guyer, Jane I. 2002. "Preface." In *Money Struggles and City Life: Devaluation in Ibadan and Other Urban Centers in Southern Nigeria, 1986-1990*, edited by J.I. Guyer, L. Denzer, & A. Agbaje, pp. ix–xvi. Portsmouth, New Hampshire: Heinemann.

Guyer, Jane I. 2017. "When and How Does Hope Spring Eternal in Personal and Popular Economics? Thoughts from West Africa to America." In Hirokazu Miyazaki and Richard Swedberg (ed), *The Economy of Hope*. Philadelphia: University of Pennsylvania Press, 147-171.

Habermas, Jürgen. 1991. *The Structural Transformation of the Public Sphere: An Inquiry into a Category of Bourgeois Society*. Cambridge: MIT Press.

Habermas, Jürgen. 2006. "The Public Sphere: An Encyclopedia Article." In *Media and Cultural Studies: Keyworks*, edited by G. Meenakshi & K. Douglas, pp. 73–74. Oxford: Blackwell.

Hage, G. 2009. "Waiting out the Crisis: On Stuckedness and Governmentality." In *Waiting*, edited by G. Hage, pp. 97–106. Melbourne: Melbourne University Press.

Hall, Peter A. 1993. "Policy Paradigms, Social Learning, and the State: The Case of Economic Policymaking in Britain." *Comparative Politics* 25 (3): 275–96.

Hall, S., and T. Jefferson. 1993. *Resistance through Rituals: Youth Subcultures in Post-War Britain*. London: Routledge.

Haller, D., and D. Shore. 2005. *Corruption: Anthropological Perspectives*. London: Pluto Press.

Hallisey, C. 2015. "Ethics and the Subject of Corruption." *Contributions to Indian Sociology* 49 (3): 337–39.

Halperin, C.J. 2019. *Ivan the Terrible: Free to Reward and Free to Punish*. Pittsburgh: University of Pittsburgh Press.

Han, C. 2012. *Life in Debt*. Berkeley: University of California Press.

Hanafi, A. 2018. "Lords of the Parks: Lavish Lifestyles of Lagos 'Big Boys' Transporters." *Punch* June 30.

Hann, C. 2016. "The Moral Dimension of Economy: Work, Workfare, and Fairness in Provincial Hungary. Working Paper 174. Halle, Germany: Marx Planck Institute for Social Anthropology.

Hansen, Hans Krause 1995. "Small Happenings and Scandalous Events: Corruption and Scandal in Contemporary Yucatan." *Folk* 37: 75–101.

Hansen, T.B. 2006. "Sounds of Freedom: Music, Taxis and the Racial Imagination in Post-Apartheid South Africa." *Public Culture* 18 (1): 185–208.

Hansen, T.B., and F. Stepputat. 2001. *States of Imagination: Ethnographic Explorations of the Postcolonial State*. Durham, North Carolina: Duke University Press.

Hart, Jennifer. 2016. *Ghana on the Go: African Mobility in the Age of Motor Transportation*. Bloomington: Indiana University Press.

Harvey, D. 2013. *Rebel Cities: From the Right to the City to the Urban Revolution*. London: Verso.

Hasty, Jennifer. 2005a. "The Pleasures of Corruption: Desire and Discipline in Ghanaian Political Culture." *Cultural Anthropology* 20 (2): 271–301.

Hasty, Jennifer. 2005b. "Sympathetic Magic/Contagious Corruption: Sociality, Democracy, and the Press in Ghana." *Public Culture* 17 (3): 339–69.

Healey, P. 2000. "Planning Theory and Urban and Regional Dynamics: A Comment on Yiftachel and Huxley." *International Journal of Urban and Regional Research* 24 (4): 917–21.

Heap, S. 2010. "'Their Days Are Spent Gambling and Loading, Pimping for Prostitutes and Picking Pockets': Male Juvenile Delinquents on Lagos Island, 1920s–1960s." *Journal of Family History* 35 (1): 48–70.

Hect, David, and AbdouMaliq Simone. 1994. *Invisible Governance: The Art of African micropolitics.* New York: Autonomedia.

Heidenheimer, A.J., M. Johnston, and T.V. Le Vine, eds. 1989. *Corruption: A Handbook.* New Brunswick, New Jersey: Transaction Publishers.

Heinze, R. 2018. "'Taxi Pirates:' A Compartive History of Informal Transport in Nairobi and Kinshasha, 1960s-2000s." In *Transport, Transgression and Politics in African Cities: The Rhythm of Chaos,* edited by D.E. Agbiboa, pp. 19–41. London: Routledge.

Hepworth, B. 1996. "Sculpture." In *Art in Theory, 1900–1990,* edited by C. Harrison and P. Wood. Oxford: Blackwell.

Hibou, B. 1999. "The 'Social Capital' of the State as an Agent of Deception or the Ruses of Economic Intelligence." In *The Criminalization of the State in Africa,* edited by J.-F. Bayart, S. Ellis, and B. Hibou, pp. 69–113. Oxford: James Currey.

Hickey, S. and A. du Toit. 2007. "Adverse Incorporation, Social Exclusion and Chronic Poverty." CPRC Working paper No. 81. Manchester UK: Chronic Poverty Research Center, University of Manchester.

Highmore, B. 2002. "Introduction: Questioning Everyday Life." In *Everyday Life and Cultural Theory: An Introduction,* edited by B. Highmore, pp. 1–34. London: Routledge.

Hoffman, D. 2007. "The Meaning of a Militia: Understanding the Civil Defense Forces in Sierra Leone." *African Affairs* 106 (425): 639–62.

Hoffman, D. 2011. "Violent Virtuosity: Visual Labor in West Africa's Mano River War." *Anthropological Quarterly,* 84(4): 940–75.

Hoffmann, L.K., and R. Patel. 2017. "Collective Action on Corruption in Nigeria: A Social Norms Approach to Connecting Society and Institutions." Chatnam House Report. London: The Royal Institute of International Affairs.

Holmberg, S., and B. Rothstein. 2011. "Dying of Corruption." *Health Economics, Policy and Law* 6 (4): 529–47.

Holmes, L. 2015. *Corruption: A Very Short Introduction.* Oxford: Oxford University Press.

Holston, James. 2007. *Insurgent Citizenship: Disjunctions of Democracy and Modernity in Brazil.* Princeton, NJ: Princeton University Press.

Honwana, A. 2012. *The Time of Youth: Social Change and Politics in Africa.* Sterling, Virginia: Kumarian Press.

Hooper-Greenhill, E. 2000. *Museums and Interpretation of Visual Culture.* London: Routledge.

Houeland, C. 2018. "Between the Street and Aso Rock: The Role of Nigerian Trade Unions in Popular Protests." *Journal of Contemporary African Studies* 36 (1): 103–20.

Hough, D. 2017. *Analysing Corruption: An Introduction.* Newcastle Upon Tyne, UK: Agenda Publishing.

HRW. 2006. "'They Do Not Own This Place': Government Discrimination against 'Non-Indigenes' in Nigeria." April.

HRW. 2007. "Criminal Politics: Violence, 'Godfathers' and Corruption in Nigeria." 19 (16A): pp. 1–121. New York.

HRW. 2010. "Everyone's in on the Game: Corruption and Human Rights Abuses by the Nigerian Police Force." August.

HRW. 2011. "Corruption on Trial? The Record of Nigeria's Economic and Financial Crimes Commission." August 25.

Hughes, E. 1958. *Men and Their Work*. The Free Press of Glencoe.

Hume, Lynne, and Jane Mulcock. 2004. *Anthropologist in the Field: Cases in Participant Observation*. New York: Columbia University Press.

Humphrey, C., and D. Sneath. 2004. "Shangaied by the Bureaucracy: Bribery and Post-Soviet Officialdom in Russia and Mongolia." In *Between Morality and the Law: Corruption, Anthropology, and Comparative Society*, edited by I. Pardo, pp. 85–100. Farnham: Ashgate.

Huntington, S.P. 1968. *Political Order in Changing Societies*. New Haven: Yale University Press.

Hyden, G. 2006. *African Politics in Comparative Perspective*. Cambridge: Cambridge University Press.

Hyden, G., J. Court and K. Mease. 2004. *Making Sense of Governance: Empirical Evidence from 16 Developing Countries*. Boulder: Lynne Rienner.

Ibekwe, N. 2013. "Drivers, Conductors of Lagos Commercial Buses to Wear Uniform." *Premium Times*, November 11.

ICG. 2007. "Nigeria's Election: Avoiding a Political Crisis." Africa Report No. 123. March 28.

Idemudia, U., T.A. Liedong, D.E. Agbiboa, and K. Amaeshi. 2019. "Exploring the Culture and Cost of Corruption in Nigeria: Can Africapitalism Help?" In *Africapitalism: Sustainable Business and Development in Africa*, edited by U. Idemudia & K. Amaeshi. New York: Routledge.

Ikoku, S.G. 1985. *Nigeria's Fourth Coup D'état: Options for Modern Statehood*. Enugu, Nigeria: Fourth Dimension.

Ilevbare, T. 2013. "Okada Ban and the Insensitivity of State Governors." *Daily Post*, June 17.

Isawumi, M.A., C.O. Adeoti, J.N. Ubah, I.O. Oluwatimilehin, and R.A. Raji. 2011. "Occular Status of Commerical Drivers in Osun State, Nigeria." *African Journal of Medicine and Medical Sciences* 40 (4): 405–11

Isichei, Elizabeth. 2004. *Moral Economy and the Popular Imagination*. Rochester, NY: Rochester University Press.

Ismail, Olawale. 2009. "The Dialectics of 'Junctions' and 'Bases': Youth 'Securo-Commerce' and the Crises of Order in Downtown Lagos." *Security Dialogue* 40 (4-5): 463–87.

Ismail, Olawale. 2010. "Deconstructing 'Oluwole': Political Economy at the Margins of the State." In *Encountering the Nigerian State*, edited by W. Adebanwi & E. Obadare, pp. 29–54. New York: Palgrave Macmillan.

Ismail, Olawale. 2013. "From 'Area-Boyism' to 'Junctions and Bases': Youth Social Formation and the Micro Structural of Violence in Lagos Island." In *State Fragility, State Formation, and Human Security in Nigeria*, edited by M.O. Okome, pp. 87–110. New York: Palgrave Macmillan.

Ismail, Olawale. 2016. "'What is in a Job?' The Social Context of Youth Employment Issues in Africa." *Journal of African Economies* 25 (AERC Supplement 1): 137–60.

ITDP. 2016. "Dar es Salaam's BRT Could Transform Urban Life in Tanzania." August 09.

Iyoha, M.A. and D.E. Oriakhi. 2008. "Explaining African Economic Growth Performance: Case of Nigeria." In *The Political Economy of Economic Growth in Africa 1960–2000*, edited by B.J. Ndulu, S.A. O'Connell, J.P. Azam, R.H. Bates, A.K. Fosu, J.W. Gunning, and D. Njinkeu, pp. 621–59. Cambridge: Cambridge University Press.

Izuekwe, C., A. Dedeigbo, and F. Toheeb, F. 2012. "4 Activists, Okada Riders Arrested." *PM News*, October 10.

Jackson, M. 2008. "The Shock of the New: On Migrant Imaginaries and Critical Transition." *Ethnos* 73 (1): 57–72.

Jackson, Robert H. and Rosberg, Carl G. 1984. "Personal Rule: Theory and Practice in Africa." *Comparative Politics*, 16(4): 421–42.

Jaffe, Rivke. 2013. "The Hybrid State: Crime and Citizenship in Urban Jamaica." *American Ethnologist* 40 (4): 734–48.

Jaffe, Rivke. 2018. "Cities and the Political Imagination." *The Sociological Review*, 66(6): 1097–1110.

Jaffe, R., C. Klaufus, C. and F. Colombijn. 2012. "Mobilities and Mobilizations of the Urban Poor." *International Journal of Urban and Regional Research* 36 (4): 643–54.

James, D. 2014. *Money from Nothing: Indebtedness and Aspiration in South Africa*. Stanford: Stanford University Press.

James, S.A. 2003. "Confronting the Moral Economy of US Racial/Ethnic Health Disparities." *American Journal of Public Health* 93 (2): 189.

Jaworski, A., and C. Thurlow, eds. 2010. *Semiotic Landscapes: Language, Image, Space*. London: Continuum.

Jeffery, Craig. 2002. "Caste, Clients, and Clientelism: A Political Economy of Everyday Corruption in Rural North India." *Economic Geography* 78 (1): 21–41.

Jega, A. 2000. "The State and Identity Transformation under Structural Adjustment in Nigeria." In *Identity Transformation and Identity Politics under Structural Adjustment in Nigeria*, edited by A. Jega, pp. 24–40. Uppsala: Nordic African Institute.

Jeganathan, P. 2000. "On the Anticipation of Violence." In *Anthropology, Development, and Modernities: Exploring Discourses, Counter-tendencies, and Violence*, edited by N. Long & A. Arce, pp. 111–25. London: Routledge.

Jeganathan, P. 2018. "Border, Checkpoints, Bodies." In *Routledge Handbook of Asia's Boderlands*, edited by A. Horstmann, M. Saxer, and A. Ripper, pp. 403–10. London: Routledge.

John, P.G., and S. Welch. 1978. "Political Corruption in America: A Search for Definitions and a Theory." *American Political Science Review* 72 (3): 974–84.

Johnston, Michael. (ed.) 1970. *Political Corruption: Readings in Comparative Analysis*. London: Routledge.

Johnston, Michael. 2001. "The New Corruption Rankings: Implications for Analysis and Reform." Prepared for Research Committee 24. International Political Science Association World Congress. Quebec City, Canada, August 02.

Jones, Jeremy L. 2010. "Nothing is Straight in Zimbabwe: The Rise of the Kukiya-Kiya Economy, 2000-2008." *Journal of Southern African Studies* 36 (2): 285–99.

Joseph, Richard. 1987. *Democracy and Prebendal Politics in Nigeria: The Rise and Fall of the Second Republic*. Cambridge: Cambridge University Press.

Kang, D.C. 2002. "Bad Loans to Good Friends: Money Politics and the Developmental State in South Korea." *International Organisation* 56 (1); 177–207.

Kangle, R.P. 1972. *The Kautiliya Arthasastra, Part II*. Bombay: University of Bombay.

Kano State Motor Vehicle Statistics. 1986. Kano: Government Printers.

Kaplan, Robert D. 1994. "The Coming Anarchy: How Scarcity, Crime, Overpopulation, Tribalism, and Disease are Rapidly Destroying the Social Fabric of our Planet." *The Atlantic Monthly* 44–76.

Kaplan, Robert D. 2000. *The Coming Anarchy: Shattering the Dreams of the Post-Cold War*. New York: Vintage.

Karklins, Rasma. 2005. *The System Made Me Do It: Corruption in Post-Communist Societies*. Armon, New York: M.E. Sharpe.

Katz, C. 2013. "Banal Terrorism." In *Violent Geographies: Fear, Terror, and Political Violence*, edited by D. Gregory & A. Pred, pp. 349–62. New York: Routledge.

Keane, Webb. 2002. "Sincerity, 'Modernity,' and the Protestants." *Cultural Anthropology* 17 (1): 65–92.

Keefer, P., and R. Vlaicu. 2008. "Democracy, Credibility, and Clientelism." *Journal of Law Economics and Organization* 24 (2): 371–406.

Keller, Evelyn F. 1992. *Secrets of Life, Secrets of Death: Essays on Language, Gender and Science*. New York: Routledge.

Kenyon, S., G. Lyons, and J. Rafferty. 2002. "Transport and Social Exclusion: Investigating the Possibility of Promoting Inclusion through Virtual Mobility." *Journal of Transport Geography* 10: 207–19.

Kew, D. 2006. "Nigeria." In *Countries at the Crossroads*, edited by S. Tatic. New York: Freedom House.

Khan, M. 1998. "Patron-Client Networks and the Economic Effects of Corruption in Asia." *Eur J Dev Res*, 10: 15–39.

Khan, Mariama. 2017. "'Blood Neighbours' and Border Enemies: Transport, Trade and Talibee Networks and The Gambia-Senegal Relations, 1960–2015." University of Edinburgh (MPhil thesis).

Khan, Mushtaq. 1989. "Clientelism, Corruption and Capitalist Development: An Analysis of State Intervention with Specific Reference to Bangladesh." University of Cambridge (PhD thesis).

Khan, Mushtaq. 1996a. "A Typology of Corrupt Transactions in Developing Countries." *IDS Bulletin* 27 (2): 12–21.

Khan, Mushtaq. 1996b. "The Efficiency Implications of Corruption." *Journal of International Development* 8: 683–96.

Khan, Mushtaq. 2000. "Rent-seeking as Process." In M.H. Khan & K.S. Jomo (eds), *Rents, Rent-seeking and Economic Development: Theory and Evidence in Asia*. Cambridge: Cambridge University Press, pp. 70–144.

Khan, Mushtaq. 2006. "Determinants of Corruption in Developing Countries: The Limits of Conventional Economic Analysis." In *International Handbook on the Economics of Corruption*, edited by S. Rose-Ackerman, pp. 216–44. Cheltenham: Edward Elgar.

Khan, Mushtaq. 2012a. "Growth, Institutional Challenges, and the Political Settlement in Bangladesh." (Working Paper). London; School of Oriental and African Studies, University of London.

Khan, Mushtaq. 2012b. "The Political Economy of Inclusive Growth." In *Promoting Inclusive Growth: Challenges and Policy*, edited by L. de Mello & M.A. Dutz, pp. 15–54. Paris: OECD Publishing.

Khayesi, M., F.M. Nafukho, and J. Kemuma. 2015. *Informal Public Transport in Practice: Matatu Entrepreneurship*. London: Routledge.

Kim, B.S. 1998. "Corruption and Anti-Corruption Policies in Korea." *Korea Journal* 38 (1): 46–69.

Kirkpatrick, A. 2007. *World Englishes: Implications for English Language Teaching and Intercultural Communication*. Cambridge: Cambridge University Press.

Kitschelt, H. and S.I. Wilkinson, eds. 2007. *Patrons, Clients and Policies: Patterns of Democratic Accountability and Political Corruption*. Cambridge: Cambridge University Press.

Kjaer, Anne Mette. 2004. "Old Brooms Can Sweep Too! An Overview of Rulers and Public Sector Reform in Uganda, Tanzania and Kenya." *The Journal of Modern African Studies* 42 (3): 389–413.

Klaeger, Gabriel. 2009. "Religion on the Road: The Spiritual Experience of Road Travel in Ghana." In Gewald Jan-Bart, Luning Sabine, and Walravenn Klass vam (eds), *The Speed of Change: Motor Vehicles and People in Africa, 1890-2000*. Leiden: Brill, pp. 212–32.

Klitgaard, R. 1988. *Fighting Corruption*. Berkeley: University of California Press.

Klopp, J.M., J. Harber, and M. Quarshie. 2019. "A Review of BRT as Public Transport Reform in African Cities." VREF Research Synthesis Project. Governance of Metropolitan Transport Background Paper, April.

Knapp, W. 1972. *Report of the Commission to Investigate Allegations of Police Corruption and the City's Anti-Corruption Procedures*. New York: George Braziller.

Koechlin, L. 2013. *Corruption as Empty Signifier: Politics and Political Order in Africa*. Leiden: Brill.

Kombe, W. and V. Kreibich. 2000. "Informal Land Management in Tanzania." SPRING Research Series 29. University of Dortmund, Dortmund, Germany.

Kondos, Alex. 1987. "The Question of 'Corruption' in Nepal." *Mankind* 17 (1); 15–33.

Konings, P.J.J. 2000. "Trade Unions and Democratization in Africa." In *Trajectories de liberation en Afrique contemporaine: Hommage a Robert Buijtenhijs*, edited by P.J.J. Konings, G.S.C.M. Hesseling, and W.M.J. van Binsbergen, pp. 167–83. Paris: Kathala.

Koolhaas, Rem. 2001. *Mutations*. Barcelona: ACTAR.

Koolhaas, Rem. 2007. *Lagos: How It Works*. Lars Muller Publishers.

Kopytoff, Igor. 1986. "The Cultural Biography of Things: Commoditization as Process." In *The Social Life of Things: Commodities in Cultural Perspectives*, edited by A. Appadurai, pp. 64–91. Cambridge: Cambridge University Press.

Kotef, Hagar, and Merav Amir. 2011. "Between Imaginary Lines: Violence and Its Justifications at the Military Checkpoints in Occupied Palestine." *Theory, Culture and Society* 28 (1): 55–80.

Kristeva, J. 1982. *Powers of Horror: An Essay on Abjection*. (Translated by Leon S. Roudiez). New York: Columbia University Press.

Kuah, K.E. 1999. "The Changing Moral Economy of Ancestor Worship in a Chinese Emigrant District." *Culture, Medicine and Psychiatry*, 23: 99–132.

Kulick, E., and D. Wilson. 1992. *Thailand's Turn: Profile of a New Dragon*. New York: St. Martin's Press.

Kumar, A. 2011. "Understanding the Emerging Role of Okadas in African Cities: A Political Economy Perspective." SSATP Discussion Paper, 13. Urban Transport Series.

Kumar, A., and F. Barrett. 2008. "Stuck in Traffic: Urban Transport in Africa." World Bank and the SSATP. January.

Kuran, T. 1997. *Private Truths, Public Lies: The Social Consequences of Preference Falsification*. Cambridge: Harvard University Press.

Kuris, G. 2014. "Remaking a Neglected Megacity: A Civic Transformation in Lagos State, 1999-2012." Innovations for Successful Societies (ISS), Princeton University, pp. 1–22.

Kusenbach, M. 2003. "Street Phenomenology: The Go-Along as Ethnographic Research Tool." *Ethnography* 4 (3): 455–85.

Kyei, K.G., and H. Schreckenbach. 1975. *No Time to Die*. Accra: Catholic Press.

Ladelokun, L. 2017. "Proposed Ban of Yellow Buses: The Gains, the Knocks." *Daily Times*, February 24, 1–47.

Lagos State Government. 2012. *Lagos State Road Traffic Law 2012*. Alahusa, Ikeja: Lagos State.

LAMATA. 2013. "A Decade of Transport." Lagos: LAMATA.

Lambsdorff, Johann G. 1999. "The Transparency International Corruption Perception Index 1999—Framework Document." October. .

Lamour, Peter. 2012. *Interpreting Corruption: Culture and Politics in the Pacific Islands.* Honolulu: University Hawai'i Press.

Larkin, B. 2013. "The Politics and Poetics of Infrastructure." *Annual Review of Anthropology* 42 (91): 327–43.

Lamour, Peter. 2008. "Corruption and the concept of 'Culture': Evidence from the Pacific Island." Crime, Law and social Change 49: 225–39.

Lamour, Peter. 2012. *Interpreting Corruption: Culture and Politics in the Pacific Islands.* Honolulu: University Hawai'i Press.

Larreguy, H.A., C.E.M. Olea, and P. Querubin. 2014. "The Role of Labor Unions as Political Machines: Evidence from the Case of the Mexical Teachers' Union." March.

Laurence, P. 2007. "Mbeki's Approval of Nigerian Poll Bodes Ill for Zimbabwe." *The Sunday Independent* (South Africa), May 06.

Lawal, F. 2015. "Driver Sleeps Overnight in Bus, Found Dead by Morning." *Pulse.ng,* April 03.

Lawal, I., A.M. Jimoh, T. Omotoye, and J. Alabi. 2008. "Chief Lamidi Adedibu Dies at 81." *The Guardian,* 13 June.

Lawson, L. 2009. "The Politics of Anti-Corruption Reform in Africa." *The Journal of Modern African Studies* 47 (1): 73–100.

Lawuyi, Olatunde B. 1988. "The World of the Yorùbá Taxi Driver: An Interpretive Approach to Vehicle Slogans." *Africa: Journal of the International African Institute* 58 (1): 1–13.

Lazar, S. 2005. "Citizens Despite the State: Everyday Corruption and Local Politics in El Alto." In *Corruption: Anthropologoical Perspectives,* edited by D. Haller & C. Shore, pp. 212–28. London: Pluto Press.

Le Pape, Marc. 1997. *L'Energie Sociale a Abidjan: Economie Politique de la Ville en Afrique Noire, 1930–1995.* Paris: Karthala.

Le Vine, V. 1975. *Political Corruption: The Ghana Case.* Stanford: Hoover Institution Press.

Leadership. 2015. "No Friend or Foe in the Fight against Corruption—Buhari." December 12.

LeBas, A. 2013. "Violence and Urban Order in Nairobi, Kenya and Lagos, Nigeria." *Studies in Comparative International Development* 48 (3): 240–62.

LeCompte, M.D., and J.P. Goetz. 1982. "Problems of Reliablity and Validity in Ethnographic Research." *Review of Educational Research* 52 (1): 31–60.

Lefebvre, Henri. 1987. "The Everyday and Everydayness." (Translated by C. Levich.) *Yale French Studies* 73: 7–11.

Lefebvre, Henri. 1992. *The Production of Space.* Oxford: Blackwell.

Lefebvre, Henri. 1996. *Writings on Cities.* Oxford: Blackwell.

Lefebvre, Henri. 2004. *Rhythmanalysis: Space, Time and Everyday Life.* London: Continuum.

Leff, N.H. 1964. "Economic Development through Bureaucratic Corruption." *American Behavior Scientist* 8 (2); 8–14.

Lewis, Oscar. 1996. "From Prebendalim to Predation: The Political Economy of Decline in Nigeria." *Journal of Modern African Studies* 34 (1): 79–103.

Lewis, P., and M. Bratton. 2000. "Attitudes to Democracy and Markets in Africa." *Afrobarometer,* No. 3. April.

Leys, C. 1965. "What is the Problem About Corruption?" *The Journal of Modern African Studies* 3 (2): 215–30.

Lindberg, S.I. 2003. "'It's Our Time to 'Chop': Do Elections in Africa Feed Neo-Patrimonialism rather than Counter-Act It?" *Democratization* 10 (2): 121–40.

Lindell, I. 2008. "The Multiple Sites of Urban Governance: Insights from an African City." *Urban Studies* 45 (9): 1879–1901.

Lindell, I., and O. Adama. 2020. "Visions of Urban Modernity and the Shrinking of Public Space: Challenges for Street Work in African Cities." NAI Policy Notes, 1–8.

Lindell, I., and M. Utas. 2012. "Networked City Life in Africa: Introduction." *Urban Forum* 23: 409–14.

Lipton, Jonah. 2017. "'Family Business': Work, Neighborhood Life, Coming of Age, and Death in the Time of Ebola in Freetown, Sierra Leone." London School of Economics and Political Science (PhD thesis).

Lloyd, R.B. 2004. "Nigeria's Democratic Generals." *Current History* 103: 215–20.

Locatelli, F. and P. Nugent. 2009. "Introduction." In *African Cities: Competing Claims on Urban Spaces*, edited by F. Locatelli & P. Nugent, pp. 1–13. Leiden: Brill.

Lomnitz, Claudia. 1995. "Ritual, Rumor and Corruption in the Constitution of Polity in Modern Mexico." *Journal of Latin American Anthropology* 1 (1): 20–47.

Long, N. 1999. "The Multiple Optic of Interface Analysis." UNESCO Background Paper on Interface Analysis, October.

Lonsdale, John, ed. 1986. "Political Accountability in African History." In *Political Domination in Africa: Reflections on the Limits of Power*, edited by P. Chabal, pp. 126–74. Cambridge: Cambridge University Press.

Lotman, Yuri. 1988. "Text within the Text." *Soviet Psychology*, 26 (3): 32–51.

Low, S. 1996. "Spatializing Culture: The Social Production and Social Construction of Public Space." *American Ethnologist* 23(94): 861–79.

Luckham, R. 1971. *The Nigerian Military: A Sociological Analysis of Authority and Revolt, 1960–1967*. Cambridge: Cambridge University Press.

Lugalla, J. 1995. *Crisis Urbanization and Urban Poverty in Tanzania: A Study of Urban Poverty and Survival Politics*. Lanham, Maryland University Press America.

Lund, C., ed. 2007. *Twilight Institutions: Public Authority and Local Politics in Africa*. Oxford: Blackwell.

MacGaffey, J. 1991. *The Real Economy of Zaire: The Contribution of Smuggling and Other Unofficial Activities to National Wealth*. Philadelphia: University of Pennsylvania Press.

MacGaffey, J. and R. Bazenguissa-Ganga. 2000. *Congo-Paris: Transnational Traders on the Margins of the Law*. London: James Currey.

Madugu, Y.U. 2018. "Filling the Mobility Gaps: The Shared Taxi Industry in Kano, Nigeria." *The Journal of Transport History* 39(1): 41–54.

Magee, C. 2007. "Spatial Stories: Photographic Practices and Urban Belongings." *Africa Today* 54 (2): 109–29.

Maier, K. 2000. *This House Has Fallen: Nigeria in Crisis*. London: Penguin Books.

Makeham, P. 2005. "Performing the City." *Theatre Research International* 30 (2); 150–60.

Mamdani, M. 1996. *Citizens and Subject: Contemporary Africa and the Legacy of Late Colonialism*. Princeton: Princeton University Press.

Marcus, George E., ed. 1983. *Elites, Ethnographic Issues*. Albuquerque: University of New Mexico Press.

Marcus, Richard R. 2010. "Marc the Medici? The Failure of a New Form of Neopatrimonial Rule in Madagascar." *Political Science Quarterly* 125 (1): 111–31.

Marcuse, P. 2009. "From Critical Urban Theory to the Right to the City." *City* 13 (2–3): 185–96.

Marcuse, P. 2014. "Reading the Right to the City." *City: Analysis of Urban Trends, Culture, Theory, Policy, Action* 18 (1): 4–9.

Marquette, H. 2012. "'Finding God' or 'Moral Disengagement' in the Fight against Corruption in Developing Countries? Evidence from India and Nigeria." *Public Administration and Development* 32 (1): 11–26.

Marquette, H., and C. Peiffer. 2015. "Collective Action and Systemic Corruption." Paper Presented at the ECPR Joint Sessions Workshops, University of Warsaw, 29 March–2 April, 1–28.

Marquette, M., C. Peiffer, and R. Armytage, R. 2019. "What we found out about bribery patterns in Uganda's health care systems." *The Conversation*, February 28.

Marshall, R. 1998. "Mediating the Global and Local in Nigerian Pentecostalism." *Journal of Religion in Africa* XXVIII (3): 278–315.

Marshall, R. 2009. *Political Spiritualities; The Pentecostal Revolution in Nigeria*. Chicago: University of Chicago Press.

Marshall, R. 2015. "Dealing with the Prince over Lagos." EDGS Working Paper 26. University of Toronto, January 22.

Masquelier, Adeline. 2000. "Of Head Hunters and Cannibals: Migrancy, Labor, and Consumption in Mawri Imagination." *Cultural Anthropology* 16: 84–126.

Masquelier, Adeline. 2001. "Behind the Dispensary's Prosperous Façade: Imagining the State in Rural Niger." *Public Culture* 13 (2): 267–92.

Masquelier, Adeline. 2002. "Road Mythographies: Space, Mobility, and the Historical Imagination in Postcolonial Niger." *American Ethnologist*, 29(4): 829–55.

Masquelier, Adeline. 2019. *Fada: Boredom and Belonging in Niger*. Chicago: Chicago University Press.

Massey, Doreen. 1993. "Politics and Space/Time." In *Place and the Politics of Identity: Place and the Politics of Identity*, edited by M. Keith & S. Pile, pp. 139–59. London: Routledge.

Massey, Doreen. 1994. *Space, Place and Gender*. Cambridge: Polity Press.

Massey, Doreen. 2005. *For Space*. Los Angeles: Sage.

Mathur, N. 2017. "Eating Money: Corruption and its Categorical 'Other' in the Leaky Indian State." *Modern Asian Studies* 51 (6): 1796–1817.

Mauro, P. 1995. "Corruption and Growth." *The Quarterly Journal of Economics* 110 (3):681–712.

Mauss, M. 2000. *The Gift*. London: Routledge.

Mazzarella, W. 2006. "Internet X-Ray: E-Governance, Transparency, and the Politics of Immediation in India." *Public Culture* 18 (3): 473–505.

Mbaku, J.M., ed. 1998. *Corruption and Crisis of Institutional Reform in Africa*. Lewiston, New York: The Edwin Mellen Press.

Mbaku, J.M. 2000. *Bureaucratic and Political Corruption in Africa: The Public Choice Perspective*. Krieger: Malabar.

Mbembe, A. 2002. "On the Power of the False." *Public Culture* 14 (3): 629–641.

Mbembe, Achille. 1992. "Provisional Notes on the Postcolony." *Africa* 62: 3–37.

Mbembe, Achille. 1997. "The 'Thing' & its Doubles in Cameroonian Cartoons." In *Readings in Popular Culture*, edited by K. Barber, pp. 151–63. Bloomington: Indiana University Press and Oxford: James Currey.

Mbembe, Achille. 2001a. *On the Postcolony*. Berkeley: University of California Press.

Mbembe, Achille. 2001b. "Ways of Seeing: Beyond the New Nativism: Introduction." *African Studies Review* 44 (2): 1–14.

Mbembe, Achille. 2003. "Necropolitics." *Public Culture* 15 (1): 11–40.

Mbembe, Achille. 2006. "On Politics as a Form of Expenditure." In *Law and Disorder in the Postcolony*, edited by J. Comaroff and J.L. Comaroff, pp. 299–330. Chicago: Chicago University Press.

Mbembe, Achille. 2018. "The Idea of a Borderless World." *Africa is a Country* November 11.

Mbembe, Achille, and S. Nuttall. 2004. "Writing the World from an African Metropolis." *Public Culture* 16 (3): 347–72.

Mbembe, Achille, and S. Nuttall. (eds). 2008. *Johannesburg: The Elusive Metropolis*. Durham, NC: Duke University Press.

Mbembe, Achille, and J. Roitman, J. 1995. "Figures of the Subject in Times of Crisis." *Public Culture* 7: 323–52.

McCall, J.C. 2003. "Madness, Money and Movies: Watching a Nigerian Popular Video with the Guidance of a Native Doctor." *Africa Today* 49 (3): 78–94.

McGregor, Sue L.T. 2003. "Critical Discourse Analysis—A Primer." *Kappa Omicron Nu Forum*, 15 (1). Retrieved from: <https://www.kon.org/archives/forum/15-1/mcgregorcda.html>

McKinsey & Company. 2003. *Vision Mumbai: Recommendations for Transforming Mumbai into a World-Class City*. Mumbai: Bombay First.

McMullan, M. 1961. "A Theory of Corruption: Based on a Consideration of Corruption in the Public Service and Government of British Colonies and Ex-Colonies in West Africa." *Sociological Review* 9 (2): 181–201.

Meagher, Kate. 2006. "Cultural Primodialism and the Post-Structuralist Imaginaire." *Africa* 76 (4): 590–97.

Meagher, Kate. 2010. *Identity Economics: Social Networks and the Informal Economy in Nigeria*. Oxford: James Currey.

Meagher, Kate. 2012. "The Strength of Weak States? Non-State Security Forces and Hybrid Governance in Africa." *Development and Change* 43 (5): 1073–101.

Meagher, Kate. 2013. "The Jobs Crisis Behind Nigeria's Unrest." *Current History* 112 (754): 169–74.

Meagher, Kate. 2018. "Complementarity, Competition and Conflict: Informal Enterprise and Religious Conflict in Northern Nigeria." In *Creed and Grievance: Muslim-Christian Relations and Conflict Resolution in Northern Nigeria*, edited by Abdul Raufu Mustapha and David Ehrhardt. New York: James Currey, pp. 184–222.

Meagher, Kate, and I. Lindell. 2013. "ASR Forum: Engaging with African Informal Economies: Social Inclusion or Adverse Incorporation?: Introduction." *African Studies Association* 56 (3): 57–76.

Medard, Jean-François. 1986. "Public Corruption in Africa: A Comparative Perspective." *Corruption & Reform* 1: 115–31.

Medium. 2018. "The African Commute: City Transport Trends." May 03.

Medium. 2019. "One Chance and the Insanity of Lagos, Nigeria." June 09.

Mehretu, A., B.W. Pigozzi, and L.M. Sommers. 2000. "Concepts in Social and Spatial Marginality." *Geografiska Annaler: Series B, Human Geography* 82 (2); 89–101.

Mehta, Suketu. 2004. *Maximum City: Bombay Lost and Found*. London: Penguin.

Mele, M.L., and B.M. Bello. 2007. "Coaxing and Coercion in Roadblock Encounters on Nigerian Highways." *Discourse & Society* 18(4): 437–52.

Melly, Caroline. 2017. *Bottleneck: Moving, Building, and Belonging in an African City*. Chicago: University of Chicago Press.

Merry, S.E. 2001. "Spatial Governmentality and the New Urban Social Order: Controlling Gender Violence through Law." *American Anthropologist* 103 (1): 16–29.

Meyer, B. 2001. "Money, Power and Morality: Popular Ghanian Cinema in the Fourth Republic." *Ghana Studies* 4: 65–84.

Meyer, B. 2004. "'Praise the Lord': Popular Cinema and Pentecostalite Style in Ghana's New Public Sphere." *American Ethnologist* 31 (1): 92–110.

Mieke, B. 2003. "Visual Essentialism and the Object of Visual Culture." *Journal of Visual Culture* 2 (1): 15–32.

Migdal, Joel S., and Klaus Schlichte. 2005. "Rethinking the State." In *The Dynamics of States: The Formation and Crises of State Domination*, edited by K. Schlichte, pp. 1–40 Aldershot: Ashgate.

Miller, D., ed. 2001. *Car Cultures*. Oxford: Berg.

Miller, R.A. 2008. The Erotics of Corruption: Law, Scandal, and Political Perversion. Albany, New York: State University of New York Press.

Mills, A.J., G. Durepos, E. Wiebe, eds. 2010. *Encyclopedia of Case Study Research*. Volume 1. London: Sage.

Mishra, A. 2005. *The Economics of Corruption*. Oxford: Oxford University Press.

Mitchell, Timothy. 1991. "The Limits of the State: Beyond Statist Approaches and Their Critics." *The American Political Science Review* 85 (1): 77–96.

Mitchell, Timothy. 1999. "Society, Economy, and the State Effect." In *State/Culture: State Formation after the Cultural Turn*, edited by G. Steinmetz, pp. 76–97. Ithaca, New York: Cornell University Press.

Mkandawire, T. 2015. "Neopatrimonialism and the Political Economy of Economic Performance in Africa: Critical Reflections." *World Politics* 67 (3): 563–612.

Momoh, A. 2000. "Youth Culture and Area Boys in Lagos." In *Identity Transformation and Identity Politics under Structural Adjustment in Nigeria*, edited by A. Jega, pp. 181–203. Uppsala: NAI.

Monahan, T., and J.A. Fisher. 2010. "Benefits of Observer Effects: Lessons from the Field." *Qualitative Research* 10 (3): 357–76.

Moncada, E. 2013. "Introduction: The Politics of Urban Violence: Challenges to Development in the Global South." *Studies in Comparative International Development* 48 (3): 217–39.

Monga, Celestine. 1996. *The Anthropology of Anger: Civil Society and Democracy in Africa*. Boulder, Colorado: Lynne Rienner.

Moran, J. 2005. *Reading the Everyday*. Abingdon, Oxon: Routledge.

Morgan, D. 2008. "The Materiality of Cultural Construction." *Material Religion: Journal of Objects, Arts and Belief* 4 (2): 228–29.

Morley, D. 2000. *Home Territories: Media, Mobility and Identity*. London: Routledge.

Muir, S. 2016. "On Historical Exhaustion: Argentine Critique in an Era of 'Total Corruption.'" *Comparative Studies in Society and History* 58 (1): 129–58.

Muir, S., and A. Gupta. 2018. "Rethinking the Anthropology of Corruption: An Introduction to Supplement 18." *Current Anthropology* 59 (18): S4–S15.

Mulder, Niels. 1996. *Inside Thai Society: Interpretations of Everyday Life*. Amsterdam: Pepin Press.

Mungiu-Pippidi, A. 2006. "Corruption: Diagnosis and Treatment." *Journal of Democracy* 17 (3): 86–99.

Murphy, W. 2003. "Military Patrimonialism and Child Soldier Clientalism in the Liberian and Sierra Leonean Civil Wars." *African Studies Review* 46 (2): 61–87.

Mustapha, Abdul Raufu. 1992. "Structural Adjustment and Multiple Modes of Social Livelihood in Nigeria." In *Authoritarianism, Democracy and Adjustment: The Politics of Economic Reforms in Africa*, edited by P. Gibbon, Y. Bangura and A. Ofstad, pp. 188–232. Uppsala: SIAS.

Mustapha, Abdul Raufu. 1999. "Nigerian Transition: Third Time Lucky or More of the Same? *Review of the African Political Economy* 26 (80): 277–91.

Mustapha, Abdul Raufu. 2000. "Transformation of Minority Identities in Postcolonial Nigeria." In *Identity Transformation and Identity Politics under Structural Adjustment in Nigeria*, edited by A. Jega, pp. 86–108. Uppasala: NAI.

Mustapha, Abdul Raufu. 2002. "States, Predation and Violence: Reconceptualizing Political Action and Political Community in Africa." Paper presented at the 10th General Assembly of CODESRIA, "State, Political Identity and Political Violence," Kampala, December 8–12.

Mustapha, Abdul Raufu. 2012. "The Public Sphere in the 21st Century Africa: Broadening the Horizon of Democratization." *African Development* XXXVII (1): 27–41.

Mutongi, Kenda. 2006. "Thugs or Entrepreneurs? Perceptions of Matatu Operators in Nairobi, 1970 to the Present." *Africa* 76 (4): 549–68.

Mutongi, Kenda. 2017. *Matatu: A History of Popular Transportation in Nairobi*. Chicago: Chicago University Press.

Myers, G.A. 2010. "Seven Themes in African Urban Dynamics." Nordic African Institute, Discussion Paper 50. Uppsala.

Myers, G.A. 2011. *African Cities: Alternative Visions of Urban Theory and Practice*. London: Zed Books.

Myrdal, G. 1968. *Asian Drama: An Inquiry into the Poverty of Nations*. London: The Penguin Press.

Naim, N. 1995. "The Corruption Eruption." *Brown Journal of World Affairs*, 2 (2): 245–61.

Nairaland Forum. 2006. "How IBB Wasted $12bn—Okigbo Report." September 05.

National Mirror. 2013. "No Going Back on Wars against Agberos on Highways—Lagos." June 10.

Nelson, Harold D. ed. 1992. *Nigeria: A Country Study*. Washington DC: Library of Congress.

Neto, Pedro F. 2017. "Surreptitious Ethnography: Following the Paths of Angolan Refugees and Returnees in the Angola-Zambia Borderlands." *Ethnography* 20 (1): 128–45.

Neuwirth, Robert. 2006. *Shadow Cities: A Billion Squatters, a New Urban World*. London: Routledge.

Newell, Sasha. 2006. "Estranged Belongings: A Moral Economy of Theft in Abidjan." *Anthropological Theory* 6 (2); 179–203.

Newell, Sasha. 2012. *The Modernity Bluff: Crime, Consumption, and Citizenship in Cote D'Ivoire*. Chicago: University of Chicago Press.

Newell, Stephanie. 2020. *Histories of Dirt: Media and Urban Life in Colonial and Postcolonial Lagos*. Durham: Duke University Press.

News 24. 2005. "Nigeria Winning Corruption War." October 14. Available at https://www.news24.com/Fin24/Nigeria-winning-corruption-war-20051013

Newswatch. 2013. "Agberos: Menace to Road Users?" November 18.

NewswireNGR. 2015. "Can't the Poor Live in Lagos?" Riverine Settlers Lament Over the Fashola Led Administration." March 19.

Ngwodo, C. 2005. "Nigeria: This is Lagos." *This Day*, July 04.

Nigerian Bureau of Statistics. 2018. "Road Transport Data." Available at https://www .nigerianstat.gov.ng/pdfuploads/Road_Transport_Data_-_Q2_2018.pdf.

Nigeria Transport Policy. 2010. Draft. Abuja: FCT.

Nigerian Tribune. 2018. "One Chance Drivers' New Methods to Trap, Rape and Kidnap Passengers." May 05.

Njoku, U.J. 2005. "Colonial Political Re-Engineering and the Genesis of Modern Corruption in African Public Service: The Issue of the Warrant Chiefs of South Eastern Nigeria as a Case in Point." *Nordic Journal of African Studies* 14 (1): 99–116.

Nordstrom, C. 2004. *Shadows of War: Violence, Power, and Profiteering in the Twenty-First Century*. Berkeley: University of California Press.

Novoa, A. 2015. "Mobile Ethnography: Emergence, Techniques and its Importance to Geography." *Human Geographies—Journal of Studies and Research in Human Geography* 9 (1): 97–107.

Nta, E. 2017. "Ethical Deficit, Corruption and Crisis of National Identity: Integrity of Termites." Convocation lecture delivered at the Achievers University, Owo, Ondo State, April.

Nuijten, M. 2003. *Power, Community and the State: The Political Anthropology of Organization in Mexico*. London: Pluto Press.

Nuijten, M., and G. Anders, eds. 2007. *Corruption and the Secret of the Law: A Legal Anthropological Perspective*. London: Routledge.

Nyamnjoh, Francis B. 2017. "Incompleteness: Frontier Africa and the Currency of Conviviality." *Journal of Asian and African Studies* 52 (3): 253–70.

Nyamnjoh, Francis B. 2018. *Eating and Being Eaten: Cannibalism as Food for Thought*. Bamenda: Langaa RPCIG.

Nye, J. 1967. "Corruption and Political Development: A Cost-Benefit Analysis." *American Political Science Review* 61 (2): 417–27.

Nzeza, A.B. 2004. "The Kinshasha Bargain." In *Reinventing Order in the Congo: How People Respond to State Failure in Kinshasa*, T. Trefon, pp. 20–32. London: Zed Books.

O'Brien, K.J., and L. Li. 2006. *Rightful Resistance in Rural China*. Cambridge: Cambridge University Press.

Obadare, Ebenezer. 2019. "Nigeria's Two Decades of Zero-Sum Democracy." *Current History* May. 163–68.

Obadare, Ebenezer. 2021. "A Hashtag Revolution in Nigeria." *Current History* 120 (186): 183-88.

Obasanjo, Olushegun. 2000. "The Address to the Nation by His Excellency President Olushegun Obasanjo on the occasion of the first anniversary of his democratically elected elected government." 29 May.

Obiechina, E. 1975. *Culture, Tradition and Society in the West African Novel*. Cambridge: Cambridge University Press.

Ocheje, P.D. 2001. "Law and Social Change: A Socio-Legal Analysis of Nigeria's Corrupt Practices and Other Related Offences ACT, 2000." *Journal of African Law* 45 (2): 173–95.

Ocheje, P.D. 2018. "Norms, Law and Social Change: Nigeria's Anti-Corruption Struggle, 1999–2017. *Crime, Law and Social Change* 70: 363–81.

Ochonu, Moses. 2008. "Corruption and Poverty in Africa: A Deconstruction." *Pambazuka*, November 26.

Oestermann, T., and Peter L. Geschiere. & 2017. "Coercion or Trade? Multiple Self-Realization During the Rubber Boom in German Kamerun (1899–1913). In

The Political Economy of Everyday Life in Africa: Beyond the Margins, edited by W. Adebanwi, pp. 92–114. Oxford: Boydell & Brewer.

Oha, O. 2001. "The Visual Rhetoric of the Ambivalent City in Nigerian Video Films." In *Cinema and the City*, edited by M. Shiel & T. Fitzmaurice, pp. 195–205. Oxford: Blackwell.

Ohnmacht, T., H. Maksim, and M.M. Bergman, eds. 2009. *Mobilities and Inequality*. Surrey: Ashgate.

Ojiakor, J.O. 1980. *13 Years of Military Rule, 1966–1979*. Lagos: Daily Times.

Okafor, J. 2011. "Bingeing on our National Cake." *Sahara Reporters*, September 05.

Okereke, G. 1995. "Police Officers' Perceptions of the Nigeria Police Force: Its Effects on the Social Organization of Policing." *Journal of Criminal Justice* 23: 277–85.

Olaniyan, T. 2004. *Arrest the Music! Fela and His Rebel Art and Politics*. Bloomington, Indiana: Indiana University Press.

Olawoyin, O. 2019. "In Lagos, Billions Generated as "Tax" By Road Unions are Never Accounted For." *Premium Times*, July 13.

Olivier de Sardan, Jean-Pierre. 1999. "A Moral Economy of Corruption in Africa?" *The Journal of Modern African Studies* 37 (1): 25–52.

Oliver de Sardan, Jean-Pierre. 2008. "Researching the Practical Norms of Real Governance in Africa." *Discussion Paper Overseas Development Institute* 5: 1–22.

Olowu, D. 1988. "Bureaucratic Morality in Africa." *International Political Science Review* 9 (3): 215–29.

Olukoshi, A. 2005. "Changing Patterns of Politics in Africa." In *Politics and Social in an Hegemonic World: Lessons from Africa, Asia and Latin America*, edited by A.A. Boron & G. Lechini, pp. 177–201. Buenos Aires: Clacso.

Oluwaniyi, O. 2011. "Police and the Institution of Corruption in Nigeria." *Policing and Society: An International Journal of Research and Policy* 21: 1–29.

Olvera, L.D., A. Guezere, D. Plat, and P. Pochet. 2016. "Earning a Living, but at what Price? Being a Motorcycle Taxi Driver in Sub-Saharan African City." *Journal of Transport Geography* 55: 165–74.

Omitoogun, W. 1994. "The Area Boys of Lagos: A Study of Organized Street Violence." In *Urban Management and Urban Violence in Africa*, edited by I.O. Albert, pp. 301–8. Ibadan, Nigeria: IFRA.

Omotola, S.J. 2006. "Through a Glass Darkly: Assessing the 'New' War against Corruption in Nigeria." *African Insight* 36 (3-4): 214–29.

Omotola, S.J. 2007. "The Police and the Challenges of Sustainable Democracy in Nigeria: Contributions and Constraints." *Pakistan Journal of Social Sciences* 4: 620–31.

Orock, Rodgers Tabe E. 2015. "Elites, Culture and Power: The Moral Politics of 'Development' in Cameroon." *Anthropological Quarterly* 88 (2): 533–68.

Osaghae, Eghosa 1998. *Nigeria Since Independence: Crippled Giant*. Bloomington: Indiana University Press.

Osaghae, Eghosa. 2006. "Colonialism and Civil Society in Africa: The Perspective of Ekeh's Two Publics." *Voluntas: International Journal of Voluntary and Nonprofit Organizations* 17 (3): 223–45.

Osinulu, D. 2008. "Painters, Blacksmith and Wordsmith: Building Molues in Lagos." *African Arts* 44–53.

OSJI (Open Society Justice Initiative). 2010. *Criminal Force: Torture, Abuse, and Extrajudicial Killings by the Nigeria Police Force*. New York: Open Society Institute.

Osoba, S.O. 1996. "Corruption in Nigeria: Historical Perspectives." *Review of African Political Economy*, 23(69): 371–86.

Ostrom, Elinor. 2005. *Understanding Institutional Diversity*. Princeton: Princeton University Press.

Osun Defender. 2012. "Lagos-Badagry Expressway: A 'Boko Haram' in the West." 25 October.

Otunola, B., O. Harman, and S. Kriticos. 2019. "The BRT and the Danfo: A Case Study of Lagos' Transport Reforms from 1999–2019." International Growth Center (IGC) Cities that Work Case Study. October.

Owasanoye, B. 2019. "The Legislature and Fight against Graft and Corruption." Paper Presented at 9th NASS Induction Program. April 5.

Owen, Oliver. 2015. *Lagos: A Cultural and Historical Companion* (review). *African Affairs* 114 (457): 654–55.

Owen, Oliver. 2016. "Government Properties: The Nigerian Police Force as Total Institution." *Africa* 86 (1): 37–58.

Owen, Oliver. 2017. "Risk and Motivation in Police Work in Nigeria." In *Police in Africa: The Street-Level View*, edited by J. Beek, M. Goepfert, O. Owen, and J. Steinberg, pp. 149–70. London: Hurst.

Oxford English Dictionary. 2012. "Precarious." By Peter Gilliver. August 16.

Oyowe, O.A. 2015. "This Thing Called Communitarianism: A Critical Review of Matolino's *Personhood in African Philosphy*." *South African Journal of Philosophy* 34 (4): 504–15.

Packer, G. 2006. "The Megacity: Decoding the Chaos of Lagos." *New Yorker Magazine*, November 13.

Packer, George. 2009. *Interesting Times: Writings from a Turbulent Decade*. New York: Farrar, Straus and Giroux.

Paller, J. 2014. "Informal Institutions and Personal Rule in Urban Ghana." *African Studies Review* 57 (3): 123–42.

Pandey, K., and M. Paul. 2019. "Nairobi to Soon Roll Out Bus Rapid Transit System." *Down To Earth*, July 01.

Pardo, I. 2004. "Introduction: Corruption, Morality and the Law." In *Between Morality and the Law: Corruption, Anthropology and Comparative Society*, edited by I. Pardo, pp. 1–17. London: Routledge.

Parker, B. 1988. "Moral Economy, Political Economy, and the Culture of Entreprenurship in Highland Nepal." *Ethnology* 27: 181–94.

Parry, Jonathan, and Maurice Bloch. 1989. *Money and the Morality of Exchange*. Cambridge: Cambridge University Press.

Pasuk, P., and P. Sungsidh. 1996. *Corruption and Democracy in Thailand*. Second Edition. Chiang Mai: Silkworm Books.

Paterson, W.D.O., and P. Chaudhuri. 2007. "Making Inroads on Corruption in the Transport Sector through Control and Prevention." In *The Many Faces of Corruption: Tracking Vulnerabilities at the Sector Level*, edited by J.E. Campus & S. Pradhan, pp. 159–90. Washington, DC: World Bank.

Peace, Adrian. 1988. "The Politics of Transporting: Mobility in South-West Nigeria." *Africa* 58 (1): 14–28.

Peel, M. 2010. *A Swamp Full of Dollars: Pipelines and Paramilitaries at Nigeria's Oil Frontiers*. Chicago: Lawrence Hill Books.

Persson, Anna, B. Rothstein, and J. Teorell. 2013. "Why Anticorruption Reforms Fail: Systemic Corruption as a Collective Action Problem." *Governance* 26 (3): 449–71.

Petit, P. 2005. "'La Crise:' Lexicon and Ethos of the Second Economy in Lubumbashi." *Africa* 75 (4): 467–87.

Pierce, Steven. 2016. *Moral Economies of Corruption: State Formation and Political Culture in Nigeria*. Durham, North Carolina: Duke University Press.

Pieterse, E. 2011. "Grasping the Unknowable: Coming to Grips with African Urbanisms." *Social Dynamics* 37 (1): 5–23.

Pile, S. 1997. "Introduction: Opposition, Political Identities, and Spaces of Resistance." In *Geographies of Resistance*, edited by M. Keith and S. Pile, pp. 1–32. London: Routledge.

Piliavsky, Anastasia. 2013. "Where is the Public Sphere? Political Communications and the Morality of Disclosure in Rural Rajasthan." *The Cambridge Journal of Anthropology* 31 (2): 104–22.

Piliavsky, Anastasia, ed. 2014. *Patronage as Politics in South Asia*. Cambridge: Cambridge University Press.

Pilo, F. and Jaffe, R. 2020. "Introduction: The Political Materiality of Cities." *City and Society*, 32(1): 8–22.

Pitcher, A., M.H. Moran, and M. Johnston. 2009. "Rethinking Patrimonialism and Neopatrimonialism in Africa." *African Studies Review* 52 (1): 125–56.

Ploch, L. 2010. Nigeria: A Report on a Key Strategic Partner of the U.S. Government. Congressional Research Service. June 04.

PM News. 2011. "Lagos Sacks 90 KAI Officers Over Stealing, Extortion." September 13.

PM News. 2015. "99% of Lagos Danfo Drivers are Hypertensive." December 10.

Polanyi, K. 1968. *Primitive, Archaic and Modern Economies*. Boston: Beacon Press.

Polk, M. 1998. "Swedish Men and Women's Mobility Patterns: Issues of Social Equity and Ecological Sustainability." In Women's Travel Issues: Proceedings from the Second National Conference. Washington DC: US Department of Transportation, pp. 187–211.

Pope, J. 2000. *Confronting Corruption: The Elements of a National Integrity System*. TI Source Book. Berlin: Transparency International.

Porter, G. 1995. "The Impact of Road Construction on Women's Trade in Rural Nigeria." *Journal of Transport Geography* 39 (1): 3–14.

Porter, G. 2012. "Reflections on a Century of Road Transport Developments in West Africa and their (Gendered) Impacts on the Rural Poor." *EchoGeo*, 20: 1–14.

Porter, G., K. Hampshire, A. Abane, A. Munthali, A. Robson, and M. Mashiri. 2017. *Young People's Daily Mobilities in Sub-Saharan Africa: Moving Young Lives*. New York: Palgrave Macmillan.

Portes, Alejandro, M. Castells, and L.A. Benton. 1989. *The Informal Economy: Studies in Advanced and Less Developed Countries*. Baltimore: Johns Hopkins University Press.

Prasad, Monica, and A. Nickow. 2016. "Mechanisms of the 'Aid Curse': Lessons from South Korea and Pakistan." *Journal of Development Studies* 52 (11): 1612–27.

Prasad, Monica, da Silva, Mariana Borges Martins & Nicklow, Andre. 2019. "Approaches to Corruption: A Synthesis of the Scholarship." *Studies in Comparative International Development*, 54: 96–132.

Pratten, David. 2006. "The Politics of Vigilance in Southeastern Nigeria." *Development and Change* 37 (4): 707–34.

Pratten, David. 2013. "The Precariousness of Prebendalism." In *Democracy and Prebendalism in Nigeria: Critical Interpretations*, edited by W. Adebanwi & E. Obadare, pp. 243–58. New York: Palgrave Macmillan.

Pratten, David. 2017. *This Present Darkness: A History of Nigerian Organized Crime* (review). *African Studies Review* 60 (1): 205–7.

Premium Times. 2017. "Lagos Second Least Liveable City in the World." August 17.

Price, P. 1999. "Cosmologies and Corruption in (South) India." *Forum for Development Studies* 2: 315–27.

Price, P.G., and A.E. Ruud, eds. 2009. *Power and Influence in India: Bosses, Lords and Captains*. London: Routledge.

Probst, P. 2012. "Lagos—Oshodi: Inspecting an Urban Icon." In *Afropolis: City, Media and Arts*, edited by Pinther, K., Forster, L. & Hanussek, C., pp. 138–43. Johannesburg: Jacana Media.

Punch. 2012. "Fashola Bars NURTW from Operating at Parks." August 07.

Punch. 2014a. "Lagos Under APC is an Animal Farm—Fasheun." July 26.

Punch. 2014b. "Nigeria: Ebola Threatening Relationships, Social Institutions." August 14.

Punch. 2018. "Updated: Appeal Court Commutes Dariye's 14-year Jail Term to 10." November 16.

Purcell, M. 2003. "Citizenship and the Right to the Global City: Reimagining the Capitalist World Order." *International Journal of Urban and Regional Research* 27 (3): 564–90.

Quah, J.S.T. 2006. Curbing Corruption in Asian Countries: An Impossible Dream? *Current History* 176–79.

Quah, J.S.T. 2011. *Curbing Corruption in Asian Countries: An Impossible Dream*. Bingley, UK: Emerald Publishing.

Quartz Africa. 2019. "Bike-Hailing Startups in Lagos May Soon Have to Pay Thousands of Dollars in State Fees." July 22.

Quayson, Ato. 2014. *Oxford Street, Accra: City Life and the Itineraries of Transnationalism*. Durham: Duke University Press.

Quayson, Ato. 2018. "Automobility in the Social Imaginary." *Journal of African Cultural Studies* 32 (1): 88–93.

Rademacher, A. 2008. "Fluid City, Solid State: urban Environmental Territory in a State of Emergency, Kathmandu." *City and Society* 20 (1); 105–29.

Rakodi, C. 2001. "Urban Governance and Poverty—Addressing Needs, Asserting Claims: An Editorial Introduction." *International Planning Studies*, 6(4): 343–56.

Rakodi, C. 2006. "Relationships of Power and Place: The Social Construction of African Cities." *Geoforum* 37 (3): 307–440.

Ralushai, N.V., M.G. Masingi, and D.M.M. Madiba. 1996. "Report of the Commission of Inquiry into Witchcraft Violence and Ritual Murders in the Northern Province of the Republic of South Africa (To: His Excellency The Honourable Member of the Executive Council for Safety and Security, Northern Province).

Rao, V. and M. Walton, eds. 2004. *Culture and Public Action*. Stanford: Stanford University Press.

Rasmussen, J. 2012. "Inside the System, Outside the Law: Operating the Matatu Sector in Nairobi." *Urban Forum* 23 (4): 415–432.

Reno, William. 1995. *Corruption and State Politics in Sierra Leone*. New York & Cambridge: Cambridge University Press.

Report of the Tribunal of Inquiry. 2012. White Paper. Ikeja: Alausa.

Riggs, F.W. 1964. *Administration in Developing Countries*. Boston: Houghton.

Riley, S.P. 1999. "Petty Corruption and Development." *Development in Practice* 9 (1): 189–93.

Rizzo, Matteo. 2011. "'Life is War': Informal Transport Workers and Neoliberalism in Tanzania 1998–2009." *Development and Change* 42 (5): 1179–1206.

Rizzo, Matteo. 2014. "The Political Economy of an Urban Megaproject: The Bus Rapid Transit Project in Tanzania." *African Affairs* 114 (455): 249–70.

Rizzo, Matteo. 2017. *Taken For A Ride: Grounding Neoliberalism, Precarious Labor, and Public Transport in an African Metropolis.* Oxford: Oxford University Press.

Robbins, Paul. 2000. "The Rotten Institution: Corruption in Natural Resource Management." *Political Geography* 19: 423–43.

Robinson, Jennifer. 2013. "The Urban Now: Theorizing Cities Beyond the New." *European Journal of Cultural Studies,* 16(6): 659–77.

Robertson, A.F. 2006. "Misunderstanding Corruption." *Anthropology Today* 22 (2): 8–11.

Roitman, Janet L. 1998. "The Garisson-Entrepot." *Cahiers d'études Africaines,* 38(150–152): 297–329.

Roitman, Janet L. 2004. *Fiscal Disobedience: An Anthropology of Economic Regulation in Central Africa.* Princeton, NJ: Princeton University Press.

Roitman, Janet L. 2006. "The Ethics of Illegality in the Chad Basin." In *Law and Disorder in the Postcolony,* edited by J. Comaroff & J.L. Comaroff, pp. 247–72. Chicago: Chicago University Press.

Rose-Ackerman, Susan. 1975. "The Economics of Corruption." *Journal of Public Economics* 4: 187–203.

Rose-Ackerman, Susan. 1978. *Corruption: A Study in Political Economy.* New York: Academic Press.

Rose-Ackerman, Susan. 2010. "Corruption: Greed, Culture and the State." *The Yale Law Journal* November 10.

Rose, R., and C. Peiffer. 2014. "Why Do Some Africans Pay Bribes While Other Africans Don't? Afrobarometer Working Paper, 148: 1–28.

Rosin, R.T. 2000. "Wind, Traffic and Dust: The Recycling of Wastes." *Contributions to Indian Sociology* 33 (3): 361–408.

Ross, M.L. 2015. "What Have We Learned About the Resource Curse?" *Annual Review of Political Science* 18: 239–59.

Rotberg, R.I., ed. 2003. *State Failure and State Weakness in a Time of Terror.* Washington, DC: Brookings Institution Press.

Rothstein, Bo. 2018. "Fighting Systemic Corruption: The Indirect Strategy." *Daedalus* 147 (3): 35–49.

Rothstein, Bo. And Davide Torsello. 2014. "Bribery in Preindustrial Societies: Understanding the Universalism-Particularism Puzzle." *Journal of Anthropological Research,* 70 (2): 263-84.

Routley, Laura. 2016. *Negotiating Corruption: NGOs, Governance and Hybridity in West Africa.* Abingdon, UK: Routledge.

Rowlands, M. 1995. "Inconsistent Temporalities in a Nation-Space." In *Worlds Apart: Modernity through the Prism of the Local,* edited by D. Miller, pp. 23–42. New York: Routledge.

Rowlands, M., and J. Warnier, J. 1988. "Sorcery, Power and the Modern State in Cameroon." *Man* 23 (1): 118–32.

Roy, A. 2005. "Urban Informality: Towards an Epistemology of Planning." *Journal of the American Planning Association* 71 (2): 147–58.

Roy, A. 2012. "Urban Informality: The Production of Space and Practice of Planning." In *The Oxford Handbook of Urban Planning,* edited by R. Crane and R. Weber, pp. 1–11. Oxford: Oxford University Press.

Roy, A., and N. AlSayyad, eds. 2004. *Urban Informality: Transnational Perspectives from the Middle East, South Asia and Latin America*. Lanham, Maryland: Lexington Books.

Roy, I. 2013. "Contesting Consensus: Disputing Inequality: Agonistic Subjectivities in Rural Bihar." *South Asia Multidisciplinary Academic Journal* (online). August 01, 1–17.

Roy, P. 2017. "Anti-Corruption in Nigeria: A Political Settlement Analysis." Anti-Corruption Evidence (ACE) Working Paper 002. July.

Ruud, Arild E. 2000. "Corruption as Everyday Practice; The Public-Private in Local Indian Society." *Forum for Development Studies* 27 (2): 271–94.

Sa'idu, L. 2009. "I Expected Worse from Clinton—Farida." *Leadership* August 15.

Sahlins, M.D. 1963. "Poor Man, Rich Man, Big-Man, Chief: Political types in Melanesia and Polynesia." *Comparative Studies in Society and History* 5 (3); 285–303.

Sala-i-Martin, X., and A. Subramanian. 2008. "Addressing the Natural Resource Curse: An Illustration from Nigeria." In *Economic Policy Options for a Prosperous Nigeria*, edited by P. Collier, C.C. Soludo, & C. Pattillo, pp. 61–92. New York: Palgrave Macmillan.

Samaila, A. 2015. "Cross-Border Trade in Fairly Used Automobiles (Tokumbo): A Study of the Nigerian North-West Border C. 1973–2013." Usman Danfodiyo University (PhD thesis).

Sanders, T. and H.G. West. 2003. "Power Revealed and Concealed in the New World Order." In *Transparency and Conspiracy: Ethnographies of Suspicion in the New World Order*, edited by H.G. West & T. Sanders, pp. 1–37. Durham: Duke University Press.

Schaffer, F.C. 2012. "What Is It We Do When We Ask Questions About Causes?" Committee on Concepts and Methods Working Paper Series, December.

Schatzberg, Michael. 2001. *Political Legitimacy in Middle Africa: Father, Family, Food*. Bloomington: Indiana University Press.

Scheper-Hughes, N. 2006. "Death Squads and Democracy in Northeast Brazil." In *Law and Disorder in the Postcolony*, edited by J. Comaroff & J.L. Comaroff, pp. 150–187. Chicago: University of Chicago Press.

Schieffelin, B.B. 1990. *The Give and Take of Everyday Life: Language Socialization of Kaluli Children*. Cambridge: Cambridge University Press.

Schindler, S. 2014. "A New Delhi Everyday: Multiplicities of Governance Regimes in a Transforming Metropolis." *Urban Geography* 35 (3): 402–19.

Schmied, J. 1991. *English in Africa*. London: Longman.

Schouten, P. 2019. "Roadblock Politics in Central Africa." *Environment and Planning D: Society and Space* 37 (5); 924–41.

Schouten, P., and S.-P. Kalessopo. 2017. "The Politics of Pillage: The Political Economy of Roadblocks in the Central African Republic." Copenhagen/Antwerp: DIIS/IPIS.

Schutz, A. & Luckmann, T. 1983. *The Structures of the Life-World*. Volume 2. Translated by R. Zanner and D.J. Parent. Evanston, IL: Northwestern University Press.

Scott, James C. 1969. "The Analysis of Corruption in Developing Nations," In *Comparative Studies and History* 2 (3): 315–41.

Scott, James C. 1972. *Comparative Political Corruption*. Englewood, Cliffs: Prentice Hall.

Scott, James C. 1976. *The Moral Economy of the Peasant: Rebellion and Subsistence in Southeast Asia*. Princeton: Princeton University Press.

Scott, James C. 1985. *Weapons of the Weak: Everyday Forms of Peasant Resistance*. New Haven, Connecticut: Yale University Press.

Scott, James. 1998. *Seeing Like a State: How Certain Schemes to Improve the Human Condition Have Failed*. New Haven and London: Yale University Press.

Sedlenieks, Klavs. 2004. "Rotten Talk: Corruption as a Part of Discourse in Contemporary Latvia." In *Between Morality and the Law: Corruption, Anthropology and Comparative Society*, edited by I. Pardo, pp. 119–34. London: Ashgate.

Shah, A. 2010. In the Shadows of the State: Indigenous Politics, Environmentalism, and Insurgency in Jharkhand, India. Duke: Duke University Press.

Shapin, S. 2014. "'You are what you Eat': Historical Changes in Ideas about Food and Identity." *Historical Research* 87 (237): 377–92.

Sheller, Mimmi. 2018. *Mobility Justice: The Politics of Movement in an Age of Extremes.* Brooklyn: Verso.

Sherman, L.W. 1978. *Scandal and Reform: Controlling Police Corruption.* Berkeley: University of California Press.

Shipley, J.W., J. Comaroff, and A. Mbembe. 2010. "Africa in Theory: A Conversation between Jean Comaroff & Achille Mbembe." *Anthropological Quarterly* 83 (3): 653–78.

Shore, C. 2002. "Introduction: Towards an Anthroplogy of Elites." *In Elite Cultures: Anthropological Perspectives*, edited by C. Shore and S. Nugent, pp. 1–21. London: Routledge.

Simmel, G. 1978. *The Philosophy of Money.* London: Routledge.

Simone, AbdouMaliq. 2001. "On the Worlding of African Cities." *African Studies Review*, 44 (2): 15–41.

Simone, AbdouMaliq. 2004a. *For the City Yet to Come: Changing African Life in Four Cities.* Durham and London: Duke University Press, Durham and London.

Simone, AbdouMaliq. 2004b. "People as Infrastructure: Intersecting Fragments in Johannesburg." *Public Culture* 16 (3): 407–29.

Simone, AbdouMaliq. 2005. "Introduction: Urban Processes and Change." In *Urban Africa: Changing Contours of Survival in the City*, edited by A. Simone & A. Abouhani, pp. 1–26. Dakar: CODESRIA Books.

Simone, AbdouMaliq. 2010. *City Life from Jakarta to Dakar: Movements at the Crossroads.* New York, NY: Routledge.

Simone, AbdouMaliq. 2016a. "City of Potentialities: An Introduction." *Theory, Culture and Society* 37 (7–8): 5–29.

Simone, AbdouMaliq. 2016b. "The Uninhabitable? In between Collapsed yet Still Rigid Distinctions." *Cultural Politics* 12 (2): 135–54.

Siollun, Max. 2013. *Soldiers of Fortune: A History of Nigeria, 1983–1993.* Abuja: Cassava Republic Press.

Sluga, Hans. 2005. "Foucault's Encounter with Heidegger and Nietzsche." In Gary Gutting (ed.), *The Cambridge Companion to Foucault.* 2nd Edition. Cambridge: Cambridge University Press, pp. 210–239.

Smith, Daniel Jordan. 2004. "The Bakassi Boys: Vigilantism, Violence, and Political Imagination in Nigeria." *Cultural Anthropology* 19 (3): 429–55.

Smith, Daniel Jordan. 2005. "Oil, Blood and Money: Culture and Power in Nigeria." *Anthropological Quarterly* 78 (3): 725–40.

Smith, Daniel Jordan. 2007. *A Culture of Corruption: Everyday Deception and Popular Discontents in Nigeria.* Princeton: Princeton University Press.

Smith, Daniel Jordan. 2014. "Corruption Complaints, Inequality and Ethnic Grievances in Post-Biafra Nigeria." *Third World Quarterly*, 35(5): 787–802.

Smith, Daniel Jordan. 2016. "Moral Economies of Corruption, State Formation and Political Culture in Nigeria." Book Reviews. *American Ethnologist*, 43(3): 564–66.

Smith, M.G. 1964. "Historical and Cultural Conditions of Political Corruption among the Hausa." *Comparative Studies in Society and History*, 6(2): 164–94.

Sneath, David. 2006. "Transacting and Enacting: Corruption, Obligation and the Use of Monies in Mongolia." *Ethnos: Journal of Anthropology* 71 (1): 89–112.

Solinger, D.J. 2003. "The New Crowd of the Dispossessed: The Shift of the Urban Proletariat from Master to Mendicant." In *State and Society in the 21st-Century China: Crisis,*

Contention and Legitimation, edited by P. Gries and S. Rosen, pp. 50–66. London: Routledge.

Sommers, Marc. 2010. "Urban Youth in Africa." *Environment and Urbanization*, 22(2): 317–332.

Sopranzetti, C. 2014. "Owners of the Map: Mobility and Mobilization among Motorcycle Taxi Drivers in Bangkok." *City & Society* 26 (1): 120–43.

Sopranzetti, C. 2017. *Owners of the Map: Motorcycle Taxi Drivers, Mobility and Politics in Bangkok*. Berkeley: University of California Press.

Sorace, C. 2019. "Extracting Affect: Televised Cadre Confessions in China." *Public culture* 33 (1): 145–71.

Soyinka, Wole. 1996. *The Open Sore of a Continent: A Personal Narrative of the Nigerian Crisis*. Oxford: Oxford University Press.

Soyinka, Wole. 2006. *You Must Set Forth at Dawn: A Memoir*. New York: Random House.

Spergel, I.A. 1995. *The Youth Gang Problem*. Oxford: Oxford University Press.

Spittler, Gerd. 2001. "Teilnehmende Beobachtung als Dichte Teilnahme." *Zeitschrift für Ethnologie* 126: 1–25.

Standing, G. 2011. *The Precariat: The New Dangerous Class*. London: Bloomsbury Academic.

Stasik, M. and S. Cissokho. 2018. "Introduction to Special Issue: Bus Stations in Africa." *Africa Today* 65 (2): vii–xxiv.

Stasiulis, D. 1999. "Relational Positionalities of Nationalisms, Racisms, and Feminisms." In *Between Woman and Nation: Nationalisms, Transnational Feminisms, and the State*, edited by C. Kaplan, N. Alarcon, & M. Moallem, pp. 182–218. Durham: Duke University Press.

Stein, J. 1997. "In Pakistan, the Corruption is Lethal," *International Herald Tribune*, September 12.

Stewart, K. 2007. *Ordinary Affects*. Durham: Duke University Press.

Storey Report. 1953. "Lagos Town Council." Ibadan: National Archives.

Suberu, Rotimi. 2001. "Can Nigeria's New Democracy Survive?" *Current History* 100 (646): 207–12.

Suberu, Rotimi. 2018. "Strategies for Advancing Anticorruption Reform in Nigeria." *Daedalus: The Journal of the American Academy of Arts and Sciences* 147 (3): 184–201.

Sunday Magazine. 2017. "Lagos: Residents Want State-Wide Ban of NURTW Activities." July 02.

Supreme Court. 1992. "The Road Transport Employers Association of Nigeria V. The National Union of Road Transport Workers. SC.4/1989. February 21.

Szeftel, M. 1998. "Misunderstanding African Politics: Corruption and the Governance Agenda." *Review of African Political Economy* 25 (76): 221–40.

Tabachnik, S. 2011. "Bills, Bribery and Brutality: How Rampant Corruption in the Electoral System Has Helped Prevent Democracy in Uganda." Independent Study Project (ISP) Collection. 1204.

Tankebe, J. 2010. "Public Confidence in the Police: Testing the Effects of Public Experiences of Police Corruption in Ghana." *British Journal of Criminology* 50: 296–319.

Tankebe, J., S. Karstedt, and S. Adu-Poku. 2019. "Corruption Intentions Among Prospective Elites in Ghana: An Economy of Esteem." *International Criminal Justice Review* 29 (2): 168–86.

Taussig, Michael. 1980. *The Devil and Commodity Fetishism in South America*. Chapel Hill: North Carolina University Press.

Taussig, Michael. 1999. *Defacement: Public Secrecy and the Labore of the Negative*. Stanford: Stanford University Press.

Taylor, S. 2006. "Divergent Politico-Legal Responses to Past Presidential Corruption in Zambia and Kenya: Catching the 'Big Fish,' or Letting them Off the Hook?" *Third World Quarterly.*

Techpoint.africa. 2019. "For Nigerian Motorcycle Hailing Startups, Government Seems to Have Abdicated Regulatory Responsibility." November 18.

The Cable. 2020. "The Trekkers of Today will Snatch Our Cars Today." February 10.

The Economist. 2000. "The Heart of the Matter." May 11.

The Economist. 2010. "Be Focused, Be Bold." February 18.

The Economist. 2015. "Learning from Lagos." July 04.

The Guardian. 2014a. "Nigeria: At 80 Gowon Explains 'Nigeria's Problem is Not Money, But How to Spend It." October 19.

The Guardian. 2014b. "Nigeria: The Success Story of Lagos." October 08.

The Guardian. 2015. "Agberos, a City's Untamed Monsters." March 04.

The Guardian. 2016. "Beatings and Bribes: The Corruption Behind Lagos's Traffic Jams." February 25.

The Guardian. 2017. "Lagos: Residents Want State-wide Ban of NURTW Activities." By

The Herald. 2013. "Alamieyeseigha's Pardon Encourages Corruption—Soyinka." *The Herald* (Nigeria), March 21.

The Nation. 2008. "Tribunal Seeks Stiffer Actions to Check 'Area Boys." October 28.

The New York Times. 1997. "Fela, 58, Dissident Nigerian Musician, Dies." By David M. Herszenhorn. August 4.

The New York Times. 2013. "In Nigeria's Largest City, Homeless are Paying the Price of Progress." By Adam Nossiter. March 01.

The New York Times. 2014. "What Makes Lagos a Model Megacity." By Seth D. Kaplan. January 7.

The Sun. 2014. "I Won't Ban Okada—Fayose." November 27.

The Telegraph. 2014. "Meet the Man who Tamed Nigeria's Most Lawless City." October 24.

The Village Square. 2013. "The Kidnapping of Poor Nigerians by Governor Babatunde Raji Fashola of Lagos." August 02.

Theobald, R. 1990. *Corruption, Development and Underdevelopment*. London: Macmillan.

Thieme, Tatiana, A. 2013. "The 'Hustle' among Youth Entrepreneurs in Mathare's Informal Waste Economy." *Journal of Eastern African Studies*, 7(3): 389–412.

Thompson, E.P. 1971. "The Moral Economy of the English Crowd in the Eighteenth Century." *Past & Present* 50: 76–136.

Thompson, Michael, M. Verweii, and R.J. Ellis. 2006. "Why and How Culture Matters." In *The Oxford Handbook of Contextual Political Analysis*, edited by R.E. Gooding & C. Tilly, pp. 319–40. Oxford: Oxford University Press.

Thurston, Alexandra. 2018. "The Politics of Technocracy in Fourth Republic Nigeria." *African Studies Review* 61 (1): 215–38.

Tignor, R.L. 1973. "Political Corruption in Nigeria Before Independence." *The Journal of Modern African Studies* 31 (2): 175–202.

Timamy, M.H.K. 2005. "African Leaders and Corruption." *Review of African Political Economy* 105 (5): 383–93.

Titeca, K. 2012. "Tycoons and Contraband: Informal Cross-border Trade in West Nile, Norther-Western Uganda." *Journal of Eastern African Studies* 6 (1): 47–63.

Titeca, Kristof, and Tom Herdt. 2011. "Real Goveranance beyond the 'Failed State': Negotiating Education in the Democratic Republic of the Congo." *African Affairs* 110 (439): 213–31.

Torsello, David, and Bertrand Venard. 2015. "The Anthropology of Corruption." *Journal of Management Inquiry* 25 (1): 34–54.

Torsello, David, ed. 2016. *Corruption in Public Administration: An Ethnographic Approach.* Cheltenham, UK: Edward Elgar Publishing.

Transparency International. N.D. "Petty Corruption." https://www.transparency.org /en/corruptionary/petty-corruption

Trefon, T. 2002. "The Political Economy of Sacrifice: *Kinois* & the State." *Review of African Political Economy* 93/94: 481–98.

Trefon, T., ed. 2004. *Reinventing Order in the Congo: How People Respond to State Failure in Kinshasa.* London: Zed Books.

Triesman, D. 2007. "What Have We Learned About the Causes of Corruption from Ten Years of Cross-National Empirical Research." *Annual Review of Political Science* 10: 211–44.

Turner, S. 2007. "The Precarious Position of Politics in Popular Imagination: The Burundian Case." *Journal of Eastern African Studies*,1 (1): 93–106.

Tyner, J.A. 2012. Space, Place, and Violence: Violence and the Embodied Geographies of Race, Sex and Gender. London: Routledge.

Udo, R.K. 1970. *Geographical Regions of Nigeria*. Berkeley: University of California Press.

UN Habitat III. 2016. New Urban Agenda. Quitto: UN.

Underkuffler, L. 2005. "Captured by Evil: The Idea of Corruption in Law." *Duke Law School Legal Studies Paper* 83: 1–73.

United States Department of State. 2012. "2012 Country Reports on Human Rights Practices—Nigeria." April 19.

UNODC. 2017. "Corruption in Nigeria: Bribery, Public Expenditure and Response." Vienna: United Nations Office on Drugs and Crime.

Urry, John. 2007. *Mobilities*. Cambridge: Polity.

Utas, Mats. 2005a. "West-African Warscapes: Victimicy, Girlfriending, Soldiering: Tactic Agency in a Young Woman's Social Navigation of the Liberian War Zone." *Anthropological Quarterly* 78 (2): 403–30.

Utas, Mats. 2005b. "Building a Future? The Reintegration and Remarginalization of Youth in Liberia." In Paul Richards (ed.), *No Peace No War: An Anthropology of Contemporary Armed Conflicts.* Athens: Ohio University Press and Oxford: James Currey.

Utas, Mats, ed. 2012. *African Conflicts and Informal Power: Big Men and Networks.* Uppsala: Zed Books.

Uyieh, J. 2018. "'Eko Gb'ole o Gbole': A Historical Study of Youth and Tout Culture in Shomolu Local Government Area, Lagos, 1976–2015." *Journal of African Cultural Studies* 30 (3): 323–38.

Van de Walle, Nicholas. 1999. "Economic Reform in a Democratizing Africa." *Comparative Politics*, 32(1): 21–41.

Van de Walle, Nicholas. 2001. *African Economies and the Politics of Permanent Crisis, 1979– 1999.* Cambridge: Cambridge University Press.

Van de Walle, Nicholas. 2007. "Meet the New Boss, Same as the Old Boss? The Evolution of Political Clientelism in Africa." In H. Kitschelt & S.I. Wilkinson (eds), *Patrons, Clients and Policies: Patterns of Democratic Accountability and Political Competition.* Cambridge, UK: Cambridge University Press, pp. 50–67.

Vanguard. 2011a. "Anger, Shock Greet Lavish Reception for Bode George." February 28.

Vanguard. 2011b. "How Prominent Nigerians saw PDP's Lavish Celebration of Bode George's Freedom." March 05.

Vanguard. 2012a. "Ban on Okada: Fashola Challenges Supporters of Unregulated Okada Operation." October 24.

Vanguard. 2012b. "Government Lied to Okada Riders—ANACOWA." November 03.

Vanguard. 2013a. "14,300 Lagos Drivers Are Partially Blind." September 17.

Vanguard. 2013b. "Alcohol, Smoking Rule Night Life at Motor Parks." September 14.

Vanguard. 2013c. "WARNING: Poor People Are not wanted in Lagos Megacity." By Femi Aribisala. September 07.

Vanguard. 2013d. "Why Local Gin Sellers Get More Patrons at Night." September 13.

Vanguard. 2014a. "Babatunde Raji Fashola: What You See is What You Get." May 08.

Vanguard. 2014b. "Fayose and Stomach Infrastructure." July 8.

Vanguard. 2015. "Stomach Infrastructure: The Newest Vocabulary in Nigeria's Political Vocabulary." 27 March.

Vanguard. 2018. "Dirt, Disease and Death: How Lagos is Losing its Beauty, Tourism Potentials." July 21.

Velasquez, Manuel. 2004. "Is Corruption Always Corrupt?" In *Corporate Integrity and Accountability*, edited by G.C. Brenkert, pp. 148–65. London: Sage Publications.

Verrips, J., and B. Meyer. 2001. "Kwaku's Car: The Struggles and Stories of a Ghanian Long-Distance Taxi Driver." In *Car Cultures*, edited by D. Miller, pp. 153–84. Oxford: Berg.

Vigh, H. 2006. *Navigating Terrains of War: Youth and Soldiering in Guinea Bisau*. New York, Oxford: Berghahn Books.

Vigh, H. 2009. "Crisis and Chronicity: Anthropological Perspectives on Continuous Conflict and Decline." *Ethnos: Journal of Anthropology* 73 (1): 5–24.

Vigil, J.D. 2003. "Urban Violence and Street Gangs." *Annual Review of Anthropology* 32: 225–42.

Vigneswaran, Darshan, and Joel Quirk, eds. 2015. *Mobility Makes States: Migration and Power in Africa*. Philadelphia: University of Pennsylvania Press.

Wade, R. 1985. "The Market for Public Office: Why the Indian State is not Better at Development." *World Development* 13 (4): 467–97.

Wainaina, Binyavanga. 2006. "How to Write about Africa." *Granta 92*. Retrieved from: <https://granta.com/how-to-write-about-africa/>

Walker, A. 2016. *Eat the Heart of the Infidel: The Harrowing of Nigeria and the Rise of Boko Haram*. London: C. Hurst & Co.

Watson, V. 2009. "The Planned City Sweeps the Poor Away: Urban Planning and 21st Century Urbanization." *Progress in Planning* 72: 151–93.

Watts, Michael J. 1983. *Silent Violence: Food, Famine and Peasantry in Northern Nigeria*. Berkeley: University of California Press.

Watts, Michael. 2008. "Oil as Money: The Devils Excrement and the Spectacle of Black Gold." In Barnes, T.J., Peck, J., Sheppard, E. and Tickell, A. (eds). *Reading Economic Geography*. Oxford: Blackwell, pp. 205–219.

Watts, Michael J. 2019. "State as Illusion? A Commentary on *Moral Economies of Corruption*." *Comparative Studies of South Asia, Africa and the Middle East* 39 (3): 551–57.

Weate, J., and B. Bakare-Yusuf. 2003. "Ojuelegba: The Sacred Profanities of a West African Crossroad." In *Urbanisation and African Cultures*, edited by T. Falola & S.J. Salm, pp. 323–42. Durham, North Carolina: Carolina Academic Press.

Weber, M. 1978. *Economy and Society Vols. I & II*. Berkeley: University of California Press.

Weber. 2012. *Collected Methodological Writings*. New York: Routledge.

Weekly Trust. 2006. Newspaper published by the Media Trust, Kaduna, February 18–24.

Weiner, T. 1998. "U.S. Aides Say Nigeria Leader Might Have Been Poisoned." *The New York Times*, July 11.

Werner, C. 2000. "Gifts, Bribes and Development in Post-Soviet Kazakstan." *Human Organisation* 59 (1): 11–22.

Williams, Gavin. 1980. "Political Consciousness among the Ibadan Poor." In *State and Society in Nigeria*, edited by G. Williams, pp. 110–20. Idanre: Afrografika Publishers.

Williams, R. 1983. *Key Words: A Vocabulary of Culture and Society*. Revised Edition. New York: Oxford University Press.

Williams, S.H. 1954. "Urban Aesthetics: An Approach to the Study of the Aesthetic Characteristics of Cities." *The Town Planning Review* 25 (2): 95–113.

Wilson, Stephen. 1977. "The Use of Ethnographic Techniques in Educational Research." *Review of Educational Research*, 47(1): 245–65.

Wolf, E. 1977. "Kinship, Friendship, and Patron-Client Relations in Complex Societies." In *Friends, Followers and Factions: A Reader in Political Clientelism*, edited by S.W. Schmidt, J.C. Scotts, C. Lande & L. Guasti, pp. 175–76. Berkeley: University of California Press.

Wolfensohn, James D. 1996. "Annual Meeting's Address by James D. Wolfensohn, President of the World Bank." Washington, DC. October 1.

Woodward, K. 2008. "Hanging Out and Hanging About: Insider/Outsider Research in the Sport of Boxing." *Ethnography* 9 (4): 536–60.

World Bank. 2010. "Silent and Lethal: How Quiet Corruption Undermines Africa's Development Efforts." Africa Development Indicators. Washington DC: World Bank.

World Bank. 2011. "Case Studies: Lagos, Nigeria." Toolkit on Fare Collection Systems for Urban Passenger Transport.

World Bank. 2020. "Combating Corruption." https://www.worldbank.org/en/topic/governance/brief/anti-corruption

World Development Report. 2015. "When Corruption is the Norm." World Bank, 60–61.

Wrong, M. 2009. *It's Our Time to Eat: The Story of a Kenyan Whistle-Blower*. New York: Harper.

Wutich, A. 2011. "The Moral Economy of Water Examined: Reciprocity, Water Insecurity, and Urban Survival in Cochabamba, Bolivia." *Journal of Anthropological Research* 67: 1–25.

Xiao, A.H and Adebayo, K.O. 2020. "Cohabiting Commerce in a Transport Hub: Peoples as Infrastructure in Lagos, Nigeria." *Urban Studies* 57 (12): 2510–2526.

Yagboyaju, D.A. 2020. "Egunje (Nigeria)." INF, May.

Yai, O.B. 1994. "In Praise of Metonymy: The Concepts of 'Tradition' and 'Creativity' in the Transmission of Yoruba Artistry over Time and Space." In Rowland Abiodun, Henry J. Drewal, and John Pemberton III (eds), *The Yoruba Artist: New Theoretical Perspectives on African Arts*. Washington, D.C.: Smithsonian Institute Press.

York, Geoffrey. 2015. "How not to fight Islamist Extremism." *The Globe and Mail*, February 27.

Young, Crawford, and Thomas Turner. 1985. *The Rise and Decline of the Zairian State*. London: The University of Wisconsin Press.

Youtube. 2013. "Lagos, Africa's Big Apple." June 11.

Zizek, S. 1996. "'I hear you with my eyes': Or, the invisible master." In R. Saleci & S. Zizek (eds), *Gaze and Voice as Love Objects*. Durham, NC: Duke University Press, pp. 90–126.

Index

Note: The following abbreviations have been used – f = figures/illustrations; n = footnotes